THE COMPLETE
FLY FISHER

THE COMPLETE
FLY FISHER

Edited by Peter Lapsley

SELECT
EDITIONS

This edition published 1992 by
The Promotional Reprint Company Limited
exclusively for Selecta Book Limited
Folly Road, Roundway, Devizes,
Wiltshire SN10 2HR

Printed in Great Britain by Butler & Tanner Ltd, Frome and London

ISBN 1 85648 0569

CONTENTS

Colour plates of most of the flies mentioned in the text may be found between pages 160 and 161.

Acknowledgements

We are grateful to the many kind friends who have provided advice and encouragement during the making of this book. In particular, we wish to record our thanks to:

Fred Buller, for his enthusiastic support for the project from the outset, and for his wise counsel during the planning stages. And Roy Eaton, for his advice and for his editorial help as the work progressed.

Brian Clarke, for his photographs of the Kennet on page 97 and of his remarkable grayling on page 166. John Goddard, for his generosity in allowing us to use so many of his marvellous photographs in Neil Patterson's chapter, 'The Angler and the Insect'. Arthur Oglesby, for his photographic sequence of the Spey cast in Chapter 8. And Dermot Wilson for his photograph of the Avon on page 87. The wood engraving by Thomas Bewick is reproduced on the title page by courtesy of the Bridgeman Art Library.

Bob Enever, for his colour plates of the flies and for the cover photographs. And Andrew Witkowski of Farlows of Pall Mall, for having provided the tackle for the cover photographs.

Mrs Brenda Elphick, for the tube flies she tied for Plate 2, and Mrs Irene Ross for the salmon flies she dressed for Plate 1.

Sidney Vines, for having provided the biographical note on Oliver Kite in the preface to Chapter 4.

Rodney Paull, for his patience and dedication in producing such excellent line drawings from our photographs and (sometimes very) rough sketches.

Dr Martin O'Grady of the Central Fisheries Board in Dublin, for his advice on brown trout populations in Irish loughs.

Dr Ross Gardiner, Scientific Officer to the Grayling Society, for his advice on the grayling's history and distribution. And Louis Noble, for the information he provided on grayling in stillwaters.

And, to our wives and families, for their forbearance and for giving us the time to fish and to write.

EDITOR'S PREFACE

In the early 1960s, the late Commander C. F. Walker drew together a team of nine fly fishers, each an expert in his field. Together they wrote a compendium volume covering all aspects of their sport — from salmon and sea-trout fishing through the pursuit of brown trout in chalk streams and rain-fed rivers to fly fishing for grayling, sea-trout and trout in lakes, lochs and reservoirs, and from casting, entomology and fly dressing to river fisheries management.

The book was published in 1963 under the not inappropriate title, *The Complete Fly-Fisher*, and was an immediate success. Its popularity with the angling public is best judged by the fact that it was re-published in a second, fully revised edition in 1969 and that it was reprinted no less than five times, most recently in 1984.

Inevitably, though, this outstanding work has been overtaken by events, particularly in the fields of stillwater trout fishing and of the materials used for rod making. When it was originally conceived, Grafham Water was little more than a twinkle in a civil engineer's eye, Rutland and Bewl Waters had not even been thought of, and the widespread use of carbon fibre rods — which has so revolutionized the ways in which people fish — was still ten years or more away.

So, feeling that the book now needed completely re-writing, rather than simply revising, the publishers decided to gather together a new team and to start afresh. I consider myself greatly privileged to have been invited to orchestrate and co-ordinate the new project as its editor, and I am immensely grateful, both to my fellow scribes and to Roddy Bloomfield and Marion Paull of Stanley Paul, the publishers, for having made my task such a pleasant and relatively straightforward one.

The team itself is remarkable. Every member of it is widely acknowledged as a master in his field. Inevitably, in the relatively modest amount of space we have been able to allocate to them, the chapters of this book represent no more than a distillation or précis of each writer's knowledge. Each of the authors could produce a volume or more on his subject; several of them have done so. I have therefore invited each one to provide a short list of appropriate books at the end of his chapter to help those who would delve more deeply into any particular aspect of our sport. And it was respect for their expertise, rather than any other motive, that led me to ask the authors not to be unduly reticent about including their own works in these lists.

Although this is essentially a completely new book, we have been particularly happy to have been able to keep two links with the original editions of *The Complete Fly-Fisher*.

There have been few if any significant changes in chalk stream fly fishing during the past thirty years. Although there are several fine fishing writers alive today, any one of whom could have written a first class chapter on the subject (at least three of them being amongst those already providing chapters for this book), we concluded that none could have bettered Major Oliver Kite's contribution, which we have therefore retained from the original work.

And nobody could have been more delighted than I when Peter Deane, the author of the chapter on fly dressing in the 1963 and 1969 editions, agreed to write a completely new one for this new work. Everyone involved with the project owes him a very considerable debt of gratitude, for having so cheerfully tied so many flies for the colour plates and for having taken so much trouble in supervising the actual taking of the colour photographs themselves, as well as for having made so marvellously lucid and logical a contribution to the text.

I know that my fellow authors would wish to join me in pointing out that you cannot learn to cast or to fish simply from the printed word, no matter how knowledgeable or authoritative the writer may be. Crafts and manual skills can only be taught by explanation, demonstration and practice. Fly fishing is no exception. We hope that this book may go some way towards meeting the first of these requirements. But we would recommend most strongly that the beginner should build upon what he or she may have absorbed from it by going to a qualified instructor, particularly in order to learn to cast. It is most unwise to seek tuition from self-styled and unqualified 'professionals'.

Two organizations in the United Kingdom examine would-be game angling instructors and certify their competence; the Association of Professional Game Angling Instructors (APGAI) and the National Anglers' Council (NAC). Their addresses are given in Appendix B, and either organization will gladly direct you towards conveniently located representatives.

Finally, we very much hope that this volume will help and encourage aspirant fly fishers and that it will provide useful guidance to those who, being familiar with certain types and styles of fishing, may wish to try others. If it goes even part of the way towards making your days at the waterside happier and more productive, it will have achieved its purpose.

Peter Lapsley
May 1990

Neil Graesser

Neil Graesser was born in 1928 at Froncysllte in the Llangollen valley, close to the banks of the River Dee. With encouragement, support and tuition from his parents, he soon became an ardent fisherman, catching his first salmon when he was six years old. Even as a boy, he had begun to make salmon his life's study and salmon fishing his prime hobby.

He has fished a very large number of salmon rivers in Scotland, England and Wales, as well as many Scottish lochs, taking several thousand salmon in the process. He moved up to live at Rosehall in Sutherland in 1950, and has lived there, above the junction of the rivers Cassley and Oykel, ever since.

Neil began to practise as a freelance Fishery Consultant in 1948, specializing in salmon. This work has taken him all over the country and has allowed him to study salmon, their environment and their unpredictable taking habits in minute detail.

He has been a member of the Council of Scottish District Salmon Fishery Boards since 1964, and was Chairman of the Council from 1969 to 1989. He has been a member of the Management Committee of the Atlantic Salmon Trust since 1969. He is a member both of the Institute of Fisheries Management and of the Government's Salmon Advisory Committee, and he is Chairman of the Highland River Purification Board.

Neil Graesser has been co-author of the books *Salmon Rivers of Scotland* and *Salmon Fisheries of Scotland*, and has written three books on salmon fishing himself — *Fly Fishing for Salmon, Advanced Salmon Fishing* and *Finer Points of Salmon Fishing*.

He was awarded the OBE in 1990 for his services to salmon fisheries management.

1

SALMON FISHING

Neil Graesser

INTRODUCTION

Unlike most other fresh water species, the salmon is migratory. Born in fresh water, it spends the first few years of its life in the nursery areas of the main river system and its tributaries, feeding on the limited food supply available. When it is a mere few inches in length, it takes on a silver coating over its scales – becoming known as a smolt – and begins its outward migration to sea. It wends its way down river to the estuary, pauses briefly to acclimatize its system to its new environment, and then heads out to its sea feeding grounds many miles from our shores.

Whilst at sea it feeds voraciously on crustacea, plankton and small fish. Its growth rate at sea is remarkably high, with a good food conversion–weight gain ratio.

Some of the fish mature after only one winter at sea and return to their rivers of origin, mainly between June and August, weighing 4–8 lb; these are known as grilse. Those that spend two or more winters at sea weigh anything from 6–40 lb when they return, and are known as salmon.

Both grilse and salmon return to fresh water for the sole purpose of regenerating their species. In order to ensure the safety of the species, nature has given grilse and salmon the ability to survive entirely without feeding on their return to fresh water. Given the numbers and sizes of the salmon and grilse that return annually to their rivers of origin, it is inevitable that they would drastically reduce the young fish life in the rivers, including members of their own species, if they had to feed daily like other freshwater species.

With millions of anglers in the British Isles and those from overseas all looking for places to fish and fish to fish for, the demand for angling waters and the pressure on fish stocks increases annually.

To catch a salmon is the ambition of many anglers. Some fly fishers start their salmon angling careers at very early ages. Many more take up salmon fishing as complete novices later in life. But the largest numbers start their angling apprenticeship fishing for coarse fish, sea fish or trout and progress steadily onwards until they finally pit their more knowledgeable wits against the salmon. There is no doubt that the latter class do have a limited advantage over the inexperienced, in both river-craft and the ability to play and land fish. However, when it comes down to either fly fishing with a salmon rod or using the knowledge they have acquired about the feeding habits of their previous quarries, they very soon find that this information can often be as much a disadvantage as an asset.

The very fact that the salmon does not require to feed on its return to fresh water makes its taking habits completely unpredictable. The trout fisher's study of entomology, feeding times or the habits of his quarry gives no useful lead when fishing for salmon, and nor does much of the rod craft learned in other types of fishing help him to use a double-handed rod. In fact, one can really say it is back to the drawing board for all and sundry, whether they be novices, young or old, or experts in another field. A clean sheet and starting from scratch is often the best way to eradicate bad habits learned elsewhere. Nothing can replace patience, persistence, confidence and the will to ring the changes when it comes to salmon fishing.

THE NATURAL HISTORY OF SALMON

I was brought up to believe that there were four main runs of salmon — winter, spring, summer and autumn. Winter runs enter the rivers around the close of the previous season, between the end of October and the end of December. Modern scientists, however, now term these as early running spring fish.

Each run has a three-to-four month duration, and the runs therefore overlap each other. On rivers that can accommodate all four runs, the runs can merge, with salmon entering the river daily throughout the year.

Winter run fish do not spawn until the autumn of the following year. Therefore, this run and the spring run are the most valuable that any river can accommodate, as the fish are available in the river system for anglers to exploit for the longest period of the angling season, in some cases from 15 January to 15 October.

The summer and autumn runs include a certain grilse component, and rivers that only accommodate such runs have much shorter angling seasons, from June to 30 November.

The angling season on rivers which do not enjoy autumn runs normally closes on 30 September, or 15 October at the latest.

Two main criteria control the potential stock of a salmon river. The first is the amount of spawning gravel available in the river system; the second, the number of salmon fry and parr that the limited food supply in the river can sustain to the smolt stage. It often follows, but is not always the case, that the longer the river is the more seasonal runs it can accommodate. A river usually fills from top to bottom; that is to say, the winter and spring runs ascend to and stock the headwaters and their tributaries while the summer run occupies the middle reaches of the river and the autumn run the lower reaches. Grilse components of these runs penetrate to their appropriate areas.

Rivers such as the Wye and Tay are large enough, with their numerous tributaries, to accommodate all runs. Rivers such as the Tweed, Spey and Dee can hold three runs. Smaller rivers on the east coast often have a spring and summer run. And short, rapid, west coast rivers, usually with very limited spawning facilities, can only accommodate one run, a summer one.

Exceptions to these rules are rivers with impassable falls that debar the passage of salmon into the upper catchment system, and rivers with very rock-strewn beds and a dearth of spawning gravel. In both cases, productivity will be severely limited. In contrast, where a river has a wealth of spawning gravel and unusually high feeding capacity, it may well be far more productive than its length suggests.

As the autumn approaches, most fish have arrived at their destinations and are lying in holding pools close to the spawning fords where they will deposit their eggs. Forsaken now are the deep rock pools; instead the fish tend to favour the shallower pools with gravelly tails or fords upstream of them. Gone are their shining silver coats. Instead they wear pink, purple or black hues; nature's way of camouflaging them in peat-stained water against gravelly surroundings. Some fish will have paired even before they left the sea, and those that have lost their partners during their homeward migrations will pair with new mates.

Once they are ready to spawn, the fish move quickly on to the spawning fords. Their main requirement of these areas is good, clean, open gravel, free of silt or sludge, which is both workable and stable. The gravel must not be in too deep water as the female relies heavily on the current speed at river-bed level to move the pebbles away from her working, and thereby to enable her to cut her redd to the required depth of 6−9 inches. Ideal depths for spawning vary from 9 inches to 3 feet beneath the surface. Such areas can often be found at the tails of long, gravelly pools or on the down-gradient between pools in the main river, or in the many side burns and tributaries, no matter how small, provided there is clean gravel to spawn on.

The female is the worker and while she makes her exploratory cuts and then selects her redd, the male cruises round chasing off any intruders that come too close. Once she has perfected her first depression, the female goes into the crouch position and opens her mouth, whereupon the male comes close alongside her. Ejections of eggs and milt are then made simultaneously, the female immediately moving just upstream and starting her next indentation in the gravel to receive a further deposit of eggs. The debris from the second cut thus covers the eggs in the first. A female normally deposits about 2000 eggs per ejection and often needs to cut four depressions to empty herself and a fifth to glean gravel to cover the eggs from the fourth. Once spawning has been completed, the fish become known as kelts.

Immediately after spawning, a very large percentage of the males and a substantial number of females die, many from furrunculosis, often caused by stress and exertion. Those that survive fall back to the holding pools to recuperate and, during the winter months, take advantage of spate flows to move down river on their way back to the sea. Some pass out to sea quickly whilst others linger on in lower reaches of the river until March or April before finally leaving.

The kelts that stay on are usually hens, by now well mended and silvery grey in colour. It is often only their emaciated shape and lack of lustre on their scales and fins that distinguishes them from fresh fish. These kelts take lures freely at the start of the season.

Kelts that survive to return to fresh water and spawn again only constitute a tiny percentage of the annual stock of a salmon river. Nearly all the second return fish are female, males being extremely rare. The Hebrides, where the rivers are extremely short, probably has the greatest survival rate in Britain.

The eggs lying nestled under their gravel covering are very fragile at this stage and are easily destroyed by excessive vibration or movement; they remain so until the eyed stage is reached.

The incubation period of the egg varies considerably and depends upon the mean water temperature. In a mean of 45°F the eggs will eye in approximately 45 days and hatch in approximately 90, but if subjected to a mean 37°F they will eye in approximately 80 days and hatch in approximately 140. This is probably nature's way of ensuring that the high catchment eggs do not hatch until there is sufficient food bloom in that part of the river to sustain the newly hatched fry.

When an egg hatches, 6−9 inches below the surface of the river bed, the little fish is known as an alevin. Attached to the underside of its gill casing is a little yolk sac. This is its food supply to sustain it as it worms its way through the gravel to the surface of the river bed. Once the yolk sac has been absorbed, the little fish is known as a fry and, after a few months, a parr.

The fry begin to forage for themselves and feed on freshwater plankton, waterborne invertebrates and terrestrial insects blown on to the surface of the water. Food availability is largely controlled by the pH value of the water. Where the water's pH level is between 6.5 and 7.5 invertebrates with high food value can be supported; in water of pH 5.5−6.5 invertebrates of lower food value will be found; where the pH is between 4.6 and 5.5, fry depend chiefly on terrestrial insects to support them. Where the pH level is lower than this the water is unacceptable to salmonids. Growth rates of fry and parr depend mainly on the density of the population the food supply has to support and the quality of the water.

When the time comes for parr to migrate to sea, they take on a silver guanine coating over their scales and descend downstream. In the estuary, they pause briefly to adjust to their new environment before heading off to feeding grounds far from our shores.

In rare cases, some parr will smolt at one year old, but the norm is two to three years old, whilst in very poor quality water or extremely high catchment areas, some may reach the age of four to five years before smolting. Wild smolts vary in length and are usually between 4 and 6 inches on average.

Once the smolts reach the sea they head out for rich feeding grounds in the Atlantic Ocean. Those that will mature as salmon often feed in the Newfoundland–Greenland area; those that will mature as grilse generally remain closer to our shores. This is because the period the fish remain at sea does not allow them time to travel to far distant feeding grounds and then return to their rivers of origin at their scheduled times.

When the fish mature, the urge to reproduce causes them to stop feeding at sea and to begin their homeward migration to their rivers of origin, in some cases thousands of miles away across the ocean. Tagging experiments over many years have shown that the vast majority return to the same rivers in which they themselves were born. We do not fully understand how they navigate, but their navigation is uncannily accurate. Once in the river, they devote all their efforts to ascending to the precise areas in which they themselves were born and where they spent the first few years of their lives.

The winter and spring fish have plenty of time to reach their destinations, but the later runs entering the rivers during drier seasons of the year can, on occasions, be held up in the sea or even in the river by low water flow rates during droughts. These fish may therefore be forced to hurry to reach their destinations in time. Some rivers have obstructions such as weirs or natural falls which the fish have to negotiate, and, early in the year, in low water temperatures, these can delay the upstream migration considerably. The most formidable falls cannot be negotiated until the water temperature has reached 52°F, and others can only be ascended at temperatures over 45°F.

In the old days, there were two main categories of rivers: the short, spate rivers with little or no reservoir capacity, and the long river systems with good water reserves and more stable flows. Now, with numerous river catchment areas harnessed for either hydro-electric or water supply purposes, many rivers no longer have natural flow regimes. Instead, some are subjected to controlled compensation flows whilst others have their spate flows diverted into neighbouring catchments and are, therefore, denuded of valuable water resources. All of these man-made changes have altered the natural distribution of salmon stocks within the river systems. And in some cases badly sited or designed fish passes curtail the ascent of salmon into previously well-populated parts of the catchment areas. In other cases, a lack of fish passes can prevent the fishes' ascent and the upstream areas can no longer be populated naturally.

On their return to their rivers of origin, winter and spring fish are beautiful creatures with silver flanks and blue backs, in perfect shape and condition. Maybe it is because after the long close season the angler is impatient to fish again; or maybe it is because of the condition and appearance of his quarry; whatever the reason, spring fishing is always in tremendous demand. Even a drastic decline in the numbers of early run fish has not reduced the angler's appetite to fish for them.

The early run fish which enter the river in October and November often forge on upstream before the water temperature drops as the colder winter weather takes a grip. These are the fish often caught on opening days in places like Loch Tay. Later running early fish, often faced with snow bree and colder temperatures, take more time to ascend and are often delayed low down the river systems. These fish favour the deep, slow moving tails of the pools and may lie in one pool for several months before being drawn further upstream by warmer water and spate flows.

By mid-May, the early fish become reddish pink and lose their silvery sheen. Even sea-liced fish straight from the sea lack the silver sheen of the earlier fish but wear a duller silver hue instead. As the months progress the camouflage of their coats increases rapidly to red or purply-black. Even fresh fish straight from the sea will take on a coloured coat in a short space of time. Generally, these later run fish favour faster, streamy, shallower pools, but they may also be found in canal-like, deep pools in low water flows.

As the season progresses the wise angler will explore every inch of his water and will often find small resting pools and shallow runs far more productive than the main holding pools.

Scale reading is a fascinating subject. It can provide details of the length and duration of the fish's early life in fresh water, its age at migration and its sea feeding life, as well as of the number of times it has spawned. Scales are read in much the same way as the life of a tree can be read once it has been cut. The most readable scales are the larger ones taken from above the lateral line from the shoulder of the fish.

Tagging of smolts and adult fish either prior to their migration to sea or whilst on the sea feeding grounds has provided useful information on their migratory habits and on the timing of their homeward journeys. And, recently, radio tagging devices have been used to monitor the fishes' movement and behaviour within the river systems.

TACKLE

Rods

The rod is undoubtedly the piece of equipment that must be chosen most carefully. If the angler makes the right choice it will stand him in good stead for many a day and be a delight to fish with. An unwise choice, on the other hand, can make a toil out of a pleasure. An angler must always remember that he will be fishing in all kinds of weather and he must therefore be sure that the rod he finally selects is adequate to deal with even the most adverse conditions.

The types of water the angler means to fish on and the times of year at which he means to fish will have a heavy bearing on the type of rod he chooses. Let us assume that he intends to fish sporadically throughout the season, and that he will be using both sunk lines and floating lines. My advice in this case would be not to be under-rodded. Always make sure you have plenty of rod power. If you don't require it, no harm is done but, if it is needed, at least you are sure you have it. I would choose a 14 or 15 feet rod, depending on your physique and age. A long rod not only gives you more

casting power and control of your fly whilst it is fishing. It also enables you to execute any type of cast you wish.

The angler who fishes frequently throughout the season should equip himself with an 11–12 feet rod for summer fishing, for fishing on small rivers or for loch fishing, and a 14–15 feet one for fishing larger rivers, rivers in spate or spring fishing.

Strength is another important factor for long line or sunk line fishing. Lifting power is essential as it is the clean take-off of the line from the water at the start of the cast that makes or mars it. It is the centre of the rod that takes the most strain at this point. If it bows under the strain or is spongy, the cast will almost inevitably be imperfect. Again, if the tip or butt sections lack strength, overall casting ability will be lacking and the rod's performance is unlikely to be adequate to deal with adverse conditions.

Most rods are made from fibre-glass, carbon fibre or boron nowadays. Wooden rods, which have served anglers so well in the past, are fast being phased out and now enjoy only a minor share of the market.

There is little doubt that this sudden change in popularity is almost entirely due to the light weight of modern materials. At the same time, the overall quality of the carbon fibre and boron rods is improving and, with the advent of the hexograph types, their strength and power have been greatly increased. An angler can now find a light, serviceable rod of any length to suit his requirements, with which he can fish all day long without tiring. The glass-fibre rods, although very serviceable, are both heavier and slightly more clumsy than more streamlined carbon and boron ones.

These rods all have suction spiggot joints, which can be less secure than the old spliced and ferrule-locking methods. I have always found it best to wax the spiggots with candle wax before putting up the rod, and then, having firmed the joints, to bind the actual joint with adhesive tape to ensure that they cannot move.

The reel fittings on any rod are of prime importance. If a reel falls off either on a river or during transportation on a car, it may very easily be damaged – perhaps beyond repair. The only really safe fitting is the metal sleeve with a socket into which one reel flange is placed, while a ring embraces the other with a screw locking device screwing down and clamping the ring so that it cannot move. Ordinary ring fittings without the locking device are liable to loosen because the cork on the handle of the rod can be depressed.

Lines

Gone are the days when lines like the tapered Kingfisher plaited dressed silk line would serve an angler adequately throughout the entire season, merely being greased when greased line fishing was necessary, and used in its normal state at other times. Nowadays, we are faced with a vast choice of lines, each one designed to meet a different set of circumstances. To mention but a few, we have various types of fast sinkers, slow sinkers and intermediate, floaters and sink-tip lines, double tapered, forward tapered, level or shooting heads. It is not surprising that some angler's minds boggle when they have to select one.

One major step forward is that rod makers now mark their rods with the size of line to which it is best suited. Too light a line will make it impossible to develop the full power of a rod, while a rod fitted with too heavy a line can easily be damaged or even broken by being over-stressed. Of course, anglers must make up their own minds and choose the type of line they think will best serve their needs. Personally, I firmly believe that a double tapered intermediate line and a double tapered floating line, matched in weight to both the angler's rod, are all one needs to fish out an entire season. Lead-cored lines, shooting heads and sink-tips seem to me to be quite unnecessary and perhaps even counter-productive as they can impair the angler's casting ability and may even strain his rod if incorrectly used.

Reels

The reel is second only in importance to the rod. Unless it is working smoothly the angler may as well pack up and go home. My advice, therefore, is to buy the best you can afford.

First and foremost I like a wide drummed reel, capable of accommodating a full line of any size and a plentiful supply of backing. This type of reel requires less effort to wind in fish, which is a small but nevertheless important consideration. The narrower the drum, the more likelihood there is of damaging the line or the reel, through overloading it.

Most modern reels are made of very light metal alloy and in spite of the lightness of modern rods they often fail to balance them. There is nothing more tiring on an angler's wrists than trying to counterbalance a rod and reel which has its weight forward. In the old days, with brass or zinc reels, this was never a problem. It is sometimes wise, therefore, to buy a good second hand reel of the heavier type to overcome this problem.

A reel with interchangeable drums is useful as it enables an angler to change his line from floating to sunk or vice versa, without having to change his reel.

Leaders

These are now made exclusively from nylon monofilament. Once again, balance is the most important factor. Light nylon and a heavy fly are a bad combination as the leader will be unable to lead the fly through a wind. The larger the fly the heavier should be the breaking strain of the nylon used, and vice versa.

In the springtime, a collar of plaited nylon, about 4 feet long, between the point of line and the actual leader (which may be shorter than usual), can be a great asset, instead of a full 9 feet leader of similar strength cast. With modern monofilament, there is no need to use leaders finer than 10−12 lb breaking strain, and even this may be too light on occasions.

I much prefer the stiffer makes of nylon. They are not nearly so liable to kink and curl as the more supple makes, and they have the necessary bone to lead a fly through the wind.

Flies

There is a wealth of flies of every conceivable colour and pattern for an angler to choose from and build up a selection to meet all his requirements. They are tied on single irons, double irons, Waddingtons mounted on trebles and tubes to which one attaches trebles, and there are dressed flies tied on long shank treble hooks.

For spring fishing, Waddingtons or tube flies with treble hooks are infinitely preferable to the old 6−9 degree flies dressed on heavy single irons. They are also easier to drive home than the old flies were. Whether we land more fish on them is a matter of question because a fish being played on a treble may get off due to leverage if all the hooks are not embedded in its mouth. There was little risk of leverage with flies tied on single irons. I believe we lost far fewer fish in play on single irons than we do on today's trebles.

Another advantage of the single hook was that the gape of the hook was large enough to encircle the salmon's jaw-bone, thereby enabling it to embed in a soft part of the mouth. With a treble, the gape of each individual hook is insufficient to do this. This invariably means that unless it is embedded in the fish's tongue or in the hinge of the jaw, only one of the legs of the treble (or two at the most) will take a grip in the skin surrounding

the fish's jaw-bone. Under such circumstances, the hook can be wrenched free either by leverage of the loose leg, or legs, of the treble against the jaw-bone, or by pressure exerted by the angler at the wrong time.

Careful consideration should be given to these points whenever salmon flies or double or treble hooks for use with tube flies are being chosen.

Accessories

Other necessary accessories include two cast spools of differing strengths of nylon; also fly boxes, which are available in numerous and varied types. You will need a box for the tubes, and for this I use either an old tobacco tin or a plastic container with separate compartments. The latter can easily be obtained from a friendly doctor or vet, as they discard many suitable containers. You will also need a tin, preferably with a screw top, to carry trebles.

You may wish to carry a thermometer and weight scales in your bag as well; also a pair of scissors. The latter are best carried on a lanyard either round one's neck or attached to a button, so that they are easily accessible. Cover the blades of course.

To land a fish, many anglers use a gaff. You can carry one of the telescopic variety either attached to a belt, or on a long staff. The staff may also be used as a wading stick. A net − once again a collapsible type with its frame made of light metal alloy − can easily be carried on your back. Finally, you may want a tailer. Again, the telescopic kind can be attached to the belt.

Personally, I never carry any of these when I am by myself. I find them too cumbersome and rely on beaching my fish. If unusual circumstances obliged me to resort to any aid. I would choose the tailer.

One item I always carry, however, is a bass, rolled up and tied with string and attached to my belt or braces. This is not only useful for carrying fish, but also keeps it in prime condition, provided the fish is washed clean before being placed in the bass. A fish left lying on the bank for any length of time often dries out and its quality deteriorates.

WHY FISH TAKE FLIES

On its return to fresh water, a salmon can survive for up to twelve months by living off its own fat.

Why then, you may ask, do these fish take a fly? There are many theories. Perhaps the salmon does it from annoyance, playfulness, his predatory nature, or memories of his feeding periods both at an early age in the river and, more recently, at sea. Which theory, if any, is correct none of us will ever know. If I had to hazard a guess, it would be the memory of feeding. One thing we do know, however, is that salmon will take, Sporadically and unpredictably for the most part but sometimes, in the right conditions, very freely.

What is even more perplexing is how a salmon's choice of diet changes with water temperatures, because in cold water − below 42°F − he prefers a fly 2−6 inches in size, and above 50°F a fly from ¼ inch to 1 inch. Between these ranges of temperature he is not so choosy and may take any size, often having a preference for a more colourful fly in spring and autumn, and a sombre drab one during the summer months. This may well reflect the type and size of the food he is used to finding during his sea feeding life in the differing temperatures of the oceans, when his wandering takes him through the warmer Gulf Stream currents into the cooler climes of the northern hemisphere.

No fly fisherman can really believe that the lure he is casting out can ever, except on the rarest occasions, behave like a fly. Their movements are simply too difficult to imitate. So he must try and decide what other type of creature he is trying to simulate whilst fishing with it. In spring and autumn, the large flies we fish with must simulate the movements of fish of varying sizes, and in the summer our small flies should do likewise. When you are using small flies in warm water, you may wish to imitate water-borne invertebrates or even plankton.

When the angler fluffs, trips or drags a fly on the surface in what we call the 'dibbling' method (see page 27), this resembles the behaviour of a flying insect struggling to get off the surface of the water.

The natural movements of whatever lifeform the angler has chosen are transmitted, through rod tip or the handling of the line, into his fly. If he wishes his lure to move like a fish he makes his fly work accordingly as it traverses the width of the pool. If, on the other hand, he wishes the lure to simulate plankton, it must hang literally inert in the current.

The main thing is for the angler to present his lure in a life-like manner and to hope that its actions in the water will stir a memory from the fish's past feeding life.

SPRING FISHING

In the early part of the year, many anglers believe that fly fishing is a waste of time and turn to other methods. The exception to this rule is the far northern tip of Scotland, where rivers such as the Kyle of Sutherland group, the Helmsdale, Thurso, Halladale, Naver and Borgie, open earlier than any other rivers in the United Kingdom, on either 11 or 12 January. Strange to say, but by a longstanding proprietors' agreement, these rivers allow no other form of angling *but* fly fishing, a tradition of which they are very proud. Their successful

catch-results throughout the first three months of the season, often in appalling conditions, with lines freezing in the rings of the rod, water temperatures as low as 34°F and snow flurries swirling down the valleys for good measure, go a long way to belie the notion that fish cannot be caught on a fly early in the season.

Similarly on the Tweed, famed for its spring and autumn runs, a 'fly fishing only' rule comes into effect from 1 to 15 February and again from 15 September onwards, although the angling season does not end until 30

November, and Tweed anglers are often faced with testing conditions at the start of the season and again in late autumn. One learns mainly by experience to adjust one's methods to deal with the widely varying circumstances. This, after all, is the very essence of salmon fishing or, for that matter, any type of fishing.

There are two main schools of thought on how best to catch fish on the fly in cold water temperatures, which are often combined with high water flows. The first theory is that one should fish slow and deep and, if necessary, use a weighted fly to reach the fish. The second school of thought holds that one should never fish one's fly more than 12–18 inches under the surface and that one should use a much larger fly to bring the fish up, rather than sink the fly to the fish. Both can be effective on their day, but I am a strong advocate of the latter method, having found it to work well on northern rivers.

The advantage of the large fly fished close to the surface is that the fish always sees it clearly silhouetted against the sky, which is the lightest background at all times for contrast. Also, if the fish is tempted to move to a fly fished in this manner, he must move with considerable impetus in order to be able to catch it. This allows for a firm contact if the fish takes, and, more importantly, if he misses, a telltale blemish or boil is left on the water surface, which alerts the angler to the fact that he has moved or risen a fish. This allows the angler the chance to re-present his fly to the fish,

which will often take it successfully the second time.

When fishing the deep fly method, the angler is purposely sinking his fly in the hope of getting it down to his quarry. The fly, therefore, is no longer silhouetted against the sky, but instead is often against the darker background of the landscape or even the underwater banks of the river, and at the same time seen through a wall of turbid water. This can reduce the fish's chances of getting a clear view of the fly. If the fish does see the fly and wishes to take it, he rarely has to use the same impetus to intercept it as it is much closer to him. Therefore, contact is not so definite. If the fish moves to the fly and misses it, the angler is rarely alerted and may be quite oblivious to the fact that he has moved a fish. Therefore, he passes the fish by as he works on down the pool, denying the fish a second chance of taking the fly.

How then does one fish the deep fly? On most occasions, in the early part of the season, the river is likely to be swollen by either snow melt or rainfall. Therefore, the current speed on the surface will be fast. In order to allow his fly to have time to sink before the line is caught by the current and swept quickly across the pool, the angler must cast fairly square across the river and at the moment his fly lands,

Squaring the rod tip across the current as soon as the fly has landed to enable it to hesitate momentarily before beginning its traverse across the pool

slacken off the tension on the line. This enables his fly to sink quickly to the required depth before the line between his rod tip and his fly is caught by the current. Whether the angler creates this slack line by moving his rod tip quickly downstream, or by actually letting off loose line, is a matter of choice and circumstance. One sure thing is that whether his fly is weighted or not, if he puts out a long cast at 45° downstream and across – because his line between the rod tip and the fly is then taut – the moment the fly lands on the surface of the water it will then have no chance of sinking to the desired depth, but will be swept across the pool just below the surface. I have often seen inexperienced anglers believing, quite wrongly, that they are fishing deep when casting at this angle.

However, if the 90° or 60° cast, straight across or slightly down and across, is employed, the fly is given adequate slack to attain the required depth before it swings across the pool.

Once the fly has traversed the width of the pool, the angler must handline to bring his fly to the surface before re-casting; if he does not, his sunken fly may snag as he re-casts, resulting in a broken rod.

When employing this method, it is best to keep the point of the rod down close to the surface of the water to help slow down the movement of the fly and allow it to fish at the optimum depth. A high rod tip only helps to keep the fly more buoyant in the water, and in high water or windy conditions this error can again defeat the purpose. As the river drops to lower flow rates, the angler must adjust his angle of cast and the amount of slack line he gives to his fly as it lands on the water, in order to prevent his fly sinking too deep and then snagging the bottom. Or, if he prefers, he may reduce the weight and size of his fly to make this adjustment.

The angler who wishes to fish his fly closer to the surface can either cast at 60° across and

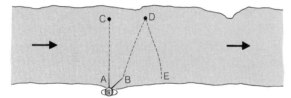

Figure 1   *Fishing a weighted fly deep in high water flow. The angler casts his fly square to the current from A to C, then moves his rod point downstream from A to B as soon as his fly lands. The fly then has slack line to enable it to sink, and begins to traverse the pool at the correct depth between D and E*

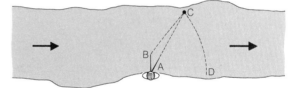

Figure 2   *Fishing an unweighted fly. The angler casts at 60° to the current from A to C. Then he moves his rod tip upstream to B, so that his rod tip lies square to the current. He then allows his fly to traverse from C to D. This movement allows his fly to hesitate fractionally before beginning its traverse across the pool*

Fishing a low rod tip with a sunken line

Using a low rod tip to prevent wind slap on the line on a blustery day

slightly downstream, then square his rod tip to make sure his fly is buoyant, or else cast at 45° down and across the river, and lead his fly across the width of the pool with his rod tip pointed downstream. In the former case, his fly will pause for a vital moment before it begins to traverse the width of the pool, and it can then be helped across the river by the aid of handlining. This also keeps the angler in contact with his fly all the time. In the latter case, the moment the fly lands it will be caught by the current and swung across the pool with no momentary pause and generally at an adequate speed. It rarely requires the aid of handlining to help it on its way.

The rod tip should be kept low to the water no matter which method is employed, both to prevent excess buoyancy and needless risk of wind slap on the line hanging between the tip of the rod and where it enters the water. In high water levels, a quick mend of the line across the current the instant the fly lands on the water is a good method of slowing down the immediate traverse of the fly across the current. This, however, can only be accomplished once when a sunk line is being used, just as the fly lands; after that, the line will grip the water and sink below the surface, making mending impossible. If a floating or greased line is being used, mending can be achieved the whole time if necessary, because this type of line lies on the surface of the water.

Mending is accomplished by lifting the rod tip up and outwards to throw the line out across the current. The line is then lying more perpendicularly downstream. This will reduce the angle and thereby prevent the current from punching a bag in the line and dragging the fly round too quickly.

In lower water flows, many anglers who choose to fish the shallow fly discard their sunk line for a sink-tip, whilst others even resort to a floater. Personally, I believe in using a full sunk line up to mid-April, or certainly until the water temperature is over 42°F. The angler who believes in fishing a deep fly slowly has no other choice but to use a full sunk line if he is to fish it effectively.

Wading is an advantage if one is fishing from the shallow side of a river, but only if the pool cannot be covered adequately from the shore. By narrowing the width of the water to be covered, the angler, especially with a long rod, has far better control over his fly as it fishes the width of the pool. Many anglers, however, are inclined to wade in too deep, sometimes to the extent that they actually disturb fish, and this is a bad mistake. If the pool is very wide, it often pays to fish it down first wading at approximately half thigh depth. Then, if need be, and only if one has not reached the full extent of the fishable water, it can be fished down a second tie, wading slightly deeper.

Tackle

Tackle required for early spring fishing is a good powerful rod, 14−15 feet in length, a wide drum reel with the capacity to house 100 yards of backing, and a No. 11, 40-yard sinking or intermediate line. You will also need a strong nylon cast of 2−3 yards in length and an ample supply of weighted and unweighted tubes, with suitable trebles, Waddington or single iron flies. Probably the most important factor is to make sure everything is balanced. You should have good reel to suit the rod, the right weight of line to suit the rod, a strong leader capable of leading out even the heaviest fly and, finally, a rod which can cope with the most adverse weather conditions.

If the line does not suit the rod, or if the rod is incapable of lifting a reasonable length of sunk line off the water, or if the leader is too light and cannot lead the heavy fly through the wind, the angler is at a severe disadvantage and cannot do justice to the water he is fishing.

When choosing flies, remember that size is usually more important than colour and 2−4 inches is the norm, though colour at certain times of the season does play an important part. However, there is no doubt in my mind that it is the body of the fly which is crucial. It is this part of the fly that reflects light as the fly is gyrated and buffeted by the current flow. This glint or glitter alerts the fish to the fly's presence in exactly the same way as a light shining on a hillside would draw our immediate attention. Once fish have focused on the fly their interest increases, and this often leads to their eventually making a mistake and taking it.

In the spring, the flies which have been traditionally regarded as most effective are the Green Highlander, Yellow Torrish, silver-bodied flies such as the Silver Grey, Dusty Miller or Mar Lodge — by far my favourite of all — and a dark fly such as the Black Doctor, Jock Scott or Thunder and Lightning. Obviously, individual anglers have their own particular favourites which may well not be in my 'old-fashioned' list.

Nowadays, the emphasis is very much on hair-winged flies instead of ones dressed with feather, mainly for the sake of economy, but there is also no doubt that hair wings do scintillate and produce more movement in the water. Tubes or Waddingtons with treble hooks have also largely replaced the old single hook (meat hook) size 6 to 10 fly, and it could be said that modern anglers have a reduced selection from which to choose.

Spring favourites are now Stoat's Tail, Garry Dog, Black and Yellow, Willie Gunn and the long-winged varieties such as the Collie Dog and Tadpole. A reliable bunch, but if one had to criticize, it would probably be the lack of unveiled bodies — apart from the last two.

The old adage 'dark fly for dark day' and 'bright fly for bright day' has long been a golden rule. Strangely, however, I have always favoured the opposite. My advice to any angler would be to fish the fly you have most confidence in first, regardless of light. If that fails, try obeying the adage — or disobeying as I do.

If all should fail with different presentations, you can put it down to the unpredictable taking habits of our quarry, or to lack of fish.

Hooking a fish

At this time of year when large flies are the norm, whether trebles or single irons are being used, the hooks have a considerable gap between the point of the hook and the point of the barb. Therefore, when a fish takes the fly make sure that the barb is securely embedded in its mouth. Raise the rod firmly so as to ensure that the barb is set. In other words — strike. If you do not do this, there is a danger that only the point of the hook will penetrate and that, after a few shakes of its head, the fish may discard the fly. Only if you are very lucky and the point happens to contact a soft part of the mouth will the barb set itself.

It is also best to keep the forefinger on the line so that you are in immediate contact with your fly and, therefore, feel the fish the instant it makes contact. You should then immediately close your forefinger and trap the line against the rod butt before raising the rod. If you do not, there is a danger that the line will run off the reel on contact, and thereby reduce the power of the strike.

There are, however, still some anglers who firmly believe that one should hold a loop of loose line in one's hand, and when the fish takes, allow this line to be drawn out before tightening. The theory behind this is that the fly will slide in the fish's mouth so that it is positioned to hook the fish in the hinge of its jaw when the angler finally tightens. Whether this can actually happen in practice, when a large treble or single iron is being used, or whether the fish will feel these large objects and spit them out when it closes its mouth on them, must be a matter of question. Hence the age-old controversy over whether to strike or not.

What a salmon angler must *not* do, is to strike at a rise before he feels the pull from the fish (except in unusual circumstances) because then he is likely to pull the fly out of the fish's mouth.

Playing a fish

Once the fish has been hooked, you should keep the point of your rod well up and at the same time keep a steady pressure on the fish. It is then wise to walk down the bank until you are opposite the fish. If the fish moves upstream you should move up too, keeping level with it. Likewise, if the fish moves downstream. By doing this there is far less chance of the line getting snagged behind a rock if the fish turns quickly, or of the line being drowned − both of which are real dangers if the fish is allowed to get too far above or below you.

At the start of the battle, I believe in keeping a steady pressure on the fish while, at the same time, allowing it to dictate the style of play. You should then get firmer and firmer on the fish as it begins to tire. If one is too hard on a fish at the start, there is a real chance of it being panicked into making a quick, unsuspected movement, thereby taking you unawares. This may result in a broken cast or in the hook being wrenched free. The first sign the angler will see of the battle drawing to a close is the fish's tail swirling close to the surface; this is the time to increase the pressure steadily. But do not try, even at this stage, to pull the fish ashore too soon. Wait until its head comes to the surface and then try to keep it above water as you swing the fish quietly into your chosen landing place.

If the fish makes a final bid for freedom, allow it to take out line again, and then reel it in until its head is back on the surface once more. If you are accompanied by a gillie or an accomplice, try and swing the fish across the current and downstream towards him, in order to avoid undue pressure on the hook hold. Keep the fish on the surface until it is either in the net or has been gaffed. Once the fish has been secured, slacken the line immediately to avoid any risk of the rod tip being broken by any sudden movement by your accomplice and to avoid pulling the fish out of the net or off the gaff.

If you are on your own and there is a good gravel bank or beach available, it is probably easier to beach the fish by swinging it firmly up the shallows and on to the shingle. Keep firm pressure on the fish until it lies inert, and then pick it up by the tail. If no suitable landing place is available, make sure that you play the fish completely out so that it is lying on the surface before you attempt to tail, gaff or net it. Then move down quietly and slip the tailer over its tail, draw it head first into the net, or impale it on your gaff. I believe in placing the gaff point underneath the fish and then drawing it up-wards into the soft underbelly. Gaffing a fish in this way damages the flesh less.

SUMMER FISHING

Once the water temperature rises to 48°F and above, salmon favour much smaller flies. Size 6−12 is the norm, or ½−1 inch tubes. Instead of sunk flies, flies fished close to the surface are also now much preferred. This is partly because, with the warmer water and weather conditions, fish now prefer to lie in a shallower water in the more streamy parts of the pools, either at the head or tail of the main holding pools or in the smaller runs and resting pools. This sudden change of preference from large to small flies is probably related to what they were used to at sea. In the colder climes they fed on larger fish whilst in the warmer Gulf Stream they fed on smaller food farms.

This change in preferred diet opens up a whole range of differing methods which an angler can now use to present his fly to his quarry in an attractive manner. He can virtually stow away his sunk line and large flies for he will not need them again until the water temperatures drop in the autumn.

Instead, he will require a floating line − in the olden days we used to grease ordinary lines for this purpose. In high water flows or when fishing deep, gorgy sections of the river, the angler may prefer to use a sink-tip line. He will need casts of varying strengths from 10 to 18 lb breaking strain, and a wide range of ordinary flies and tube flies in the smaller range of sizes. In the past, one had the choice of flies dressed on single or double irons, either normal dressings or low-water dressings for summer fishing. Today, as well as these varieties, we have a wide selection of tube flies, Waddingtons and patterned flies dressed on Esmond Drury treble hooks, to choose from.

Obviously, the experienced angler will long since have chosen a small selection of patterns that have proved successful to him in the past, and, for the most part, he will use these during the summer months. Advice to the inexperienced: it would seem that on the whole salmon prefer drab, dull colours at this time of year in clear water conditions. Flies like the Stoat's Tail, Hairy Mary, Lady Caroline, March Brown, Logie, Blue Charm, Silver Blue, Mar Lodge and Thunder and Lightning, amongst many others, will fill the bill. If, however, the water is discoloured, either by peat or by turbidity, a coloured fly is often an advantage. I have always found that a gold or copper-bodied fly shows up better in these conditions than silver-bodied ones do, and an orange or yellow fly can also do well. The Dunkeld, Member, General Practitioner, Willie Gunn, Black and Orange and Garry Dog, all come into this category.

Rods, again, are really a matter of choice, which will be influenced by circumstances. In the past, we used to discard our heavy 15−16-foot split cane or greenheart rods in the summer, often gratefully choosing lighter ones from 12 foot 6 inches to 13 foot 6 inches. Today, with carbon fibre and glass fibre being the norm (and being very much lighter than their predecessors), the angler has a wide choice. He can fish on perfectly comfortably throughout the year with his spring 15 foot rod if he wishes, or he can choose from a wide range of 12−14 foot rods. If he prefers, he can choose an even smaller 9−11 footer, with which he (or she) can cast single-handed.

My advice, however, and regardless of circumstances or seasons of the year, would be for the angler who only fishes occasionally to choose a 14−15 foot rod that can be used in any situation, and which is also capable of coping with the worst weather conditions likely to be encountered. If you are fishing fairly regularly throughout the year in widely differing circumstances, I would suggest either a 10½−11 foot carbon for the smaller river and

loch fishing; a 13−13½ foot for summer fishing; and a 15−17 foot carbon one for use in the spring and autumn and in high water conditions at other times of year. All these rods should have the power to cope with the strongest winds because, as any angler knows, weather conditions can change very quickly. When they change for the worse it is most frustrating for an angler to find that he is under-rodded, with the one he is using being incapable of casting his fly to where the fish are lying.

Presentation

There are four main methods of presentation for use in summer fishing.

1. The normal fly fishing method with a greased or floating line, with or without a sink-tip.
2. The greased line method.
3. Dibbling or dragging the dropper or tail fly on the surface of the water.
4. Backing up a pool.

Each of these methods can be very effective on its day, and each presents the fly to the fish in entirely different ways.

The floating line

The angler should pause briefly before he starts fishing a pool, to identify the most likely lies. As a guide for the inexperienced, fish are likely to lie on either side of the fast current at the head of the pool, off promontories or rock ledges, upstream of or behind swirls or blemishes denoting underwater obstructions − such as rock ledges or large stones − and again, in the draw at the tail of the pool.

When you start fishing you should literally begin with the length of line you have on the rod and make a very short cast, working the fly with the rod tip. Then, standing in the same place, lengthen the line a yard at a time and fish out each cast carefully until you have sufficient line out to cover the full width of the pool, the fishable water in the pool, or the water you can cover from that position. Having

Figure 3 *Fishing with a floating line. The angler should cast at a 45° angle downstream and across the current between A and C. Then lift his rod tip up and outwards to mend his line across the current moving his rod to point B. His line will then lie parallel to the current and traverse from C to D. This movement slows down the speed of his fly's progress across the pool and can be repeated if necessary*

fished out these initial casts, you then move on down the pool, a yard or two after every cast. If you do not fan out your fly in this way, but instead lengthen line quickly until you reach the far side of the fishable water before starting to fish, you will miss all the fish lying within the arc between you and your fly as it lands in the water. This arc may be as much as 10−20 yards at the neck of the pool, which, in some water heights, is one of the most likely taking areas in the pool during the summer months.

The angle of cast must vary according to the current entering the pool. Usually, I prefer to cast at an angle of 60° downstream and across the current. This allows the fly to pause and to be sized up by fish lying close to where it alights on the surface of the water, before it is swept across the current and away. Other fishermen, however, prefer a more-angled, 45° cast downstream and across current but, unless one mends one's line immediately, the fly will begin to traverse the current immediately on landing, allowing little chance for fish lying on the far side of the current to see it clearly.

An angler fishing with a floating line or sink-tip has a big advantage over the sunk line fisherman because he can mend his line at any time during the fishing out of the cast. He is, therefore, able to slow down or speed up the traverse of his fly at will. By mending line and using rod-tip control, he should be able to hold his fly, albeit momentarily, over the most likely taking places in the pool and, by doing so, to

improve his chances, particularly in high water conditions.

It is also important to fish the fly in as close as possible to the bank on which one is standing because fish, in certain water heights, may well be lying close to the bank, or may follow the fly for some distance. In this latter case, they often take as the angler handlines to make his re-cast, because this last-minute increase of speed by the fly resembles a creature trying to escape and attracts a predator to pounce on it.

It pays, sometimes, to fish down a very wide pool first with a medium-length line, combing the nearside of it carefully, and then to fish it down again with a full length of line, paying more attention to the main body of the pool this time. If you attempt to fish the full width of the pool in one fishing, it is almost inevitable that you will lift your fly off the water to re-cast before it has properly covered the water close in to the near bank.

Even when fishing a floating line, I still believe in squaring my rod tip across current immediately after my fly has landed, or I have made my first mend, ensuring that my fly is buoyant and that I am fully in contact with it. I then believe in handlining to ensure that I keep in absolute contact. In the summer, however, I retrieve only 2−4 inches of line per draw, instead of 1 foot to 18 inches in the spring.

The size of fly depends largely on water conditions. A size 8 or 6 is probably the norm in high water, a 10 or 12 being usual when the water is low. I am quite certain, however, that most anglers err on the large side; I have been guilty of this myself.

Many anglers believe in fishing a dropper as a second fly at this time of year. I follow this practice and always use a No. 9 Hairy Mary or silver-bodied Stoat's Tail for my dropper. As the dropper is fishing higher in the water than the tail fly and is also presented entirely differently (because it is stabilized by the short length of cast to which it is attached), the angler who uses it has the advantage that he can fish the pool down with two different flies, presented in contrasting ways.

The pattern to use on any particular day depends on what inspires the angler's confi-

Using a high rod tip to fish a glide at the tail of a pool with a floating line

dence or what is advised by the gillie. If these choices prove fruitless, my advice is to ring the changes.

When a floating line is being used, a higher rod tip is acceptable, but if it is very windy I still lower my rod tip to avoid windslap on the length of line between the tip and the water.

In high water flows, fast streamy water or narrow deep gorges, where swirly buffeting surface currents and eddies are usual, it pays to use a sink-tip. This length of sunk line grips the water and stabilizes the movement of the fly just below the surface, preventing the fly from skating across in an erratic manner.

Striking, playing and landing a fish when using a floating line do not really differ from the spring fishing technique, except for the fact that the angler is using lighter tackle and must, therefore, scale down the pressure he exerts accordingly.

The grease line

It is necessary to use a full floating line in order to fish this method properly. The cast should be 9 – 12 feet, and a size 8 – 12 fly is the(norm6 Thik is uainly because medium to low water flows suit this particular type of floating line technique best.

The object of this method is to fish one's fly so that it hangs motionless in the current. I believe the technique was devised in an attempt to imitate plankton. These microscopic creatures, found both in fresh and sea water, are known to be part of a salmon's favoured diet during its feeding life. Because plankton is fairly immobile in the water, remove any drag or untoward movement from the fly by allowing it merely to hang inert below the surface as it floats across the width of the pool.

To achieve this, it is necessary to cast one's fly at 45° down and across the current and to mend immediately, so that the fly and line are lying perpendicular up and down-stream, parallel to the current flow. As soon as any quirk, bag or kink appears in the line, causing the fly to drag, the line must be remended immediately. Sometimes, in streamy water, five or more mends may have to be made while fishing out one cast; on smoother water, fewer mends will be required.

The angler using this method should hold his rod tip up and out over the water whilst his fly is fishing, because if he tries to lead the fly with the rod tip this in itself could cause his line to drag.

When a fish takes, the angler will often see his floating line tightening on the surface before feeling the actual pull. Many anglers believe in having a loose loop of line in their hands and allowing the fish to take out this loose line before tightening; others prefer to keep a high rod tip and to lower it to give slack line as the fish takes, just before tightening. Because the fly is not being dragged by the current, the current cannot help to set the hook firmly in the fish's mouth, so the angler himself must exert sufficient pressure to set the barb.

Many anglers believe that a dark, dull or drab pattern of fly is the most effective for use with this method, and certainly if we are right in believing that we are simulating plankton, this would be in keeping with its colour.

The Lady Caroline, March Brown, Sweep and Blue Charm were some of the old favourites used in the past for this purpose; today, the Hairy Mary, Munro Killer and Stoat's Tail are all eminently suitable. Either single or double flies, mounted as low water dressings, were thought in the past to be the most effective, before tube flies and dressed flies mounted on treble hook shanks came into fashion. It is really a matter of personal choice.

Dibbling

Dibbling or trailing the tail fly on the surface is fairly new to salmon fishing. It is really akin to raising the bob fly on to the surface of the wave when fishing from a boat on a loch. Undoubtedly, this method is intended to imitate a flying insect, struggling to take off again after having been blown on to the water's surface. In mild weather conditions it can be very effective, and often attracts fish when nothing else will. Everything depends on rod tip control, because when the fly lands the rod tip is raised to pull it up on to the surface, when the tail fly is being used, only the hooks are trailing, and when the dropper is employed the dropper fly is fluttering on the surface. This method is most effective in the streamy necks of pools or on fast narrow runs, where the full width of the river can be covered with a short line. Once the pool widens out and the current dies, these methods are not nearly so efficient.

When dibbling with the dropper, it pays to use a slightly heavier tail fly to act as an anchor. This stabilizes the leader and allows the dropper to flutter over the surface in a pendulum movement. The dropper leg is tied to the leader, usually 4–4½ feet above the tail fly, and should be about 4 inches in length. The overall length of the leader should be 9–10 feet, with a breaking strain of 12–15 lb. The choice of line is really immaterial as this seldom, if ever, touches the water, apart from when a fish is being played. It is best, however, to use a floating line so that the angler can continue fishing on down the pool in the normal manner, once the dibbling area has been covered.

Flies range from No. 6 in high water flows, to sizes 9 to 12 in normal conditions. The pattern is really the angler's choice, but I prefer a fly with a silver or gold full body, or part body, in order to reflect light. Hairy Mary, Silver Stoat, Blue and Black and Munro Killer are all favoured on the River Helmsdale, where this method is widely used.

When a fish takes, it is best to momentarily drop the point of the rod and then to tighten straight away. This allows the fish to submerge and turn before the strike. In most cases the angler will see the fish as it takes, so he must steel himself not to pull the fly out of its mouth by striking too soon.

Flies for use when the trailed tail fly method is adopted are much larger tubes, varying from 1½ to 2 inches in low to medium water, and from 2½ to 3 inches in high water. The Willie Gunn is my favourite pattern, but the Collie Dog or Tadpole can be equally effective. The method of striking is identical to that used when dibbling.

For both these techniques a long rod offers an obvious advantage.

Backing up a pool

This technique is useful regardless of the season of the year. It was originally devised to enable the slack tail of a pool to be fished with ease when insufficient flow prevented the fly from traversing the width of the river when the usual fly fishing method was employed, or in slack, canal-like pools where there was little or no current. It is obviously best to fish these areas of a river when the surface is ruffled by

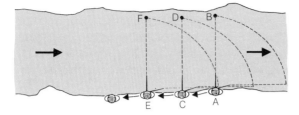

Figure 4   *Backing up a pool. The angler starts at the tail of the pool at point A, casts square to point B, then takes four steps upstream towards the head of the pool to point C, whilst his fly traverses the pool. He then recasts and repeats the performance as many times as is required to fish the pool from tail to head.*

wind; under these conditions this method can be very productive.

Instead of fishing the pool down, the angler starts at the tail of the fishable water and backs up towards the head of the pool. He should cast fairly square across the pool and move up the pool some five short paces as each cast is being fished out, handlining in in draws of 6–12 inches at the same time. It is the angler's movement upstream, combined with the handlining, which creates sufficient impetus to enable the fly to traverse the width of the pool. In fact, these movements upstream are a substitute for the current needed to swing the fly across when the pool is being fished out.

It is important to swing the fly right across the pool and close in to the bank from which you are fishing before recasting, because some fish follow the fly across the pool while others may be lying close in to the bank. Once you reach the head of the pool, you should finish off by winding in 5 yards of line per cast. This is similar to fanning out one's fly at the start of fishing a pool down; in fact, it is fanning out in reverse and if the angler fails to add this last finesse, he will have missed the opportunity of presenting his fly to all the fish lying in the first 20 yards at the head of the pool.

Part of the effectiveness of this method is that the fly is being taken away from the fish, instead of coming towards it. This is always attractive to any predator. Quite often, the fly simply appears from behind the fish's head and moves quickly away, enticing him to grab it before it escapes.

I use this method not only for fishing dead water with no current, but also, quite often, as a matter of practice having just fished down a pool, quickly backing up it again, often to remarkable effect, without even changing my fly. Also, when confronted with a very long pool, I rarely fish it down but, instead, back up it in order to save time. This method can fish out a pool just as thoroughly as fishing a pool down can, and takes only a third of the time.

The type of equipment required is exactly the same as for normal fishing at the same season of the year. Fly size and colour usually remain unchanged, too. However, if all else fails, it often pays to try shock tactics, such as putting on an unusually large long-winged fly, and then backing it up as the final fishing of a pool. A very large Collie Dog is ideal for this purpose. Quite often, an angler who turns to this radical tactic will find that fish will move to the large fly. Sometimes they will take it, at others they may merely rise to it. In the latter case, the angler should change down and back the pool up again with a normal-sized fly of a similar pattern, as the fish which moved to the radical sized fly will be fully alerted, and may now take this one.

AUTUMN FISHING

Early autumn fishing does not differ much from summer fishing but, as the nights grow longer and colder, water temperatures begin to drop once again. Floating lines are first replaced by sink-tips, then by intermediates and finally by full sunk lines. Fly sizes also drop, until in late autumn similar sizes to those used in early spring are often the order of the day. Orange or red are effective colours in the autumn, and all the normal favourites can be relied on. If the water is peaty or turbid, a yellow fly will show up well.

Gravelly bottomed pools are a favoured habitat as the spawning season draws nigh, and rocky, rugged pools are now less attractive to the fish and are often deserted. Shallow tails of pools, and runs between pools, often neglected earlier in the season, are now popular haunts.

Methods of fishing are exactly the same as for earlier in the season, when similar water and water-temperature levels prevailed. Finally, as overall advice for all periods of the year: do not be too conservative and fish in one monot-onous manner. Be adventurous and ring the changes, not only in fly size and colour, but also in presentation. See how fortunate beginners always seem to be! I firmly believe that this is due to their inconsistency as they try to master the art. No one cast is fished in a similar manner to the previous one, and because of this, their flies may be presented in numerous different ways as they fish down one pool. This is more likely to contribute to their success than the popular belief in 'beginners' luck'!

There is surely a lesson for us all to learn from this.

LOCH FISHING

Salmon lochs throughout the UK vary tremendously, both in size and depth, and so do the salmon stocks available in these lochs. Lochs Tay, Ness and Lomond are probably the largest of the famed salmon lochs in the British Isles, but there are also salmon fisheries on similar-sized loughs in Ireland.

On the east and north coasts of Scotland, spring fish can be caught in Lochs Tay, Ness, Brora, Achnemoine on the Helmsdale, More and Beg on the Thurso, and Loch Naver. All these lochs can be productive throughout the season. There are many good salmon lochs on the west coast rivers, and also on the islands off the west coast, most of which fish best from June onwards. Many of these lochs, on both west and east coast rivers, have relatively short river systems connecting the lochs to the sea, so many fish entering the lochs are fresh; and some will even carry sea lice.

As with all other forms of successful salmon angling, the most important factor is an intimate knowledge of the water one is fishing. For fly fishing on a loch this is even more crucial, and at the same time much more difficult to attain. The main criterion for success or failure is usually the depth of water. A depth of 2½–5 feet is probably the most productive, and salmon can be caught freely on a fly up to a depth of 8 feet, but in depths greater than that, the fish are usually very difficult to tempt with a fly.

There are some obvious pointers to where these taking places are likely to be, such as in bays, off burns, around the main feeding tributaries or outlets, and around off-shore islands. But in the case of the larger lochs, such as Tay, Ness and Lomond, obvious taking places are often few and far apart. In most lochs, for every obvious taking place there are many, many shallow banks that cannot be read by sight, hidden under the surface of rippling waves. That is why the loch fisher for salmon is at a far greater disadvantage than his counterpart who fishes a river. The loch fisher can often waste a large part of his day – or even the entire day – fishing over water that is too deep, whilst his counterpart on a river has only to recognize a pool to stand a good chance of success.

Therefore, the best advice any loch fisher can be given is to procure the services of a gillie who has an intimate knowledge of that loch, if only for the first day of his fishing holiday. At least he will then be guided to areas of the loch where he stands some chance of success; after that, he has the opportunity of building on this knowledge. Obviously, the longer he can employ the gillie, the sooner will he learn the vital characteristics of the loch.

Anglers should always be aware, however, that the level of a loch will fluctuate, rising and falling after rainfall, in exactly the same manner as a river. As taking areas are related so critically to depth, they are liable to change frequently, according to the fluctuations of the loch levels. Obviously, as the loch rises, the deeper taking areas become too deep, and the shallower ones also become deeper. Those which previously were too shallow to fish may now be the most productive. The same thing happens when a loch is drawn down by prolonged drought. The prime areas at normal loch level become too shallow or high and dry, whilst some which were normally too deep to be of use may become productive.

Sometimes gillies, especially experienced ones, are difficult to find. If this is the case, the angler who wishes to fish from a boat can only get over this problem by hiring a boat and purchasing a depth-meter. He should spend part of his first day charting the loch for himself and, once he has pinpointed suitable areas, then he should start to exploit them. At least, having done this, he stands some chance of success. The angler who wishes to fish from the bank must rely on being able to read the loch sufficiently and then concentrate his efforts on obviously shallow areas.

When the loch is high, fish often rest at the loch mouth having just entered it, and in and around the mouths of burns or larger tributaries, or in bays close to them. The inflow current from these burns often helps the shore angler to work his fly. In a lower loch, bays, burn mouths and the water off promontories are all worth exploring.

If need be, the shore angler should be prepared to wade out a short distance in order to cover water between 2 feet 6 inches and 8 feet deep. He should not, however, use body waders as they may tempt him to wade in good fishing water, thereby disturbing his fish.

Wind direction and strength are both important factors in fly fishing for salmon on a loch. Strong, steady winds are generally the best, with a real trough between the waves a bonus. For day-time fishing, anything less than a 3 inch wave, although ideal for trout fishing, can be insufficient for salmon. But a 'trouty' ripple in the early morning or late evening can be productive and even a 1 inch wave at dawn or dusk can be acceptable. The wind direction often serves certain banks and bays better than others; again, intimate knowledge of the loch is of great benefit in this respect.

An onshore wind blowing into a bay, promontory or burn mouth can be an asset to the boat fisherman but these conditions may, at times, be a disadvantage to the angler on the shore, unless he can position himself to fish either across the wind or with it. Sometimes the advantage is reversed when there is an offshore wind, unless the boat can be squeezed in between the shore and the fishable water without disturbing the area to be fished. Under these conditions, it can pay the boat fisherman to land a short distance away from the fishable area, and to fish it first from the shore, returning to his boat to fish the rest of the water when he has done this. Blustery conditions, or days when the wind direction changes frequently, are seldom compatible with good taking. However, there is always an exception to any rule.

Other climatic changes – sunshine, thunder and variations in water temperature levels – have much the same effect on loch fishing as they do on river fishing. Salmon rarely take well on the first and second days after heavy rain, especially during the summer months, because they are sickened by the high acidity levels. But as the loch levels drop, they will usually begin to take more freely once again.

Tackle

For early season loch fishing, a boat angler requires a 12-feet rod with plenty of bone, whilst the bank angler will have more command over his flies if he uses a 15-feet rod. Carbon or glass fibre rods are lighter than wooden ones and generally serve well.

A wide-drummed reel is best fitted with 150 yards of backing and an intermediate or sink-tip line. This amount of backing is necessary as fish being played in large expanses of water can make longer runs than they normally do in the more confined areas of pools on a river.

Ideally, leaders should be of 15–18 lb breaking strain, 6–9 feet in length, in the spring, depending upon whether one or two flies are being used. Most lochs have a favoured pattern or two of their own, such as the turkey-winged varieties popular on Loch Lomond. Otherwise, use the fly you have confidence in – the Hairy Mary, Stoat's Tail, Mar Lodge and Silver Grey are my favourites. Sizes: tail fly 1–9 according to water temperature; on the dropper, 9–12.

In summer time, the boat angler can either continue to use a 12-foot rod, or do as I prefer and change to a single-handed one of 9½–11 foot. I still prefer a light intermediate line with a plentiful supply of backing, but others use either a sinktip or a full floater, which in mild weather conditions are quite adequate.

Shore fishermen can now reduce to a 12-foot rod, or smaller if they wish, but a 15-footer has more casting power which is an advantage if wind conditions are adverse. Casts of 10–15 lb are the norm, again according to conditions.

I prefer No. 8 sea-trout flies at all times when loch fishing in the summer and I only change if very windy conditions prevail, when I put a No. 6 on as a tail fly. I always lift my bob fly to the surface on mild, warm days. For the bob fly, I use a Black Pennel or a Soldier Palmer, and a Loch Ordie on a rough day. On the tail position a Greenwell, an Invicta or a Grouse and Claret are my favourites, but on rough days I use a Worm fly or a Muddler. Others prefer to use salmon flies, among which Hairy Mary, Stoat's Tail, Munro Killer, Willie Gunn and Mar Lodge are all favoured, and many place great faith in either Black or Brown Muddlers. Of course, if the loch one is fishing happens to have a favourite pattern or two, it is sensible to try them. Quite often when I am using a Stoat's Tail tube fly, I put on a Silver Treble to contrast with the dressing. In fact, when I use dull-coloured tube flies I often attach gold and silver trebles to them for this purpose.

Method

For boat fishing, undoubtedly the best combination is a single angler accompanied by a gillie. In this way, the gillie can control the speed of the drift of the boat so that the best water can be fished both unhurriedly and meticulously. When a fish is hooked, the gillie can row away from the fishable water and play the fish in deep water where it will not disturb others. If a fish is risen and does not take, the boat can be rowed into the wind a few yards and this allows the angler to re-present the flies to the fish without creating a disturbance.

For this method, it is best for the angler to sit on a bench or swivel seat with his back to the

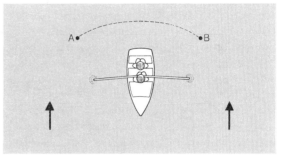

Figure 5 *Fishing a loch with one rod and one gillie in the boat. The angler sits in the stern of the boat with his back to the gillie. He covers the water between A and B fishing a different segment with alternate casts, whilst the gillie holds the boat into the wind*

Side casting from the stern of a boat with the angler sitting with his back to the gillie

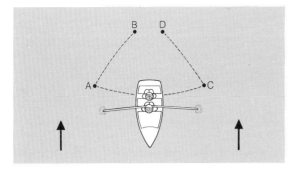

Figure 6 *Side casting as the gillie rows between beats. The angler sits in the stern with his back to the gillie. He either casts to long line A and allows his flies to traverse to B when he recasts, or alternatively casts to C and lets his flies traverse to D. Casting to A if he prefers to use his right shoulder, and to C if he prefers his left*

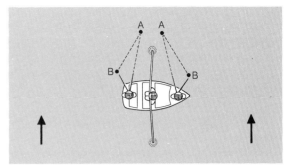

Figure 7 *Drifting down wind with a gillie and two anglers in the boat. One angler sits in the stern, the other in the bow. Each casts down wind to point A, and they then work their rods out and away from the boat, lifting their flies at point B*

gillie, which gives him complete freedom of movement to cast over a wide arc either to the right or left of its stern, or directly behind it. The gillie can row quietly head into the wind or angled across it slightly either way, so that the angler does not drift too quickly over the best places, and in this way can comb it literally inch by inch. With an onshore wind, salmon will lie with their tails almost touching the bank or sand, and these fish are easily covered in this manner. When moving between drifts the angler can, if he wishes, side cast by casting square and allowing his fly to sweep round in an arc behind the boat. This method can sometimes be quite effective; at others fish seem to disregard it entirely.

If, however, a boatman has two anglers instead of one in the boat, he has no alternative but to drift broadside down wind in order to give them both a fair chance. This allows both anglers to cover the water in front of them. Alternatively, the boatman may row quietly across the wind. This gives him very little chance of controlling the speed of the drift unless he puts a drogue out behind the boat. In some conditions this method gives both anglers a fair chance of good sport, but it is hard for the gillie to search his water as thoroughly as he would have been able to with only one angler present. If there are two experienced anglers in the boat it is possible for them both

to side cast, but they must be competent enough to be able to time their individual casts to avoid catching each other's lines.

I have always favoured the short line method and lift my bob fly to the surface of the wave, but the long line can be effective, usually on days with lighter winds or when colder conditions prevail.

When a salmon rises to the angler's fly he must give the fish time to turn with it and must delay his strike until he either feels the pull or has given the fish time to submerge. 'Quietly count three under your breath and then strike,' is often sound advice. When a salmon is hooked, the angler should keep steady pressure on it at all times. The gillie will probably row quietly away from the fishing area and, if two rods are in the boat, the one who is not playing the fish should wind in and lay his rod flat, so that the angler playing the fish has complete freedom of movement. Sometimes the fish will make a wild run, whilst at other times it will just bore deep. If a fish does run, just let it go, for the boatman will follow and it will soon tire. Just wind it back when it does. I prefer to try and get my fish behind the boat as soon as possible after I have hooked it, so that it is away from the best water, but one must be careful not to let it dive under the boat or snag a loose fly. Many people like to go ashore to land a fish, and this is often the safest method, but it is just as easy to net or gaff a fish alongside the boat, provided nobody panics and tries to land it too soon.

The shore angler can either fish out into the loch quite normally and handline his flies back to him, with or without raising his dropper, or, alternatively, he can back up the shore line in exactly the same way as he would back up a pool. This is the method I prefer. One is able to cover much more water in this manner, and I believe it gives one a much better chance of success.

If a floating line is being used, either from a boat or from the shore, the angler will often see the line on the surface tightening and beginning to move away as the fish takes, long before he feels the pull from the fish. Some anglers will be fishing with a loop of line in their hand, and will let the fish take this out before tightening, just as they would in a river. Others strike immediately on contact. The timing of the strike always has been and always will be controversial, but I for one strike as soon as I feel my fish.

The bank angler must approach his water carefully, as fish can at times be lying very close to the shore. It is often best to stand well back and make the first few casts to cover the water close in before moving nearer to the water.

Evening and early morning fishing can be very productive around the mouths of tributaries and in bays, even though these places may have been more or less lifeless during the daytime. Especially in the evening, fish often come out of the deep and nose around these burns at dusk, and they may still be there at dawn.

Finally, another method to try for salmon in warm water conditions on a loch, is the dap on a floss line. This is great fun if it works and can, on occasions, move quite a lot of fish, but they do not always take.

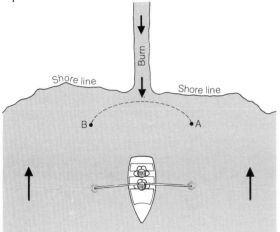

Figure 8 *Fishing a burn mouth or bay with an onshore wind. The angler sits in the stern of the boat with his back to the gillie, whilst the gillie holds the boat into the wind and the angler fishes the arc between A and B in segments with alternate casts. Having fished the first arc out, the gillie eases the boat 2 yards nearer the shore, and then the process is repeated*

Further reading

G.P.R. Balfour-Kinnear, *Flying Salmon* (A. & C. Black, 1937).

H. Falkus, *Salmon Fishing: A Practical Guide* (H. F. & G. Witherby, 1984).

Neil W. Graesser, *Advanced Salmon Fishing* (Boydell Press, 1987).

—— *Finer Points of Salmon Fishing* (Boydell Press, 1989).

—— *Fly Fishing for Salmon* (Boydell Press, 1982).

Moc Morgan

Moc Morgan started fishing at the age of nine and has spent much of his time fishing for trout, grayling, sea-trout and salmon ever since. His summers have been spent chiefly in pursuit of sea-trout in all parts of the British Isles and he has now fished for this marvellous species in more than seventy rivers and still waters.

Moc has captained the Welsh National Fly Fishing Team on ten occasions and has won the Welsh Fly Fishing Championship twice.

In terms of fishing journalism and authorship, Moc is becoming something of a legend. A regular contributor to *Trout and Salmon* and to *Trout Fisherman*, he also writes articles for some ten other periodicals, two of which are in Welsh, his native tongue. He has written five books and made substantial contributions to three others. He appears regularly on television and radio, presenting programmes both on angling and on the countryside.

For seven years, he had his own weekly radio programme on country matters.

He is also deeply involved in angling administration, having been Chairman of the Welsh Anglers' Council, Director of Coaching for Angling in Wales, and President of the International Fly Fishing Association; and he was largely instrumental in setting up the youth, ladies' and disabled international fly fishing matches.

At present, Moc is Secretary of the Welsh Salmon and Trout Angling Association and a member of the prestigious Salmon Advisory Committee, which advises Government on the management needs of salmon and sea-trout fisheries. He is also a member of the Management Committee of the Atlantic Salmon Trust and Chairman of its Educational Sub-Committee. In his spare time, Moc is a Councillor, and a Governor of seven schools − a hang-over from his schoolmastering days!

2

SEA-TROUT FISHING

Moc Morgan

The cows were settling down in the lush grass after crossing the river to the greener pastures that always lie on the other side as I tackled-up on the bank of one of my favourite beats of the Towi. I had been lucky to arrive when I did. The water still had a tinge of colour from the cattle's disturbance of the river-bed as I made my first cast across the neck of the run downstream.

I let my flies swing round just beneath the surface. The spot I was concentrating on was where the stream cut sharply under the far bank and the flow made the flies move quite fast. They were two patterns in which I had every confidence, an old Welsh dressing, Harry Tom, size 12, on the point, and a small Black Pennell on the dropper of my 5 lb leader.

I saw the flash of the fish as it came from the deeps and took the point fly with slow determination. The line pulled away, I tightened, and I was into a good sea-trout. As it took line and raced back into the pool, I realized that in my anxiety to take advantage of the colour, I had quite forgotten my net. Luckily, I was standing on some nice shingle, and eventually was able to beach the fish.

It was then that I realized just how lucky I had been. Had those cows crossed the river half an hour earlier, I would not have caught that sea-trout. I had been fortunate in meeting the all-important factor in any form of sea-trout fishing: right place, right time.

Why is the sea-trout so special? The oft-asked question came to me again as I placed the fish on the grass and looked at it admiringly. It is such a simple question. Would there was an equally simple answer. We all know of the migratory habits of the sea-trout, and that it spends half its life in the sea and the other half in fresh water. We encounter it as it comes back from salt water after its period of indulgence, moving upriver, whence it came, to spawn. Theories about it are legion, but no amount of scientific data will help us catch it. The knowledge needed is of its habits in the environment where the contest takes place. How it finds its own estuary is of interest, but of little use to us when we try to catch a fish.

This particular sea-trout had moved upriver some ten days previously, pushing through despite the comparatively low water. I recall seeing sea-trout moving upriver on the same stretch one evening with their backs out of the water. It is almost impossible to appreciate the urgency that drives some fish upriver, while others are content to remain in the lower reaches until spawning time.

The bigger sea-trout generally move into the river systems in April and May, while the smaller shoal fish appear in July. But generalizations are dangerous, especially with a creature as unpredictable as the sea-trout. I know a number of ardent sea-trout anglers who start fishing on their own river on a certain date every year irrespective of conditions, and they seldom miss out.

The sea-trout I'd caught on this evening was a perfect specimen – small head, strong shoulders and a powerhouse of energy. Once in a river system, sea-trout expend little energy as they lie in deep holes, making the occasional lunge or splash seemingly just to relieve their boredom. They seem to know they are safe in these deep holding spots. They are the 'stock ponds' whence the big fish move out at night; it pays to know where they are.

Each river has a somewhat different pattern of sea-trout run. Some smaller rivers have no sea-trout until July, when both big and small fish run together. But most rivers have a run of small sea-trout in summer, and some have a good run in September, although care is needed then in fishing for them, as fish will be near to spawning. Many sea-trout in a river system in September and October will have been upriver for a few months and will not be worth fishing for. Their flesh will be generally soft and white, and they'll make poor table fish. But really fresh sea-trout will still be superb.

A lad came down the meadow and opened the gate, and the ever-faithful sheepdog proved his versatility by rounding up all the cows and herding them out of the field. The 'lowing herd', I realized, no longer heralds nightfall.

I fetched my bass from the car and put the fish into it. It is important to keep fish in good condition, and not to put them in evil-smelling plastic bags. Sea-trout deserve better shrouds.

This fish had marks across its shoulders where scales had been removed. Some anglers, on seeing such damage, might blame the commercial netsmen. I'm not sure they would be right. I'd spent a morning with the commercial netters a few days previously and had seen that many of the fish they had taken bore similar marks. A terrible toll is taken of our sea-trout by illegal drift-nets which sweep the bays under cover of darkness, and I believe that the percentage of sea-trout bearing such scars indicates the extent of the problem of illegal netting. The

marks might have been made by a seal – I had seen seals taking fish in the estuary – but I think not.

The sea-trout's back also carried a big healed scar. The wound must have been made a year or two earlier, perhaps by a heron, kingfisher or cormorant, all of which are on the increase in the Towi valley following some mild winters. On the other hand, it might have been made by the latest predator to become established in the valley – the goosander. This bird, a recent immigrant, is a great fisher, certainly in the same class as the heron. But despite its trials and tribulations, this particular sea-trout had made it back to the river of its birth and had survived innumerable dangers only to fall victim to my pleasure.

More big sea-trout are about these days than at any other time in the last fifteen years. Many anglers believe that, pound for pound, no fish gives a better scrap than does a sea-trout. It is certainly the most volatile fighter of all, and the fact that sea-trout tend to 'explode' on feeling the hook is why so many gain their freedom.

The Dyfi (Dovey) is one river that has an impressive record for big sea-trout. The late Peter Vaughan one night took two of 16 lb and

The hatchery that members of the Glaslyn Angling Association built in order to enhance sea-trout stocks on the River Glaslyn

17 lb, surely the best brace of sea-trout ever taken at one outing in the British Isles? In the 1924 and 1925 seasons, Dr Thomas Davies, also fishing the Dyfi, recorded two sea-trout of 13 lb, two of 14 lb, one at 16 lb and three of more than 17 lb. Some fishers believe that these big sea-trout can be taken only late at night on quick-sinking lines and huge lures. Such a technique is a good one, but the fish can be taken also on small flies, and the angler must really be ready at all times to encounter a big one.

Salmon disease killed off many of the better sea-trout in the 1970s, but more recent seasons have seen a dramatic enhancement of sea-trout stocks on rivers such as the Towi, Dyfi, Teifi, Taf, Dwyfor, Conwy (Conway), Mawddach, Rhiedol and Ystwyth. All these waters produce fish into double figures each season. Big sea-trout, incidentally, do not necessarily take viciously. Sometimes a big fish will take so gently that the angler doesn't realize that he has a good one on.

Two important factors in successful sea-trout fishing are luck and confidence. Most of us get our fair share of good and bad luck, and I'm sure that over the seasons they even themselves out. Confidence is another matter. I have known some great sea-trout anglers in my fifty years of fishing, and they all had confidence to a greater or lesser degree – not cockiness, but just faith that they would 'catch'. This quality – a positive mental attitude it might be termed – may not be considered important by everyone, but I am convinced that the angler who adopts a positive approach to catching sea-trout generally does better than the angler who takes things more casually.

Some years ago I was subjected to considerable ribbing by my colleagues because I invariably carried four rods on my nightly outings on the river. My reason for this apparent overload was that I might want to use different types of line, and I loathed the time-consuming task of changing from one to the other. My aim at that time was to prove to myself – and to those who did me the honour of reading my essays – that the type of line used has an important bearing on the catching of sea-trout.

If a good fish moved, I would make three or four casts over the spot where the fish had shown with each of the four rods – if I didn't get a take, that is. Using only one rod, and with the need to change lines, rather than just rods, would have completely defeated my purpose.

The four lines I used were floating, intermediate, slow-sink and fast-sink. I also had three sink-tips of variable lengths which I could attach to my floating line. Some anglers, including some extremely good catchers of sea-trout, swear by one type of line or another. They fish right through the season with just that and would never dream of changing. But I believe we have a lot to learn from reservoir anglers, who may change lines quite often during a day's fishing. It is the fish that decide at what level in the water they want to take, and the only way to achieve the right depth is to use the right line. I am convinced that not to do so often accounts for lack of success.

The use of the quick-sinking line is probably the biggest development in sea-trout fishing in recent years. When I put up such a line, I know full well that I shall not use it much, but that it is a 'must' for one particular pool with a huge dip into a deep hole. It is a spot which has given me a few big sea-trout from time to time, and I would feel ill-equipped if I hadn't the line to cope with it.

I was introduced to the advantages of the quick-sinking line in the early 1970s on the Nith. Two anglers from the Midlands, en-

Figure 9 *Lines and flies*

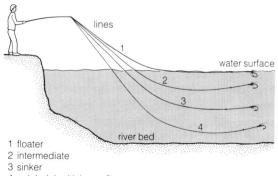

1 floater
2 intermediate
3 sinker
4 quick sink with hover fly

amoured with the late Dick Walker's methods, had adopted his static-fly technique for their sea-trout fishing. Being something of a Doubting Thomas, I joined them one night and saw that they really were taking a lot of fish. Their technique was to cast a huge Black Lure far out and allow it to sink to the bottom. Although they did nothing to move their flies, I was not convinced that they were completely static. The slow current through the deep pool must have exerted some pressure and pull on their leaders, and this in turn must have resulted in some movement of the flies. There was also a chance that an apparently immobile fly could be moved by the acquatic life at the bottom of the pool. But I was convinced that the ledgered fly did work. Other anglers strip their lures along the river-bed on quick-sinking lines — a method demanding a high work-rate — and yet others work their flies slowly in the deeps.

Many anglers favour the floating line, probably because of its ease of casting and pick-up off the water, and, of course, its bulk, which feels nice in the hand. I would certainly use a floater when tackling the tail of the pool after dark. Having said that, however, I have to confess to having a soft spot for intermediate lines, because some of my best catches in recent years have been taken on them. They do, of course, differ considerably between makes. Some sink to quite a low level in the water, while others, which I favour, hold up just below the surface. They usually cast well and handle nicely, which is important, as the angler often depends on the pressure on the line to tell him what is going on at the far end.

Anglers with long memories will recall the days of silk lines. Am I right in thinking that they were more sensitive than are the modern plastic lines? Or is my hankering really after the days when my reflexes were more finely tuned? Some sea-trout anglers still opt for silk lines (yes, they are still available) and maintain that with them they are better equipped than are anglers with plastic lines. A sea-trout's take can on some nights be as gentle as a kiss, registering only the slightest pressure on the line, and it is likely to go undetected unless the angler is really in touch with his fly.

But lines are only half the battle. What about flies? It seems to me that sea-trout anglers often indulge in something of a lucky dip when they choose their flies, yet each must have a principle which governs his choice. In the early 1970s I was privileged to act as boatman for two of the most respected gillies in these islands, Jim Kelly, from Ireland, and Tom Stark, from Scotland. Jim, then in his eighties, had been a gillie on Lough Conn from the age of twelve, and Tom Stark was a 'living legend' on Loch Leven. Between them they had more than 120 years' experience as gillies.

I shall treasure the memory of that day for the rest of my life. I learned a lot about boat fishing, but that wasn't all. In mid-afternoon, when things had become a little slow, I invited them to try some of my flies. From what must have been a few hundred colourful feathered creations, each of them took about a dozen, mainly palmered flies with good-quality hackles.

Jim Kelly picked the flies that he said 'buzzed' in the water, and Tom Stark said his selection had enough 'kick' in them. These may have been somewhat unusual descriptions, but they were certainly explicit. And I have to say that I agreed with their choice. My flies may lack clinical perfection, but I, too, like them to have life. I want flies that are fussy, fidgety, vivacious, frisky, agitated and bustling as they work through the currents in a river. When a fly is retrieved across the river, the current pulls, pushes, presses, opens, lifts and lowers it, and it must react to these pressures. Sea-trout have good vision, and if a fly is not taken, it is not necessarily because the fish has failed to see it. Yet there are times when I believe a fly or lure does go unnoticed, and I like to think that my flies have a presence that makes them more detectable at such times.

Figure 10   *Fly*

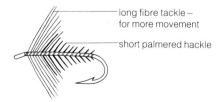

long fibre tackle – for more movement

short palmered hackle

Most anglers develop their own style of fly-dressing, yet there is a tendency for them to retain something of their teacher's influence. My teacher was the great Dai Lewis, of the Teifi, a professional fisher and dresser of flies. His flies had to have the 'kick' he so revered.

It's the hackle that gives a fly its lively qualities. A fly may appear to have bulk when viewed in its dry form, but that's not how sea-trout see it. They see it being worked across or against the current, and all flies dressed with good hackle lose their bulkiness when they are viewed in transmitted light. The qualities that most anglers look for are translucency, glint, gleam and life.

My old teacher, Dai, had an ingenious method of enhancing his flies. He would achieve the necessary gleam and glint in the hackle by adding one or two turns of cree hackle. This had the effect of making the points of the hackle gleam, giving a distinct impression of life and movement. He would also use a turn or two of long, soft hackle as a collar around the normal hackle, adding to the impression of life.

Three seasons ago, on the Camel, I came across the same principle in a Teal, Blue and Silver dressed as a palmered pattern, the teal used as hackle over the shorter blue hackle. It looked good and worked a treat, yet the principle of dressing flies that 'buzz' and 'kick' should be considered not as a Moses-like commandment, but nearer the teaching of the New Testament: Blessed are they who give sea-trout things lively and kicking, for they shall be rewarded.

Many anglers like their flies and lures for sea-trout to be dressed on the 'slim-line' principle, with just wisps of wing, a few false hackles, and the hook-shank painted silver. I shared a pool one night on the Coquet with an angler who swore by his very slim flies, and I have to admit that he did much better than I did with my patterns. I suffered similar 'whitewashes' on the Lynher and the Teign at the hands of anglers using 'slim-line' flies. Perhaps we should accept the teaching of my old mentor, Dai, who said that pattern was at

times irrelevant. What mattered were the flies' size and the manner and speed of their fishing.

I envy anglers who dress their flies and place them in row upon row in huge purpose-built boxes. I keep my sea-trout flies in four rather old tobacco tins, and my 'filing system' leaves a lot to be desired. But these are the patterns I find most useful.

Box 1 (for floating lines): Zulu, Bumbles, Connemara Black, Green Peter, Black Pennell, Invicta, Teifi Terror, Dai Ben, Teifi Topper.

Box 2 (for sinking lines): Alexandra, Squirrel series, Silver March Brown, Butchers, Red Mackerel, Pryf Llwyd, Haslam, Teal series, Mallard and Silver, Cert, Blackie, Black-and-silver Waddington, Peter Ross.

Box 3 (for surface work): Muddlers, Floating Lure, Surface Lure, Loch Ordie, Wake lures.

Box 4 (for fast-sink lines): Black Waddington Lure, Hover Lure, Tandem Blackie, Peacock-and-blue Lure, Marchogs, Silver Muddler Waddington, Beauty.

Sea-trout are often thought of as fish which are caught only at night, but daytime fishing for them can be just as exciting, given a breeze and water that has not been disturbed by other anglers. I favour working upriver, simply because it allows a more careful approach, but if the water is carrying some colour, then the downstream wet fly is the better method. I've never done well fishing at night in coloured water, but daytime fishing in high, coloured water with a wet fly can offer capital sport. All one need do is to adopt a normal wet-fly technique and work the flies just a little faster than one would normally for brown trout.

Daytime fishing with worm and spinner can also be rewarding, both techniques demanding skills which some fly fishers are reluctant to acknowledge. I remember one day, as I sat checking my four fly outfits, noticing another angler working his way down a stretch of water some quarter of a mile above me. I knew at once he was fishing a running worm, and immediately recognized him for his style. He was an expert catcher of sea-trout, who used a fixed spool reel and thin nylon line with just one shot to keep the worm near the river-bed. Through my binoculars I could see that he was letting his worm trundle downriver with the current, keeping well back from the fish's line of vision. He was making that worm fish every corner and eddy in the river, and I had no doubt that it was travelling downriver in a very natural manner. I do not fish the worm, but I can appreciate the art of this type of fishing. This particular angler's success — and it is outstanding success — is based on his 'link' with the worm. Some might describe it as telepathy. Do we fly fishers have this same close affinity with the fly?

Fishing the run into the pool, the angler quickly took a brace of sea-trout. Undoubtedly he knew the good holding spot there, and I made a mental note of it for future reference. One can learn a lot about the taking spots by watching other anglers! That particular spot had been ignored by me many a time. But I wonder if the taking spots are the same for worm anglers as they are for fly-fishers?

On this occasion, the angler I was watching fished his way down to the neck of the next pool and then did a sharp about turn, changing to a small spinner. Using the same rod, reel and line as before, he hurled the lure upstream with accuracy and then brought it spinning back at speed. He showed great river-craft as he fished his way upstream, covering sections that he had avoided when fishing the worm. One could but compare his approach with that of a fly-

fisher and realize that he could cover sections of river protected by trees that fly-fishers could not fish. He had gone further: he had chosen which sections fished best to spinner and which best to worm.

Again I saw him tighten into a sea-trout, this time in a deep glide near a huge obstacle in a heavily tree-shadowed stretch. That fish was netted rather unceremoniously, and on the very next cast another was hooked but kicked away. Two casts later the rod bent again, but this fish was to get away as well. However, the incident demonstrated how, on occasions, the spinner is responsible for an angler hitting a lot of fish.

The speed at which he retrieved the spinner was incredible, and I realized why a fly cast upstream and stripped back at top speed is sometimes so effective. I also noticed that he would change the speed of retrieve quite often and would bend its path, tactics adopted by fly-fishers.

Considerable stretches of river are left un-fished because of bankside trees and obstacles. This is good, as it takes the pressure off the sea-trout, which need areas of sanctuary. Yet often enough stretches which we fly-fishers ignore can be fished by Spey-casting and roll-casting. I have since fished the spot among the trees which I've mentioned and I've done quite well, despite a few hang-ups.

I always use chest-waders for sea-trout fishing, an excellent pair which are glove-like in their snugness, and I carry all I need in my waistcoat pockets. I favour two flies, which keeps my set-up simple, especially if I get a tangle (but more of that later). On the point I might put a size 8 Black Squirrel single, and on the dropper a size 10 Haslam, completing a favoured combination of one light pattern and one dark. The Squirrel series in fact includes a number of variations, and I tend to ring the changes on difficult nights.

Once in the water, I cast my intermediate line across river and let it swing across and down with the current in the manner that makes some anglers describe wet-fly fishing downriver as a chuck-and-chance method. That, of course, is rubbish. Would that those

Figure 11   *Good taking places in a pool*

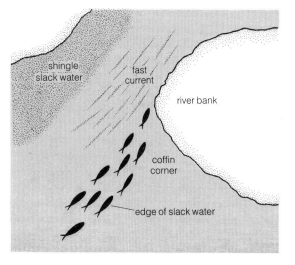

shingle
slack water

fast
current

river bank

coffin
corner

edge of slack water

Moc, footloose and fancy free on an Irish river, on a sea-trout safari to the Emerald Isle — where he has found his sea-trout technique so effective

who hold such a view could see a master of this type of fishing at work. They would soon change their minds.

Now begins the all-important retrieve of the flies across the river. As the current takes the line and pushes it down and back across the river, there is a tendency for the flies to be whipped across the stream unless the angler applies a break to the fly speed by judicious use of rod and line. I use a figure-of-eight action when I retrieve line. It is important to be in contact with the fly, and to think all the time about what the fly is actually doing.

If it is important for tackle to be well-balanced for daytime fishing, then at night it is essential. Most modern rods are far more tolerant of differing weights of line than were the old cane and glass rods, but when fishing in the dark you must be able to feel the weight of the line and appreciate the pressure being put on the rod. Some anglers like to use heavy lines. This has an advantage in terms of casting, despite its distinct drawback in terms of presentation. By overloading a rod, a night-angler is better able to feel the weight of the line and to gauge the length of his cast more accurately. The great thing is to retain one's normal casting action and timing, which some newcomers find difficult, and not to try to cast too long a line. With experience, casting in the dark becomes more of a reflex action, whereas at first one tends to be slightly disorientated and to increase casting speed.

I have started many anglers on night-fishing for sea-trout by suggesting that they should have a casting lesson. The drill I follow is to have them cast in daylight while blindfolded. Their initial indignation is usually replaced by astonishment as they realize the problems of casting by feel only. Much practice is needed to achieve the comfortable presentation that is the hallmark of an experienced night-fisher.

One angler who wanted to take up night-fishing for sewin asked if he could accompany me for a night's fishing, just to observe. After a dour hour of fishing, he asked why was I forever bringing the line in and running my hands down the leader and flies. I was not really aware that I was doing this, but then I realized that after a few casts I actually did run my fingers down the leader, checking both the leader for knots and the flies for weed.

This part of my fishing drill has developed over some fifty years and is now habit – and it is a vital one on windy nights, when it is easy to fish for some time with a tangled leader or a twisted fly unless a check is made. The drill eliminates the disappointment of having a strong pull from a fish and finding that the flies were caught up on the leader.

Windy nights are my personal aversion. They make presentation difficult, cause wind-knots in the leader, and make it impossible to keep in close contact with the flies. Lately, however, I have found braided leaders a great boon. Last year, on the Deveron, I went through four hours of night-fishing without mishap in a difficult wind gusting upriver, while my partners spent half the night undoing tangles in their nylon.

For me the important feature of braided leaders is their near-perfect turnover. Nevertheless, I tailor them to my own needs by reducing their length to about 4 feet 6 inches and then attaching nylon tippets of 6–9 feet by pushing the nylon up the hollow braid and making a suitable knot. I use two flies, one on the point and the other 4 feet up the tippet. It is important to standardize one's leaders and to become so familiar with them that one is able to judge the length of the cast when casting towards dark shadows on the far bank.

Some anglers attach their dropper to the braid itself. I shared a boat on a lough in Connemara with an angler who did just that and was somewhat surprised when he took more whitefish (sea-trout) than I did.

I am excited by the opportunities offered by the use of a sinking braid. I have never liked sink-tip lines and for years have worked on modifying them as I have found their presentation unsatisfactory at distances over about 20 yards. Some years ago I started tailoring my floating lines with loop knots to which I could attach sink-tips of different lengths. The experiment was born out of desperation, but it worked.

Already the sinking braid has proved its worth, especially to those who have problems with casting in the dark. What we need now is plenty of experimentation with braids of various lengths.

Sometimes, when I've been fishing a deep, slow pool and a big sea-trout has shown, I've wondered whether stillwater tactics might be the answer. Unfortunately, we have little opportunity to fish for sea-trout in stillwaters in England and Wales, and I recall how helpless I felt in my early outings on sea-trout loughs in Connemara. The only advice we were given was to look for water of between 4 feet and 15 feet deep. Following that abortive trip, I obtained a contour map of the lough and set about colouring the all-important areas of the correct depth. My second visit was far more productive.

It's always useful if you can follow a local angler and make notes about the various drifts and their landmarks, although when I first tried that, I soon learned that it was not as simple as it seemed.

After the customary break for lunch, and tea brewed in a Kelly's Kettle, we started to fish confident that I had the knowledge to ensure that our boat would drift the correct areas. Unfortunately, the wind had changed during our lunch-break, and so had the productive drifts!

Many years ago I was privileged to fish famous Loch Maree, then one of the finest sea-trout lochs, and it was there that I learned of the need to be quiet in a boat. I recall the boatman's insistence on absolute quiet, and at the slightest noise, he would say, 'That's another one we've lost!' However, most modern reservoir anglers are well-equipped for boat fishing for sea-trout. Indeed, there is little need for any change in tactics in fishing for sea-trout in stillwaters from the normal approach to fishing for brown trout on a reservoir.

When I last visited Loch Lomond, a number of anglers favoured extremely long rods, some up to 15 feet. The late Bill McEwan was one, and who was I to argue with such an authority? He explained that a long rod gave him much greater control over the bob-fly, and that he could work it at a good distance from the boat.

I shared a boat with one long-rod enthusiast, and he did seem to have far better control than I did with my 10-footer. He took about one sea-trout of every two that boiled or swirled, while I was able to manage only one out of every five. The long rod seemed to give him ample time to tighten on to a swirl on the surface in a positive manner.

One other advantage of a long rod is that it allows the use of a very long leader, and here the spacing of the droppers could be an important factor in getting fish to take an interest. But the long rod is of little use for long casting with a sinking line, and is an awkward weapon to keep in a boat unless it is dismantled.

On Irish loughs the boatmen always seem reluctant to go back over a productive drift, which seems strange to me. Many a time I have wanted to go back over fish we had raised and missed, but the boatmen have been adamant that to repeat the drift would be a waste of time.

It is amazing how much one can learn about a lough by fishing with a local for a couple of days. I was fortunate to do just that, and as he was a great thinker, it was stimulating to be with him. He convinced me that one of the most important factors in sea-trout fishing in stillwaters is the light on the water. Three days on Lough Currane gave me the opportunity to appreciate the effects of many different kinds of light. I'm sure his theories were sound, and it is such advanced thinking that lifts fishing above being merely a fish-catching exercise.

Back on my native Towi it is the hooting of the owls and the flighting bats that can be regarded as the start of night-fishing proper. Many anglers then start at the tail of a pool, but I tend to work my way down from the 'belly' of the pool towards the shallows in the tail. I use a slow-sinking line for this fishing, which gives me a chance to latch on to one of the big fish that often move around the pool at dusk. This may be something of a long shot, but long shots do occasionally come off! And what a thrill when they do! On some nights, however, the sea-trout do not automatically move to the tail, and it is always worth giving the in-between area a try.

I like handling my slow-sinking line, and to feel the line pulling the flies around is most satisfying. I believe that flies are shown at their best when the line pulls them 'round the bend'. My flies might well be a Cert on the point and a Haslam on the dropper. Each has a good record on the Towi, although the Cert has had exceptional success on the Teifi, too. It is difficult to understand why some flies seem to do better on one river than on another, but sometimes they do. The Cert has a dismal record in Ireland, but it has provided some outstanding nights on Nith and Lune. The Lynher sea-trout also appreciate it.

Flies are personal items, and the Cert was devised by a committee. It is said that a camel is a horse designed by a committee, and that is no recommendation for a fly so designed. The four members of the committee considered what they thought to be the all-important trigger points in a sea-trout fly, and the Cert was the result.

Its body has two sections, the rear half being silver, and the front half having black seal's fur ribbed with flat silver. The seal's fur is tied

Figure 12 *Boat fishing*

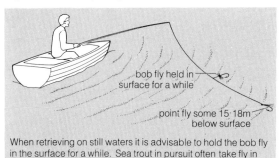

bob fly held in
surface for a while

point fly some 15-18m
below surface

When retrieving on still waters it is advisable to hold the bob fly in the surface for a while. Sea trout in pursuit often take fly in this position bulkily, and a black hackle and black wing are tied in a manner that ensure a lively action in the water. An overlay of green peacock sword feathers and jungle-cock eyes are tied in the head for maximum visibility.

The Haslam is an old-established pattern, but the body should have a white hackle, making for a light-coloured pattern and thus providing contrast between the two when they are used together.

It is always advisable to let a hooked sea-trout fight in deep water if possible. It is when it indulges in surface skirmishes that there is most danger of it kicking off. Another danger-ous moment is when the fish is being brought towards the net and one tends anxiously to add that little extra pressure to 'make sure of it'. But it is when a fish is on such a short line, and it becomes aware of the angler, that there is the greatest danger that if it makes a last-minute struggle, and with little line to absorb the shock, it will kick off.

For many years I was guilty of undervaluing the worth of a landing-net. Experience is a good school but an expensive one, and the loss of what would have been the sea-trout of a life-time taught me to have my net within reach at all times when I'm sea-trout fishing. Now I use a firm, half-moon-shaped net which I strap on to my back and which I'm able to release simply by slipping the loop off the handle — one flick, and the net is ready. It is, without doubt, the simplest net to use, and it has never failed me. A net should always be big enough to take the biggest fish you might catch, and it is better to err on the big side. I have two sizes, the bigger of the two being used when I fish rivers with a reputation for big fish.

When I've fished the 'belly' of a pool and move into the shallows, I opt for my floating line. Here I might use a Beauty dressed on Waddington hook on the point and a Muddler on the dropper. The Muddler is probably the one universal sea-trout fly, and I've done well with it at most locations. It is equally effective on floating and sinking lines. My favourite is one with a silver body, though others favour gold or black.

One angler who has exceptional faith in the

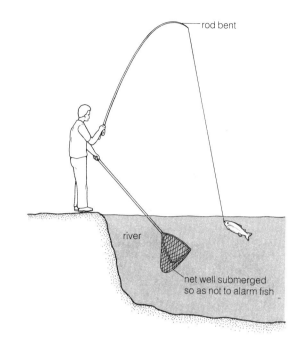

Figure 13   *Sea-trout need great care, when being netted. Many gain their freedom as a result of not taking the net low enough and of keeping too tight a line*

Muddler fishes on the Taf. His approach to sea-trout fishing is delightfully simple. He goes for a drink every night, leaves the pub at 'stop tap', picks up his rod from the garage, walks 100 yards to the river, and fishes the same pool every night. He is home never later than mid-night, yet he takes between fifty and sixty sea-trout every season.

The floating line is essential in a low river. Some anglers claim that it gives more life to a fly than do other lines. I wonder? Certainly once the river drops below a certain level, the floating line is the only one that can be fished in the tail of a pool, and it makes it simpler to detect a gentle take. The glide at the tail of a pool usually flows evenly, and hence the flies work in a steady manner, becoming more active where an eddy or obstacle offers a holding spot for the sea-trout.

It is always important, when fishing the tail of a pool, to keep a watchful eye on the lip, as sea-trout moving into the pool from below can often be seen. These newcomers generally need a little time before they will take. They seem to like to move some yards into the body of the pool, perhaps 30 yards, before they do.

If I've fished the shallows for about an hour and feel that I'm fishing empty water, then I move to the body of the pool, and change line and flies once more.

The sea-trout angler must be convinced that his water is good and holds fish. Once that confidence disappears, he is seriously handicapped and his chances of catching fish diminish dramatically. If the move pays off, especially with those fish seen coming into the pool, then all well and good. If it doesn't, then I take stock and perhaps decide that for the next hour or so I ought to move to the head of the pool and try a Floating Lure on a floating line.

The Floating Lure that I have been using for the last couple of seasons was developed from Floating Fry used on reservoirs. It is dressed on a tube with Ethafoam cut to the shape of an arrowhead, the wide base, or tail, providing the bulk to carry the treble. I'm still improving this lure and, although I am not yet fully satisfied with it, I believe it is the best that I have ever used. It is certainly more manageable than a lure made of pieces of cork and quill.

I use the Floating Lure as a change from more usual methods, and often as an indicator of where sea-trout are holding up. Indeed, I normally resort to it only when everything else has failed. Perhaps if I used it when the sea-trout were really on, the results would be spectacular. As it is, it often succeeds when all else fails.

The Floating Lure is difficult to cast, but judicious movement of the rod will keep it fishing in a steady current for a long time, without need to recast. Indeed, it is possible to hold it in the current all night without having to resort to casting at all! It is the wake it causes which is the important factor.

Because it is a comparatively poor hooker, I use an outpoint treble as on a normal tubefly, but without a stiffener, thus allowing the hooks to hang down. Some anglers use two trebles, but the hooking qualities are still disappointing. Perhaps the sea-trout simply play tip-and-run with it. Whatever the case, the potential of the method is great, and some find it such a fascinating method that they use nothing else.

One great sea-trout angler with whom I've had the privilege of fishing simply greases up his cast, puts a huge Loch Ordie on the point and a Muddler on the dropper, and casts this combination all night, letting the flies swing out and down over the water. It is a simplistic approach, but he is invariably 'top rod'.

Sea-trout fishing provides many contradictions. Often in the early hours I will give the Surface Lure a try and then follow it immediately with a deep-sunk lure fished on a fast-sinking line. Even more contradictory is the fact that I often use the same lure for both types of fishing, except that they are known by different names. Used on a fast-sinking line I call it Hover Lure; on a floating line I term it a Floating Lure.

Modern fast-sink lines really do get the fly down. Over the years I have used many differing types of sunk lure, and even today have no firm favourite. No sooner than I have discovered one which seems effective than I find another to try. I readily acknowledge the effectiveness of the standard Sunk Lure, with its long feathers and trebles.

It is over the last two seasons that I have used the Hover Lure on a fast-sinking line. This, too, has great potential in that one can keep it 'hovering' just off the river-bed, generally avoiding the snags and just above the eye-level of the sea-trout − and hence in a highly visible position. This is a principle which has proved successful on reservoirs with Boobies. The problem with them, however, is that the treble weighs down the tail of the lure. The arrow shape of the Hover Lure has effectively eliminated this problem.

There is something refreshing about being on a river-bank at the dawning of another day, with everything fresh and unspoiled. But the edge may be taken off the experience if neither the Floating Lure nor the Hover Lure has been producing fish. In this circumstance I change to a size 12 Black Squirrel and a size 10 Teifi Terror and fish them slow and deep. A brace of sea-trout taken now are ample reward for the night's work.

Daytime sea-trout fishing – upriver to avoid disturbing the fish. The positive strike is all important and bending the rod solidly into the fish

Some anglers claim they can forecast the taking times of sea-trout at night. How I wish I were so blessed! Sea-trout are an enigma, and the more you study them, the more you realize how little you know.

Few nights of sea-trout fishing are of identical pattern, and it is unwise to be dogmatic. In April 1989, sea-trout anglers on the Towi were taking bags of fish of 4–10 lb apiece well before midnight. We attributed the lack of post-midnight activity to a sharp drop in air temperature, yet some anglers did extremely well again at daybreak, when the temperature showed no increase.

In 1970 I compiled graphs to depict my night-fishing excursions. I was anxious to discover a 'magic' formula for successful sea-trout fishing during darkness, and I was sure that the taking times of 300-plus sea-trout would provide valuable information. I was even 'green' enough to believe that my studies would enable me to concentrate on the most productive period. The resultant graphs seemed to prove that sea-trout taken in the pre-midnight period were the smaller fish and that the big sea-trout were generally taken in the post-midnight period. They showed also that the most productive hour was from 2 to 3 a.m.

I was sure that my findings had something to do with the fact that my fishing was mainly on waters managed by angling associations. Sea-trout in association water do not always behave as do those in private water. One pool which I fished regularly was used by the village young-sters as their bathing pool. The lads were in the pool until dusk, and I seldom took a sea-trout from it until dawn. Another pool which I fished regularly never produced sea-trout until after midnight. One night I decided to watch the pool from 9 p.m., so that I could find out more about it. At 11 p.m. a gentleman came along the river-bank for his evening stroll with his Labrador. At the pool he threw in a stick and in went the Labrador to fetch it. The exercise was repeated three times. There was the explanation for the pool's later performance.

Graphs drawn up for fishing on private stretches were completely different. More than 65 per cent of the sea-trout caught were taken before midnight. I'm convinced that sea-trout in private stretches respond better to the angler's effort, especially during daylight. On some association waters they tend to become frightened, which precludes them taking boldly. Sea-trout that are continually harassed will ignore everything.

Sometimes I take a sea-trout just at the 'link' between the tail and the 'belly' of a pool. I think that some fish move about a pool at night, and these 'roamers' provide the occasional success when the angler seems otherwise to have lost out. Another school of thought maintains that once sea-trout have taken up station for the night, they remain there. But this is not borne out in my experience. I have often taken a fish from a location which was empty half an hour earlier. One particularly interesting experience of sea-trout behaviour during darkness was with a fish which had been lost after being hooked on a float-fished maggot. The nylon broke, leaving the sea-trout lip-hooked with the float, some 4 feet up the nylon, acting as an indicator of its position. The location of the float at different times during the night confirmed that the fish was on the move throughout. Other proof of roaming sea-trout has come from the radio-tracking of two fish which revealed considerable movement, up to a couple of hundred yards, at times during the night.

On one popular pool of the Mawddach I have seen rods sitting waiting with their worms and maggots ready. They would each take a sea-trout in turn, and this was accepted as proof that the fish were roaming around the pool. A similar situation occurs on the Aeron, where worm anglers will line the side of a pool and, if one takes a sea-trout, often the others get a fish in turn. This, too, is accepted as

showing that the sea-trout roam around the pool.

One of the most famous sea-trout pools in the Principality is Rhydgalfe, on the Teifi at Llandysul. If one had the power to construct the perfect pool for sea-trout, this would be prototype. At its head are some 50 yards of rocky pool with an average depth of more than 12 feet. Then it shallows out for about 80 yards into a wide tail strategically placed at the head of a long run. The tail of the pool has changed somewhat over the last fifty years, but the deeps at the head have remained constant because of the rocky structure.

The sea-trout leave the deeps at dusk and work their way back to the shallows. Along this 80 yards are 'hot-spots' where anglers are able to intercept the sea-trout as they move from one part to another. Anglers fishing the midway 'hot-spot' often take fish as they move down to the shallows in the first hour or so, and then the anglers at the tail start to catch fish.

However, rods midway go on taking fish well after the first exodus and for most of the night. These seem to be the roamers which are on the fin at various times during darkness. It is easy to understand why the first rods to arrive opt for this particular spot. It is sometimes good also at dawn, when many of the sea-trout head back to the deeps. Sea-trout do roam at night, and anglers can benefit if they know their routes.

Figure 14   *Ideal pool (Rhydgalfe on the Teifi)*

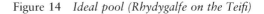
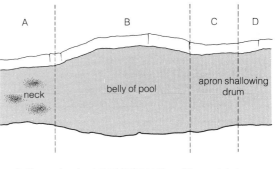

A The angler should tackle the section of the pool during
   dusk and dawn period

B The belly fished with a quick sinker can be productive

C-D When darkness falls the anglers fish the apron out to the tail

Good fishing can be enjoyed in the upper reaches of the river late in the season provided *the angler ensures that he returns all dark fish*

A long-held belief in Wales is that the best time to take a fish on a worm, especially in summer, is at crack of dawn. In the early years of this century, keepers on Towi valley estates often had to catch fish to order for the house. Captain Hughes, of Llandeilo, told me that all the charge hands thus ordered would be out fishing at crack of dawn, and they invariably got their fish. Why this should apply equally to fly fishing, I do not know.

It is curious that it is possible to take three or four fish of quite different appearance from the same pool. The reason is, of course, that they have been in the river for different periods. One may have come off the tide a few days previously; one may have been upriver for at least six weeks; and the other two for periods in between. It is easy to distinguish between fresh sea-trout and those that have been upriver for a while, and the difference is in behaviour as well as appearance. Fish fresh off the tide behave much as do newly-stocked rainbow trout in small ponds. They react to anything thrown at them and are no test of an angler's skill. This 'mad' period does not last long, but some big bags can be made by unscrupulous anglers. Many fish fall victim to gaudy spinners flashed across the river, but fly can be equally devastating, especially the more colourful offerings.

But sea-trout learn quickly, and soon become creatures of their environment. After they have been upriver for perhaps three weeks, they begin to present a real challenge to the angler, and not least to the angler who fishes through the night. It is a demanding pursuit, both physically and mentally. With luck, the reward comes at dawn, when a brace or two of sea-trout are laid on the bass and catch the light of the rising sun before the homeward journey and the inevitable post-mortem: Why did I do this? Why did I do that? Next time I'll do this. Next time I'll do the other. New theories are concocted, and old theories exploded. We're all so clever in retrospect. But the bottom line remains as always: we sea-trout anglers have a long, long way to go fully to understand the humour and mood of our quarry. If the day — or night — comes when we do understand, then fishing for them will become even more wonderful.

Or will it?

Further reading

W.B. Currie, *Days and Nights of Game Fishing* (George Allen & Unwin).

Hugh Falkus, *Sea Trout Fishing* (H.F. & G. Witherby).

Harris and Morgan, *Successful Sea-Trout Angling* (Blandford Press).

T.C. Kingsmill Moore, *A Man May Fish* (Smith Ltd, Gerrards Cross, Buckinghamshire).

Bill McEwan, *Angling on Lomond* (Albyn Press, Edinburgh).

Mike Weaver

Mike Weaver started fishing seriously at the age of fifteen, his quarry being the coarse fish of the Severn and Avon around Tewkesbury. Within two years the sight of rising chub and dace in summer had tempted him to buy his first fly-rod and to catch his first fish on fly – a chub at Tewkesbury Weir. Soon after this, he took his first trout on fly at Chew Valley Lake, when it opened in 1957, and in the following year he started his river trouting on the Usk.

During the past thirty years, Mike has fished widely in Great Britain, Ireland, Europe, North America and the Falkland Islands, mostly in pursuit of trout, developing an awareness of the challenges presented by rivers of every type. He now lives close to the River Teign in the Dartmoor National Park and, although much of his fishing is on the rain-fed rivers of the south-west, he is a frequent visitor to chalk and limestone streams.

Mike has been Chairman of the Upper Teign Fishing Association for almost ten years and is now a member of the Regional Fisheries Advisory Committee of the South West Region of the National Rivers Authority.

Mike Weaver has contributed to two books, *West Country Fly Fishing* and *The Haig Guide to Trout Fishing in Britain*. He has reported on the Devon scene for *Trout and Salmon* for over fifteen years, and he has contributed many feature articles to that magazine. His articles have also been published in *Salmon, Trout and Sea-trout*, *Fishing*, *The Fly-fishers' Journal*, the American magazine *The Fly-fisher* and the county magazine, *Devon Life*. He is a keen photographer and thousands of his pictures have been reproduced with his own articles and elsewhere.

3

BROWN TROUT IN RAIN-FED RIVERS

Mike Weaver

Rain-fed rivers come in many forms. They can be broad stately streams, tiny rushing torrents, smooth weedy rivers with the appearance of chalk streams, or sluggish little brooks meandering through lowland meadows. The one thing they have in common is that most of their flow derives from surface drainage, rather than the springs that well up from chalk and limestone. The true nature of a rain-fed stream can be readily seen if you are on the river-bank after heavy rain; before long it will take on colour and then rise rapidly, something we have all experienced after driving many miles for our day's fishing.

In these islands, most of the rain-fed trout streams are to be found in Scotland, Ireland, Wales, the Welsh Marches, northern England and south-west England. Fortunately the rivers of these areas have remained reasonably unpolluted and many, possibly a majority of them, still offer that priceless commodity – the wild brown trout. On the whole, the trout in these streams are not big, though there are exceptions, but they are numerous, frequently more free rising than tradition would have it, and often offer fishing at a remarkably reasonable price.

The streams themselves include some of our most famous rivers like the Tay, Tweed and Wye, which can offer excellent trout fishing that is often overshadowed by their fame as salmon fisheries. At the other end of the spectrum are the countless tiny torrents that tumble down from the mountains and moorlands, where the size of the trout reflects a combination of optimum breeding conditions and limited food supply. Then there are streams which are famous for their trout, like the Usk or Don, even though they have significant runs of salmon. On some streams, like the Eden or the Eamont in Cumbria, the Derbyshire Wye or the Culm in Devon, the small upwinged flies emerge in often prolific numbers from among the weeds that wave in the current, giving the feeling that you have found your way on to a chalk stream.

These and many other rain-fed rivers offer endless opportunities for the versatile and exploring angler, whether running a team of wet flies across the stream in spring, bouncing a bushy dry fly down a mountain torrent, covering a rising fish on a silky lowland river, or casting a sedge in the last light of a summer evening. And the fly fisher most likely to achieve consistent success is the one who can adapt fluently from one technique to another and acquire mastery in the skills required – fly casting, river craft, identifying hatching insects, fly tying, wading, fish location, tackle selection, and so on.

THE RIGHT APPROACH

It is often said that 10 per cent of the fishermen catch 90 per cent of the fish. Whether or not that is an exaggeration, there is no doubt that most trout on the rivers are taken by a minority of anglers who have developed an approach and technique that give them a very real edge over other fly fishers. So, if you want to succeed, the first step is perhaps the philosophical one of really wanting to catch trout and, in particular, lots of them.

In Britain there is a long tradition of being satisfied with a brace or two of trout and, on the face of it, such an approach makes sense in the name of conservation. The trouble is that fishing to a small bag limit also sets a limit on the development of your skills and gives a sense of artificiality. On a really good day, when the flies are hatching and the trout are rising, any skilful fly fisher is likely to fill his limit very quickly, just when things are getting interesting.

Catch and release

The imposition of a bag limit assumes that the angler is going to kill his trout but, especially on rain-fed rivers, why should this be the case? Most rain-fed streams provide the conditions required for trout to reproduce and, therefore, maintain a stock of wild fish. Except on the most prolific streams, too many anglers killing the trout they catch, even if there is a limit, will inevitably lead to the reduction of stocks and, if funds are available, the replacement of wild trout with hatchery fish — not a very good trade. On many occasions I have fished streams where the stocks of wild fish are way below what they should be, or a travesty of trout fishing is maintained by stocking with flabby fish which are easily caught. Why fly fishers

A 14-inch brown trout is returned to the River Teifi near Llandysul

should tolerate substandard fishing when the answer is in their own hands by adopting a no-kill policy is beyond my comprehension. Even with heavy fishing pressure, a catch-and-release policy can result in excellent trout fishing — and it is a lot cheaper than stocking!

For about fifteen years I have virtually given up killing trout on rivers with the capacity to reproduce them, relying on the occasional trip to my nearest put-and-take pool when I want to kill a few trout for the pot. Far from feeling deprived by returning trout to the stream, I have enjoyed my fishing all the more and I am sure that the removal of the artificial constraint of a bag limit has vastly improved my fishing. Returning a wild trout to grow bigger and reproduce is surely a simple example of enlightened self-interest.

Barbless hooks

Of course, if you intend to return trout alive, there is little point in doing so if they have been so badly treated that they soon die, so you do take on the responsibility to think about how you handle fish. First of all, forget about barbs. Barbless hooks penetrate easily, hold perfectly well if you keep a tight line, and are quickly removed. With the smaller fish, all you have to do is reach down to the hook shank when the trout is ready and remove it with a quick jerk. With bigger fish, net them in the usual way and then hold the trout in the mesh, remove the hook and return the fish without your hand coming into direct contact with it.

Above all, play the fish as hard as your tackle will allow and get it to the net as fast as you can. Biologists tell us that prolonged playing is harmful to trout and can be fatal, so never prolong the fight for your personal gratification. Whenever an angler boasts about the length of time it took to subdue a trout, I can only think that he is admitting his own lack of skill.

Once you have made the decision to return your trout alive, you no longer have to place any restraint on your instinct to catch fish and can apply your mind to maximizing the catch.

A 1¼ lb brown trout is slipped back into the Torridge at Sheepwash

Having broken with tradition already, let us now cast down a few more idols, as many anglers restrict themselves unnecessarily by sticking to ideas and methods which have long outlived their usefulness. Fishing on rain-fed rivers really has moved on since the age of Stewart.

The dry fly

A newcomer to this branch of fishing could still be excused for thinking that the angler on the rain-fed streams usually fishes with a wet fly, fishing the water rather than the rise, and uses only a few standard patterns throughout the season. This approach has its place and I use it where appropriate — but at least 90 per cent of my trout are taken on a dry fly, more than half are taken by casting to rising fish, and whenever appropriate I try to match my fly to the hatching insect. There is no sense of self-denial or purity in this approach; its sole purpose is to catch more trout, which it most certainly does. It is also infinitely more enjoyable than just going through the motions — and fishing should be fun!

Fishing a dry fly to a rising fish offers a tremendous advantage over just working your way along a stream fishing the water. With a rising trout in front of you, one of the most basic problems in all types of fishing has been solved — that of fish location. Whenever I have fished hundreds or even thousands of miles from home, I have always concentrated on fishing for rising trout, so that I am not running the risk of fishing empty water. That is really important when you are in a strange place and time is limited. In this way you also build up a detailed picture of where the trout lie, so that when nothing is rising and you are forced to fish the water, you have a good idea where to cast your fly.

My last thoughts on the approach to fishing the rain-fed streams, before getting down to the practice, concern the overall attitude to this branch of the sport. Just before writing this introduction I looked through some of the books of trout fishing reminiscences in my library and many of them start with the writer's angling adolescence on the moors before moving on to their maturity on the chalk streams. Perhaps unwittingly, they give the impression that the rain-fed rivers are a soft touch and that their trout are easily fooled. Such an attitude is unlikely to be rewarded with any degree of success.

Most rain-fed rivers are able to reproduce trout naturally and that means plenty of small and innocent fish that come readily to the fly. But, if you want to make good catches of trout of decent proportions, you should treat your fishing on these streams just as seriously as when you are on a chalk stream. Over the course of a season I move back and forth between chalk streams and rain-fed rivers and never think of one type of fishing as superior to the other.

Fishing a dry fly into the pockets between the boulders on the East Lyn, Devon

FLIES—NATURAL AND ARTIFICIAL

Far too often, entomology takes a back seat on the rain-fed rivers and is looked upon as some esoteric study pursued by chalk stream anglers. Certainly, fly hatches are less reliable or prolific, and a single species of insect is less likely to dominate and induce preoccupation by the trout. However, an attempt to match the hatching insects is likely to produce success on rain-fed streams far more often than is realized by many anglers and that means that a working knowledge of entomology really pays off, and adds immensely to the pleasure of a day out on the river. The inquisitiveness that leads you to identify the insects that drift past on the current surely is part of the enquiring mind that will lead to success in catching trout.

So, whenever an emergence of insects takes place, the angler should be ready to identify them and, if they induce a rise by the trout, use something that matches the naturals reasonably closely. There will, of course, be many oc-casions when not a fly is to be seen and then, whether fishing wet or dry, the fly fisher has to know how to select one of the standard patterns that is appropriate to the conditions.

The fly life of rivers is dealt with in Neil Patterson's chapter on entomology, and rain-fed rivers provide a home for virtually all of the insects that live in British rivers. However, the emphasis can be very different from chalk streams, with some insects so infrequent that they are hardly worth considering, while others are far more important. A classic example is provided by terrestrial insects, which are relatively unimportant on chalk streams but vital to summer fishing on rain-fed rivers.

The following flies occur in sufficient numbers to be worth imitating with specific patterns. For each insect I have given an approximation of its main season and some suggestions for matching standard patterns that are usually available in the shops or by mail order.

Natural fly	Season	Artifical fly (dry)	Hook size
Ephemeroptera			
Large dark olive	March, April	Rough Olive, Imperial, Greenwell, Blue Upright	16
March brown	Late March, April	March Brown	14
Olive upright	May, June	Olive Dun, Greenwell	16
Pale watery	May to end season	Last Hope, Ginger Quill	18
Iron blue	May and September	Iron Blue Dun	18
Mayfly	Late May, early June	Numerous Mayfly patterns	10, 12
Blue-winged olive	June to end season	B-WO, Orange Quill (evening) For spinner use Sherry Spinner, Pheasant Tail	16
Others			
Sedges (various)	May to end season	Richard Walker, Sedge, G. & H. Sedge, Elk Hair Sedge, Cinnamon Sedge	14, 16
Beetles (various)	June to end season	Coch-y-bondhu, Eric's Beetle	16, 18
Midges	All season		20, 22
Black gnat	May, June	Black Gnat	18
Hawthorn	May	Hawthorn	14

Artificial flies

The artificial flies listed above against the appropriate naturals will cover most of the dry fly fisher's needs, but there are also many standard patterns which imitate nothing in particular but suggest many different insects. Two that I always carry to use when no particular insects are on the water are the Grey Duster and Adams, plus a Yellow Humpy for rough water conditions when buoyancy is essential.

For nymph fishing, Sawyer's Pheasant Tail Nymph can be used in most conditions, but I also carry a simple Hare's Ear Nymph, which can be leaded for deep water.

The long tradition of wet fly fishing on rain-fed rivers means that the list of standard patterns is virtually endless, but for downstream wet fly fishing I doubt if the choice of fly makes much difference to the catch.

Although I would hate to be restricted in the range of flies that I use, I can understand that the beginner will want guidance on making an initial selection to get started, so here is a short list of six dry flies and six wet flies, all of which are available in the tackle shops.

Dry	Wet
Imperial (14, 16)	Greenwell's Glory (12, 14)
Grey Duster (14, 16)	Partridge and Orange (12, 14)
Black Gnat (16, 18)	Black and Peacock Spider (12, 14)
Coch-y-bondhu (14, 16)	Half Stone (12, 14)
Pheasant Tail (16)	Sawyer Pheasant Tail Nymph (14)
Blue Upright (16)	Soldier Palmer (12, 14)

The dressings for the patterns I use regularly on rain-fed rivers are given under the heading *Tying Your Own* at the end of this chapter.

TACKLE

Good well-chosen tackle is a delight to use and adds immeasurably to both efficiency and enjoyment. Such equipment can be expensive, but need not necessarily be so – the important thing is to take real care when you choose it, and attention should go into choosing every piece of your fishing equipment! There is little point in fishing with a superb rod and the best reel that money can buy, if your efforts are ruined by a badly designed leader. The items that cost only a few pennies can be just as important as those that cost many pounds.

Lines

The tremendous range of fly lines now available makes it possible to select the line that is exactly right for just about every purpose. For dry fly fishing, the first choice would probably be a floating line of size 5, especially in windy conditions or when casting a big fly like a Mayfly, but a size 4 gives a more delicate presentation and that is the size I now use for most of my dry fly fishing.

Either of these lines can be used for wet fly fishing on shallow streams or when the trout are near the surface, but a couple of sinking lines – one slow-sinking and the other fast-sinking – can be an advantage when you want to get down to the fish. When fishing the downstream wet fly, a strong current can result in the flies and leader skating across the surface with a wake, and then a sinker will cut through the surface film and avoid skating.

The choice between double taper and weight-forward can be argued endlessly, but I unhesitatingly recommend weight-forward for rivers. When river fishing, most casts are less than 10 yards and with a weight-forward taper the weight of the line is in the air, where it is needed, rather than on the reel.

Rods

When I bought my first fly rod, actions were often described as dry fly or wet fly; I did not know what those terms meant then and I still do not to this day. Fortunately, the tackle dealer who sold me my first fly rod was an old tournament fly caster from pre-war days and he made sure that I acquired a cane rod with a crisp positive action and not one of those sloppy monstrosities with the so-called wet fly action.

Although the inevitable collection of rods that I have gathered over the years includes greenheart, cane, glass and carbon fibre, it is the last of these materials that I now use for all my fly fishing. For the No. 4 line I use two rods, one of which is 8½ feet long and covers many of my needs, especially on the larger and more open rivers. However, for operating in confined spaces, a much shorter rod of 7 feet, also matching the No. 4 line, offers distinct advantages. When fishing a small stream, where the canopy of branches meets over the river, the shorter rod with a quick action that will cast a narrow loop, will avoid much wasted time removing flies from the vegetation. The third rod in my armoury, an 8½-footer, is rather more powerful than the other two, and rated for a size 5 or 6 line. With a WF5 line it is ideal for coping with strong winds or casting big air-resistant flies like the Mayfly.

Reels

Although I normally believe in getting the best that I can afford, I have never felt the need to spend much on fly reels, as there are plenty of well-made reels on the market at very reasonable prices. Mechanically, fly reels have very little work to do compared with multiplying and fixed spool reels, which are constantly cranked as you fish.

Choosing a small, light reel is important, as a heavy reel on a 7-foot carbon rod weighing only a couple of ounces in completely out of place. The use of materials like magnesium has made such reels readily available. Your reel should have a ratchet which can be adjusted to right or left hand wind. Being right-handed, I like to keep the rod in my right hand while playing a fish as well as for casting, so a left hand wind is essential to avoid changing hands.

Leaders

While the choice of leader for the downstream wet fly matters little, as the current will ensure that it straightens out, a well-designed leader really pays dividends when fishing the dry fly or nymph. There is little point in presenting the fly line accurately and tidily if the leader then falls untidily in a heap. The objective is to get a smooth progression from the thick fly line down to the fine leader point, so that the momentum of your cast goes right through to the fly.

Until recently I built my leaders from various thicknesses of level monofilament nylon, but now I have gone over to braided tapered material for the butt sections, which I attach to the fly line permanently. You can use the plastic sleeve supplied for this join, but I prefer to use a droplet of super-glue on the fly line, which is then pushed into the braided butt. To ensure that the braided material has a neat end, push in a needle which is then heated briefly with a match, thus fusing the material without burning it. This method of attachment makes it possible to use a leader longer than the rod, as the join passes easily through the tip ring.

The remainder of the leader is then made with monofilament nylon to meet your needs. Normally you can use whatever brand of nylon you prefer, but for the leaders that you use when a really fine point is necessary, as in high summer on a clear stream, extra strong or double-strength nylon has considerable advantages. Whenever conditions demand the use of a really tiny fly, I like to taper my leader to a point of 7X (.004 inch), which can now give the incredible breaking strain of 2½ lb.

Here are some typical leader designs that are easy to produce.

(a) *Downstream wet fly*: 5 feet braided tapered butt, 3 feet of 4X (.007-inch) nylon, 3 feet of 5X (.006-inch) nylon. 5 inches of the 4X nylon are left for the dropper at the join with the 5X nylon. On large open streams, a longer leader with another dropper can be used; just add another 3 feet of 5X nylon.

(b) *Dry fly (normal)*: 5 feet braided tapered butt, 2 feet of 5X (.006-inch) nylon, 3 feet of 6X (.005-inch) nylon. The leader can be converted for nymph fishing by extending the point by up to 2 feet, so that the nymph sinks freely.

(c) *Dry fly (fine)*: 5 feet braided tapered butt, 2 feet of 5X (.006-inch) nylon, 2 feet of 6X (.005-inch) nylon, 3 feet of 7X (.004-inch) nylon.

Joins both between the braided butt and nylon, and between nylon and nylon are made with a three-turn water knot. All of the nylon sizes given above are for extra strong or double strength material. With standard nylon, it is probably best to go up in diameter by an X all round, to give a margin of safety in strength. I like a long point for delicate presentation, but if you have difficulty with a whole yard, cut back by a foot.

Recently there have been signs of a gradual return to X ratings for leader material. American anglers have for long used these ratings, but they dropped out of fashion in Britain for many years, although they were standard in the days of silkworm gut. Such a simple system of stating the diameter of leader nylon has considerable advantages if you have difficulty in remembering a long decimal number, especially while we remain unable to decide whether we want imperial or decimal measures, so ending up with both.

For running repairs to leaders, carry spools of point material with you for frequent replacement. The fine nylon at the point cannot be expected to take too much wear and tear, and it is silly to risk the loss of a good fish for the sake of a few pence.

Waders and wading staffs

You will often read that wading scares the fish and it should only be done as a last resort. On rain-fed rivers I would suggest that the opposite is true and that wading, if carried out skilfully,

A quiet stretch of the River Teifi, near Llandysul, where deep wading is really necessary

is the key to catching more trout. Far from scaring fish, the angler who is down in the river, and not silhouetted against the sky as he fishes from a high bank, is far less likely to be spotted by the fish. As many streams are heavily bushed on both banks there is often little option – you wade or move on to a more open stretch which may not hold as many trout. Another great advantage in wading is the fact that your eyes are much closer to the surface of the stream and you have a much greater awareness of what is drifting down for the trout to eat. So, forget any inhibitions about wading, become a skilled wader and catch a lot more trout.

Most trout fishers use thigh waders, but for more than twenty years my secret weapon has been a pair of full-length body waders. In that time, deep wading has made it possible to fish effectively on stretches that could only be detoured with thigh waders and countless trout have been added to my catches.

Over the years I have used both studded and cleated waders and found neither satisfactory on rivers where the bottom is mainly rocks and boulders. The only way to wade quietly or safely with such waders is to use a third point of contact with the river bed, in the shape of a wading staff. I make up my own staff by selecting a suitable sapling, cutting it to a length of about 4 feet 7 inches, fitting a cycle grip at the top and attaching a lanyard of thick braided nylon cord through the hole of the grip. The staff is finished with several coats of varnish, to prolong its life, and a rubber walking stick button is glued to the bottom. Wading staffs can be purchased, but the lanyard attachment is usually part way down the staff and you will find that loops of your fly line will often get hooked up with the top of the staff as it floats on the surface. This is avoided if the lanyard goes into a hole at the top of the grip.

More recently I have turned to felt-soled waders; what a revelation. The sureness of grip and the quietness of wading has to be experienced to be believed. I have been aware of the advantages of felt soles for many years, having borrowed them on visits to the USA, but availability in the United Kingdom has been very limited until recently. Eventually, I bought a pair of felt-soled wading boots in the USA and use these with light-weight nylon stocking-foot waders, with a pair of thick synthetic socks in between, to avoid excessive wear. Fortunately, the last couple of years have seen an increasing number of felt-soled waders on the home market. Thanks to felt soles, I have even given up using a staff, except in deep, difficult water, or when I need to wade with extra care.

Waistcoat or bag?

Fly fishing on a stream is a mobile affair – none of the bag on the bank and landing-net stuck in the lake-bed that you often see on the reservoirs. However, you still have to carry all the equipment you will need for a fishing session which could last all day, but remain sufficiently comfortable to avoid fatigue or being cramped when casting. Long ago I discovered that the strap of even a light bag eventually bites into the shoulder and, in spite of the limitations, I got by for many years with a few items stuffed in the pockets of my jacket. Then the fishing waistcoat arrived on the scene and for over twenty years has been the ideal answer to carrying all the gear that I need.

For fishing with thigh waders, there are plenty of waistcoats available in this country, but once you don a pair of body waders and wade really deep you will find that most of them are too long. On many occasions I found that my waistcoat had dipped into the water and the fly boxes had become soaked – not the ideal way to treat the products of many hours' fly tying. I have now overcome the problem by obtaining a short American waistcoat, or vest as it is known across the Atlantic, and I use this for all deep wading. The catalogue states that this waistcoat has twenty-five pockets; certainly there are more than enough for all my needs. If you use such a waistcoat, much time can be saved by always keeping individual items in the same pocket, so that you go straight to the one you want every time.

Landing-net

Like so many anglers, my first landing-net was of the collapsible type with a clip for attaching to a ring, belt or shoulder strap, but I quickly found that for river fishing it was far from satisfactory. Apart from the inconvenience of having to throw up the net before use, I could never be absolutely sure that the net was there when I wanted it. I finally gave up one day when fishing the Usk, after the third time that the branch of a tree in the wooded stretch that I was fishing had removed the net without my

A trout safely in the net. River Barle in the Exmoor National Park, Somerset

realizing it. I went straight into the tackle shop, in those days run by Molly Sweet, and bought a net that I had seen when getting my permit that morning. It was a simple aluminium bow net with a plastic handle imported from America and cost 25 shillings – that was more than twenty-five years ago and I am still using the same net. The great advantage of this type of landing-net is that it is attached to a loop of elasticated cord which is worn over the shoulder, so there is no danger of losing it, and it is always ready for instant use. The short handle is no problem as virtually all of my fishing on rain-fed rivers is carried out while wading.

Fly boxes

My preference in dry fly boxes is for those with strips of high density foam, the gaps between the strips allowing space for the hackles to stand out without being bent over. For nymphs and wet flies, boxes with flat foam are fine. The boxes should be large enough to carry plenty of flies, yet small enough to fit into the pockets of a fishing waistcoat, so 6 inches by 4 inches is about right.

Other items of tackle

Distributed around your waistcoat can be the odds and ends that are necessary during a day's fishing. Floatants, both for flies and lines, will be required, but remember that some line floatants are reputed to have an adverse effect on synthetic fly lines; the tackle dealer should be able to tell you which to avoid.

Even if you use barbless hooks, the fly will often be lodged well back in the trout's mouth and then a pair of artery forceps make removal easy. Attach them to a length of rot-proof braided backing material or similar, which can be looped on to one of the D-rings of your waistcoat; the forceps can then be clamped on to the flap of a breast pocket, ready for instant use. You will also need clippers for cutting nylon; I like the simple type that are pressed together, with a short needle at the other end from the blades, to clear varnish from the eyes of hooks, something which I always forget to do at the tying bench. These clippers are also attached to the waistcoat by a length of braided material.

A small extending metal tape measure is useful for checking the length of trout, plus some lightweight scales if you want to weigh them – in the net, please, if they will be returned. These devices avoid you joining the ranks of those who boast of catching a trout of at least 16 inches (which really means 14 inches at most) or well over 2 lb (which would probably have difficulty in making a pound and a half).

Finally, always ensure that your hooks are needle sharp by carrying a hook sharpener. For more than twenty years I have used the same small piece of carborundum stone.

THE SEASON IN BRIEF

The middle of March is the typical opening time on rain-fed rivers, though some open at the beginning of the month and on a few the opening is delayed until 1 April. When the season starts, the country may still be in the grip of winter and the rivers are often high and cold. The trout will be lying deep, except when hatches of the large dark olives and, on a few favoured streams like the Usk, the March browns bring the fish to the surface. That means that the wet fly is likely to succeed, but always be ready to switch to the dry fly if there is a brief rise.

After a short lull in fly hatches in late April and early May, the best insect activity of the season starts around the middle of May and continues until the end of June, with ample opportunities for day-long dry fly fishing. Throughout this period you are likely to see a fly rarely seen on chalk streams but important on most rain-fed rivers, the olive upright, which is similar to the dark olive but rather lighter in colour. I have never seen a really big concentrated hatch of this insect, but it is well worth imitating. Two tiny upwinged flies are also worth watching out for – the pale watery and the iron blue, the latter often hatching on cold blustery days when the dark little duns can easily be missed. Many slower streams enjoy good hatches of mayflies and the splendid fishing that they produce. In spite of its name, the best of the mayfly fishing is likely to be in the first week or two of June.

May and early June also see huge numbers of black gnat swarming over the streams, especially those with tree-lined banks, and possibly the best prolonged surface feeding of the season on many rain-fed rivers. This tiny dark insect, like a slim house fly, is the first terrestrial insect of the season to excite the trout, and as the season progresses terrestrials will become even more important. This is one of the most marked differences between rain-fed rivers and chalk streams. The black gnat's cousin, the hawthorn, can usually be seen hovering over the hedgerows with its legs trailing at this time and when they get blown onto the river they are taken readily by the trout.

By late June, the rivers are usually dropping to low levels. Day-time fishing can become increasingly difficult and will stay that way until the end of summer. Few upwinged flies will be hatching in the day and this is the time to use a fly that suggests the terrestrial insects that now account for most of the trout's surface food. The fish lie close to overhanging branches looking out for beetles, caterpillars, wood ants and various *Diptera*, some very small as they fall upon the surface of the stream.

Now is the time for the first real evening rises as the hatches of blue-winged olives and various sedges get under way and continue until the first chilly evenings of September. On any reasonably warm summer evening you can expect both a hatch of blue-winged olive duns and a fall of its female spinner, the sherry spinner.

On most rivers, the brown trout season ends on the last day of September, a month about which it is very difficult to generalize. On some rivers there will be a real resurgence of hatches of upwinged flies and a return to prolonged surface feeding through the day. However, September can be a disappointment, especially on the moorland streams, with meagre hatches of fly and few rising trout. At such times it is probably best to return to the wet fly.

EARLY SPRING

There are days when I wonder why I venture onto the river in March. There is often a biting wind out of the north, blustery showers with more than a hint of snow can numb the fingers, and even the hardy dark olives are reluctant to appear. Yet there is something very special about those days before spring has really arrived, a sense of expectation which pulls me to the river even though I know that my catches are likely to be modest. For more than a decade I lived close enough to the Usk to open every season there, hoping first for one of its wonderful hatches of dark olives and then, with the arrival of April, the hatches of March brown which so few rivers experience. In Devon, where I now live, those early spring hatches are usually sparse and it is best to fish the wet fly, only turning to the surface when there is clearly a case for doing so.

Downstream wet fly

The basic downstream wet fly is probably the simplest form of fly fishing and one of the easiest, but in the early season, when nothing is rising, it can also be very effective. It may seem unnatural for the flies to swing across the stream, rather than drifting down the current like natural objects, but there is no doubt that this method does attract fish when a more natural presentation produces very little. It also has the advantage that when there are no rising trout to guide you, the downstream wet fly covers a lot of water. Your fly can go searching every likely spot, rather than waiting for a fish to come to you.

Unless I am visiting a river with a reputation for big hatches of fly in spring, I normally choose a medium to small river for the early season. I would also go for a stream with plenty of variety – a mixture of fast runs and pools, with plenty of boulders or other obstructions to break up the current and provide cover. Fishing a featureless stretch of even water, which may well come to life later in the season when there is plenty of fly about, can be really disheartening in early spring. At this time of year, I rarely travel too far from home, as rapid changes in the weather can easily bring already full rivers into flood and make the journey fruitless. That means that my own early outings are to rivers like the Lyn, the upper Teign and the moorland reaches of the Dart and its tributaries. Such upland rivers clear quickly after rain, so even in March there is a good chance that they will be fishable.

Tackling up

On arrival at the river, which need not be before 10 a.m., put together your rod and a size 5 line. On a really small stream, use the floating line, as little more than your leader will be on the water anyway, but on a bigger stream a sinker will avoid skating and if the river is on the high side you may even need the fast sinker. If possible, however, I prefer the floating line or a neutral density, for a reason that will emerge later.

Use the two fly leader, and make a start with a size 12 Greenwell on the point and a 14 Partridge and Orange on the dropper. In tackling up it is almost inevitable that the leader will have become slightly greasy so wipe it down with one of the sinking agents available in the tackle shops. This should ensure that leader and flies cut cleanly through the surface film.

Where to fish

Before starting to fish, take a good long look at the river. Unless you know it really well, with past experience telling you where the fish will be, you will have to read the water and decide from the look of the stream where you stand the best chance of taking some trout. The process of elimination will help you to reduce the choice quite dramatically; those slow deep pools that may look easy to fish are a waste of time, as both you and your line will be very obvious to the fish. Avoid too the fast shallow stretches which, at this time of year, will hold only small trout or immature salmon. It is the medium that you are looking for – medium current, medium depth, and a broken surface which is neither too rough nor too smooth. A steady run a couple of feet deep will be just about right.

Trying to explain where the trout will lie in a specific pool, either in words or in diagrams, is difficult, as every pool has its own special features which influence the spots favoured by trout. There are, however, certain features that occur in many stretches of river which consistently hold trout. For example, a really large boulder which diverts the current will usually have trout lying alongside it and right in the bulge at its head caused by the current, but rarely in the slack water behind it. Trout will also lie along a steep drop-off caused by a cliff

Figure 15 *A pool on the River Culm, a meadow stream in Devon. The main current runs along the undercut bank, carrying food to the trout which are mostly within two feet of the bank. Fish are also found near the big tree at the tail of the pool*

Figure 16 *A typical moorland pool on the upper reaches of the River Teign in Devon. Large boulders break up the current and provide ample shelter for the trout, many of which lie alongside and even in front of the boulders, but hardly ever in the slack water downstream of them*

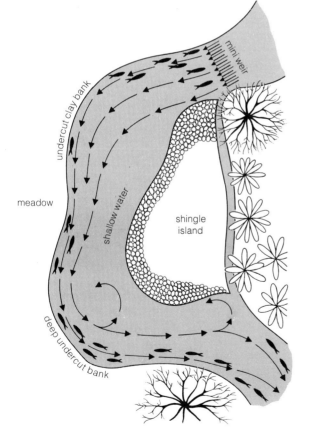

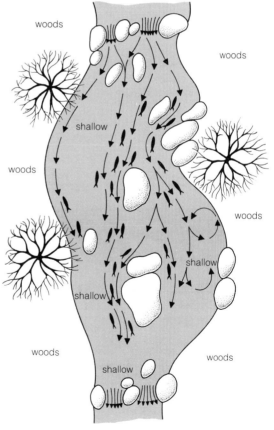

or undercut bank. Remember that the trout must lie sufficiently in the current for food to be brought to them, but they also look for something that will ease or break up the strongest flow that would use up too much of their energy in holding position. It may seem difficult at first but gradually you will develop a feel for the water and the ability to tell by looking at a pool just where the most trout will be lying. There is nothing occult in this ability − just the unconscious accumulation of experience and build-up in your memory of those spots that actually produce trout.

Searching the pool

Having selected a pool or run, look for a suitable place near the head to slip into the water. I am always more confident when wading, partly because I feel more in touch with the river and also because I know I am not silhouetted against the skyline. If you are right handed, choose the left bank for downstream fishing if you have the choice. This way, your right arm and rod are out over the water, thus keeping the flies as far as possible from bankside vegetation. Cast your team of flies straight across the current near the head of the run and allow the current to swing them across the stream until lying downstream. Then take a step downstream or lengthen the line slightly and repeat the process. If the river bottom is reasonably level you will be able to step and cast all of the way down the pool or run, knowing that you are covering most of the water with your flies.

Even the newcomer will have no difficulty in keeping in touch with the flies with this method, as the current will quickly straighten your line and leader. If all goes well, there will eventually be a sharp tug and suddenly you will be playing a fish, which might be a midget trout, a salmon parr or, with luck, a sizable trout. Fishing the downstream wet fly, you rarely know what size fish a take will produce, but as you gain intimate knowledge of a fishery you will get to know those spots where you can expect a better than average trout.

If you meet with early success, stick with your original team of flies but if after some time you have not had a pull, change the point fly to a Silver March Brown and put a Soldier Palmer on the dropper, thus really ringing the changes both in colour and style. Your failure could be due to the trout being in a dour mood, but a change of fly might just be the answer. Other wet flies which are always worth a try include Pheasant Tail, Half Stone, Infallible or a black pattern like William's Favourite or Black and Peacock Spider.

A hatch of fly

Around noon, even on a moorland stream where spring hatches are sparse, you may see a few dark olive duns drifting down the stream and, if the hatch develops, several rises as they are eagerly taken by the trout. Some anglers will continue to fish the water and ignore the rises, but I can never pass up an opportunity to cast to a rising trout. At this point, you could change quickly to a dry fly outfit, but these early spring rises can be very short-lived, so to save time I often stick with the wet fly outfit. That is why I prefer always to fish with a floating or neutral density line in spring, which will not drag the flies down when I wish to fish at the surface.

If necessary, change to a couple of wet flies that suggest the dark olives, like a Greenwell and a Half Stone, and cast to the nearest rising fish, ideally upstream of where you are standing. As the flies drift back towards you, lift the rod and recover line in your spare hand to keep in touch, and watch for a boil as the trout takes. If you manage to keep in touch and tighten slightly as the fish takes, very few should be missed.

When the rise slackens off you can return to the downstream wet fly, but the trout will often stay near the surface for some time. Eventually, however, towards late afternoon, the takes will get fewer and fewer and then stop altogether. Early spring fishing is usually confined to a few hours around the middle of the day, so keep at it while the going is good; a break for lunch could cost you the best of the day's sport.

The dry fly in spring

If you are fortunate enough to be fishing a river with a reputation for big hatches of dark olives and March brown, it will often pay to turn to the dry fly outfit towards noon. In the days when I opened each season on the Usk, I often tackled up with the dry fly outfit on arrival and awaited a hatch of fly, providing it was a reasonably soft day when a decent hatch could be anticipated. The opportunity to go straight into the season with fishing a dry fly to rising trout was too much to resist.

One of the problems with early season fishing is wind, especially when it blows downstream, so the tackle needs to be capable of punching a dry fly into a stiff breeze. In these conditions I use a slightly stronger rod than usual, rated for a five or six line, but using the weight-forward five. To help presentation, the usual yard-long leader point is reduced to no more than 2 feet.

If and when a hatch takes place, there is no problem in identifying the fly on the water, with only two upwinged flies to choose from. Usually the dark olives will hatch first and be in greater numbers, and if the March brown appears it will be spotted immediately, being considerably bigger and, as its name suggests, distinctly brown.

Providing fortune smiles upon you and there is a good hatch, you are likely to enjoy some of the easiest fishing of the season, with the trout taking any reasonable imitation with the eagerness you would expect after the poor feeding of the winter months.

THE CREAM OF THE SEASON

The months of May and June usually see the best fishing of the year on the rain-fed rivers and this is an ideal time for the beginner to make a start. Fly hatches are coming to a peak, the rivers have dropped to ideal fishing level, the trout are coming into prime condition and are feeding heavily at the surface at every opportunity. The fact that the countryside is at its sparkling best is an added bonus.

To make things really easy for yourself, try a day at the very end of May or the beginning of June, when you will probably see more species of those insects that are taken by trout than at any other time in the season. You can expect to see olive uprights, pale wateries, iron blues, mayflies, black gnats, hawthorns, early sedges, and several other insects. This is the period when fishing some of the more fertile lowland streams comes closest to chalk stream fishing, with the opportunity to spend most of the day casting to rising trout.

The two great carnivals of this period are the black gnat and the mayfly, but the latter is confined to those rivers which run slowly enough for sediment to settle and provide the conditions required for the mayfly larvae. The black gnat brings the fish to the surface with its sheer numbers, while the mayfly attracts them with its large size.

Finding the trout

For the newcomer, or indeed the experienced angler on a new river, locating the fish can be a real problem. You will quickly learn that trout are not evenly distributed along a river, but concentrated in a relatively few places, especially those better than average fish you are looking for. In May and June, the problem of location is usually taken care of by the sight of rising fish, so a walk along the bank with your eyes wide open, should quickly tell you where to make a start.

By this time, the dry fly has come into its own and from May until the end of the season I rarely use anything else on rain-fed rivers. The size 5 floating line used for the wet fly will still do, but dropping to a size 4 will give greater delicacy. If the river you are fishing is fairly open, use the 8½ foot rod, but on those little streams with a canopy of trees which can produce some of the best black gnat fishing, a shorter rod of 7 feet can avoid trouble. If it has a quick action which throws a narrow loop so much the better; a wider loop is likely to catch the overhanging branches unless you are very careful.

This time, when you enter the water, you will be fishing a dry fly upstream, so it makes sense to fish the right bank if you are right handed. This will once again keep your false casting over the river and well clear of the trees.

Except on the rocky torrents of moor and mountain, of which more later, you should be looking for rising fish right from the word go, especially if you have left your arrival to around mid-morning. By then, enough insects should be hatching to get the first trout taking surface food, and if you can identify the dominant insect, try an imitation right away. However, the trout may well be taking a variety of insects, so try a good general pattern like a size 16 Adams or Grey Duster, and cover any rising trout within reach.

In late May and early June, the numbers of black gnats will be building up by mid-morning and will gradually increase as the day progresses, until by the afternoon there may be huge swarms producing a virtual haze over the water. These swarms are usually over the quicker water at the head of a pool and some of the smaller trout will be seen leaping frantically to take the black gnats in mid-air. The bigger fish that you are looking for should be rising more sedately, not only under the swarms but all down the pools and runs. This constant feeding will often continue until early evening, providing the best prolonged surface activity of the season. This fishing to trout steadily taking the black gnat has a wonderful timelessness, with none of the frantic racing against time of a brief spring hatch of dark olives or a fall of sherry spinners as the light fades. The black gnat has given me some huge catches of trout on many rivers and some of my best fish.

The other great carnival at this time is the mayfly, but this wonderful insect rarely appears in large numbers on the rougher streams. Its larvae need a reasonable amount of sediment for their two years in the river, so that means

that it is on the slower streams that you will find the best mayfly fishing. The best of the hatch is usually in the afternoon, but I always try to be on the water from mid-morning, especially after the hatch has been under way for a few days. By then the trout will have developed a taste for the big duns and are likely to take an imitation as soon as a few naturals start hatching. At the peak of the hatch, hectic fishing should continue until late afternoon or early evening and then, just as the rise to the duns begins to slow, the female spinners will return to the river to lay their eggs and drift down the current, dead or dying at the end of their life cycle. This should produce another rise for an hour or so. A day during the mayfly hatch can be long and tiring, but make the most of it as there will be years when the hatch will be sparse and spasmodic.

Presenting the fly

Once you have located a rising trout and decided on the fly you are to use, whether an imitation of the hatching insect or a more general pattern, you are faced with an aspect of dry fly fishing which you just have to get right if you want to succeed – presentation. The first advice is not to rush it; it is all too easy for the beginner, in the excitement of seeing a rising trout, to cast his fly at it without a moment's thought and, almost certainly, send it darting for cover or at least put it on its guard.

This is the time to stay your hand and give some thought to how you will take the fish; if it is really on the feed, it will not swim away in a hurry. Before you even cast, think about where you will cast from. If, for example, the trout is rising in water of moderate flow, but with a strong current between you and it, your fly will drag almost immediately after alighting and that is fatal. By quietly wading across the stream into a position downstream of the fish, you can drop your line on to slower water that will allow your fly to drift naturally over the rising trout.

The excitement may also make you forget that what is behind you is almost as important as what is in front. There is nothing more frustrating than extending your line to cover a rising trout and then, as you are making the final delivery, hanging up on a branch with your back cast. Unless you are on an open stretch of water, check for any such obstacles and move into a position where your back cast is clear.

If I had to choose the ideal position from which to cover a rising trout it would be that which allowed me to cast across stream, or up and across. Such an angle makes it easier to get a drag-free drift over the fish. However, trout can be covered from any angle and there will be many times when considerations like current, wind or overhanging trees will make it necessary to cast in every direction, even downstream.

Let us assume that conditions are kind and allow you to cast to your first rising trout of the day from an easy position downstream and across from the fish. At this point you have to decide where to drop the fly. It is all too easy to cast instinctively to the ring of the rise, but a moment's thought will make it clear that on a moving stream you need to cast upstream of the fish — but how far? As a rule of thumb, the faster the current, the farther the fly should be above the trout, otherwise you may be casting downstream of where the fish is actually lying. Conversely, in slow clear water, the fly should alight only inches upstream of the fish, so that it has little time to study your offering. If you are immediately below a fish, casting too far above it will give it the chance to see your whole leader, especially the thick part of it.

If all goes well, the trout will suck in your dry fly as it drifts down on the current and, once more, the beginner can easily let excitement spoil the opportunity, probably by snatching the fly away from the fish or striking so hard that the leader will break even on a half-pound trout. Trout on rain-fed rivers are reputed to be quick risers and that is certainly the case with small fish on mountain torrents, but a good trout rising quietly on slower water will take the dry fly slowly and deliberately, little different from the chalk streams, so you have to adapt to the conditions. When I try to analyse what happens when I hook a trout, it can best be described as a steady lifting of the rod to tighten on the fish — the word strike that is often used is probably misleading and suggests something far more violent than is really necessary. Fortunately, the excitement of the rise of a trout to your dry fly is something that never palls even after decades of fishing, but with experience you learn to control the excitement and develop the restraint that is necessary to hook trout successfully.

Caterpillar interlude

On any stream that runs through heavily wooded country, a phenomenon to look out for around the beginning of June is the little green caterpillar. I first became aware of this little creature nearly a decade ago when I saw one descending on a gossamer thread from a bankside tree until it touched the water, when it instantly vanished in the swirl of a trout. Later that day I killed a fish and when cleaning it discovered that it was crammed with green caterpillars. That year the caterpillars reached almost plague proportions in the Teign valley, as they attacked the fresh leaves, and for a couple of weeks the fishing was fantastic, both for quantity and quality.

For a couple of years more there was an early June carnival and then the caterpillar population collapsed. Since then these insects have been scarce, but even modest numbers are enough to trigger off heavy feeding by the trout, so it is always worth keeping a few imitations in the fly box.

Unlike dry fly fishing, which is best done in the streamier water, the caterpillar works best in the slow smooth water at the tail of a pool and under the bankside trees out of the current. The overhanging trees which provide the supply of food also supply the shade which is necessary for success in water that is usually gin clear, smooth and often only a few inches deep. Cast into every likely spot, doing everything possible to avoid wading ripples. The very tail of each pool should be covered thoroughly, thin water that you would rarely fish with other methods.

Although the caterpillar dressing that I use sinks, it is usually taken almost immediately, often with a visible rise as it hits the water. The little splash as it hits the water often excites the fish to move a considerable distance to take it, and nearly all takes are within a couple of seconds of the fly hitting the water. The leader is greased along its whole length so that any sub-surface take can be spotted by the leader skating along the surface. This really is exciting fishing but only worth trying if the trout are feeding on caterpillars. The imitation that will draw trout from several feet at the right time, will send them rushing for cover when there are no naturals.

A stretch of the East Lyn at Rockford (Devon), where the boulders provide plenty of cover for a large head of trout

Fishing the water

Not all fishing in May and June is casting to rising trout, especially in the moors and mountains where even during this bountiful period the insect activity may be relatively sparse. Nevertheless, I still stick to the dry fly on these waters and find that it not only takes the most fish but also the bigger trout. This fishing differs from that on the lowland streams in that you cannot hope to confine your efforts to casting to rising trout; on many pools and runs, not a fish will be seen rising, but as soon as you drop your dry fly on the stream, a trout will be there in a flash. Clearly you have to learn to identify those spots which are likely to produce trout – the technique usually known as 'fishing the water'.

The problem of selecting the right location can be eased considerably by the process of elimination. As in early spring, those big slow pools with a glassy surface, where the trout can easily be seen, will often beguile the beginner into wasting much time, but this temptation should be firmly resisted. Those fish may look attainable but they are more difficult to hook than any other trout I know of, so pass on to more profitable pastures. You can also by-pass the stretches of thin broken water only a few inches deep where cover is insufficient to hold anything but small fish.

As in the early part of the season, you are looking for water of moderate depth and moderate speed, with the surface sufficiently broken to help conceal any slight deficiencies in your presentation. Many moorland streams have stretches which are broken up by large boulders, and these provide cover for the trout and concealment for the angler. Such stretches can be full of trout, with the fish lying in the deeper pockets among the boulders.

The moorland torrents

One of my greatest pleasures at this time of the year, and in the summer months, is to work up a really tiny upland stream which tumbles down from pool to pool. The trout taken on such a day may not be big, but on a good stream they will be very numerous and once in a while a relatively huge fish will emerge from cover and suck in your fly.

For this fishing you need a fly that floats well and this can be achieved by using buoyant material like deer hair or producing a bushy fly by giving the hackle a few extra turns. As soon as possible after the fly has been tied or purchased, give it a good application of floatant. My favourite moorland dry flies include the Adams, Hair Wing Sedge, Grey Duster and Humpy.

HIGH SUMMER

Around the beginning of July there comes a distinct change in the pattern of fishing. In a normal year, the rivers will have become progressively lower and clearer, with the trout becoming increasingly difficult to approach or deceive during the daytime. They are perfectly easy to locate, especially on a sunny day when trout can be seen virtually anywhere in the river, lying below the surface waiting for whatever the current brings their way. The problem is that they will usually spot you long before you can even get into casting position and move quickly away to deeper water. But do not give up – they can still be caught even on the brightest day, with sufficient care and application.

Another change is the growing importance of the evening rise, due mainly to the blue-winged olive and a variety of sedges. There will have been some evening activity as early as May and certainly by early June most evenings will see some sort of rise, but I find the daytime fishing in those months so productive and fascinating that it is usually late June before I really turn to evening fishing.

Daytime dry fly

But first, what can be done to make the most of daytime fishing? Those fish that you can see quietly sipping in food on the quieter stretches, especially where there are plenty of overhanging trees and bushes, are eating something, even though there is little sign of anything hatching. And there lies the answer – very little is hatching, but there is a steady flow of insect life falling from the trees. As the daytime hatches of upwinged flies decline,

the onset of summer sees an explosion in the numbers of terrestrial insects, often all too evident in the case of those that pester us. Fortunately, many of these terrestrials end up

A tree-lined stretch of the River Teign, Devon, in high summer, when terrestrial insects are prolific

in the rivers and are well liked by the trout, which can expect to see a varied diet of beetles, bugs, caterpillars, ants and *Diptera* coming their way. An examination of the trout's stomach content at this time of year will reveal the variety of food items that it takes and that sheer variety means that the fish are seldom preoccupied with a single species. This means that you can choose to use a fly that suggests any of these groups of terrestrial insects, and my own favourite is the beetle.

Netting a good wild trout on the River Teifi at Maesycrugiau. In fast water like this, felt soles give added security

On the more broken stretches of river, a traditional hackle beetle like a Coch-y-bondhu or Eric's Beetle will work well enough, but on the smoother stretches where more trout can be spotted, such patterns will often be refused. Take a close look at the rising trout and you will see that they are just sipping, hardly breaking the surface, a sure sign that they are taking insects that are trapped in the surface film. When the trout are taking hatching duns or sedges they know that their prey may take off at any time and the rise is quicker and often splashier, very different from the almost lazy rise when a drowning land insect is taken. What this all means is that terrestrial patterns should float right in the surface film, and not cocked high on stiff hackles.

The beetle that I have come to rely on is the American pattern often known as the Crowe Beetle, which uses buoyant hollow deer hair for the whole fly. It really looks like a beetle, floats well and, in sizes 16 and 18, is a great fish catcher. Another American pattern which represents a beetle and doubles up by suggesting a variety of *Diptera*, is the Jassid, which has on many occasions come to my rescue with difficult trout. Even in sizes as small as 18 and 20, the peacock eye feather, which is used for the flat wing, is easily seen.

There will be frequent occasions in the heat of a summer day when the trout are feeding steadily on very tiny midges and other insects that can barely be seen. If you fancy a real challenge, try these fish with a very small midge pattern – you will be surprised to find that trout which are usually described as impossible can be taken on a 22 or even 24 fly. My favourite pattern for such occasions is a very simple black midge with no hackle, but a tiny white wing to aid visibility.

There is, of course, little point in fishing these small terrestrial patterns on the smoother stretches of river unless you use suitable tackle, and that means a light line of size 4 or less, and a leader point which is as fine as you feel you can handle. The new extra-fine nylon makes it possible to go finer than ever before, while retaining a reasonable breaking strain. Presenting a fly to a rising trout on the smoother stretches of a stream in high summer is a real test of your casting ability and puts an absolute premium on getting the first presentation absolutely right. The slightest blunder will probably be fatal; the trout may not move away but it has probably been warned and the next cast will send it racing for cover. Get the first cast right and you might just get your fish.

Another and easier dry fly technique for high summer is to seek the roughest most oxygenated water you can find and work up it with a bushy high-riding hackle pattern like a Grey Duster. For this purpose a variant often works well — a fly with the hackle rather longer in the fibre than usual. This is one time when the trout will often be in surprisingly thin water, providing it is not too far from cover.

Fishing the nymph

'But what about the nymph?' I hear you say — the stand-by for the chalk stream on a hot summer day. The fact is that on the clearer moorland streams I have found the dry fly more effective. Where the nymph has worked well for me is on the quiet meandering little meadow streams that often carry quite a lot of colour — the upper Torridge and tributaries of the Tamar like the Carey and Thrushel are good examples, as are the brooks in Herefordshire that I fished many years ago.

On these streams, a weighted nymph cast into a sluggish little pool that looks quite dead will frequently attract trout after trout. The classic fly for this type of fishing is Frank Sawyer's Pheasant Tail Nymph, but I also use a Hare's Ear Nymph with a little lead wire around the hook shank. The cast should be well greased so that when the trout takes, the draw of the leader is immediately apparent.

A form of nymph fishing which can work well on the clearer streams is the sunk beetle, which sometimes performs better than the floating deer hair beetle in very smooth water. This fly is fished exactly like the green caterpillar, where trees overhang the river, and the take is usually immediately after the beetle hits the water.

The evening rise

In high summer, many anglers prefer to confine their activities to the evening, an exciting if often exasperating time. From mid-summer until they become chilly, many evenings will see some sort of hatch of blue-winged olives, a fall of sherry spinners and some sedge activity, and all of these insects are loved by the trout. The problem is that right from the moment that the fish start rising, time is running out rapidly, so a cool head is called for. A few bad casts, a lost fish or two, a tangled leader — such normally minor irritations can easily result in the rot setting in as daylight fades, and your fishing can quickly become ragged. Conversely, if you can just settle down and achieve a smooth rhythm in your fishing, you can expect to enjoy an hour or two of concentrated and productive sport.

In July, 7.30 p.m. is early enough to be on the river and even then there may be little rising. Some sedges will already be hovering over the stream and I usually start with a size 16 hair wing sedge, which often produces a fish or two before the main activity of the evening, especially if you fish the quicker broken water. Soon you should see the sherry spinners building up over the stream and as they fall to the surface after egg laying they will be taken avidly by the trout. Surprisingly, this opportunity for imitating the spinner is often ignored by anglers on rain-fed streams, many of whom do not carry any spinner patterns. Various standard patterns will certainly take some fish, but, by using a spent-wing imitation fished flat on the surface, you are likely to take far more fish. There is also likely to be a hatch of blue-winged olive duns and quite often both the duns and spinners will be on the water at the same time. When this happens, I have found that the Sherry Spinner imitation is usually the more effective.

The best way to deal with a hatch of blue-winged olive duns has intrigued anglers for decades, especially in the choice of the colour of the fly body. Tradition favours an orange-bodied fly and that is what I use for late evening fishing. However, the blue-winged olive is not only an evening fly; on rain-fed rivers, some of the biggest hatches take place in the afternoon, especially in June and September. One of the best catches I ever enjoyed on Dartmoor was on a dull afternoon on Black Brook. Around 2 p.m. the blue-winged olives started hatching and continued for nearly three hours, creating a prolonged rise with trout feeding in places I had never seen fish before. For these daytime rises, a more natural colour scheme works better than the orange body.

THE BACK END

September is the last month of the season on most rain-fed rivers, a period about which it is difficult to generalize. Many years ago I enjoyed some golden September days on the Usk above Abergavenny, when around noon the blue-winged olive duns started hatching and continued without a break until early evening. On those soft afternoons without a breath of wind, trout were quietly sucking in the duns all across the river and I enjoyed dry fly fishing as close to perfection as I could ever hope for.

The last weeks of the season can also see a revival in the hatches of pale wateries and, particularly on an overcast day with an autum-nal chill in the air, the iron blues.

In complete contrast, many streams become very dour in September, with the season ending on a low note. There are late season days on my local Dartmoor rivers when nothing seems to happen and even a rigorous search of the water with a wet fly produces very little.

The answer is to adapt to the changing conditions. If the weather is benign, you can enjoy splendid fishing reminiscent of May and June, but if autumn comes early you are faced with conditions similar to early spring, and your tactics may have to return to those you would use at that time.

SOME FINAL HINTS

The margin between real success and relative failure on rain-fed streams can be a very small one. Consistent success comes as a result of getting a variety of things right, and the more you get right, the more trout you will catch. Here is a reminder of a dozen hints and tips that have appeared in this chapter, a combination of which will not only increase your catches but, I hope, add to the enjoyment of your fishing.

1. *Take the rain-fed rivers seriously.*   Fishing on them can be every bit as demanding as on chalk streams and the trout are usually more difficult to approach. If you look upon fishing these streams as second best, your catches will reflect this attitude.

2. *Aim high.*   If you are willing to settle for a brace or two of trout in a day, your results will reflect your aspirations. On any reasonable day you should be expecting a dozen decent trout, with more than twenty fish within your reach when the trout are taking readily. If you really want to catch a lot of trout and develop the skills to achieve your aim, the time will come when you will find yourself in the right place at the right time, and that is when your catch may top forty or fifty fish and provide one of those days that live in the memory for ever.

3. *Fish the dry fly.*   Once the fish start feeding at the surface, change to the dry fly and stick with it whenever conditions permit. A competent dry fly fisher will probably take

more fish and bigger fish over the course of a season than the wet fly angler.

4. *Fish the rise.*   The opportunities to fish to rising trout may not be as frequent as on the chalk streams, but they come more often than you may think. Time spent looking for rising trout is rarely wasted.

5. *Match the hatch.*   Trout on rain-fed rivers may not often have the chance to become preoccupied with a huge hatch of a single species of insect, but attempting to imitate the predominant insect gives you an advantage, and it is more fun, too.

6. *Be mobile.*   There are no prizes for sticking in one spot hoping the trout will come to you, like many anglers do on the lakes. Go in search of the fish, even if other anglers look askance at the time you spend walking rather than fishing. You will probably end up catching more trout than them.

7. *Wade deep.*   Wading, and at times really deep wading, can put you in touch with trout that rarely see an angler's fly. Used skilfully, a pair of felt soled body waders will increase your catches like few other items of equipment.

8. *Think small.*   Many anglers on rain-fed rivers do not carry any flies smaller than size 16, thus excluding them from any hope of real success when the trout are feeding on tiny insects, especially in summer. Make sure that you have patterns down to size 22, and become an all-season fly fisher.

9. *Fish fine.*   There is no merit in fishing fine for its own sake, but when the trout are taking really small flies you have to scale down your tackle accordingly. That means a light rod, light line and fine leader point to match the tiny flies that become necessary.

10. *Fish in the surface film.*   When trout are taking spinners or other insects that drift right in the surface film, that is where your fly has to be. Always carry some spent-winged spinners and small terrestrial patterns that will fish where those sipping trout are expecting them.

11. *Make the first cast count.*   Make sure that your first presentation to a rising trout is accurate and touches down lightly. Compensating at the second attempt, after a clumsy first cast, is rarely successful.

12. *Catch and release.*   The quality of fishing on even the most prolific rain-fed stream can eventually decline if too many trout are killed by too many anglers. My final piece of advice, far more important than all the tips on taking trout, is to do all you can to maintain the priceless asset of so many rain-fed rivers — the wild brown trout. More and more anglers are realizing that once you have enjoyed the excitement of deceiving and catching a wild trout, its place is back in the river alive, to produce more of the same. Catch-and-release may be catching on slowly in Britain (and is still opposed by many) but my prediction is that its growth on suitable streams is inevitable.

TYING YOUR OWN

The angler who ties his own flies will usually have an edge over those who do not. Striving to imitate or suggest the natural insects upon which trout feed is such an integral part of the whole experience that I now find it difficult to contemplate fly fishing without fly tying.

Professional fly tyers have to stick to those patterns that have a high level of demand and a quick turnover, so that rules out most of the unusual patterns like beetles and caterpillars — it is even quite difficult to get good spinner

imitations in many shops. Really small flies are also hard to get hold of. The only answer is to tie your own if you want to carry a really comprehensive range of flies to meet most eventualities.

Another advantage of producing your own flies is that you can, if you wish, tie them on barbless hooks. I went barbless a decade ago and have complete faith in these hooks and their ability to hold fish, providing you keep a tight line until the fish is in the net. The ease of unhooking a trout, or even the cuff of your sweater, is a revelation and I would never go back to the barbed hook. A bonus is the fact that the barbless hook penetrates more easily, an advantage when using fine leaders.

If your favourite hook is not available without a barb, it is easy to crush down the barb with very fine pointed pliers, but do this before tying the fly to avoid the exasperation of breaking a hook after tying is complete. Fortunately, the English hook manufacturer, Partridge of Redditch, offers a range of barbless hooks. For normal length dry flies I use the Roman Moser Arrowpoint (code CS20) and for those dry flies like the Mayfly that require a longer shank I use the barbless Hooper Long Shank (code E3AY). If you prefer barbed hooks, use the Hooper 1X Short (code E6A) for standard dry flies and the Hooper L/S (code E1A) when a longer shank is needed. For wet flies I crush down the barbs on the Sproat Forged Wet Fly (code G3A).

Here then are the specifications for the flies that I use regularly on rain-fed rivers, a mixture of attempts to imitate specific insects or families of insects, plus a range of standard patterns.

The knowledgeable angler will quickly spot some omissions and wonder why I have left out imitations of some insects. For example, you will find no imitations of dry stone flies here, even though these insects can often be seen in large numbers fluttering over the rockier streams. The reason is that I have rarely seen a trout take a stone fly, so I see no point in tying an artificial to match it. Similarly, I have often read that the alder is a great favourite with the trout, but until I experience a rise to alder it will find no place in my fly box.

Although I have tried to stick to materials that are easily available, there are some dressings that use less common materials. For the bodies of small dry flies, seal's fur is inclined to be rather coarse, so I prefer something finer, whether natural or synthetic. Poly yarn for wings usually has to be obtained by mail order, although the first supply I ever used came from a sewing materials shop. Fine quality deer hair is a problem and all of my best material was obtained in the USA, and then only after

looking through a large selection. If the ends are uneven they can be tapped in one of the old Magic Marker caps or one of the new hair stackers. For wet flies, hen hackles are usually specified, but I am happy to use cock hackles which are not up to dry fly standard. Inevitably, all fly tyers collect plenty of these over the years.

Finally, never be afraid to vary these or other writers' fly dressings. If you think that the recommended shade of body fur, the position of the hackle, or anything else could be improved, then do it — that is the way that fly tying develops.

Dry flies

Large Dark Olive

Hook: 16
Tail: Dark blue dun cock hackle fibres.
Body: Dark olive fur dubbed on yellow silk, with a few turns of silk exposed at the rear.
Hackle: Dark blue dun cock. The hackle is wound further back from the eye than usual, with a few turns of the body material wound in front.

The setting back of the hackle, with some of the body in front of it, is a personal preference developed over the years. Whether it catches more trout or not is open to question, but I like the look of the result and one of the advantages

Figure 17   *Side view of dun showing the position of the hackle favoured by the writer, with a few turns of body material at the front*

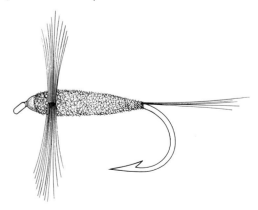

of tying your own flies is the opportunity to indulge your preferences — always providing the trout agree. This technique is used for most of my hackle dry flies.

March Brown

Hook: 14.
Tail: Brown cock hackle fibres.
Body: Dubbed hare's ear with ribbing of very fine gold wire.
Hackles: Brown and grizzle cock, one wound through the other.

This is the pattern that worked well in the days of a quarter of a century ago when I started every season on the Usk, and I keep it in the fly box for occasional visits to those few fortunate rivers with a hatch of March brown.

Olive Upright

Hook: 16.
Tail: Blue dun cock hackle fibres.
Body: Medium olive fur dubbed on yellow silk, with a few turns of silk exposed at the rear.
Hackle: Blue dun cock.

This dressing is essentially the same as the Dark Olive, but with lighter shades to suggest the natural.

Iron Blue

Hook: 18.
Tail: Slate blue cock hackle fibres.
Body: Mole's fur dubbed on crimson silk, with a few turns of silk exposed at the rear.
Hackle: Slate blue cock.

Tied as a wet fly on a heavier hook, this becomes the Infallible, a traditional Devon fly.

Pale Watery

Hook: 18 and 20.
Tail: Pale blue dun cock hackle fibres.
Body: Dubbed light olive fur, sometimes with a touch of yellow mixed in.
Hackle: Pale blue dun cock.

Mayfly

Hook: 12 long shank.
Tail: Three or four fibres of dark brown moose hair.
Body: Dubbed cream fur with ribbing of dark brown silk.
Hackles: Medium olive and well marked grizzle cock, one wound through the other.

If moose hair is not available for the tail, the traditional cock pheasant tail fibres can be used. I tie some mayflies with a pink body and this works very well at times.

Mayfly Spinner

Hook: 12 long shank.
Tail: Three or four fibres of dark brown moose hair.
Body: Rear two-thirds dubbed natural sheep's wool with ribbing of black silk. Front third dubbed black fur, wound behind and in front of wing.
Wing: Light grey poly yarn, tied horizontal at right angles to the hook shank. The black body material is wound figure-of-eight around the wing, thus forming a distinct thorax.

Poly yarn is ideal for spinner wings, making it quick and easy to tie even the smallest spinners. The winding of the body material in figures-of-eight around the wing makes a really neat fly.

Figure 18 Overhead view of poly-wing spinner, showing a small ball of body material at butt, to ensure that a forked tail is achieved

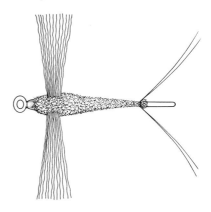

Blue-Winged Olive

Hook: 16.
Tail: Slate blue cock hackle fibres.
Body: Dubbed orange *or* yellow/green fur.
Hackle: Slate blue cock.

The orange body is used for evening fishing and the yellow-green body for daytime hatches of blue-winged olives. The latter colour is often described as ripe greengage.

Rusty Spinner

Hook: 16 and 18.
Tail: Honey dun or pale ginger cock hackle fibres.
Body: Dubbed reddish-brown fur.
Wing: Pale grey poly yarn, tied horizontal.

This pattern covers most of my needs for a spinner, with size 16 used for falls of sherry spinner. It is easy to vary the body colour if necessary.

Black Gnat

Hook: 18.
Body: Dubbed black fur.
Wing: White or pale grey poly yarn, sloping back over body.
Hackle: Black cock.

For the Hawthorn I use this same dressing on a size 16 hook, without attempting to suggest the dangling legs of the natural.

Hair Wing Sedge

Hook: 14 and 16.
Body: Dubbed hare's ear. A short butt of yellow or green wool can be added.
Wing: Natural deer hair, sloping back over body.
Hackle: Brown cock.

A simpler and very effective version can be produced by leaving out the hackle. The butts of the hairs used for the wing are left lying forward and then clipped to a tiny muddler-type head.

Deer Hair Beetle

Hook: 16 and 18.
Body, back, legs and head: Black, green or brown hollow deer hair. A clump of hair is tied down along the shank of the hook with most of the excess pointing to the rear. The hair is brought forward from the rear, over the back and tied down hard just behind the eye, so that it flares. A muddler-type head is created by clipping, with three or four strands of hair left at each side to suggest legs. The back is given several coats of varnish.

Jassid

Hook: 18 and 20.
Body: Fine black fur ribbed with short fibred black cock hackle, clipped top and bottom.
Wing: Peacock eye feather, lying flat over body. A spot of glue between wing and body helps to keep the wing in place.

Black Midge

Hook: 20, 22 and 24.
Body: Dubbed black fur.
Wing: White poly yarn, vertical and slightly back from eye

Adams

Hook: 14, 16 and 18.
Tail: Mixed grizzle and brown cock hackle fibres.
Body: Dubbed grey fur. The original specification states muskrat, but I am happy to use grey rabbit.
Wings: Two grizzle cock hackle tips, upright and divided.
Hackles: Grizzle and brown cock, one wound through the other.

This ubiquitous pattern is possibly the most popular dry fly in the USA. I often exclude the wings and find the resulting fly just as effective.

Grey Duster

Hook: 14, 16 and 18.
Body: Dubbed rabbit fur.
Hackle: Badger cock.

Tie a few with extra-long hackles for rough water. In very small sizes like 20 and 22 the Grey Duster is an excellent adult midge imitation.

Coch-y-bonddu

Hook: 14 and 16.
Butt: Flat gold tinsel.
Body: Bronze peacock herl, fairly bulky.
Hackle: Brown cock with black centre. Alternatively, use two hackles, brown and black, with one wound through the other.

Eric's Beetle

Hook: 14 and 16.
Body: Underbody of yellow wool with bronze peacock herl wound over, leaving a little of the yellow wool showing at the butt.
Hackle: Black cock.

Yellow Humpy

Hook: 14 and 16.
Tail: Moose hair, about 6 fibres.
Underbody: Pale yellow floss or dubbed fur.
Overbody or back: Natural deer hair.
Wing: Natural deer hair, upright.
Hackles: Brown and grizzle cock, one wound through the other.

This fly is widely used on the rough rivers of the Rocky Mountains, so it is ideal for rapid moorland streams.

Nymphs

Green Caterpillar

Hook: 12 long shank.
Body: Lime-green fluorescent wool wound well into the bend. A ribbing, which can be fine

copper wire, helps to prolong the life of the fly.

Although this fly will be used infrequently, it produces spectacular sport at the right time, so keep several in the fly box.

Sawyer Pheasant Tail Nymph

Hook: 12, 14 and 16.

The whole nymph is tied with fine copper wire instead of silk and four fibres of red-brown cock pheasant tail. To quote Frank Sawyer, whose classic dressing has become the standard nymph for many situations, the fly is tied as follows: 'Hold the fibres by their tips and tie them on so that the fine ends stand out about ⅛ inch to form tail. Spin the fibres on to the wire and wind fibres and wire to the eye. Separate fibres from wire and wind wire back to point behind which thorax is to be made. Bend fibres back and fasten, then bring wire to point behind eye once more and take fibres forward to it again. Fasten with a dozen turns of wire and cut away spare fibres.'

Hare's Ear Nymph

Hook: 12, 14 and 16.
Tail: Three or four fibres of cock pheasant tail.
Body: Dubbed hare's ear with gold wire rib.
Thorax: Dubbed hare's ear, thicker than body, with wing case of crow or heron herl.
Legs: A few fibres of brown speckled partridge.

To ensure that this fly sinks, lead should be added to the hook shank, in variable amounts for differing depths and currents.

Sinking Beetle

Hook: 16 and 18.
Body: Peacock herl wound over a little lead.
Back: Crow or heron herl, tied down front and rear.

Sometimes, a beetle which drops with a little 'plop' and then sinks works better in really smooth water than the floating deer hair version.

Wet flies

Half Stone

Hook: 12, 14 and 16.
Tail: Blue dun cock hackle fibres.
Body: Rear half yellow silk or floss. Front half dubbed mole's fur.
Hackle: Blue dun

One of the best Devon patterns, which is also useful when olives are emerging. It also works well as a dry fly.

Greenwell (variation)

Hook: 12, 14 and 16.
Tail: Coch-y-bonddu cock hackle fibres.
Body: Dubbed yellow-olive fur, ribbed with fine gold wire.
Wings: Two blue dun cock hackle points, sloping back.
Hackle: Coch-y-bondhu.

A variation on one of the all-time classic flies.

Partridge and Orange

Hook: 12, 14 and 16.
Body: Dubbed orange fur ribbed with fine gold wire.
Hackle: Speckled brown partridge.

This fly can be varied by the use of yellow or green bodies, and a hare's ear body turns it into a wet March brown.

Pheasant Tail

Hook: 12, 14 and 16.
Tail: Pale blue dun or honey dun cock hackle fibres.

Body: Cock pheasant tail fibres, ribbed with fine gold wire.
Hackle: Pale blue dun or honey dun.

Tied as a dry fly, size 16, this makes a useful spinner imitation.

Soldier Palmer

Hook: 12, 14 and 16.
Body: Dubbed scarlet seal's fur, ribbed first with a short-fibred brown cock hackle and then fine gold wire to lock in the hackle.
Hackle: Brown cock, rather longer in fibre than body hackle.

Tradition has it that this is the fly to use on the moors when rain has produced peat stain. A very good variation is produced by using grizzle hackles instead of brown.

Black and Peacock Spider

Hook: 12, 14 and 16.
Body: Bronze peacock herl.
Hackle: Black.

A simple fly for those days when the trout want something really dark.

Further reading

Anne Voss Bark (ed.), *West Country Fly Fishing* (Batsford, 1983).
David Barr (ed.), *The Haig Guide to Trout Fishing in Britain* (Collins [Willow], 1983).
Maj. Kenneth Dawson ('West Country'), *Salmon and Trout in Moorland Streams* (Herbert Jenkins, 1928).
H.H. Edmonds and N.N. Lee, *Brook and River Trouting* (privately published, Bradford, 1916).
Peter Lapsley, *River Trout Flyfishing* (Unwin Hyman, 1988).

Oliver Kite

Oliver Kite (universally known as Olly) was certainly one of the best fly fishermen of his time. Halford said that, in casting to an educated fish, it was necessary to be right first time; Olly Kite nearly always was. He was a splendid fishing companion – skilful, witty, helpful, seeing all the flora and fauna and a mine of information about it. He was an extrovert, a raconteur, the life and soul of any party. When he was invited by Southern Television to do a weekly wildlife programme, he was an instant success. His warm and friendly personality and attractive Monmouth accent, with a fertile brain forever producing new angles, meant that he could educate and entertain at the same time. No one who saw him catch grayling in October, make a wood fire, and fry them in butter with wild mushrooms by the riverside, will forget it.

Olly was a fluent writer with the ability to explain clearly the new (at that time) doctrine of fishing the sunk nymph, which he did in his book, *Nymph Fishing in Practice*, published in 1963. But he was not an original thinker: he had not the dogged determination of Frank Sawyer, who over many years evolved the theory of the sunk nymph, and who designed the artificials required to turn that theory into practice. Kite (Sawyer's neighbour at Netheravon) acknowledged this, saying in his introduction that the whole book was a tribute to Sawyer.

Olly Kite knew, some years before he died, that he had a heart condition and that he was unlikely to reach old age. He worked hard, with writing and television, to leave enough to provide for his wife and daughter. He had a final heart attack beside the Test at Overton on 15 June 1968. He died beside the river, mercifully and with dignity, as all fishermen would wish to do.

Sidney Vines

The text that follows is taken from pages 113 to 145 inclusive of the 1984 reprint of the 1969 edition of *The Complete Fly-Fisher*, edited by C.F. Walker (Barrie & Jenkins).

4

BROWN TROUT IN CHALK STREAMS

Oliver Kite

Oliver Kite

INTRODUCTION

Chalk stream characteristics

Chalk streams are spring-fed rivers characterized by naturally filtered alkaline water of great clarity, conducive to the production of such nourishing protein trout food as freshwater shrimps, crayfish and a variety of molluscs. These rivers are not so liable to sudden fluctuation in level as rain-fed rivers and are less subject to discoloration. They support a lush growth of waterweed for much of the year and this helps to keep up the water level during the summer months, when it also gives rise to various problems in fishery management. Weed affords good cover for the fish and many of the creatures on which they feed.

Maintenance of trout stocks

In some chalk streams, the Wylye being a good example, the natural regeneration of trout is adequate to maintain a sufficient stock of wild fish in the river to meet the requirements of carefully controlled private fisheries. Elsewhere, for example on the expensive but hard-fished waters of the middle Test, periodic re-stocking is carried out with mature trout raised in adjoining hatcheries. Hatchery trout are, of course, easier to catch than wild fish when first turned into the river but they very quickly learn to be discreet, or die.

Importance of fly production

Regardless of the stock of trout it may hold, the sport afforded by a chalk stream fishery depends on the presence of fly in sufficient quantity to attract feeding fish, for unless the trout are willing to take natural insects it would be difficult, if not impossible, to induce them to accept artificial flies. Although the amount of fly varies from season to season and river to river, indeed from place to place on the individual fisheries of a river, chalk streams in general provide suitable conditions for the breeding of many Ephemerid species. It is on the nymphs, duns and spinners of these flies that the chalk stream fly fisher relies for his sport, augmented at times by sedge flies which also breed freely in these waters, and by a few other important insects of other orders. The key to the successful management of a chalk stream fishery is therefore the production of fly.

Limitations on fishing methods

Since it is possible to catch trout using imitations of these flies, either floating to represent them in the winged stages of their development, or beneath the surface to represent the later larval or nymph forms of the upwinged flies, and since two methods of fly fishing have been devised which are selective and allow the angler to fish for individual trout believed to be of takeable size, other forms of fishing, including spinning, bait fishing, and wet fly fishing, are normally strictly prohibited on the chalk streams.

The limitation of fishing to these highly specialized methods, the tolerably easy dry fly fishing and the less easy nymph fishing, may or may not be right, but there can be no doubt that it commands the support of the overwhelming majority of chalk stream anglers today.

The chalk country

Chalk streams are to be found in a number of English counties, especially in the south and, more especially, in Hampshire, Wiltshire, Berkshire and Dorset. Waters with many similar characteristics are found in several other counties. It would be wrong to assume that chalk streams resemble one another closely in character. Nothing could be further from the truth. They vary from the broad, swift-flowing Test to the impounded, canal-like reaches of the Itchen above Winchester, immortalized by the late G. E. M. Skues who fished the Abbot's Barton water from 1883 to 1938; from the crystal-clear, gravelly shallows of the Bourne at Hurstbourne Priors to the sedate and weedy Kennet at Ramsbury; from the tiny Ebble in the Chalke valley of Wiltshire to the many-faceted Upper Avon of Salisbury Plain.

The Wylye flowing through the heart of Wiltshire. This lovely river sustains a fine head of wild brown trout and is still largely unstocked

The end and the means

Chalk stream trout may, or may not, be more difficult to catch than trout elsewhere. Chalk stream fly fishers are, in any case, usually strictly limited in the number of trout they may keep each day and they are often less concerned with how many trout they catch than the manner in which they catch them. If it were otherwise, the chalk streams would quickly be denuded of their native trout stocks.

BASIC METHODS

Dry fly fishing

In the late Victorian times, a number of scholarly and inventive fly fishers with enviable opportunities to fish the classic waters of the great chalk streams like the Test, the Kennet and the Itchen, evolved a pattern of chalk stream fishing, the influence of which has persisted to this day. Francis Francis and G. S. Marryat set the stage for the more detailed work of F. M. Halford who, more than anyone else, formulated the cult of the dry fly, made feasible by H. S. Hall's invention of the eyed hook.

Halford's knowledge was profound and his writings were lucid and instructive, if somewhat dogmatic in his later works. He classified natural flies by types rather than by species, and for each type of upwinged fly he dressed separate artificial patterns for the male and female dun and spinner. He also suggested a number of patterns for artificial sedge flies and other insects, to be fished floating on the surface. In this way, he laid down a dry fly code which implied that artificial flies should always be imitations of natural flies in their *winged* stages and should always be fished floating on the surface.

Such fishing was and is known as dry fly fishing, to distinguish it from fly fishing in which one or more artificials are fished beneath the surface. Halford further defined dry fly fishing as offering a trout the best possible imitation of the insect on which it is seen to be feeding, floating on the surface in the position which fly fishers call 'cocked'. It is clearly implicit in this definition that before fishing can begin, a trout must first be seen to rise, the type of fly on which it is feeding must be identified correctly, and a suitably matched artificial must be tied on the cast and presented to the trout floating on the water. And this is how some chalk stream anglers practise dry fly fishing to this day.

It is still customary to fish the rise rather than the water. On nearly all chalk streams there is a minimum size below which trout should not be taken, indeed, should not be fished for. By studying the rising fish, it is usually possible to determine whether it is of takeable size. With regard to matching the fly on the water, some chalk stream anglers take this very seriously: others are content to rely on a few favourite well-tried patterns and hope to deceive the fish by delicate and accurate presentation of the fly. In these busy times, they find the Halford approach to dry fly fishing unnecessarily complicated and sometimes their entomological knowledge is scanty. But they may still catch fish.

Halford was a great man and he invested dry fly fishing with a scholarly and almost ritualistic charm which, for many, is a large part of its fascination. Yet it is almost certainly true that dry fly fishing evolved on the chalk streams for the simple reason that it was an easy way of catching trout. It is probably the easiest of all fly fishing methods, which is not the same as saying that chalk stream trout are the easiest of all to catch. Some of them are indeed easy, and some are uncommonly difficult.

Some of Halford's followers, who have been referred to as dry fly purists, held, and still hold, that the only rewarding, indeed the only legitimate way, to catch a chalk stream trout is to fish for it with a floating imitation of the type of fly on which it is feeding. The snag is that the trout often elects to feed beneath the surface on flies which are still in the underwater stages of their development. Such trout may not be willing to rise to the surface at all, either to natural hatched fly or to artificial dry flies, especially when they are feeding on nymphs. The dry fly purist accepts this with resignation, and may not cast a fly all day long. His fortitude commands our respect. The nymph fisherman, no purist, tries to catch these trout with artificial nymphs.

Nymph fishing

Nymph fishing owes its inception to G. E. M. Skues. His advocacy of a form of wet fly fishing, specially adapted for use on the chalk streams, brought him into acrimonious conflict with Halford and Halford's disciples. Skues discovered that a trout feeding below the surface which would not rise to an artificial floating fly would sometimes take the same fly if it became waterlogged and sank. This discovery led him to experiment with flies fished wet to individual trout seen to be feeding underwater. He published his early conclusions in 1910 in *Minor Tactics of the Chalk Stream*.

Skues's methods were every bit as selective as those of the most orthodox dry fly fisherman but it is, perhaps, understandable that in an age at once more formal and conventional than our own, they were viewed with disfavour by many of his contemporaries. Some scorned his methods as ineffective; others feared they would be dangerously efficient; above all, his critics looked on them as unsporting. Some of them were guilty of an intolerance which threatened to bring discredit on the specialized but overtly simple art of chalk stream fly fishing, of which some trout fishers elsewhere cherish a distorted impression to this day.

Despite the hostility he aroused, Skues persisted with his experiments and began to dress imitations of the nymphs which he found in the stomachs of the fish he caught. He published a number of other books including *Nymph Fishing for Chalk Stream Trout* (1938) in which he recommended a series of dressings of nymphs based on direct imitation of individual species.

It was from Skues's early discoveries and experiments that the modern technique of upstream nymph fishing was evolved at Netheravon by Frank Sawyer, since 1926 head river keeper of the Officers' Fishing Association which controls six miles of the Upper Avon. This fascinating technique, which is discussed in some detail in the section on nymph fishing later in this chapter, is fully explained in Sawyer's second book, *Nymphs and the Trout* (1958). His first book, *Keeper of the Stream* (1952), had earlier drawn attention o its possibilities and had attracted to Netheravon outstanding fly fishers of several nations to learn at first-hand the simple but effective methods which Sawyer had devised. Later, especially in France, manufacturers turned their attention to the production of suitable tackle expressly designed for modern nymph fishing.

It is important to understand the difference between wet fly fishing, as practised elsewhere, and upstream nymph fishing as permitted and practised on the chalk streams. In wet fly fishing, artificial flies are fished sunk in such a way as to represent various kinds of underwater trout food, including natural nymphs, but are not necessarily fished to a selected individual trout, as is the case in upstream nymph fishing. Wet flies, which may be fished singly or in teams of two or more, are dressed either as winged or nymphal patterns but generally include a certain amount of hackle to give them an appearance of life and thereby increase their effectiveness as lures. Artificial nymphs employed in the Netheravon style of nymph fishing are characterized by a complete absence of hackle of any kind. They are, in short, fished as nymphs, calculated to deceive, and not as lures, designed to attract.

In nymph fishing, as in dry fly fishing, only one artificial is employed at a time. The term 'upstream' should not be taken literally. Although fishing a nymph downstream and across, with a dragging action, is barred on the chalk streams, the artificial nymph is fished directly across the stream, or up and across, at least as often as it is fished directly upstream. The point to note is that it is always fished to an individual trout believed to be of take-

Sir Michael Hordern on the Wiltshire Avon, just downstream of the Services' Dry Fly Fishing Association water where Oliver Kite did much of his fishing and where Frank Sawyer was keeper for over 40 years

able size and seen to be feeding *beneath* the surface.

Upstream nymph fishing is therefore three-dimensional fly fishing and, as such, presents a range of problems additional to those of the dry fly. It is more difficult to master and it calls for good eyesight and constant practice to bring the art to perfection. Once mastered, it is an indispensable asset to the chalk stream fly fisher, particularly during the long bright days of July and August.

On most chalk stream fisheries today, nymph fishing and dry fly fishing are regarded as complementary and both are tolerated on an equal footing. There are still one or two fisheries and a number of private waters, however, where nymph fishing is either not allowed at all or is confined to a limited period during the season. It is therefore as well to ascertain the rule applicable when visiting a strange water before attempting to employ an artificial nymph. When in doubt, stick to the dry fly rather than risk offering offence.

THE CHALK STREAM SEASON

Duration

In general, the chalk stream trout fishing season lasts from May Day to Michaelmas but there are many exceptions at both extremities. Some Hampshire fisheries and parts of the Wylye open as early as mid-April but fishing does not start on the upper Test until May. Much depends on the usual spawning dates. The earlier the fish spawn, the sooner they can be expected

The Itchen at Martyr Worthy, still one of our finest chalk streams

to recover condition. On late spawning rivers, the season may be extended to mid-October.

Most chalk stream trout contrive to regain condition by mid-May and young fish make noticeable growth by the end of June. The trout of these rivers are generally at their best in July and early August. Appropriately, this is when they are usually hardest to catch!

Towards the end of the season, trout, and female trout especially, feed up hard preparatory to spawning. They then become rather vulnerable to the skilful fly fisher and somewhat ripe and ill-conditioned. The great Skues consistently refused to fish for them after August for this reason, but his Itchen water, just above Winchester, was usually regarded as an early one and Skues used to begin fishing about a month earlier than we start on the middle Wylye.

Main phases

The chalk stream trout season comprises three main phases: the first lasts from the beginning of the season until after the mayfly hatch is over, in other words until early June; the second from early June until mid-August; and the third from mid-August until the end of the season.

First phase

This phase takes in the sweet of the year and, we optimistically believe, coincides with an abundance of natural fly. It is a biological fact that certain important species of upwinged flies, on the English chalk streams, produce their spring generation at this time. Consequently, when climatic conditions are suitable, their duns and spinners can be expected to appear on the wing in good numbers. Moreover, heavy falls of black fly may occur during this opening phase, if conditions are conducive, and these insects, hawthorn flies and black gnats, are beloved by trout above all others.

If fly does materialize, fish can be expected to rise freely, to suitable artificials as well as to natural winged insects, for they have not yet been hammered by fishermen into a state of extreme caution, as will be the case on popular fisheries later in the season.

In April, hatches of duns may be concentrated into a short period of an hour or so and may not begin until after noon. In May, the hatches tend to draw out and by the end of the month may last for much of the day.

It is only towards the end of May that a regular evening rise can be expected. Indeed, the earliest big evening rises may occur at mayfly time when the spent spinner is on the water.

The dry fly is supreme during the first phase. Indeed, on some fisheries nymph fishing is not allowed before 1 July. In any case, it is not normally necessary to use it before June. My diary records that on the Upper Avon, where nymph fishing is permitted throughout the season, my first thirty-two trout of the 1961 season were all taken on the dry fly. Not until 24 June did I employ an artificial nymph to catch a trout from this water.

Second phase

This lasts from about mid-June to mid-August, is marked by a diminution in daytime small-fly hatches, coinciding with the end of the mayfly period. The two are unrelated. Certain important chalk stream species, some of the olives and iron blues among them, produce two main generations; one in spring and one in the autumn. Accordingly, the duns of these species hatch in the greatest numbers early and late in the trout fishing season. They give way during the second phase to daytime flies like the pale watery duns, the small spurwings and the slow-water olives[1] and to flies which hatch well on some evening at dusk, notably blue-winged olives and pale evening duns. At last light, sedge flies may hatch in considerable numbers, prolonging the evening rise until darkness.

Spent spinners may be coming down in considerable numbers throughout the day, and on most evenings, bringing on an evening rise. On waters where the blue-winged olive is plentiful, there may be a fall of sherry spinners on most evenings around sunset.

Trout may feed all day long on natural nymphs, especially over beds of water celery and in the runs at the tail of trimmed ranunculus beds. Indeed, nymph fishing assumes great importance during this second phase, when it normally takes precedence, by day, over the dry fly. On the Upper Avon, between 24 June and 17 August 1961, I took thirty-one trout on the nymph and only eleven on the dry fly, and, of those caught on the dry fly, all were taken in the evening: six on the Pale Evening Dun and five on the Red Spinner.

Third phase

This begins about mid-August but can be somewhat retarded in a hot, dry summer. It is characterized by increasing hatches of duns as the autumn generation of certain species begins to appear, by day-long hatches of blue-winged olives, by occasional falls of ants, by the appearance of numbers of willow flies, by generous sprinklings of black gnats, especially on muggy days in August, and by the continuing hatches of sedge flies at dusk on warm evenings. The month of September is traditionally one of the best for fly of the whole season and it witnesses the increasing employment of the dry fly by day to the exclusion of the artificial nymph. On the Upper Avon between 24 August and 30 September 1961, I took twenty-seven trout, all by day, twenty on the dry fly and only seven on the nymph.

---

[1] The lake and pond olives of Harris, which are found in certain slow-flowing reaches on some chalks streams — Ed.

THE CONTENTS OF THE FLY BOX

Introduction

Beware of those who pontificate on the subject of flies, those who say you should always use this or you never need that. 'Always' and 'Never' are terms of rather limited application to chalk stream fishing. The contents of your fly box can be as diverse or as uniform as you care to make them. If you want diversity, study the works of Halford, or Hills, or Carey, on the dry fly, and Skues on the nymph. If you want simplicity, you can have that, too, and still be successful for much of the time, especially if you know what you are doing, and why.

The nymph in relation to the dry fly

The chalk stream fly fisher generally likes to relate his artificial to what he thinks the trout are feeding on. Trout obtain a high proportion of the insect content of their diet beneath the surface of the water and if you examine their stomach contents, especially during the summer months, you often find that nymphs greatly outnumber hatched flies. It therefore stands to reason that a fly fisher operating regularly and evenly throughout a chalk stream season may end up by catching more trout on the artificial nymph than on the dry fly. I do so myself, in most years.

Your choice of artificial nymph patterns is unlimited, if you are tempted to try exact imitation. I use only one, Sawyer's Pheasant Tail, dressed on hooks of sizes 14 and 16, but mostly on No. 16. Others may be necessary, somewhere, but not on the chalk streams which are our concern here. In 1961 this pattern yielded me good trout from the Avon, Bourne, Anton, Test, Itchen, Nadder, Wylye and Shal Bourne (a Kennet tributary), and no less than 551 of the 951 takeable fish I caught in 1957–61. Nymph fishing in the Netheravon style turns not on pattern but on the manner in which the artificial is fished. I believe, however, that chalk stream fishermen should aim to master the dry fly completely before they concern themselves with learning nymph fishing; I do not know anyone who fishes the nymph well who is not also a competent performer with the dry fly.

All-round dry fly patterns

Certain dry fly patterns, in competent hands, are capable of taking trout feeding on the surface on a variety of insects. An expert rod, using an artificial of this kind, can be counted on most days to catch more trout than a fly fisher of moderate ability who commands a whole range of nicely dressed patterns. Successful all-round patterns include the Red Quill, which Halford recommended as the dry fly man's sheet anchor on a strange river, the spent-winged Lunn's Particular, and the Pheasant Tail Red Spinner, with white tails, a body and thorax of pheasant tail herls, red tying silk, and a dark red hackle.

These three artificials are effective because they are reasonable imitations of female olive spinners, and some of these natural insects, of which there are six fairly similar species, may be on the water every day of the fishing season. Trout expect to see them, spent, dead, and easy to capture, and are rarely averse to eating them. There is no other way of explaining my consistent success with the Pheasant Tail Red Spinner when trout are taking blue-winged olive duns.

My old friend, Colonel Peter Hammond, a distinguished fly fisher who in these days operates mainly on the Abbot's Barton water on the Itchen, now contents himself with using a small Black Gnat and, sometimes, a Ginger Quill for variety. He still catches his share of trout: he is, of course, a master with the dry fly. There are decided advantages in this straightforward approach for skilled fly fishers whose sight is no longer as keen as it was.

Some trout are more selective than others, even on the same river. On some chalk streams, they tend to be particularly finicky and easy to put down in the evenings, although on some evenings they can be relatively free-rising. Trout can also be momentarily rather choosey, just as a fly fisher who enjoys Stilton cheese might not care to sample some when half-way through a bowl of strawberries and cream.

There are times, however, when trout settle to feed on one particular species of fly: black gnats, perhaps on muggy August days, or may-flies, or pale evening duns in the warm dusk of a summer evening when various other duns and spinners may be on the water. It is then that you feel the need for suitable related patterns to tempt them, although even when this happens, you can sometimes find the odd fish who is less pernickety than the rest. This knowledge may help to fill your basket, but the true chalk stream fly fisher does not readily

acknowledge defeat by the selective feeder: a quarry worthy of his skill.

When you fail to induce a trout to rise to your fly, do not take it for granted that the pattern is at fault. Perhaps it is. But it could also be failure on your part to conceal from the trout that you are trying to catch it: by a faulty approach; by allowing the fish to see your line or cast, or their shadow on a bright, sunny day; by using the right pattern dressed on too big or too small a scale to look realistic; or by that most common cause of betrayal, drag.

Remember Hill's injunction to fly fishers never to allow educated chalk stream trout to see drag: you are lucky, in some ways, if you have access to chalk stream fishing where trout are still naïve. You can get away with drag on some rivers to an astonishing degree, but if you think chalk stream trout will put up with it, test your theory at Leckford, on fish lying under the far bank on one of the broad fast-flowing beats of this beautifully kept middle

Fishing on the Piddle, one of several delightful small chalk streams to be found in Dorset

The River Test, a Mecca for fly fishers the world over, but much threatened nowadays by abstraction and pollution

Test water, or on one of the tearing, racing fisheries of the upper Itchen or middle Wylye, or the Bourne just above its confluence with the Test, or the Avon below Figheldean Mill. There you may learn how drag affects chalk stream trout, and how to overcome it. And thereafter you have a pretty good idea when your pattern is at fault, and when you are, yourself. But never be put off by the prospect of drag.

Although you may confine yourself, if you so wish, to the use of one or two patterns, and still catch trout, I believe that in so doing you may forfeit much of the pleasure, the funda-

mental charm of chalk stream dry fly fishing. Is there, then, a happy mean, somewhere between the one or two patterns favoured by some, and the comprehensive but formidably complex assortment advocated by Halford and others? Of course there is.

The happy mean

In practice, not more than a dozen dry fly patterns are needed during the course of a full chalk stream season. The simplified table may explain this more clearly. I believe it is more helpful to the beginner to teach him the practical use of a few sound patterns than to confuse him with a wide range, some of which have little practical value. Once he has mastered these, it is up to him to employ as many, or as

Natural fly	Scientific name	Recommended artificial and hook size	Remarks
		First Phase – April to Early June	
Large olive dun	*Baëtis rhodani*	Olive Dun (1)	Good hatches possible well into April; body darker in cold conditions.
Small olive dun	*B. scambus*	" " (00)	Early hatches sometimes occur in April;
Olive dun	*B. vernus*	" " (0)	Peak hatches occur late April to late May.
Hawthorn fly	*Bibio marci*	Hawthorn Fly (3)	Especially when wind follows sunshine in late April and early May.
Spring black gnat	Bibionid species	Black Gnat (0)	" " " " " " "
Iron blue dun	*Baëtis niger pumilus*	Iron Blue (0)	Sometimes hatches well in rough, showery conditions.
Red spinners	*Baëtis* species	Pheasant Tail Red Spinner (0)	A pattern for evening use as a matter of course.
Mayfly	*Ephemera* species	Mayfly (5)	Mid-May to early June on some rivers.
Spent mayfly spinner	" "	Spent Mayfly Spinner (5)	Evenings in late May and early June, if naturals are on the water.
		Second Phase – mid-June to mid-August	
Nymphs	*Baëtidae*, all species	Pheasant Tail Nymph (00 to 1)	Most days, during the daytime when trout are feeding under water.
Pale watery dun	*B. bioculatus*	Pale Water Dun (00)	For those occasions when trout take the natural duns.
Small olive dun	*B. scambus*	Olive Dun (00)	" " " " " " " "
Red spinners	*Baëtis* species	Pheasant Tail Red Spinner (0)	Most evenings and, sometimes, during the day if trout take spent fly.
Blue-winged olive dun	*Ephemerella ignita*	" " " " (1)	Most evenings at dusk. Orange Quill is the accepted imitation.
Sherry spinner	" "	" " " " (1)	Most evenings around sunset, if naturals fall on the water in numbers.
Pale evening dun	*Procloëon pseudorufulum*	Pale Evening Dun (00) or (0)	Occasionally on warm evenings after sunset in slow water.
Sedge flies	Order Trichoptera	Sedge Fly (3) " " (1)	When too dark to see the Red spinner on the water. For daytime use, especially in carriers; or use Lunn's Caperer.
Black gnat	Bibionid species	Black Gnat (00)	Sometimes, on muggy days, especially in August.

Third Phase – mid-August to the End of the Season

As for the second phase but add olive dun (0) and iron blue (00), especially on damp, showery days in September

Notes: (i)   A fall of ants is always a possibility in August.
   (ii) This table is only one possible effective combination favoured by one fly-fisherman and may be varied or augmented to suit both local conditions and personal inclinations.
   (iii) For the benefit of those who dress their own flies, the dressing of the Pheasant Tail Red Spinner is given on page 90. My dressing of the Pale Evening Dun is given on pages 95–6 and of a Sedge Fly on page 98.

few, as his fancy dictates. I respect any individual's estimate of the number of patterns he requires. I use only ten myself, those listed in the table less the Spent Mayfly Spinner, and I'll use that if I ever need it. In most cases I like to relate my artificial to what I reckon trout are feeding on.

The natural flies which the regular chalk stream angler may encounter are briefly discussed below. I have grouped them, for convenience, in the orders to which they belong: *Ephemeroptera*, or upwinged flies: *Trichoptera*, or sedge flies; *Diptera*, the order to which hawthorn flies and black gnats belong; and Other Insects to cover a few species outside these three orders. My aim is to show which are important to the fly fisher and which I have found to be of less significance.

Upwinged flies (Ephemeroptera)

I have recorded twenty-one different species of upwinged flies on the chalk streams in recent years. Six of these are uncommon. Some, indeed, have no English names. Two others, the yellow May dun and the turkey brown, although becoming increasingly familiar to chalk stream anglers, rarely feature in the diet of trout. Then there are two species of iron blue which may, for all practical purposes, be treated as one. This leaves us with twelve species, and only a fly fisher who fishes most of the chalk streams and is on the water most weeks throughout the season is likely to see all of them.

Four are different species of olive duns. The olives – nymphs, duns and spinners – are the foundation of chalk stream fly fishing. The iron blue is their closest relative. Another is the pale watery dun. The small spurwing, the slow-water olive and the pale evening dun also belong to the same family. All these flies have two tails. Finally there are three flies which have three tails: the mayfly, the blue-winged olive and the *Caenis*, or broadwing as it is now called.

Some of these twelve species are of significance to the fly fisher only at certain times of the year. Some, indeed, are usually on the water at certain times of the day or evening as well. Some are more likely to be found on one river than another. Some prefer fast water, others prefer slow. These notes on the natural flies are intended only as an introduction to a subject which can only be satisfactorily studied at the waterside.

Olive duns

There are six species of olive duns. Omitting the rare *Baëtis buceratus*, and *B. tenax*, inseparable from *B. vernus*, the common chalk stream olive, in the dun stage, we are left with four species which the chalk stream angler is likely to encounter some time during the season. These are: the (common) olive (*B. vernus*), the large olive (*B. rhodani*), the dark olive (*B. atrebatinus*), and the small olive (*B. scambus*).

Dark olives, although widely distributed and locally abundant in the chalk country, are usually only seen in numbers in the autumn. They are therefore important to the grayling angler but of limited significance to the trout fisherman who, for practical purposes, can think of his olive duns in terms of three sizes: large, medium and small. This explains the use of the widely recognized terms, large dark olive, medium olive and small dark olive, to describe them. In fact, the body coloration of these olives is so variable, being darker when the water is cold, that I neither use these terms nor teach them. You should, however, understand what they mean.

I use only one pattern of olive dun, dressed on hooks of sizes 14 and 16, to represent all

the olives. Others prefer to differentiate between them.

Large olives may still be seen hatching in good numbers on chalk streams which open for fishing by mid-April. From about the end of this month medium olives are increasingly in evidence and the large olive disappears temporarily, to return again towards the end of September at the tail of the season. May is usually a good month for hatches of olives. September is another. Some olives may be seen at any time during the season, for they hatch in every month of the year.

Small olives, too, may be seen throughout the fishing season. The time of the peak hatches varies from river to river and season to season. Sometimes good hatches occur as early as April; Skues called the little fly the July dun, and I see quite a few at that time too; but small olives are generally most plentiful in September and October. The females are almost as large as iron blues and are sometimes mistaken for pale watery duns. The males are much smaller and also consistently much darker.

Iron blue dun

Darker still is the iron blue dun, a fly which no two writers seem able to describe in identical terms. This is understandable for it, too, varies slightly in size and, to some extent, coloration. Its comparatively small size and two tails, coupled with its distinctive blue-black wings and very dark purple-brown body, make it one of the easiest of all flies to recognize.

There are nearly always one or two days in the second half of May when iron blues come up in good numbers on both the Avon and the Wylye but it is a matter of chance whether one is out fishing on those days. They are usually wet, nearly always very windy, and not, in my experience, cold. Iron blues have not been very important on the Wiltshire streams in recent years although there are signs that they are on the increase again.

In Hampshire, it is different. The iron blue hatches well on some Itchen fisheries and the Test also enjoys frequent, and at times, good hatches. The fly is much in evidence on the

Leckford water, higher up at Longparish, and on the topmost beats of the Laverstoke estate during late May and much of June. Curiously enough, the Hampshire Bourne, which Plunket-Greene linked for ever with the iron blue in his book, *Where the Bright Waters Meet*, seems to produce few hatches of this fly nowadays.

The somewhat smaller iron blues of September and October come up in rather less concentrated fashion than the flush broods of May and June but again you see the biggest hatches on wet, windy days. Once the weather turns cold, you have seen the last of the iron blue until the spring.

Pale watery dun

Although the natural insect, *Baëtis bioculatus*, hatches freely on all the chalk streams I fish from about the end of May until early September, I have found little need for an artificial dry fly pattern. This dun shares with the spurwings and the slow-water olives the characteristic of transposing so rapidly from nymph to dun that trout simply do not waste their time and hard-earned calorific energy in pursuing the rapidly escaping duns.

Like so many matters appertaining to chalk stream fishing, it is dangerous to generalize. Once in a while, I encounter an evening hatch of pale wateries and when this happens, the duns seem to sit a little longer on their shucks. Then, if fish come on to the duns to feed, you may be glad of a Pale Watery in your box.

There are also some chalk stream fisheries where anglers do quite well with the artificial during a hatch of these small, pale duns. At Bossington, on the middle Test, a Pale Watery dressing, Fairey's Irresistible, accounts for many good trout. It was devised by the late Sir Richard Fairey, whose favourite pattern it was.

The trout of the Wiltshire chalk streams generally show little interest in pale watery duns and I have known day-long hatches of the fly at Itchen Stoke and Abbot's Barton to be ignored by Itchen trout. The nymph is another matter. I reckon to catch a great many trout every summer when they are taking pale watery nymphs.

Spurwings

The large spurwing (*Centroptilum pennulatum*) is rarely seen in considerable numbers on any of the chalk streams and the average chalk stream fly fisher need not concern himself with this insect. The small spurwing (*C. luteolum*) is common on most of these rivers, where it may be seen hatching from February to November, being most in evidence during the summer and early autumn.

Although the small spurwing is important in the scheme of daytime nymph fishing, it is of little consequence in the dun stage to the dry fly fisherman because it spends little time on the water. I have therefore not found it necessary to carry a separate pattern of dry fly. In any case, if I did, my pale watery dressing would probably serve the purpose well enough. The spurwings were, for many years, regarded as pale wateries.

Slow-water olives

These olives (*Cloëon spp.*) occur locally on some chalk streams in the slow-flowing reaches, sun-warmed backwaters and, in one case, in the old gravel pits through which the head waters of a Test tributary flow. Although common in stillwaters in the chalk country, slow-water olives are known to comparatively few chalk stream anglers. As in the case of the spurwings, emergence from nymph to dun is rapid and the flies take wing so quickly that trout do not seem to bother much with them in the dun stage, even when they are hatching in fair numbers. Again, I have not found it necessary to carry an artificial dry fly pattern. Trout take the nymph well at times.

Pale evening dun

Some chalk streams experience occasional heavy hatches of this crepuscular insect (*Procloëon pseudorufulum*), a fly I have yet to see on the Itchen. I usually see it on warm evenings from about the beginning of July to the end of August, especially from the impounded reaches above mills and hatches. The duns generally emerge at dusk and may continue to hatch after the light has failed. I have also seen a good hatch on a wet September evening. On such occasions, trout positively indulge in selective feeding and to take them, consistently, you need a suitably dressed whitish artificial.

I have devised an effective pattern which, for the benefit of those who dress their own flies, is: hook, 16; silk, white; hackle, cream cock; tails, cream cock; body and thorax, grey goose herls.

A heavy hatch of pale evening duns is one of the few occasions when I find it necessary to use a pattern other than the Pheasant Tail Red Spinner in the evening. Given a simultaneous hatch of blue-winged olives and pale evening duns, trout, in my experience, usually elect to feed on the latter alone, and they obligingly take the hatched dun so that you don't have to contend with the difficult problems of nymphing in the failing light.

Mayfly

The natural mayfly again reached a low ebb in 1959 in its customary fluctuating cycle. I saw few good hatches that year, and not many more in 1960. More seemed to hatch in 1961, but the days when sport was good were few and far between on most chalk stream fisheries. Parts of the Kennet fished well at times and there were some good hatches on one or two beats at Bossington and elsewhere on the middle Test. Slight improvements were noted on the Wiltshire rivers, especially the Nadder, but it may be a few years before we shall again enjoy the slightly barbarous excitements of an old-fashioned mayfly season. When people tell you they dislike the mayfly, watch their faces work when you reply that you won't offend them, in that case, by asking them to fish your water at mayfly time!

Although in recent years I have not seen a fall of spent mayfly spinners heavy enough to interest trout, you could be more fortunate and I would certainly advise fly fishers visiting mayfly water to carry spent patterns with them.

I never go anywhere, at any time of the year, without a small fly dressing kit in my car and if ever I should need spent mayfly spinners or ants or anything else unexpectedly, it wouldn't take many minutes to turn them out.

Blue-winged olive

The blue-winged olive is one of the commonest of all chalk stream flies, much commoner than is generally realized, for there is scarcely a day in the whole year when a few cannot be found hatching. The main emergence period occurs from about mid-June to the end of October. We may further generalize by saying that during that time, big hatches of this fly may be expected at about dusk in the evening from mid-summer to mid-August. Thereafter, good and prolonged daytime hatches are often recorded.

The attitude of trout to the blue-winged olive varies considerably and is not always consistent on one river, or even on one fishery. Sometimes a big dusk hatch brings on a good rise; sometimes trout ignore the fly almost completely or, to complicate matters, they take the nymph and disregard the dun.

It usually pays, when fishing the evening rise, to take advantage of the afterglow, if possible. You achieve this automatically by fishing upstream on most beats of the Kennet, Wylye, Nadder and Ebble and by opting for the east bank on the Test and Avon. The Itchen, above the Worthy villages, does not lend itself to this strategy.

Against the reflected afterglow, you can see the tall, backward-slanting wings of the blue-winged olive duns clearly silhouetted, and you know when trout are taking them. I catch such fish on all the chalk streams on the Pheasant Tail Red Spinner. This pattern is not an imitation of a blue-winged olive, but I do not allow this to distress me. The natural fly, which occurs in two distinct types, varies so much in size and coloration, within each type, that I question whether any other pattern, including the popular Orange Quill, could possibly serve me as well. Whether it would always be as

The Kennet in Berkshire; perhaps the prettiest of the major chalk streams

effective in other hands is open to question. But many of my pupils now do very well with it on all the major chalk streams.

Broadwings

Broadwings, as *Caenis* species are now called, sometimes hatch in great numbers early on summer mornings.[1] The only time I see them is if I am on the water long before breakfast-time. Fish seem fond of them but they are small flies, difficult to imitate, and the average chalk stream angler need not concern himself with them unduly.

[1] Some species of *Caenis*, however, emerge in the late evening – Ed.

Spinners

So far we have considered only the dun, or subimago, stage of the important chalk stream upwinged flies. To the dry fly fisherman, however, the adult imagines, or spinners, are of considerable importance too. They lay their eggs in, on, or over the water, according to species, and thereafter perish and drift down, spent and lifeless, easy and acceptable prey to hungry trout. Male spinners, except for those of the small spurwing, only rarely occur on the water in appreciable numbers, but do not overlook the importance of spent female spinners in the scheme of dry fly fishing.

It would complicate matters considerably, and clutter up the fly box no end if it were necessary to carry separate patterns of each female spinner. It isn't. Reference has already been made to the advisability of including spent mayfly patterns at mayfly time. The early-rising specialist might find the need for *Caenis* spinners and a case could no doubt be made for carrying a suitable pattern representing the apricot-coloured spinner of the slow-water olive (*Cloëon dipterum*) in some localities. Apart from these exceptions, it is fortunate that the female spinners of other chalk stream species share many common similarities and the Pheasant Tail Red Spinner, to mention only one effective pattern, is an adequate representation of them all, when dressed on hooks of appropriate size.

There is, however, no reason at all why those who like variety should not provide themselves with patterns representing the female olive, or red spinner, female iron blue, or little claret spinner, female blue-winged olive, or sherry spinner, and so on, if they think they need them. I don't.

Sedge flies (Trichoptera)

These moth-like insects hatch from all the chalk streams, but are more abundant on some than on others. The grannom, a small spring sedge fly, is locally important but much less common than in days gone by. The Kennet is tradition-ally a great sedge river and there are occasions, especially late on warm summer evenings, when trout may take natural sedge flies on almost any chalk stream fishery.

There are so many different species of sedge flies that it is clearly impracticable even to begin to imitate them with separate artificials. Indeed, I content myself with one pattern, dressed in two sizes: hook No. 12 or 14; tying silk, brown; body, pheasant tail herls; hackle, dark red, dressed palmer-fashion.

The smaller version may come in handy for daytime use in the summer, rather like Lunn's Caperer, the popular Test pattern, especially for luring trout in carrier streams. The larger version, named after me, was responsible for the capture of more large Avon trout (over 3 lb) than any other evening pattern in 1961.

Diptera

Two insects of this order are of importance to the chalk stream angler: the hawthorn fly (*Bibio marci*) and the black gnat, a convenient fisherman's name for several species related to but smaller than the hawthorn fly.

Hawthorn fly

This ungainly, leg-drooping insect is of great importance on some chalk streams, more especially in Wiltshire, but appears to be of less significance on the Hampshire rivers. Its short season lasts from mid-April to early May. When you get a good hawthorn fly season, as we did in Wiltshire in 1959 and again in 1961, it may provide the best sport of the year. The prospects are usually good after a mild winter and spring, for the hawthorn fly is a land-bred insect, like the black gnat.

You do best when there is some sunshine first thing in the morning to bring these ugly insects out on the wing. Then you hope for wind to blow them on to the water. I look to the artificial hawthorn fly to give me my limit of three brace on the morning of May Day, which it does most years.

Skues once dismissed the hawthorn fly, in one of his minor works, as being of little account to the chalk stream fly fisher. He learned its worth eventually, but only when he came to live in Wiltshire, and in April 1943, almost at the end of his fishing career, we find him on the banks of the Nadder, mourning the untimely death of his old friend and fishing companion, Norman McCaskie, and deploring his absence from the water during a great rise of trout to the hawthorn fly.

Black gnat

Several closely related species of black gnat occur on the chalk streams, in appearance looking like smaller versions of the hawthorn fly. Black gnats and hawthorn flies are sometimes on the water together during the opening days of the chalk stream season. Trout seem very fond of all these black flies.

Black gnats are most likely to be present on the water in numbers again in August, especially on close muggy days. Many fly fishers will remember how abundant black dipterans were on the chalk streams of southern England in August 1953. In September, too, you may be glad of this pattern, for grayling as well as trout fishing.

Other insects

A fall of ants is a possibility which has to be reckoned with, especially if you are fishing in the month of August. Some heavy falls did, in fact, occur on the Test at Bossington and elsewhere late in August 1961. For some reason, trout seem to be fond of ants.

I carry no 'Other Insect' patterns myself. Certain other insects are often plentiful along the banks of the chalk streams; alder flies in late May and June, and willow flies in September; but in my experience, they rarely seem to feature in the diet of chalk stream trout.

Winged and hackled flies

All my dry flies are hackled patterns. I do not use winged flies, although it is always a joy to be shown the fly box of a fly dresser who commands the time and skill to dress winged patterns. As to which are more effective, individual fly fishers must decide for themselves.

CLOTHES AND TACKLE

Dressing the part

Anglers visiting a chalk stream for the first time are usually struck by the exceptional clarity of the water which, except in the deeps above the hatches or in reflected light, makes it possible to see trout clearly and to establish whether they are of takeable size. Equally, of course, the fish find it easy to see the fisherman, unless he takes care to hide himself from them. They may also hear him unless he treads very lightly as he moves along the river-bank. Wading is not allowed on many chalk stream fisheries because it may disturb the water, interfering with sport downstream, or it may damage the banks, or it may cause the destruction of small living creatures on the bed of the river.

The main factors to be considered when deciding how to dress for chalk stream fishing are:

(a) The paramount importance of hiding from the fish.
(b) The dirt and damp expected along the banks.
(c) Temperature and the weather generally.
(d) Rules regarding wading.

Avoid light-coloured clothes and shiny material. Be thorough about this. It is pointless to invest in an expensive willow-coloured fishing suit and then wear a white shirt with it. Khaki green, dark olive and such drab colours are the best for fishing clothes, shirts included. Expect to get wet and dirty while stalking your quarry, and dress accordingly. A cap may help to hide the face. Rubber knee-boots are useful if the banks are marshy. Wear thigh waders if wading is allowed; these are also useful if the banks are very wet and you wish to keep your knees dry when kneeling.

The working tools

Carry no more than absolutely necessary to enable you to fish effectively and to deal with the trout you win by your skill. Some men fish the better for the comforting knowledge that they have come prepared for all emergencies. Good luck to them. But your requirements in fact, are few.

The rod and line

The length of the rod should be between 8 feet and 9 feet 6 inches, suited to the line you propose to use, rather than the other way about. The point is that if you only propose to use one rod for nymph fishing and dry fly fishing, it is not a bit of good buying a rod so stiff that you need a #7 line to make it give of its best. You cannot master nymph fishing technique with a #7 line. Buy a #5 or 6 line and then a suitable rod to handle it. Nymph fishing really demands a #4 line and an appropriate rod, but I manage very well without either, by using a # 5 or 6 line for both nymph fishing and dry fly work. I have handled some exquisite French tackle expressly designed for modern nymph fishing, for those who can afford it. For dry fly work alone, of course, a stiff rod which takes a #7 line enables you to throw prodigious distances and once in a while you want to do just that. More often, you will find yourself casting 12–15 yards. Farther than 20 yards, hooking fish on the dry fly is not easy. Hooking them on the nymph is hardly 'on' at all. The reel should balance the rod in the usual way and should carry enough backing to fill it.

Bear in mind that chalk streams are notoriously windy rivers, both the Test and the Wylye especially so, and that you will expect your rod to put a fly into the wind, once you have mastered the elements of casting. A soft rod can be an abomination on a rough day. Expensive split cane rods are sometimes a delight to handle. This season, however, I have killed good trout on all the principal chalk streams using a glass rod. My only experience with a steel rod was unfortunate. It broke for no apparent reason except, perhaps, metal fatigue.

Editor's note: It should be remembered that Oliver Kite wrote all this long before the advent of carbon fibre.

The leader

I recommend a cast of about 9 feet, consisting of four or five links, of which the thickest should be at least 3 feet and the point at least 3 feet. The breaking strain of my point is 3.6 lb (5X) until after mayfly, thereafter (6X). Changing the fly and shortening the point to eliminate wind knots and frayed ends soon reduces the length of the point to less than a yard. Once it drops below 2 feet 6 inches, I have it off and tie on another, using the treble blood knot. When I am fishing, I always carry a roll of point-strength nylon in the right breast pocket of my shirt. Then if it is a hot day and I am tempted to leave my coat off, I do not find myself engaged in, literally, pointless activity half a mile upstream of my car.

If you do not tie your own leaders, you need some spare ones with you: quite a few of them if you fish rivers badly overhung with trees. If you have no teeth, you might also be glad of a small pair of scissors.

Landing-net

You need a big landing-net for chalk stream fishing. A satisfactory net is hard to find. Folding nets are for ever catching in barbed wire with which chalk stream fisheries seem to abound, or you fall over them, or they won't open when you want them to, or they won't shut. An inexpensive net recently on the market may, in time, be developed to meet this very real requirement of the chalk stream fly fisher.

Bag

This is for carrying the fish in. Chalk stream trout are quite heavy enough to carry about in your bag. I see no point in cluttering it up with anything else.

Flies and nymphs and something to carry them in

You don't need anything elaborate. The only fly box I have ever possessed is an old tobacco tin, enamelled black without and white within, with a little grid made from pipe cleaners which provides horizontal bars on which the flies rest. There is also a magnetized needle for lifting them out and clearing eyes of hooks of bits of old nylon. I have always carried my nymphs in a little round pink box which, I think, once held face-cream: my wife gave it to me when it was empty.

Amadou and oil

I carry on me a bit of amadou, with which I dry my fly, and a little bottle of silicone floatant with which I anoint it to make it float better.

Ruler and spring balance

Carry whichever is appropriate to keep you above the size limit of the water you intend to fish. If weight is the criterion the fish should, of course, be weighed in the landing-net without being handled, in case they have to be returned to the water, the weight of the net then being subtracted.

A case could no doubt be made for burdening yourself with a great deal of paraphernalia over and above these few items. All I have set out to do is to indicate the items which I find necessary. The individual fly fisher will add to this to suit his fancy. He is, I think, unlikely to be content with less.

__ THE DRY FLY IN THEORY AND PRACTICE__

Basic theory

The basic theory of dry fly fishing is simple: you arrive on your beat; put your tackle together and pull on the appropriate footwear; start at the downstream end, unless you have a particular reason for beginning elsewhere; watch for a trout feeding on the surface; when you find one, satisfy yourself that it is a takeable size, creditable as well as takeable; decide what it is eating — dun, spent spinner, sedge fly, dipteran, ant or various; tie on the appropriate artificial, using a Turle knot, dressed on a hook of suitable size; oil the fly; approach the fish quietly and cautiously and not too closely, taking full advantage of available cover and background; present your fly so that it alights delicately on the water near the trout's head; and when the fish takes the fly, give it time to get its head down, then tighten smartly with a light movement of the wrist which is calculated not to break the point of your leader at the fly. Thereafter there is nothing unduly specialized about the procedure.

Preliminaries

Whenever you go to fish a chalk stream, do give yourself a fair chance. You may already have formed a poor opinion of chalk stream trout on some underfished private water where the fish are naïve and easy to deceive, or on one of the great fisheries a day or two after stock fish have been turned in. Broaden your mind with a day on the Upper Avon around August Bank Holiday or, if you can get there, with a day engaging the big wild trout, shy as maidens, of the upper Test.

If you haven't fished for some time, loosen up with some preliminary casting practice *before* you go to the river. Nothing beats an open-air swimming pool for this, but a pond, a canal, a lawn, a park, a field, a parade ground, a big garage, a hangar, all will serve.

Try to arrive at your beat suitably dressed and equipped. You may be fortunate enough to receive helpful advice and suggestions from your host or his keeper as to where and when you are most likely to find worthwhile fish on the feed. Listen carefully to what they have to say. Unless you are visiting underfished private water, remember that you are faced with the problem of deceiving trout who owe their very survival to their caution, much of it inculcated by rods who have already failed. Accord the trout the respect they deserve, and resolve to teach them a lesson.

Making a start

Tackle up and tie on a fly appropriate to the season of the year. Hook the fly on to the second ring up from the cork handle. Run your fingers from the fly down the point of your leader to your reel and take the cast around it. Then reel up gently until all is taut. Make sure you have your bag, with a ruler or spring balance aboard; your net; spare nylon for renewing your point; amadou to dry your fly; silicone oil to oil it, and, of course, your fly box.

Choice of bank

If you can cast effectively back-handed or, better still, if you are left-handed, choose the left bank of the river (left, that is, when looking *downstream*) because fish under that bank are generally less educated than those under the right bank, which is the one normally favoured by right-handed rods. If you are out of practice, or if trees and other obstructions make the left bank difficult, settle for the easier right bank and accept the disadvantages of shyer trout.

Your choice may also be affected by wind. The worst wind to contend with is the one blowing from between a point directly down-stream and directly across from you. I would rather have a cross wind at my back than in my face, and I prefer a light downstream wind to a light upstream wind. Strong winds are always tiresome, but they have to be faced, often, during the course of a chalk stream season.

Locating a trout

Having made your choice — and you can always reverse the decision if you so wish — begin at the bottom of your beat and keep an eye on the water upstream for signs of a rising fish. Pay special attention to the water under the banks. Trout like to feed close to cover. Wherever there are likely hide-outs, near weed rafts, tree stumps, cattle bridges, in the runs at the tail of trimmed ranunculus beds, in gravel pockets on beds of water-celery and starwort, in the eddies of hatch pools, under bridges, near groynes and hurdles, below carrier in-flows, and near the abutments of disused hatches, there you may expect to find trout and to see them rise during a hatch of duns or when spent fly is coming down.

If you cannot spot a rise although a hatch is on, look at the duns themselves and follow their course with your eye, noting where the current tends to set towards the bank, stringing them beneath it. You may see one or more being sucked down by a fish making hardly any disturbance in the water. A good many trout also lie out in mid-stream during a hatch of duns, especially on the smaller, shallow chalk streams.

Fish in hatch pools may be facing in any direction, according to the set of the currents. Trout sometimes come up out of these pools and lie just above the hatches, where they feed on spent spinners which have earlier laid their eggs by dipping in the sluggish impounded reaches above.

The main problem

When you have found a sizable trout on the feed, do not imagine the main problem is to deceive it into mistaking your artificial fly for a natural. It is not. *The main problem on a hard-*

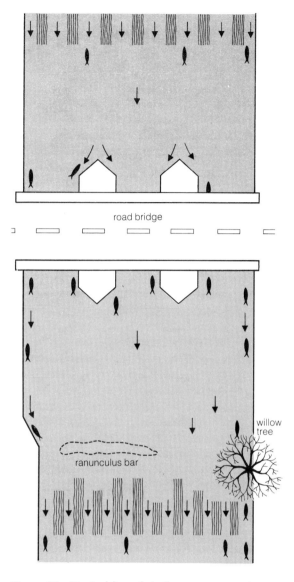

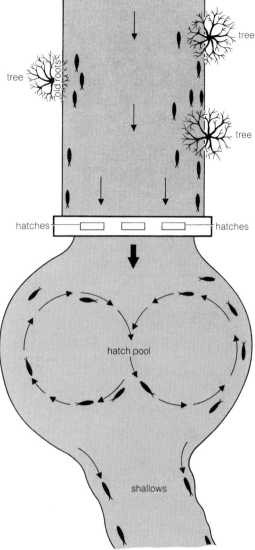

Figure 19   *Typical lies of chalk stream trout above and below a road bridge*

Figure 20   *Typical lies of chalk stream trout above and in a hatch pool*

fished chalk stream is usually how to present a fly without the trout knowing, or quickly coming to know, that you are at the other end of the line. This, I know, surprises many visiting anglers who are apt to ascribe their failure to catch fish to many other causes. They fail to realize that, in most cases, the game was up before they ever began to cast.

You may betray yourself in various ways. The most obvious is to let the trout see you by boldly walking along the bank instead of moving forward slowly and cautiously and getting down on your knees before you begin to cast. Occasionally you may be able to fish standing up, behind a screen of rushes, for example, or when you have a really good background of trees to conceal you if you are dressed appropriately, or late in the evening when you are fishing an artificial sedge fly as the light is failing, or in the daytime if wading is allowed, which is not quite the same thing.

You may carry out a model approach but station yourself too close to the trout, so that the fish sees you or your rod the moment you begin to get out line. There are obvious gaps here and there among the bankside herbage and it doesn't take long to appreciate that these are usually related to the lies of feeding trout. Stop short of these before you start to cast, and try to throw the extra yard or two. Trout get to know these gaps very well.

You may not be using a long enough cast, so that if you throw a shade too far, the thick line waves above the trout's head, in which case it will see it, whether the line touches the water or not. Or your cast may be all right but you may mistime your delivery and slam it down hard on the water and scare the fish in that way. Scared trout do not necessarily leave their lies; but you have the devil of a job to make them rise.

Reconnaissance

When you find a fish on the feed, don't be in too much of a hurry to put a fly over it. Watch it for a bit. Satisfy yourself that you know what manner of fly it is taking, to convince yourself that your own artificial is appropriate. If, when you left your starting point, you tied on a fly to anchor your line to your rod, do not hesitate to change it if your fish is clearly looking for something quite different. On some occasions, it may be.

Opening fire

When you do cast, aim to put the fly as close to the trout's head as your hands will allow. Above all, put it down lightly, and be inaccurate behind rather than in front of your fish. It helps if the first cast can be made to tell.

Aim always at an imaginary point three feet above (overhead) and slightly beyond the fish and shoot your line so that there is a bit of recoil, at the end of which the fly parachutes down like thistledown and alights on the water on the tips of its hackles, as susceptible to a breath of wind as a fragile dun. Never, ever, let anyone persuade you this is difficult. With practice, it becomes automatic.

Provided a chalk stream trout is unaware that it is being fished for, it will often turn aside a yard or go back a foot to take an artificial dry fly presented in this way.

Take comfort in this knowledge as you prepare to engage. The late William Lunn said to a friend of mine, 'It's better to change the fish than the fly.' What he meant was that a fish, once alarmed, is no longer receptive to artificial offerings. Equally, a trout, carefully approached, may well accept a nicely presented, reasonable-looking artificial.

If the trout refuses your fly, it does so for one of two reasons. Either, despite all your care, something has happened to make it suspect that it is being fished for, or your artificial itself does not appeal to it as being good enough to eat. It is usually possible, by observation, to deduce which of these two reasons underlies the trout's refusal. If the fish has not been scared, it will continue feeding quietly and confidently and, if you are careful, you should know that such fish can generally be caught, however difficult they may seem, provided you have the patience to do nothing to give the game away.

You do better to change your fly frequently rather than accustom the trout to one particular pattern, and in cases like these, by no means uncommon on the chalk stream, you may be glad you do not restrict yourself to one or two patterns. You may change your fly many times before you eventually induce the fish to rise. I have caught a trout after forty or more casts, on an artificial which it had seen several times before and refused. If you watch some of these difficult trout, you notice that they allow many naturals to pass over them untaken. You can't hope to improve on the Creator's work, and you need patience to do as well.

It is always debatable whether you would not do better, in the long run, to pass on to less difficult quarry. If feeding fish are few and far between, you may have little choice. Then, of course, if you have found an exceptional fish for the water, one which is worth catching even if it means forfeiting a chance of several smaller trout, go ahead and persevere.

If you do rise the fish eventually, but miss it, you probably will not rise it again if you have pricked it severely, but if you mistime your strike and do not even scratch the fish, you may still succeed. On the Upper Avon in September 1961, I worked patiently on a good trout rising in shallow water below the lip of a hatch pool. Eventually it took a Red Spinner, and I missed it, being rather tired. I waited a few moments, rose the fish again and missed it once more. I gave it, and myself, a few minutes rest, cast, rose the fish again and this time hooked it firmly. It is a shameful thing to be beaten by a trout.

Some advice

If you are impatient and become fed up with trying to tempt a difficult fish, you may prefer to look for a less sophisticated trout elsewhere. You would certainly be well advised not to waste too much time over notorious Aunt Sallies; trout such as those who seem to be for ever feeding near popular car parking sites and the junction points between beats. These fish are usually subjected to a hammering by most of the rods who frequent the water and they become educated to a superlative degree. At the other end of the scale, you may find good fish, especially in summer, in the carriers and side-streams, particularly lying out just below foot bridges. A small sedge fly may be their undoing.

Smutting fish

Smutting fish, taking tiny insects on the surface, are not easy to catch. Sometimes all the trout seem to be engaged in this manner of feeding and it is not easy to tempt them with artificials, least of all with black gnats which are so much bigger, and basically unlike the tiny smuts. But I have found that such trout also intercept occasional olive spinners as they come down spent in the surface film and I prefer to tackle smutting fish with a spinner than to try to imitate the smut, a very difficult thing to do.

Nymphing fish

If a fish is clearly nymphing, or feeding on something invisible to you beneath the surface, and will have nothing to do with your floater, do not bombard it with dry flies. Either try it with a nymph or pass on to more responsive quarry.

Handling a hooked trout

Trout vary tremendously in their reactions to being hooked. The struggle they put up is not always related to their weight, but when fish over 1½ lb decide to run, there is not much you can safely do to stop them. Indeed I always feel happier about my chances of eventually landing a fish that does run hard than about recovering one which turns down into thick ranunculus the moment it feels the hook. The more acrobatics a fish indulges in and the faster it rushes about, the sooner it will tire.

Do nothing to alarm a trout once you have hooked it. Play it quietly and firmly but do not try to hold it hard, unless some fearful snag is close at hand. In principle, it pays to be firm rather than light. Far more fish are lost in weed than by the hook pulling out, though both account for a good many getting away during the course of a chalk stream season. Remember that nothing takes the steam out of a trout like towing it downstream.

Sometimes a fish can be quietly coaxed over the net before it ever begins to fight seriously, but with large fish this can be a dangerous game, and if they are well hooked and the coast is clear, play them out before you try to net them. Very large trout, over 4 lb, say, may decide to head for refuge some considerable distance away. You may then be obliged to go with them, at a respectful distance, especially if you have only a very fine point on your cast. You may end up by netting such a fish more than 100 yards from the spot where you hooked it.

Weed is the great snag on most chalk streams. Try to keep the fish's head up from the moment the hook takes hold. A fish fighting for its head has little thought for weed. If a fish tries to get into ranunculus, hold the rod low over the water and exert downstream pressure to comb it, as it were, through the weed tresses.

When a fish goes to weed, your best ally in coaxing it out is the fish itself. Do not lose patience. Alternate between pressure and relaxation. Use your net to liven things up. Don't neglect handlining, and rapping the rod. And when, eventually, you do get your trout, you may congratulate yourself on earning it the hard way.

Fish to be returned to the water should not be handled, if possible. Kill a trout by striking it firmly on the head and weigh the fish at once, while it is fresh. Then wrap it in a generous piece of muslin, to keep it fresh, and put it in your bag. If the keeper comes along, he may be able to ease your load by taking the fish in for you. Trout do not improve in condition by being carried about in the hot sun all day. But do not leave fish cached about the river-bank. Cats or rats nearly always find them. Don't kill more trout than you need for yourself or your friends and see that any you do kill are given to those who will appreciate and make good use of them.

NYMPH FISHING TECHNIQUE

Natural nymphs

The nymphs of many species of upwinged flies occur in the English chalk streams, but the fly fisher is concerned only with those which commonly feature in the diet of the trout and, more especially, with those on which trout regularly feed during the daytime in the summer months, when dry fly fishing is least rewarding. There are relatively few of these.

They belong, for the most part, to the genus *Baëtis* (the pale watery, certain olives, and perhaps a few belated iron blues), *Centroptilum* (the spurwings, and especially the abundant small spurwing) and *Cloëon* (the slow-water olives). All except the latter occur in fast-flowing reaches which are a feature of most chalk streams. Spurwings also occur in the sluggish waters above hatches, mills and other obstructions, together with slow-water olives.

When the insect first hatches from the egg, and during the first instars, or stages, of its larval existence, its species may be impossible to determine. Up to the time when its wing-pads first appear, it is known as a larva. After the wing-pads appear, it is properly called a nymph. A nymph is designated young, half-grown or full-grown, according to the length of its wing-pads.

Nymphs of different generations of the same species vary considerably in size. Structural differences have already been explained. In addition, nymphs undergo colour changes, in whole or in part, at various stages in their development. These facts have naturally influenced the dressing of modern artificial nymphs.

Artificial nymphs

Pattern is of much less significance than size and careful construction to imitate the general appearance of natural nymphs in the water. The artificial nymph is dressed to sink quickly and is fished *under* the surface in such a way as to simulate the behaviour of the natural nymph it is intended to imitate.

This method, the Netheravon technique devised by Sawyer, differs from the style of nymph fishing first advocated by Skues. His numerous patterns were dressed as exact imitations of ripe, full-grown nymphs of various species about to transpose into duns, and were intended to be fished in or just beneath the surface film. Skues was primarily concerned with the full-grown nymph during the last few moments of its subaqueous existence. The Netheravon-style nymph fisherman is concerned with the nymph throughout its existence as such, a period taking in several instars and amounting to days, or even weeks. A knowledge of the habits and behaviour of the natural nymph during its underwater lifetime is therefore essential for its practical application.

Patterns necessary

Few patterns are required. Sawyer himself advocates three, and there are obvious advantages to being able to ring the changes a bit, but for all that, I only use one of them, the Pheasant Tail, dressed in sizes 14 and 16. I take most of my fish on a size 16 hook. Pheasant tail herls are wound on over a core of gossamer-fine nymph wire which gives the artificial its characteristic outlines and ensures its free-sinking capability which is so essential. These wire bodied nymphs, an original and imaginative construction evolved by Sawyer, are the very foundation of modern nymph fishing. Even after the pheasant tail herls have worn away completely, I catch many trout on the almost bare hook, merely by fishing it in an appropriate manner.

When trout are feeding freely on or close to the surface, they often take natural duns and hatching nymphs impartially. Pale watery, spurwing and slow-water olive nymphs, all of which transpose rapidly, are often taken a moment before emergence, especially on a fine, warm day when the transition from nymph to dun is very swift indeed. When trout feed in this way, they accept nymph-like patterns fished in the surface film, including patterns such as Skues devised for his impounded Abbot's Barton water where these species commonly hatch. This canal-like fishery has little in common with the fast, shallow, well-aerated reaches of many chalk streams, including the upper lengths of the Itchen itself where artificial nymphs of the kind Skues devised are whirled away downstream like confetti on the surface, and achieve but modest success.

A test of suitability

Natural nymphs live *under* water. That is where artificial nymphs should be fished. You can test the suitability of your own artificials at home, with the aid of a glass of clean water. Place your artificial gently on the surface film of the water. It should sink to the bottom at once, without dithering. Unless it does, it is unsuitable, indeed useless for nymph fishing in the modern style.

Tackle

Nymph fishing calls for a fairly fine line, not thicker than #5 or 6. You can catch trout on the nymph on a #7 line – I catch a good few myself when demonstrating with other people's tackle – but you handicap yourself in speed of reaction to the take by doing so. The rod should be suited to the line.

Use a yard, at least, of fine nylon on the point to allow the artificial to sink freely and rapidly after entering the water. Do not allow any oil or grease to come into contact with the point, or its sinking capability will be impaired. During fishing, keep the point well rubbed down with soft mud to give it a good entry into the water.

When to fish the nymph

Provided its use is permitted, the artificial nymph should be fished to any trout, believed to be of creditable size, which can be seen feeding consistently beneath the surface. A nymphing trout visible to the fly fisher can be seen making little movements, lifting slightly in the water from time to time and half turning sideways to intercept food particles which may not themselves be visible. Such fish are 'on the fin', as fishermen say, and their tails are working busily to keep them balanced for interceptory movements.

Nymphing trout, in fact, are usually feeding on a variety of creatures borne down by the current but, more especially, on freshwater shrimps, migrating snails and the nymphs of upwinged flies at various stages in their development, as you discover when you catch them by the score and examine the contents of their stomachs.

Even if it is not possible to see the trout itself, in reflected light or other circumstances, it may be possible to estimate its size either from the nature of the swirls as it moves under water or from past experience of the trout which usually occupies its lie.

Windy days

On very rough days, when duns are hatching in numbers but fish are frustrated in their attempts to seize them on the wind-whipped surface, nymph fishing may be the only practicable way of making a basket. This sometimes happens in September during what should be good dry fly fishing time. It was so in mid-September 1961. In these conditions, when it may be impossible to see the trout, it pays to grease the thicker links of the leader to make it lie more visibly in the rough water on the surface and so act as a float to give you some indication of the whereabouts of your artificial.

Tailing trout

It is during the daytime in July and August that nymph fishing is most necessary, but it may sometimes be helpful to use the nymph earlier in the season, especially if trout are seen 'tailing' − feeding on the bed of the stream with their tails showing occasionally through the surface. Such trout are easy to catch with an artificial nymph, provided you offer it to them when their attention is momentarily withdrawn from the bottom. It was in these circumstances that I employed the nymph for the first time this season (1961), at Polhampton Mill on the upper Test on 6 June as the guest of Mr J. C. Marsden. Although there was no hatch of fly on that hot, bright day, and the large trout were shy and difficult to approach, an almost bare size 16 hook yielded me six weighing over 14 lb.

Tailing trout, feeding on caddis, snails and so on, are usually vulnerable to the nymph fisherman with quick-sinking artificials. So, occasionally, are trout minnowing on the gravelly shallows when the little fish are spawning at mid-summer.

Evening nymph fishing

Sometimes the nymph is useful in the evening, especially early on before the presence of much spent fly brings on the evening rise proper. After the light begins to fail, however, the indications of a take are not easy to detect and nymph fishing then imposes a strain on the fly fisher who may be seeking relaxation after an arduous day.

Basic technique

The basis of modern nymph fishing technique is deception. The nymph fisherman relies for success on deceiving the trout with a representation, similar in outline, size and general appearance to the nature nymphs it is expecting to see, fished where it expects to see them, and behaving as it expects them to behave.

The first problem, then, is to deceive the trout into taking the artificial. The second is detecting when it has done sp. The third is hooking it when this has been established. To be successful, the three must take place almost simultaneously.

Nymphs in fast water

The natural nymphs which a trout expects to encounter in fast water during the daytime in summer are primarily those of the pale watery and small olive, with some common olives and small spurwings. All belong to the swimming group of nymphs and, indeed, are closely related.

Trout intercept these nymphs over beds of water celery, in the gravel runs between clumps of starwort and close under the banks and, more especially, in the runs at the tail of ranunculus beds which have been barred during the main summer weed cutting operations in June. Such nymphs are fairly helpless in the faster currents by which they are borne to the waiting trout. It follows that the artificial must also swim down freely, unimpeded by lateral drag which, in these circumstances, would appear unnatural and alarming to the fish.

Nymphs in slow water

The two most important species occurring in slow water in summer are the abundant small spurwings and the locally common slow-water olives, mainly *C. dipterum*. These nymphs, especially the latter species, are fast swimmers which dart about among the weed fronds in which they live and from which they periodically emerge into open water, perhaps to frolic. Trout take them at all levels and the artificial should accordingly be fished at the depth at which the trout can be seen feeding. Unless favourable conditions of light and background enable you to see into deep water, trout feeding well below the surface may be quite invisible. This is the case on some reaches of the middle Test where opportunities for employing the artificial nymph may be limited.

Trout in slow water may take an artificial as it is sinking, like a natural nymph settling back into deep water, or, if the fish seems likely not to notice the artificial, movement may be imparted to it with the rod-tip to simulate the sideways dart or the upward glide of a natural nymph, and so induce the trout to take.

Nymph pitching

Casting a nymph is in some ways the opposite of casting a dry fly. Whereas the latter should be aimed at an imaginary point above the water and from there drop lightly on to the surface on the tips of its hackle, the artificial nymph should be pitched, as it were, to arc over and into the water with the minimum of surface disturbance to interfere with vision — an otter's entry.

According to the speed of the water and the depth at which the trout is judged to be feeding, the nymph may have to be pitched into the stream anything from a few inches to 15 yards above the fish's lie. The aim is to present the nymph in front of the fish at its own level and correct for line, without treacherous lateral drag. Fish directly upstream to overcome the latter, whenever this is possible.

Timing the strike

Nymphing trout see the artificial with astonishing speed, especially during the summer months, the moment it penetrates the surface to their approximate level and they may shoot forward several feet to take it with savage

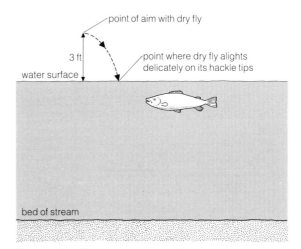

Figure 21 *The correct point of aim for a dry fly so that it falls lightly on the surface*

Figure 22 *A nymph should be pitched directly into the water so that it sinks immediately*

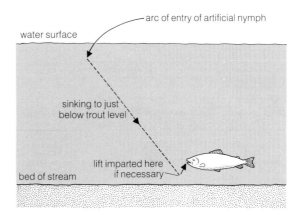

eagerness. Stock fish seize a nymph with great deliberation and are easy to hook. Wild trout eject an artificial with a rapid movement of the jaws and you must be keyed up to strike the moment they take to have any chance of hooking them consistently.

The first requirement is to gather in the slack line as the artificial is drifting down to the fish, so that your strike, when you make it, is immediately effective. You must also be prepared for forward acceleration by the trout as already described. When the trout does shoot forward to take, you do well to strike at once, for if you wait to see what happens when it reaches your nymph you may be too late. Trout hardly ever hook themselves in nymph fishing, as is quite common in wet fly fishing.

Although you may not be able to see your artificial in the water, you can follow its progress by watching the dipping-point of your floating cast – the place where the fine nylon or gut turns down into the water over and above the position of your drifting nymph.

When you judge that your artificial has reached the fish's head, you can and should expect the trout to take it, whether or not you see any sign of this. If your cast has been accurately gauged, the trout should take first time and it therefore pays to assume that it has and strike as a matter of course. Every season I catch a good many trout in the presence of other fly fishers who see no sign of a take. Very often there is no sign, but usually there is some slight indication recognizable with experience.

A visible trout generally lifts slightly or turns aside a little as it intercepts the artificial. The more accurate the cast, the less it needs to do so. In favourable conditions, the take may be clearly seen as the trout's mouth whitens when it opens its jaws to seize the nymph. In reflected light, when the fish cannot be seen, the indication of the take must be obtained by watching the dipping-point of the cast. This will check and draw under as the fish grips the nymph momentarily. The strike must follow at once to be effective.

Once a trout has ejected an artificial due to a delayed strike, it is not easy to persuade it to take it a second time until it has forgotten the incident. This may take anything from some minutes to a day or more. Always wait a little before trying again, preferably until the trout

has restored its confidence by taking several natural nymphs.

Should a trout refuse an artificial nymph, after appearing to show interest in it, it may pay to put on an artificial dressed on a slightly smaller hook. Once again, give the fish a chance to take a few naturals before you offer it the smaller artificial.

Practice

Good eyesight is essential for effective nymph fishing. Even this, in itself, is not enough. The eyes must be trained to detect the take in reflected light, in rough conditions, and in poor visibility and they should be helped to achieve this (and protected) by the use of polarized glasses. Train them at grayling time, in the autumn, when these obliging quick-taking fish readily accept an artificial nymph during the murk and gales of wet November and December days. After that, nymph fishing for trout in the clear water and bright weather of July and August may be found less difficult.

Further reading

Brian Clarke and John Goddard, *The Trout and the Fly* (Benn, 1980).

F.M. Halford (modern edition by Barry Shurlock), *Dry Fly Fishing in Theory and Practice* (1895).

John Waller Hills, *A Summer on the Test* (Hodder & Stoughton, 1924).

Oliver Kite, *Nymph Fishing in Practice* (Jenkins, 1963).

Frank Sawyer, *Nymphs and the Trout* (A. & C. Black, 1974).

Dermot Wilson, *Fishing the Dry Fly* (Unwin Hyman, 1987).

Peter O'Reilly

Peter O'Reilly spent his youth on the banks of the River Annalee in Co. Cavan, where fish and fishing were part of daily life at the family corn mill. He has been fascinated by trout and their watery environment for as long as he can remember.

Peter joined the staff of the Inland Fisheries Trust in 1978 and is presently an Angling Officer with the Central Fisheries Board. He is a member of all three sections (Salmon, Trout and Fly Dressing) of the prestigious Association of Professional Game Angling Instructors and, when royalty or foreign heads of state visit Ireland to fish, he is frequently called upon to ensure that their holidays are successful.

For many years, Peter has had a particular passion for brown trout. As a competitive fly fisher, he has captained his province to All-Ireland success, and he has achieved every competitor's ambition — to represent his country at international level.

His overwhelming interest in fly fishing and entomology quite naturally led him to master the craft of fly dressing — so much so that he is now generally recognized as one of Ireland's leading fly dressers.

As an acknowledged authority on Irish game fishing, Peter O'Reilly has become a noted angling journalist, contributing regularly to Irish, British and Continental angling magazines. His book, *Trout and Salmon Loughs of Ireland: A Fisherman's Guide*, has been widely acclaimed by the critics as an example of what a good angling guide should be.

Peter is very enthusiastic about catch-and-release tactics on wild trout loughs and is ever conscious of the limited resource our wild brown trout represent.

5

LOCH AND LOUGH TROUT

Peter O'Reilly

What is it that makes lough fishing for wild brown trout so interesting? Anglers you question will give a whole range of answers and each answer will contain one or more of the reasons that make this fishing so fascinating.

Lough fishing offers the prospect of catching a big average size of trout and this has its attractions for some. A moderately limestone lough offers prospects of trout averaging 1–1¼ lb, while a rich limestone water can produce trout averaging 2 lb, with plenty of fish to 3½ lb and a 6 or even a 7-pounder always a possibility.

Spot the difference. Both over 5½ lb, the top trout has been stocked, the bottom one is wild

For others, the attraction lies in the non-stop action that can be experienced on a moderately acid water where large numbers of relatively small trout can make for protracted sport that will keep the fisherman on the edge of his seat, literally, in anticipation of the next lightning rise.

For many, the attraction lies in the sheer ease with which lough fishing can be enjoyed. There is no climbing over fences involved, or balancing precariously on slippery rocks. It may involve no more than being seated comfortably and being rowed and guided by an experienced gillie, or drifting all alone effortlessly before a soft breeze with the comfort of an outboard motor to take you up to the top of the next drift.

Perhaps the greatest attraction of all lies in the fact that fishing for brown trout on a wild natural lough is the original form of stillwater fishing. The angler pursues the wild trout in its natural habitat. It is a challenging, exciting form of fishing, calling for a combination of skills. He must be able to read all the signs of wind and light, temperature and fly hatches. The variety and combinations are endless. The challenge is in getting all the pieces of the jigsaw to fit. Reservoir fishing for freshly stocked trout pales by comparison.

Lough fishing, of its nature involves fishing high in the water, whether the methods employed be dapping, wet fly, dry fly or nymphing. Only when the fisherman decides to go after the big ferox trout is deep fishing called for and this is really a minor tactic of lough fishing, only practised by a few and not very frequently.

There is no doubt that the variety of challenges presented by the trout lough is a source of constant challenge to the fly fisher. No two loughs or no two fishing days are ever the same. Constant changes of weather and water conditions have to be coped with as do the seasonal variations of the fly hatches and their consequent effect on fish behaviour. Every set of circumstances calls for its own particular tactical approach and part of the enjoyment is choosing the right tactics.

Perhaps the greatest attraction of all is the great beauty of the wild brown trout itself and the clean unspoiled surroundings in which we fish for it. Modern stocked lakes and put-and-take reservoirs are man's artificial answer to the natural lough; rainbow trout and triploids fill a need in modern trout angling, but when you hold a truly *wild* Sheelin, Leven or Corrib trout in your hands, you can admire the fin-perfect product of 10,000 years of genetic engineering. There is nowhere better to get away from the maddening throng than a big lough, with only the hills and the islands for company and the challenge of the wild trout to keep the mind fully occupied.

And what a challenge these lovely places and their spotted inhabitants present. First the angler must learn the habits of the trout in its watery environment. Then he must become familiar with the various food organisms that the trout feeds on. It is only by tempting them to take a hook disguised as food into their mouths that they can be caught. There is the marvellous challenge of creating an object out of silk, fur and feather which will either imitate or suggest food to the trout. Finally, the lough fisher must present this object to the trout with rod and line at a depth and in a manner that is likely to entice the trout to eat it.

Two of the attractions of chalk stream trout fishing are the large average size of the trout and mastering the entomology of the river; then being able to identify individual food items and offer suitable imitations. A limestone lough can hold trout of equal size to the chalk streams and sometimes even bigger. The food chain is equally complex and to become a competent lough angler, it is necessary to have a good working knowledge of the changes that take place in the water through the season. This requires a knowledge of the behaviour and life cycles of the shrimp, snails, water lice and small fish that form part of the trout's diet as well as being well informed on the behaviour

Fin perfect

and times of emergence of the various insects.

It is a well-recognized fact that brown trout are primarily bottom feeders. The greater part of their lives are spent on or near the bottom. There they feed among the vegetation, rocks, etc., and examination of their stomach contents invariably reveals a predominant diet of bottom living creatures. However, for reasons best known to themselves, they will *sometimes* feed at the surface on emerging insects, ovipositing or dead insects, or on a fall of terrestrials. I emphasize *sometimes* because occasionally they will ignore even the most prolific fly hatch, as they sometimes do in the case of the duck fly hatch on Lough Ennell in Ireland. But, by and large, a hatch of insects usually brings the trout up. It is for the angler to learn the times and locations of these hatches if he is to be in the right place at the right time. The great advantage to be gained in fishing the rise is the opportunity it offers the fisherman to place his fly in the vicinity of and even in view of the trout. If the trout is feeding, his chances of catching it are greatly improved. As I said earlier, lough fishing is all about fishing the top, whether it be dapping or fishing a dry fly, a wet fly or a nymph in the top few feet of water. The successful fisherman must get his flies in the trout's field of vision.

Rising trout make the task easy. But what if trout are not rising? This calls for a change in tactics. The first alternative is to fish the shallows – along by the shore line, around islands and over areas of known shallow water with a depth of from about 2 to 8 feet (deeper for dapping). When the lough angler is not fishing to rising fish, he must become a hunter, searching out his trout in areas that experience tells him hold fish. This explains why local knowledge, familiarity with the contours of the lough bed and an understanding of trout habits and habitat are so important. When fishing from the shore, he must keep on the move and similar rules govern boat fishing. The boat must be allowed to drift over known fish holding areas and the only alteration necessary in its course is when it leaves fish holding water.

Now, all water appears the same on the surface and only experience can tell the angler when he is in the right place. This experience is gained either by frequently fishing a given lough or even a portion of a lough under varying weather and seasonal conditions or by employing the knowledge of a good local boatman. The experienced angler will have his marks – rocks, islands, headlands and onshore features – which tell him when he is on or off productive water.

LOUGHS, RESERVOIRS AND STILLWATERS

A lough is a large inland body of fresh water and may owe its origin to a number of different causes. These causes have mainly been geological processes, the chief ones being glacial activity, earth movements, volcanic activity, deposition of sediments and finally human activity. There are other causes too, but it is not necessary to go into them here. Man-made reservoirs are the modern equivalents of loughs, being the result of human action rather than of natural causes. It is the natural loughs that interest us here.

The structure of the vast majority of the loughs of Ireland and Great Britain was determined by the last Ice Age. During the last Glaciation, which ended about 10,000 years ago, these islands (Great Britain and Ireland) were either totally covered in ice or experienced conditions of permafrost. The ice reached a depth of more than 1,000 metres. As the ice melted and retreated, it scooped out hollows which are now valleys and loughs and left ridges which are now hills and mountain ranges. It also left mounds of moraine which gave us hills or drumlins and this moraine caused dams which formed further loughs.

If the angler observes the line of the hills and ridges around many of the glacial formed loughs and relates them to the islands and rocky reefs, he can easily plot the underwater

Lough Corrib − a great, Western lough

contours of the lough and with a little experience, plan his fishing drifts accordingly. This is particularly true of the great loughs − Corrib, Mask and Conn in the West of Ireland.

On the bottom of these loughs, and especially along the shore line and on the perimeter of islands, the retreating ice left a wild chaos of boulders of every size from a football to a small house. The propensity of these rocks and boulders to snag anglers' hooks is further enhanced in limestone loughs by the results of the action of the water on the rock, hence the futility of trying to fish lead lines or deep nymphs in these circumstances. Such tactics are quite impossible and utterly frustrating, so the angler's aim is to attract the trout up to his flies rather than to get the flies down to the fish.

LOUGH TYPES

The geological structure of the countryside in which a lough is situated determines type and productivity of the water and the size, quality and population density of the trout. Just as the productivity of the countryside is determined by the underlying geology and climate, and the land can range from rich pastures and tillage crops to bare mountain and acid moorland, so too with the loughs. Their natural productivity is basically determined by the surrounding geology − hence we have poor loughs and rich loughs, loughs that hold small populations of tiny trout and those that have big stocks of trout of a large average size.

In between, the average size and population density ranges through the complete scale. Basically, loughs that lie on limestone have a high pH value and usually sustain a population of fast growing trout with an unusually high average weight. As the pH value of the water drops, so too does its trout producing capacity. For example, some large loughs may lie partly on limestone and partly on granite. Here the trout population may be quite prolific but the average size will be smaller. At the other end of the scale are the acid loughs found mainly in mountainous regions of granite or other acid rock and surrounded by bog and peat land. These loughs will have a low pH value and carry stocks of small, poorly fed trout, often averaging three or even four to the pound.

THE TROUT'S LIFE CYCLE

Brown trout are the most widespread species of fish in these islands. They are to be found in many and varied freshwater locations from limestone loughs and chalk streams right up to quite inaccessible mountain loughs, thousands of feet above sea level. The main factors determining trout stocks in loughs are the amount of spawning and nursery area available to the trout in the inflowing streams; the numbers of competitors (perch, roach, etc.) for food that they have to contend with; if they are heavily preyed on by pike; and finally, the size and average depth of the lough they inhabit. In too deep a lough, the light cannot penetrate enough for vegetation and invertebrate life to flourish; too shallow a lough and the wave action will reduce the plant and hence the invertebrate population. It is therefore considered by fishery scientists that a limestone lough with an average depth of about 9 feet is the optimum for sustaining a good head of trout. They would claim that the extent of water six to twelve feet deep is the principal controlling factor in determining a trout population. In fact, some would say that extensive areas of suitably shallow water (6–12 feet) are more important than pH in determining stock densities.

Brown trout live their lives entirely in fresh-water. The hen fish leaves the lough and spawns in the gravel of an inflowing river or stream. The young fish usually live in the river for two to four years before dropping down into the lough where they mature after a further one or two years and, in turn, migrate upstream to start the cycle all over again. Their growth rate is very much governed by the relative abundance of food and genetic strain. For example, the ferox trout seem to have a genetic propensity for fast growth in the first three or four years of their lives and at the age of four they change from an invertebrate diet to become fish eaters. They have been known to grow to well over 20 lb in a relatively short time.

The colour of trout varies greatly from lough to lough and, even within a single large lough, trout of differing colorations may be found. It is my opinion that the colour pattern is primarily related to the environment they inhabit. In some loughs, the primary food organisms may also influence coloration. Anyway, the colour can vary greatly from the more common dark brown back, silvery flank with large brown spots and pearl-white belly of the limestone lough trout to the red-spotted golden trout of a moderately acid water.

TROUT POPULATIONS

The stock density of trout in a lough is a point of major importance to the angler and is probably only surpassed in importance by how prolific the fly hatches are on a given water. The greater the stock density of trout in a water, the better chance the angler has of meeting a fish. However, the more prolific the fly hatches are, the more trout come to the surface, giving the angler an opportunity of presenting his fly in the path of a feeding trout.

Dr Martin O'Grady of the Central Fisheries Board in Ireland carried out pioneering work in estimating lough trout populations in the 1970s and 1980s. He found a trout population of over 100,000 trout in Lough Sheelin, equal to, or greater than 8 inches and over 500,000 trout (over 8 inches) in Lough Conn in more recent times.

What is important to realize, however, is that the trout are not spread evenly throughout a lough. They are concentrated in specific areas and the areas of greatest concentration are those where food is most readily available. Thus, it is not unusual to find a stock density of well over 150 trout per acre in parts of some Irish wild lough fisheries.

Finding the big concentrations of trout is, perhaps, the greatest challenge presented to the angler. Get among the trout and you are in with a chance. You have no chance whatever fishing barren water – and barren water exists, even in the most densely populated trout loughs. Local knowledge is the key to learning about a lough. The newcomer would be well advised to arm himself with as much local knowledge as possible. The best sources are local anglers who fish the water on a regular basis and local boatmen. After that, maps are a help, especially those showing the depths and bottom contours. The newcomer to a lough would be well advised to fish close to the shore, along by islands and rocky outcrops, across the points of headlands and over and across shallow bays. Other signs worth noting are a grouping of local boats in a specific area. Gulls swooping and diving as they feed can be an almost infallible sign of a localized hatch of fly and you may be lucky enough to find the trout and the gulls eagerly competing for the emerging flies.

A knowledge of the contours and substratum of a lough can only come with experience. But it is knowledge vital to the angler. I like to think of a lough as a large vegetable garden. Each different plot produces at a different season. So too with the lough: the shrimp and freshwater louse are to be found in the shallows in spring; a month later the duck fly is found coming off over the deep holes; and the big sedges are a bit like the bats, they only come out at night.

Figure 23   *A hypothetical lough showing islands, shallows and a 10-foot contour line along by the shore, around islands and on shallows*

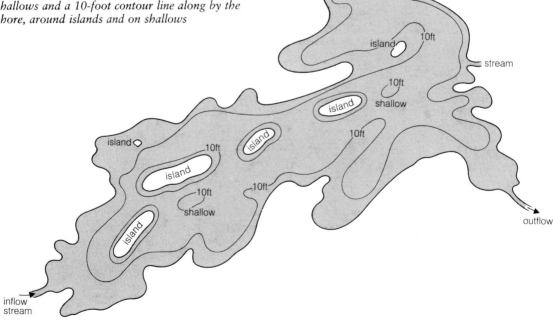

TACKLE

Where tackle is concerned, anglers can have very fixed ideas, and you see a great variety of fishing gear among lough fishermen. In my opinion, the wet fly rod should be made of carbon fibre and have a soft action. It can vary in length from 10 feet to 12 feet, depending on the physical strength of the angler's arm. It is a case of 'horses for courses'. It is a good idea to have a second rod for dry fly and nymph work and 9 feet 6 inches is adequate for these purposes. At least two double-tapered lines are necessary, one a good floater and the other a slow sinker or sink-tip. The reel should carry 75–100 yards of backing and should be well engineered. By that I mean that it should be capable of playing a big, strong, fast running brown trout without the danger of breaking a light tippet. A butt piece should always be attached to the line. Braided butt pieces help

the leader to turn over beautifully in the hands of a competent caster.

The strength of the leader material is a vexed question. In a big wave on a dark day, you will get away with 8 lb breaking strain; 6 lb seems more sensible unless the trout are very big. But in a small ripple, in calm conditions or when dry fly fishing, it may be necessary to go down to 4 lb or even 3. This poses a great problem in terms of potential breakage if you expect to catch trout of 3 lb or better. This is why I emphasize the need for a free-running reel, and I find it helps to insert a short piece (9 inches) of power gum between the butt piece and the leader when fishing with a fine tippet.

The colour of the monofilament is important. I favour the clear, matt-finished brands because I believe the darker monofilaments frighten trout.

ANGLING METHODS

Angling methods on loughs fall into five distinct categories – wet fly, dry fly, nymph, dapping and trolling.

Wet fly or lough-style

Wet fly fishing, sometimes referred to as lough-style fishing, is one of the oldest methods of fishing a lough. It is generally, although not exclusively, performed from a boat. Basically, it consists of an angler casting a team of two, three or four wet flies in front of or to the side of a drifting boat.

Since this is likely to be the most frequent style of fishing used by the lough fisher, it is important that the tackle be suitable and comfortable to use. The ideal rod is hard to define, especially as regards length and strength. For instance, let us consider two anglers of identical build: one fishes every evening, the other only occasionally. The former will build up strength to use with ease a

rod that the latter would find very tiring after a short time. For this reason, I would say that the range of rods can vary from 9 feet 6 inches to 12 feet, depending on personal physique

A sturdy, safe, clinker-built boat

and on the frequency with which the individual fishes. There is, however, one characteristic that all of these rods should have in common if the fishing is to be enjoyed. The rod must have a relatively soft action. This makes for much more comfortable and enjoyable wet fly fishing than a stiff rod that requires the angler to work hard with every cast.

The choice of fly line is very much dictated by the fishing conditions and whether or not the trout are feeding deep or at the surface. Having said that, one man's meat is another man's poison, and you will find people using everything from a floater to a fast sinker. Personally, my first preference is for a slow sinker or a sink-tip. I should perhaps add that a sink-tip is not the most pleasant line to cast and that, while it is effective, the slow sinker is a more comfortable line to use. Of course, there are days when a fast sinker may be responsible for putting an extra fish in the boat or helping to avoid a complete blank, and in certain conditions, when trout are on the top feeding on emerging insects, a floating line will often provide the answer.

The length of the leader is determined very much by the wave or ripple conditions and the angler's casting ability. We'll assume that most fishermen use a butt piece, 1½–2½ feet approximately of either braided nylon or strong (20 lb) monofilament. In a strong wind, with a big wave to hide the fly line, a 9-foot leader is adequate. In a small wave or a ripple, it is important to get the flies away 'as far as possible' from the line and 'as far as possible' means having a leader you can cast comfortably and that straightens out on the water. No good having a leader so long that much time is spent undoing tangles. Reasonably competent casters should have no trouble turning over leaders 12–18 feet long.

The number, size and choice of fly pattern is again governed by weather conditions and by the trout's feeding pattern at a particular time in a given location.

There is a tendency among anglers to fish the maximum number of flies – which is four under international fly fishing rules. I am not sure that this is always wise and personally I often feel happier with three on the cast. Moreover, under very light wind conditions, I think there is a definite advantage to be gained by only fishing two, provided, of course, that they are near – in terms of size and hue – to what the trout wants.

The flies the trout want are, of course, the sixty-four thousand dollar question. Traditional wet flies are, by their nature, suggestive of food. In themselves, they look like nothing a trout eats – well, some of them. Yet thousands of trout, indeed the majority of trout, are caught on them every season. The trick is to offer the trout flies of a size and shade of colour closely related to what it is feeding on or likely to feed on. Fortunately for us, trout are very catholic in their choice of food. Someone once said a trout will eat anything from a midge to a mouse, and he was not far wrong. Certainly, it is unusual, when one examines the stomach contents of trout, not to find more than one form of food organism. What you usually find is a predominance of one form of food and then a small number of different organisms. For example, a trout may be stuffed with chironomid pupae or mayfly nymphs, but it may also contain a few caddis larvae, some shrimps and maybe a couple of beetles.

The angler will occasionally meet a situation in which trout are feeding selectively on a particular insect at a given depth or even on the surface. In these circumstances, he must be able to present his trout with a fairly close imitative pattern if success is to be achieved. Only experience can tell the angler which flies to put up on his leader and in what order and that is something we shall deal with later.

There is another factor, and possibly a third, which influences a trout to take food, and hopefully your fly, into its mouth. The first is aggression and the second curiosity. These two influences come into play very much when trout are not seen to be feeding at or near the surface, and the angler who can spot this and fishes his flies in a manner likely to induce aggression or curiosity is likely to be the one to bring home the trout. On days when nothing is moving, the angler has to provoke either hunger, aggression or curiosity in the trout. He may have nothing more to go on than a rule of thumb; when all else fails, mine is, 'dark flies for a dark day and bright flies for a bright day.'

Wet fly fishing at its simplest involves casting a team of wet flies from a boat (or from the lough shore). Note I don't say in front of the boat, because on occasions, you may be required to cast to a rising fish to the side or even behind the boat. The angler who fishes alone from a boat is at liberty to cast in any direction. When fishing with a partner, the angle is limited to 90°, for good manners does not allow one to cast into the other man's water, though you may cast well to your own side or even behind to a rising fish, provided you have an understanding with your boat partner.

There are various techniques for fishing the wet fly. The simplest is to cast a short line — say about 7 yards — directly in front of the boat and retrieve it back in short pulls of about 14 inches each. When about half the line is retrieved, the angler stops pulling by hand and raises the rod tip, thus changing the pattern of the retrieve and hence the movement of the flies from a stop-start action to steady draw as the line and flies are drawn in by the steady lifting of the rod tip in preparation for the next cast. A variation on this technique is to 'quarter' the water, casting at a different angle each time in order to cover the maximum area.

The next technique involves 'bobbing' or 'dibbling' the first or top dropper fly. In this instance, a relatively short line is cast in front of the boat and the retrieve commences with

Figure 24 *Bobbing the dropper, with suggested lengths and spacing of droppers*

the rod angled at about 30° to the water. First the line is retrieved as before in a series of short pulls. The speed of these pulls can be varied from slow to fast. In a slow retrieve, the flies remain stationary as the boat drifts towards them; in the fast one, they are stripped back quickly. When half of the line is retrieved, the rod tip is raised slowly, drawing the bob fly to the surface. This fly is then 'bobbed' or 'dibbled' in the surface of the water back towards the boat, sometimes just under the surface, and then on top giving the appearance of an insect drowning, struggling or even sitting on the surface of the water. The technique of performing this action properly is only slowly acquired. Most people lift off too soon. Being able to hold the bob fly as long as possible at the surface is of the essence in traditional wet fly fishing. The master of this technique will still have his fly bobbing on the surface long after a less experienced angler has lifted off to cast again. But, very often, it is those vital final seconds that will entice or provoke the trout or perhaps just gives it time to make up its mind to take the fly. As a rule, this method works best when flies are hatching or later in the season when trout expect to see terrestrial flies on the water.

A variation on this cast is what I term the 'Deacy flip', called after the late Christy Deacy from Lough Corrib, who was a marvellous

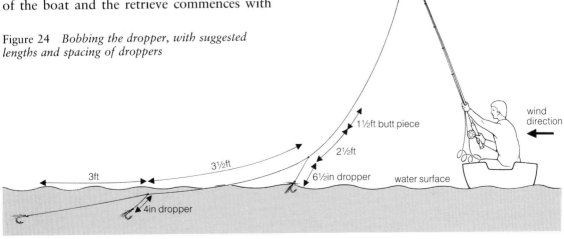

exponent of the technique. With the boat moving along nicely, riding on a good wave in front of a force 5 or 6 wind, he would flick the flies to the side over the bow or stern of the boat. The next action was to raise the rod slowly and draw the flies across the wave. The final bobbing of the flies was imparted by the boat bobbing like a cork on the waves. The effect of this method was to present the flies completely out of the line of the boat and draw them across the trout's nose. If done properly, and if trout are on the move, it rarely fails to get a response. Again, the psychological moments seem to be those last few seconds with the fly bobbing on the surface, when the less experienced would have lifted off and cast again.

A fourth method of retrieve is one I call the 'competition technique'. It is one that is rarely spoken of or written about except in disparaging terms, though why anglers should wish to denigrate it or its exponents, I don't know. Again it is a technique to deal with a situation – namely when no trout are showing, there are no flies about and the wind is light. The requirement for this method is the ability to cast a very long line at least 25 yards. The line must be either a sink-tip or a sinker. When the cast is made, the flies are allowed to sink for between five and ten seconds – or more – depending on the depth of water being fished. They are then retrieved back in very fast pulls till about 5 yards of line remain in the water. The retrieve then stops abruptly and the rod tip is raised, thereby changing the direction in which the flies are travelling from the horizontal to the vertical. The flies are then slowly drawn to the surface and bobbed back to the boat in traditional fashion. The takes usually come underneath as the flies start to ascend or during the bobbing process.

The final and well proved wet fly technique is what is termed 'side casting'. In order to perform it properly, the boat must be rowed along and slightly into the wind. It does not work if the boat is rowed downwind. Using a sink-tip or slow-sinking line, the angler casts with the wind and, instead of retrieving, allows the boat to pull the line around until the flies

reach a point directly behind the boat. The takes usually come as the flies speed up before straightening out and the strike must be delayed to allow the fish to be hooked properly. A quick strike and the fish is usually lost!

While on the subject of setting the hook, I find it important to strike a trout at the psychological moment – slower in the case of large trout than for a small one. But rest assured, if you don't set the hook smartly in the case of wild trout, they will very quickly eject it. This is a point well worth remembering by anglers who have begun their trout fishing with stocked fish.

Figure 25   *Side casting*

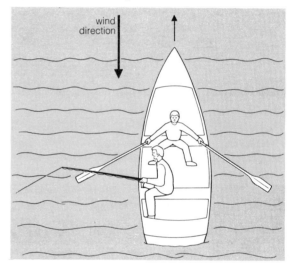

The dry fly

It has constantly amazed me how little attention has been paid to dry fly fishing on loughs in recent times. In fact, the very first trout I ever hooked on a lough was on a dry fly, and on the Irish Midland loughs, where I learned my trout fishing, the use of the dry fly was regarded as an essential part of lough fishing. The dry fly can be used with success when trout are taking their food off the surface and this occurs frequently throughout the season. Trout feed on adult chironomids, olive and mayfly duns and their spinners, on black gnats, sedge and *caenis* and occasionally on terrestrial flies like daddy-long-legs or moths. Dry fly fishing on a lough

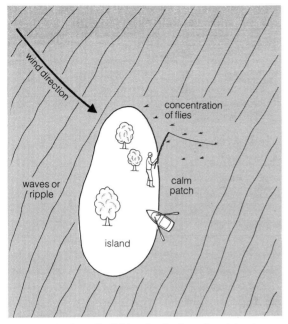

Figure 26 *Dry fly fishing in the lee of an island*

must be one of the most satisfying forms of trout fishing. It ranks equal to dry fly fishing on rivers in my opinion and calls for a high standard of skill in boat handling and presentation. You see your fish rise, plot his course by observing a further series of rises, get the boat in position, make the cast to present the fly to a point where you judge the trout will rise next, watch him take it, allow time for him to close his mouth and turn down – and only then do you set the hook.

Dry flies for lough fishing must match in size the natural insects they represent and should

Figure 27 *The ideal conditions for dry fly sedge fishing at dusk with offshore wind*

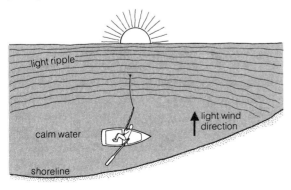

be dressed on good quality, light wire hooks. Ideally, they should be treated with floatant before being put in the fly box. This way, they have plenty of time to dry properly and so float well. A 9- or 10-foot leader with a butt piece will do. The tippet should be as fine as is practical to deal with the size of trout you expect and the shine should always be removed from the last 2 feet with fuller's earth. Usually, only one fly is fished. It should closely represent the natural it imitates and ride high or be low in the surface film, as in the case of the natural. Similarly, as regards movement, it should be fished static or moved slowly, after the manner of its natural counterpart on the water.

Fishing the nymph

Nymph fishing has become very popular in recent years on stillwaters, due in no small measure to the pioneering tactics and writing of its great exponent, Arthur Cove. It has an equally important role to play on loughs, though almost exclusively during hatches of chironomids.

There is one big difference between nymphing on still water and on loughs. Much of the stillwater nymphing is done from the bank, while loughs are generally fished from the boat. The bank nymph fisher is 'anchored' as it were, in one spot, whereas the boat fisherman is drifting freely and, in many situations on loughs, it is necessary to anchor up or at least use a drogue if the nymph is to be fished successfully. Proper anchors with a 6-foot length of chain are best – one at either end of the boat – but a large stone or a concrete block will sometimes substitute if the wind is not too strong.

Nymph fishing can be deadly during a hatch of chironomids when trout are feeding on the emerging flies at the surface. It can work in a flat calm, but a small ripple makes it much easier. The trick is to find a patch with trout feeding at the surface. These patches are often quite localized and local knowledge is essential. Get as near as possible to the trout without putting them down. The ideal tackle is a 9½-foot rod to take a No. 6 floating line and as

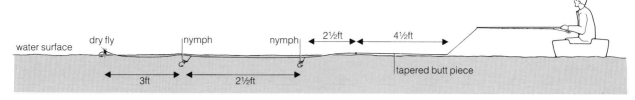

Figure 28   *Nymph fishing*

long a leader as the angler can comfortably manage. The nymphs used should approximate in size and shade of colour to the size and colour of the hatching naturals. Two nymphs and a dry fly on the point or three nymphs are mounted on the leader on short droppers and cast in the path of a feeding trout or sometimes into the rings of its previous rise, if it is observed that the trout is moving only very slowly. The angler then keeps a tight line – by retrieving any slack between him and the nymphs – and watches for the trout to rise again in the vicinity of nymphs, or for the end of his fly line to move away from him. As soon as he notices any movement, he tightens immediately to set the hook and to prevent the trout from ejecting the artificial nymph. This it will do very quickly and good timing of the strike is all important.

When trout feed on emerging flies, they appear to zone in on their food very close to the surface. Thus their window of vision is quite small. Hence the necessity for good and accurate presentation of the nymph and also the need to keep it on or near the surface. If it is 4 inches down, it *may* be too deep and will be ignored.

Nymphs can be fished high in the water,

either by greasing them or by greasing the leader between the droppers. A dry fly fished on the point is another ploy to keep the leader on top. Generally speaking, nymphs should be fished without being moved. In some circumstances, a slight twitch of the rod tip can induce a take but this must be done with great care not to disturb the trout in very calm conditions. It is important to use a fine leader material and 4 lb ordinary monofilament or 5 lb double strength is about right – and remember to be very careful about tying the knots.

Nymph fishing is not very effective in a big wave when practised from a drifting boat, though a nymph fished on the point with a team of wet flies can produce results. Like all the other techniques, there is a time and a place for it, and it is up to the angler to decide from experience what is the opportune time and situation.

Dapping

Dapping must be one of the oldest methods of fishing a lough. Essentially, it involves holding

Figure 29   *The trout at (a) has a full view of angler's flies but the trout at (b) has no view because the nymphs have sunk too deep*

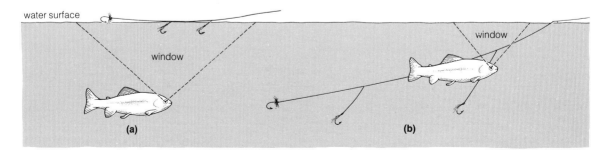

Above: *Dapping*

Figure 30   *Dapping outfit*

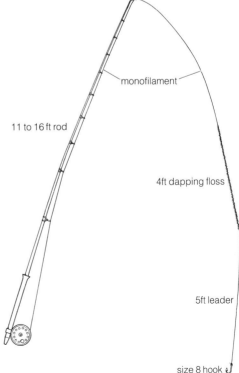

monofilament

11 to 16 ft rod

4ft dapping floss

5ft leader

size 8 hook

a natural fly, impaled on a hook, on the surface of the water by means of a blow line in front of a drifting boat. When natural flies are not available, an artificial representation of the natural will often do.

The first requirement for dapping is a good breeze. You can't dap in a light wind or a flat calm. The rod can vary in length from 11 feet to 16 feet. Longer rods become very tiring and I wouldn't recommend more than 14 feet. A fly reel or even a spinning reel filled with monofilament will do. With a fly reel, attach about 10 yards of 12 lb or 15 lb monofilament to the end of the fly line and thread it through the rod rings. Attach a 4 feet length of dapping floss to the end of the monofilament and a 4½−5 feet leader of 6 or 8 lb monofilament and a size 8 wet fly wide gape hook. The only other require-

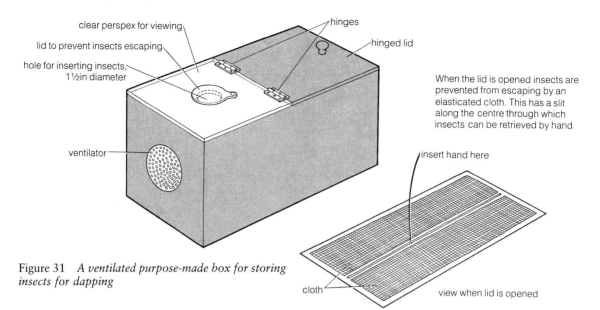

clear perspex for viewing

lid to prevent insects escaping

hole for inserting insects,
1½in diameter

ventilator

hinges

hinged lid

When the lid is opened insects are
prevented from escaping by an
elasticated cloth. This has a slit
along the centre through which
insects can be retrieved by hand.

insert hand here

cloth

view when lid is opened

Figure 31 *A ventilated purpose-made box for storing
insects for dapping*

ment is a purpose made, well ventilated box in which to hold a store of the natural flies.

There are two periods in the season for dapping. The first is the mayfly season and the second is in August and September when the daddys and grasshoppers are in season.

Two mayflies or two daddys – but only one grasshopper – are impaled on the hook by inserting it through the thorax and the wind carries the flies out over the water using the

A dapper's fly box

floss line as a sail. The flies are held on the surface of the water and dibbled from side to side without letting the leader touch the water. When a trout takes, the rod is lowered and there is a pause for a *minimum* of five seconds before the hook is set. If an artificial fly is being dapped, the hook is set more quickly – as soon as the trout turns down with the fly.

It is useful to know how to find natural mayflies. They can be collected on the stones along the shore of the lough where they have been washed in and are sitting drying their wings before flying off to the shelter of the bushes. Alternatively, they can be collected from underneath the leaves of ash, whitethorn and briar on the sheltered side of a hedge or clump of bushes. They are rarely found on the side exposed to the wind.

Daddys are best picked in the morning in rushy fields or in the long grass by the lake shore. They can also be picked off a white wall at night if a lighted bulb is left by the wall.

Grasshoppers can be more difficult to find and local knowledge gleaned from gillies or local fishermen is essential. They are found in patches of old unfertilized pasture and in old quarries or rocky areas – even cemeteries! They can be collected on a sunny day by shuffling along using your feet to disturb them and watching the spot where you see them land. Then grab them quickly. Alternatively, on a damp or a wet day, if you know a good location for grasshoppers, from previous experience, they can be collected by carefully parting the long grass with the hands and picking the grasshoppers from among the grass stalks close to the soil.

Trolling

Trolling for big ferox trout takes place on loughs known to hold these monster fish. It is a monotonous form of fishing and is usually engaged in when conditions are not suitable for other forms of trout fishing. Ferox trout only form a very small percentage of the total population of trout in a lough, so the chances of catching one are often quite slim. Nonetheless, it is possible, and when one is captured it is regarded as a great trophy.

Either of two approaches can be adopted. The first is that of the conventional fly fisherman who, when the lough falls flat calm, rigs up a spinning rod with a large copper and silver or other spoon and begins trolling with the outboard ticking over. The water fished is usually fairly shallow — 6–16 feet. Ferox trout are caught in this manner every season but the general consensus is that many hours, even days, of trolling are required to catch one fish.

The second method is more methodical, requiring specialized equipment and a good knowledge of the lough. It is believed that ferox trout live deep — at approximately 30 feet — and their diet consists of char, perch and small trout. First the angler must get a hydrographic chart of the lough he proposes to fish and make a note of areas with a 30-foot contour line. When he goes out on the water, he uses an echo sounder to keep him over this depth. The transducer is set in the bottom of the boat in the plank next to the keel and the dial of the echo sounder is located directly in front of the person who drives the outboard motor so that he can constantly observe over what depth he is trolling. The bait or spoon should travel about 1½–2 feet above the bottom and it is maintained at this level by using lead cored line and/or a selection of weights. Once the area that holds ferox trout is located, this method is considered to be relatively successful.

Figure 32 *Deep trolling*

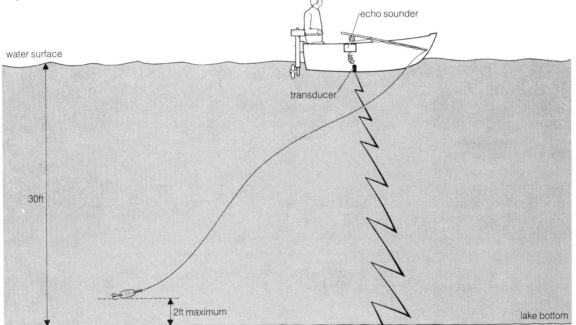

THE ANGLING SEASON

Brown trout are born in the inflowing streams and drop down into the lough at about two years old. They begin by feeding on small microscopic organisms but as soon as they begin to mature and start feeding on the insects, snails, freshwater shrimps, etc. they can be caught by the fly fisher. It is therefore important for the fisherman to have a good working knowledge of the life cycle and behavioural patterns of the major food organisms on which the trout feed – the time of emergence of major insect hatches, etc. and how the trout react and behave in relation to them. Furthermore, he must have some understanding of the effects of 'fishing conditions' and how both the trout and their food react and behave in relation to changes in water levels, light, air temperature and wind strength and direction.

EARLY SEASON

At the start of the season – February and March – feeding trout are found in shallow water in relatively sheltered areas. They feed mainly on water louse and freshwater shrimp. They may be fished for from the shore or, if a boat is being used, it should be drifted over depths from 1 feet 6 inches to about 5 feet. A team of wet flies fished on a sink-tip line will get results, and the choice can be made from a March Brown, Water Louse, Hare's Ear, Fiery Brown Spider and Sweeney Todd. The Water Louse can be a good choice for bob fly and the Sweeney Todd is always fished on the point.

THE CHIRONOMIDS

Chironomids form a very important part of the trout's diet at various periods throughout the season and are enormously important for the angler. Their life cycle is egg, larvae, pupa and adult and hatches occur through from March to September. The early season species are usually referred to on loughs as duckfly or blae and blacks and the summer species are called buzzers. The pupae and adults can vary in size from less than a quarter of an inch to well over half an inch. The chironomid hatches provide some of the best trout fishing a lough can offer. The trout feed avidly on the pupae as they ascend to the surface and as the fly – trapped in the surface film – struggles out of its shuck. They will also feed on the ovipositing females and dead flies that fall on the surface.

It is important to remember that chironomid hatches have the effect of drawing trout into shoals. The reason being that the hatches are very localized. This is caused by the substrata or bottom vegetation from which the pupa emerge to swim to the surface. It is of primary importance for the angler to ascertain and know the exact location of the productive areas. The peak emergence period of a particular species lasts for about two weeks with a ten day shoulder period at either end. Just to make life difficult for the angler, several species may hatch simultaneously.

Early season duckfly fishing can be enormously exciting and rewarding. The fly emerges in short bursts in the forenoon, afternoon and at dusk. Weather conditions play a big part in the tactics used. The best fishing will always be in sheltered areas where the air temperature is a degree or so warmer than out on the exposed water. The wind strength dictates the methods to be employed. Small wet flies like Peter Ross, Connemara Black, Bibio, Fiery Brown, Sooty Olive, Blae Sooty Olive, Blae and Black and Red Arrow can be fished in a good ripple or wave. In near calm conditions, with the trout cruising at the surface, nymph tactics are called for and successful patterns are Leonard's Hatching Duckfly and the Paisley, Orange and Ringrose pupae. Occasionally, a size 14 or 16 Peter Ross can share the leader with a pair of pupae. Towards the end of the duckfly season, a lot of dead and dying flies fall on the water in sheltered bays. Trout can be seen cruising in the calm and out as far as the edge of the ripple. This situation calls for nymph tactics and the use of flies like the Millerman, William's Favourite and a very small Blae and Black.

The early summer chironomid of buzzer hatches occur in May and on some loughs are a follow-on to the duckfly hatch. They take place over relatively shallow water − 3−10 feet − and the hatch can be quite widespread. Again it has the effect of sending the trout into a feeding frenzy for long periods in the forenoon, afternoon and especially before and after dusk.

Daytime fishing tactics are again dictated by the location of the hatch and wind strength. In a good ripple or a wave, use wet flies with shades of colour approximating to those of the emerging pupae. Useful patterns are Sooty Olive, Green Olive, Mallard and Claret, Dunkeld, Connemara Black, Kingsmill, The Paisley, Golden Olive and Hackled Golden Olive. For nymph fishing, the black, olive, claret and Apple Green pupae imitations are all useful, as well as Hob Nob and Ringrose and Orange Duckfly pupae. A phenomenon to be watched for on hot, sunny days and warm evenings is what is popularly called 'Balling Buzzer'. The buzzers swarm into clumps nearly as big as a golf ball and roll along on the water surface. They prove irresistible to the trout and in such circumstances a well oiled Balling Buzzer is called for and fished as a dry fly. Occasionally during the day and frequently before and after dusk, the trout will turn their attention to adult buzzers. In these circum-

Ready for the net

Safely aboard

stances, dry fly tactics come into their own and popular patterns are the Grey Duster, Sooty Duster and the Apple Green (dry). Night fishing in late May and early June can last till 1 a.m., or later and anglers fish 'by ear' listening for the sound of a trout as it sucks down the fly. The fly is cast in the direction from which the sound comes and after the next sound the angler pauses before lifting the rod to strike and hopefully set the hook.

Mid-summer, July and August, chironomid hatches usually occur at dawn and dusk. The dawn rise begins about forty minutes before sunrise and ends about forty minutes after first light. The evening fishing takes place in reverse order and in both situations, wet fly and nymph tactics are most likely to succeed.

LAKE OLIVES

The lake olives make their appearance in mid-April and the hatch lasts till mid-May. A second generation appears in August and September and it is worth noting that the early season olives are dark olive in colour, while the autumn variety have a paler golden olive hue. The hatches are localized and occur over relatively shallow water. The trout feed mainly on the nymphs and duns and can sometimes be notoriously difficult to catch. In windy conditions, with a good wave, wet fly fishing can often work on a wild lough where the angling pressure is light. Useful wet fly patterns are Sooty Olive, Harry Tom, Greenwell's Glory (wet), Cock Robin, Golden Olive and Woodcock and Hare's Ear. If the trout are clearly feeding on the nymph in a ripple, it is worth putting up a single Olive nymph or Hare's Ear nymph on a fine tippett and casting it into the rings of the previous rise form. A Greenwell's Glory tied parachute style will often take trout feeding on the duns and an alternative is a Lake Olive (dry).

A small Claret and Mallard will take trout feeding on hatching Claret Duns in a wave and a Claret Dun (dry) and dressed in either conventional or parachute style will take trout feeding on the duns.

Coch-y-bondhu beetles, alders and hawthorn flies often catch the trout's attention at this time of year and it is as well to have a few fly patterns in the box.

THE MAYFLY SEASON

The mayfly season in May and June probably offers the cream of the trout season on loughs. Not every lough has a hatch, but those that have one are treasures to be valued. Trout are relatively easy to catch at mayfly time – hence the term 'the duffers fortnight'. The mayfly season can vary by as much as a couple of weeks from one region to the next and anyone planning a trip is well advised to check the approximate date that the hatch is expected on a given lough. The mayfly hatch can give sport from morning till night. The fly begin to emerge in the early forenoon and continue to appear spasmodically right through till evening. Dapping, wet fly fishing and even the dry fly take fish feeding on duns for the first week or so of the hatch. When the flies begin to moult, spinner or 'spent gnat' fishing can be effective in suitable conditions from early evening till after dusk. This is dry fly fishing at its best and is generally regarded by lough anglers as the 'Rolls Royce' fishing of the season.

Wet fly fishing and dapping is most successful when the trout are feeding on the ascending nymph. Artificial mayfly nymphs are not popular with lough anglers. They seem to prefer the various wet fly patterns, which, when drawn through the water, have the profile of a nymph. The patterns are legion but I would narrow down the choice to the Gosling, French Partridge, the Mask Mayfly and the Green Drake. Other useful flies on a leader at this time are the Grey Wulff, Royal Coachman, Golden Olive Bumble, Green Peter and Teal and Yellow. Even a Bibio or a Watson's Fancy, though they don't look like anything the trout are feeding on, will often take fish. When the trout are taking duns I favour the 'two feather mayfly', the Fan Wing, or a Royal Coachman.

The Sunshine Spent is a marvellous fly to pick off trout feeding on spent gnats in quiet corners during the day. For evening spent gnat fishing, it is hard to beat the Lough Arrow Spent or Kennedy's Spent Mayfly. Spent male flies generally go out on the water very late in the evening or early in the morning and for these a dark pattern to represent the much darker male is required.

When dressing mayfly patterns, it is important to remember that the lough mayfly is smaller than its river cousin and that artificial flies for fishing a lough should therefore be tied on smaller hooks.

Dapping the natural mayfly is likely to take trout at any time. The sport can be fast and furious with the trout 'stealing' the flies from the hook. For that reason, it is advisable to have between 8 and 12 dozen natural flies in your mayfly box for a day's dapping.

Dry fly fishing at mayfly time can be both interesting and rewarding. The flies — usually two on a leader — are cast on the wave in front of the drifting boat when trout are seen to be feeding. Or fish may be found in the lee of an island where the freshly hatched flies get swept in by the breeze and currents. In these latter circumstances, it is best to fish just one fly, such as a Two Feather or a Royal Coachman.

It is worth noting that some loughs have two hatches of mayfly each season. The first in May and the second, a smaller hatch, but often are extremely important one, in August.

THE BLACK GNAT

On hot, sunny days in late May and early June a phenomenon occurs along the sheltered shores of many limestone loughs that many anglers never see. Big swarms of tiny black gnats hover over the water close to the shore in the vicinity of reed beds and other leafy vegetation. Their life span must be very short for dead flies are constantly dropping from the hovering swarm on to the calm water. The trout seem to love them and an observant angler will frequently see three or four trout quietly sipping down the dead flies. This is a situation that calls for stealth, fine tackle and a careful approach in the boat along by the bank. It is best to anchor well away from the rise and to cast a small Black Gnat on a fine leader in the direction of the nearest trout.

THE CAENIS

Every lough fisher knows the *caenis* or fisherman's curse. They emerge in swarms in June and July and cover your clothes and the boat with their little white shucks as they moult. I have rarely seen trout take them during the evening hatch, but the early morning hatch is another matter altogether. The trout feed avidly on them in the early morning sun from about 6.30 a.m. till 8.00 or 8.30 a.m. This usually happens in a calm patch, along the edge of the ripple in the lee of an island or even along the shore. Ideally, the wind should be very light and the morning air nice and warm. The trout feed on the hatching nymphs and on the dead spinners trapped in the surface film and, when they are doing so, they will often take a *caenis* imitation or even a small Grey Duster. It must be presented dry, on a fine tippet.

SEDGES

I have seen sedges hatch on loughs or in the vicinity of loughs from late February to September. Several species of sedge are often found on the water together and trout probably recognize them by their shape and colour rather than by individual recognizable characteristics. Consequently, artificial sedge patterns are more akin to suggestive patterns rather than exact imitations. Hence, anglers tend to know several species of sedge flies collectively as 'Murroughs', or 'Green Peters' or 'Cinnamon Sedges'.

What is important for the lough angler to know about sedges is that they hatch in two distinct fashions. The first and more important are those that hatch in open water. The pupae swim to the surface and emerge like mayflies or chironomids. Naturally, the species that behave so are much more readily available to the trout.

Evening sedge fishing

The second category are those that crawl ashore and emerge in the bankside vegetation. So, anglers should be aware that we have what may be termed (a) open water sedges and (b) marsh sedges.

The most important of the open water sedges are the great speckled sedge or 'Green Peter' (*Phryganea varia* and *Phryganea obsoleta*), the great red sedge or 'Murrough' (*Phryganea striata* or *grandis*), the silverhorns (*Leptocerus spp.*) and the 'Dark Caperer' (*Sericostoma personaturn*).

Because sedges emerge right through the season, it often pays to fish a sedge pattern on a cast of wet flies, either on the bob or on the point. It is for this reason that the 'Green Peter' and 'Murrough' patterns are so popular and successful on Irish loughs when fished with teams of wet flies. The Invicta, Raymond and Wickham's Fancy fit into this category too.

The big sedges (Murrough and Green Peter) provide the best of the sedge fishing. They

emerge in relatively shallow, bog bays at dusk and into the night in late May and early June and again in late July and early August. The best of this fishing is at the time when the adult fly emerges and scatters across the surface towards the nearest shore. It is very vulnerable to the trout and they take with a characteristic slashing rise. A single artificial dry fly is cast in the path of the feeding trout and retrieved slowly. It usually gets a quick response.

PERCH FRY

Shoals of tiny perch fry begin to appear about mid-June and, for a time, the trout prey heavily on them. We are now getting towards the height of the summer temperatures with bright sunshine and consequent unsuitable fishing conditions. Shoals of fry are generally found in relatively sheltered, shallow areas and sandy bays. The trout usually feed on them in short bursts. The sequence appears to be that the fry rise to the surface and the trout then come in and lash out at them with their tails. This either stuns or kills dozens of fry and they are then quietly eaten by the trout. To capitalize on this situation, the angler should cast his flies into the area of activity and fish them static or very slowly on a floating line. The best flies to use are Dunkeld Nymph, Dunkeld, Peter Ross and Alexandra, though a Green Peter may also take fish under such circumstances.

THE DADDY AND THE GRASSHOPPER

In the late summer and early autumn, in August and early September, the perch fry may still interest the trout and there will still be hatches of chironomids and lake olives, but possibly the best fishing of all is to be had with terrestrials — daddys, grasshoppers and black flies like the common bluebottle. It would be a daft angler indeed who would not have a selection of daddys in his fly box at this time. The daddy can be fished dry if trout are observed feeding on the fly as it is blown out on the lough. But even when none appear on the water, an artificial can be fished on the bob or even on the point.

Dapping the grasshopper and daddy comes into its own in August and September. Local knowledge dictates which is most effective on any given fishery.

ANTS

Very large swarms of ants often get blown on to loughs in August. It is not a frequent occurrence but, when it does happen, the trout appear to become suicidal and the angler who happens to be there with a few well-dressed ant patterns in his fly box is likely to have as good a session of dry fly fishing as he could hope for.

CORIXA

The corixa or lesser water-boatman inhabits the shallower areas of sandy bays and may be taken by the trout at any time during the season. It seems to be particularly vulnerable to trout in September, and a close imitative pattern will take fish, though I have found a small Black Zulu fished on the point even more effective.

SAFETY

Anglers who go bank fishing should exercise extreme care either when bank fishing or when wading in an unfamiliar lough. High peat banks can become undercut by wave action and collapse under the weight of an angler. Never take chances when wading. A step too far into a deep hole can be fatal. So too can wading on a marl bottom. The crust can break and if this happens, it can be virtually impossible to get out unaided.

Glasses – polaroids if you don't wear spectacles – should always be worn for eye protection.

Boat fishers should wear a life jacket or buoyancy aid and it is always sensible to obtain a weather forecast before going afloat.

In sunny weather, it is advisable to wear a cream that offers optimum skin protection now that the risks of skin cancer have been highlighted.

CLOTHING

Much has been written about what the well dressed angler should wear. The most important aspect of the matter is that it should be warm and comfortable and that it should keep him dry. Wellingtons are preferable to waders when fishing from a boat. In cold weather, tweed clothing and wool pullovers should be worn – never denims – under the waterproofs. As to the waterproofs themselves, I have finally come to the conclusion that only garments made of heavy gauge PVC with welded seams will keep an angler dry if he has to sit in a boat in heavy rain for a whole day. And waterproofs should be put on *before* the rain starts.

GILLIES AND BOATS

A good boatman makes a wonderful fishing companion and generally becomes a friend for life. He is an invaluable and indispensable aid on an unfamiliar water. Not only does he provide safe passage around the lough but, if he is a regular boatman on the water, he should know when, where and what action to expect at any given time.

The first requirement of a lough boat is that it be of sound construction, preferably made of timber and that it should drift well. It should also be clinker built, rather than flat bottomed, with the planks overlapping and fastened with copper nails. Indeed, a flat bottomed boat is a death trap, even on a small lough, if a wave blows up. For a big lough, the boat should be at least 19 feet long from stern to stern and constructed with nine planks on each side.

Most of the modern lough boats are made of

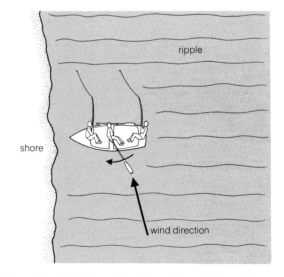

Figure 33 *Drifting a shoreline with a slight onshore wind and using the 'back' oar to prevent the boat from running ashore*

fibre glass with the mould taken from a clinker built boat. Many of these are fine fishing boats but some tend to be too light and do not drift well. It is important that a boat should drift square to the wind. To do so, the weight of the occupants must be balanced evenly. The direction in which a boat is drifting can be altered by using the 'back oar'. If an angler wishes to drift parallel to the shore in a slight onshore wind, the bow of the boat should point towards the shore. This way it is possible to keep the boat off the shore with an oc-casional stroke of the rear oar. If you drift with the bow pointing out into the lough, the boat will spin around when this exercise is attempted.

A first-time lough angler would be well advised to employ the services of a good boatman just to learn how to manage a boat when fishing. A competent boatman will demonstrate the proper way to do things and impart more information in a couple of days than a new-comer could hope to learn in a whole season on his own.

ETIQUETTE

'Manners make the man' and good manners on the lough are as important as anywhere else. Maybe more so, because here people find themselves in situations where they should be enjoying themselves, away from the cares and hassle of daily living.

The rules are simple and obvious − treat your fellow anglers as you would have them treat you. To be a little more precise, don't drive your boat across the drift of another boat and don't cut in and start drifting less than a couple of hundred yards in front of another boat. When motoring up to start another drift, give other boats a wide berth and cut the motor and use the oars if other boats are seen to be casting to rising fish. In calm conditions, row away a respectable distance from the nearest angler, rather than start the motor close to others who are still fishing.

Further reading

Hugh Falkus and Fred Buller, *Freshwater Fishing* (Stanley Paul, 1988).

H.P. Henzell, *The Art and Craft of Loch Fishing* (Phillip Allan, 1937).

Peter O'Reilly, *Trout and Salmon Loughs of Ireland: A Fisherman's Guide* (Unwin Hyman, 1987).

Bruce Sandison, *Trout Lochs of Scotland: A Fisherman's Guide* (Unwin Hyman, 1987).

Peter Lapsley

Peter Lapsley was born in 1943 and started coarse fishing on Norfolk gravel pits when he was six years old. After several years spent in single-minded but unsuccessful pursuit of the British rod-caught gudgeon record on the Grand Union Canal, he graduated to fly fishing for trout on the River Chess in Hertfordshire in his early teens. Since then, he has fished for trout, sea-trout and grayling throughout the British Isles and abroad.

Five years spent running a stillwater trout fishery in Hampshire in the early 1980s gave him the opportunity to study trout and the creatures they live on at close quarters and in detail, and to develop his own approach to the sport based on personal observation and experience seasoned with constant contact with other anglers.

Although he now lives and works in London and chiefly fishes southern chalk streams and stillwaters, he retains great affection for the lochs, loughs, rivers and reservoirs of the further flung corners of these islands. He is a member of the Association of Professional Game Angling Instructors and a National Anglers' Council Grade I Game Angling Coach.

Peter Lapsley's three books on fly fishing – *The Bankside Book of Stillwater Trout Flies*, *Trout From Stillwaters* and *River Trout Flyfishing* have all been widely acclaimed. He contributed regular fortnightly articles on fly fishing to *The Shooting Times* throughout the 1980's and in these, and in his numerous articles for *Trout and Salmon*, *Trout Fisherman*, *The Field* and *Salmon, Trout and Sea Trout* he has developed a considerable reputation for clarity of thought and expression.

6

TROUT IN LAKES AND RESERVOIRS

Peter Lapsley

INTRODUCTION

Lake and reservoir fly fishing for trout is a relatively recent arrival on the British fieldsports scene. It is essentially a product of rapid increases in affluence, leisure time and mobility over the past hundred years and of a shortage of good, natural trout lakes, lochs and rivers, especially in central and southern England. It has been made possible by rapid growth in the number of reservoirs, gravel pits and private lakes in the country and by the ready availability of farm-reared trout, particularly rainbow trout, with which to stock them.

The early reservoir anglers, those who fished Lake Vyrnwy and Ravensthorpe in the 1890s and Blagdon in the early 1900s, quite naturally adopted the tackle and tactics already widely in use on Scottish lochs and Irish loughs, and they tried other methods, too − salmon flies (the early equivalent of the modern stillwater lure), spinners and 'fly spoons' amongst them. It was not long, though, before observant and innovative men like Drs J. C. Mottram and Howard Bell began to identify the creatures that trout in reservoirs eat and to tie and fish patterns specifically intended to represent or suggest them.

The opening of several Midland reservoirs as trout fisheries in the middle years of this century − and particularly that of Grafham Water in 1967 − attracted substantial numbers of people to the sport from coarse fishing, rather than from river or loch trout fly fishing. Amongst the newcomers was a particularly imaginative and innovative group of anglers. Unfettered by the lore and traditions of fly fishing, they evolved a range of tackle and tactics specifically designed for the taking of rainbow trout from big, deep, fertile waters. Most notable amongst the techniques they developed was an assortment of lures which they fished on sinking lines of various densities in order to catch fish feeding on tiny daphnia at ever-changing depths.

So much publicity did their methods attract that they were quickly adopted almost as a panacea by large numbers of less skilful fishermen. For a while, there was a real risk that reservoir trouting would slide ever deeper into a slough of mindless lure stripping, losing credibility as a thinking man's pursuit in the process.

Fortunately, several perceptive imitative fly fishers recognized this trend and were able gradually to halt and then to reverse it by presenting the public with more interesting alternatives. Particularly noteworthy amongst this group were Brian Clarke and Arthur Cove,

Lake Vyrnwy, a deep, steep-sided, upland reservoir, closely resembling a Highland Loch in character

Blagdon, near Bristol. One of the first lowland reservoirs to have opened as a trout fishery and still one of our very finest waters

who, separately, did more for stillwater fly fishing in the 1970s than had almost anyone else in the history of the sport.

The boom in reservoir trouting in the 1960s and early 1970s induced all sorts of people to stock all sorts of lakes and gravel pits with trout and to open them to the public, either as club or syndicate waters or as commercial, day or season ticket fisheries. Inevitably, these waters varied enormously in quality and, equally inevitably, the less good ones went to the wall as anglers became more discriminating and as the increase in demand levelled off in the late 1970s and early 1980s.

One of the chief features of reservoir trouting through the 1980s was the growth of interest in competitive fishing. It was, perhaps, inevitable that an element of competition should have surfaced in a sport that had attracted so many new participants in so short time, many of them with competitive coarse fishing experience. It was probably equally inevitable that the increase in the number of competitions should have stirred up strong feelings, both for and against them. Whatever the rights and wrongs, though, there can be no doubt that widespread interest in competitions has breathed new life into loch-style fishing, upon which the rules for most of them are based.

The other major changes seen during the 1980s were an increasing tendency for the ten regional water authorities to lease out the fishing rights on their reservoirs to private management and, at the end of the decade, the privatization of the water industry and the creation of a new National Rivers Authority.

The effects of these two major developments are still difficult to judge. What is clear, though is that the days when good trout fishing was subsidized from the water rates are all but gone, and that the cost to the angler of reservoir trout fishing must inevitably rise over the next few years.

In angling terms, much of the old dogmatism has now been removed from a pursuit in which skill may best be judged by the flexibility of the angler's approach – by his ability to match his tackle and tactics to the conditions and to fish a nymph or a dry fly as effectively as a lure or a traditional pattern. Some of the experiments that have been conducted in the name of stillwater fly fishing during the past twenty years or so may have made the chalk stream, dry fly purists huff and puff a bit, but they have been the trademarks of a young and healthily evolving sport.

TACKLING UP

Rods

Until quite recently, weight was a major consideration in the selection of a fly rod for stillwater trouting, which often involves continuous casting for long periods. The introduction of carbon fibre and, to a lesser extent, boron as replacements for fibre glass and cane has changed that and has made the use of longer rods entirely practicable.

A rod of between 9 feet 6 inches and 10 feet rated for lines in the range size 6–8 should serve for most reservoir trouting. Those who chiefly fish small stillwaters, where short, accurate casting may often be necessary, may well find a shorter rod of, say, 9 feet an asset. I know of no circumstances under which there is any-thing to be said for using a rod shorter than this.

A rod's action – the extent to which it flexes and the distribution of that flexibility along its length – is very much a matter of personal preference. For myself, I abominate soft, sloppy rods, always choosing stiffish ones in which most of the flexibility comes in the top quarter. But, if you expect to do a lot of loch-style boat fishing, you may find a softer rod with an 'all-through' action more comfortable and less physically demanding than a stiff one.

Fly lines

For the novice, there is a bewildering array of fly lines available in all sorts of profiles, densities and colours.

The two truly essential lines are a floater and a medium sinker. Because delicacy is more important than distance when you are fishing at or near the surface, it is probably sensible to select a double-tapered floating line (i.e. DT6, 7 or 8F). When fishing deeper down, distance casting may be important, and it is therefore probably as well to buy a weight-forward medium sinker (i.e. WF6, 7 or 8S).

Beyond these two basic lines there is a mass of lead-cored quick sinkers, intermediates, sink-tips, shooting heads and so on. While each has its uses under particular conditions and at particular stages in the season, none is truly essential.

As is the case with most fishing tackle, the price of a line is a fair guide to its quality, and it usually pays to buy the best you can afford.

Reels

Unlike the reels used for coarse and sea fishing, a fly reel is really little more than a receptacle for line that is not in use. It should be as light as possible, big enough to accommodate the fly line and 50–75 yards of braided backing line, and it should have holes in the spool face to reduce weight and to allow air to reach the fly line. Personally, I dislike multiplying and automatic reels which seem to me to be unnecessarily heavy and which are sometimes prone to mechanical failure.

Leaders

The leader – the length of nylon used to connect the fly or flies to the fly line – must meet a number of requirements, some of them conflicting, if it is to be as effective as possible. It must distance the fly or flies from the potentially fish-frightening fly line. It must turn over properly at the end of the forward cast, laying the flies out neatly on the water. And, it must be fine enough to go unnoticed by the trout and yet strong enough to withstand the shock of a fierce take, jump or run.

Some people scrape by with simple, untapered lengths of monofilament. Others

Figure 34 *Typical stillwater leaders*

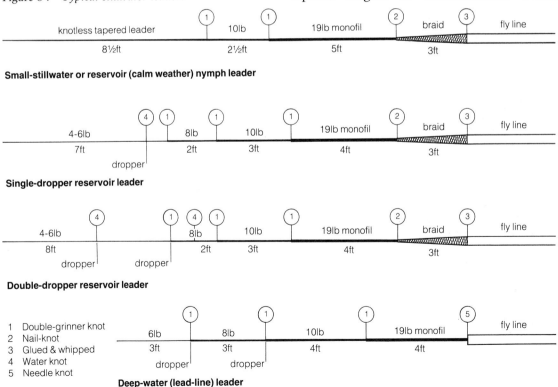

cobble their own leaders together from lengths of nylon of various strengths. Personally, I am disinclined to compromise with so fundamental a part of my tackle and almost always use commercially produced, knotless, tapered leaders or leaders with droppers.

On reservoirs, where trout can run much further than they can in rivers or little lakes, it is unwise to use a point of less than about 6 lb breaking strain. On small stillwaters, it will rarely be either acceptable or necessary to use less than a 4 lb point. Whatever some authors may have said about it in the past, there is nothing sporting about using too fine a leader and risking being broken, leaving a trout to swim off with a hook in its mouth.

I attach my leaders to floating fly lines with anything from 3–15 feet of 23 lb mono-filament, and usually put a braided butt between the line itself and this length of level nylon to improve the leader's turn-over. Long leaders are rarely necessary when fishing with sinking lines, to which I generally attach a commercial leader with a simple, 2–3 feet length of 23 lb monofilament.

Nets

Provided that it is big enough to accommodate the biggest fish you may realistically hope to catch, the choice of a landing-net is very much a matter of personal preference. If you fish waters where catch-and-release is allowed, it is vital to use one with a knotless mesh so as to avoid damaging the fish.

The priest

Where trout are to be killed, it is important that this should be done as quickly, cleanly and humanely as possible. A purpose-made priest (with which to 'administer the last rites') should be used, and it should be fastened to the fishing jacket or waistcoat with a length of cord to prevent it from being lost.

Etceteras

In addition to these essentials, every tackle shop is an Aladdin's cave of more or less useful bits and pieces – fly boxes, fly floatant, line sinkant and mucilin, scissors, clippers and artery forceps, line trays, and so on. The only firm advice I would offer is that you should take with you to the waterside only what you really need, ideally no more than can be carried in your pockets. One of the great pleasures of fly fishing is that it allows us to go lightly laden and thus to be mobile, and mobility is essential to successful stillwater trouting.

FLIES

When you consider that all the words in all the languages that use the Roman alphabet have been created from a mere twenty-six letters, it must quickly become evident that there can be almost no limit to the number of different fly patterns that can be produced from the massive range of hooks, silks, tinsels, furs and feathers available to the fly dresser.

Most fly fishers collect large numbers of flies over the years, and it is fun to do so. But it is also worth bearing in mind the widely agreed tenet that successful fly fishing has very much more to do with good presentation than with choice of fly pattern.

Most of the patterns described by Peter O'Reilly in his chapter on lough fishing, and some of those used for sea-trout and for brown trout in rivers, will serve well on lakes and reservoirs. In addition, it is as well to arm oneself with a modest assortment of stillwater nymphs and lures.

Midges and caddis flies (sedges) are the reservoir trout's bread and butter, chiefly in their larval and pupal forms but also as winged adults. Artificials designed to represent them can be effective for much of the year. In addition, patterns, designed to suggest corixae, dragonfly larvae, olive and damselfly nymphs, coarse fish fry and fresh-water shrimps will be useful at appropriate stages in the season.

Nor should we forget floating flies. A Hawthorn can be as deadly on stillwater as it can on a river in late April and in May. A dry sedge pattern can produce spectacular sport on a summer's evening. And an artificial daddy-long-legs can work wonders on breezy July and August days, as can a floating Muddler Minnow, stripped through the ripple in September and October.

Where lures are concerned, I am increasingly convinced that we need far fewer than most people seem to believe. If black does not work, white often will, except perhaps in high summer, when something like a Whiskey Fly — flashy and with a lot of orange in it — will often distract rainbow trout otherwise pre-occupied with minuscule daphnia.

At certain times of year, particularly early in the season, the fish are likely to be found at or near the bottom, often in very deep water. Until quite recently, those who fished for them with sinking lines were at constant risk of becoming snagged on weeds and other obstructions. Buoyant lures like the Booby Nymph solve this problem by floating above the end of a high density, quick sinking fly line on a leader of anything from 3 to 10 feet or so in length.

Buoyant lures fished in this way frequently take bigger than average trout, trout which have become exclusively bottom feeders and which may well be uncatchable by other means.

FISH LOCATION

There can be few sights more daunting to the novice or to the newcomer to a reservoir fishery than a vast, bleak, featureless and apparently lifeless expanse of grey water stretching away into the distance. Do not allow yourself to be daunted. Even the veriest beginner will understand that, however meticulously a water may have been stocked, some areas will prove more attractive to the fish than others, and that some areas are therefore likely to be highly productive while others are effectively aquatic deserts. The fly fisher's objective is to stack the odds in his favour by seeking to fish only the most productive water. The problem is how to identify it. The solution lies in tapping informed and benevolent local knowledge and then

Figure 35 *A typical lowland reservoir*

KEY
1. Trout tend to lie deep early in the season, when the water is cold.
2. Promontories on steeply shelving shore lines give bank anglers access to deep water, and can also attract feeding trout when the wind blows onto or along the shore line.
3. Terrestrial insects may be blown onto the water from deciduous woodland, especially in April and May.
4. Warm, shallow water will produce good midge and sedge hatches, especially in spring and summer.
5. Daddy-long-legs can provide good sport when blown onto the water from meadows or grassland.
6. Trout tend to be attracted to the mouths of feeder streams as the spawning season approaches in the autumn and early winter.

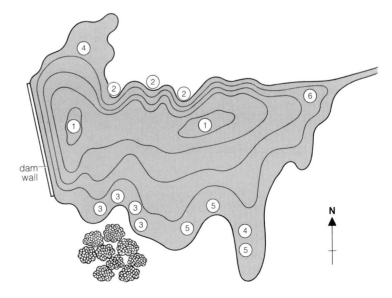

tempering it with one's own understanding and reasoning.

Satisfied customers often come back, which is why fisheries staffs want those who fish their waters to do well. Do not be shy of seeking their advice; it will almost always be authoritative, objective and honest. Be a little more cautious about seeking guidance from local anglers. Many of them will be helpful but a selfish few may be more concerned to protect their own sport than to try to ensure a visitor's success.

The fisheries offices at most major reservoirs sell large-scale maps showing underwater contours and detail of the immediately surrounding countryside. Buy one, and use it. It will show you where the deep and shallow water is, and where the shore slopes steeply down or shelves only gradually into the water, all of which is important. What is just as important, though, is that it will also enable you to work out where underwater features are likely to be found.

Where land has been flooded, submerged hedgerows, ditches, tree stumps, buildings, walls and so on remain in evidence for an astonishingly long time after being inundated. A good map will often enable you to work out where many of these drowned objects and artifacts are. And, since all of these sorts of things can be relied upon to attract and hold fish, knowledge of their whereabouts can put you at a distinct advantage.

Although there are usually far fewer visible clues to the trout's whereabouts on reservoirs than there are on streams and rivers, surface movement and the activities of birds — swallows and martins feeding on insects, gulls and terns picking up dead or injured fry — can quite often lead us to feeding trout, and make a pair of lightweight binoculars an invaluable part of the reservoir angler's equipment.

Finally, we are fortunate in that the trout's movements and behaviour are far from random. Indeed, they are almost always direct and predictable responses to a series of clearly identifiable stimuli — temperature, light, wind speed and direction, hunger, the availability of food and the reproductive urge. If we can understand these stimuli and the fishes' responses to them, we should be able to work out quite often where the fish are likely to be and what they may be expected to be doing, and to adjust our tackle and tactics to match their behaviour.

We shall use most of the rest of this chapter to see how all this may be translated into practice.

MARCH AND APRIL

Lure fishing

Fish being cold-blooded creatures, their metabolic rates — and thus their levels of activity — are governed by the temperature of the water around them. Every fish species has its own 'temperature tolerance range' and its 'preferred temperature range' — the former being the temperature range within which the fish can survive; the latter, the range within which it feeds more or less actively. The rainbow trout's preferred temperature range runs from about 8°C to about 17°C; the brown trout's is a few degrees lower.

If the winter has been cold and water temperatures are still low when reservoir fisheries open in March or April, the trout are likely to be torpid and largely inactive, mainly keeping to the deeper water. Their disinclination to come close into the shore is often reinforced by the fact that the marginal shallows, dried out and parched last summer and autumn and only recently re-flooded, will hold little or no food.

For these reasons, boat anglers tend to do better early in the season than their bank-bound colleagues, but that is by no means to say that you would be wasting your time on the bank.

Using your own knowledge and experience, an angler's map and such local knowledge as may be available, try to place yourself on a promontory on a stretch of bank which shelves

Bleak and concrete-sided it may be, but the Queen Mother reservoir at Datchet produces some of the finest rainbow trout fishing in the country

down quite steeply into deep water. If you can find a point at which the wind is blowing across your front from left to right (for right handers, of course; right to left for left handers), so much the better. It will make casting both easier and safer, keeping fast moving flies away from your face.

As the trout are unlikely to be feeding actively – in the mornings, at least – it is sensible to pander to their aggressive instincts, or to their curiosity, rather than to the feeding urge, by offering them a lure on a sinking line. My own experience suggests that a simple black lure, with a silver-ribbed chenille body and a fluffy, marabou wing will work for

something like 75 per cent of the time when the water is cold and that, when it fails, a similarly simple white lure will usually solve the problem.

If the fish really are hugging the bottom, a buoyant lure like a Booby Nymph, fished on a quick-sinking line and an 8–10-foot leader will often tempt them, and will make it possible to work the lure close to the reservoir bed without constantly picking up weed or being snagged. The chief problem with this technique – and, to a lesser extent, with all sinking line techniques – is that the curve of the line can make take detection and hooking difficult.

Start at the water's edge, without wading, casting quite a short line at first and only lengthening it gradually. Try fishing at a variety of depths and speeds, and do not be in too much of a hurry to move on if sport is a little slow in coming. Rainbow trout have a marked tendency to shoal. A little patience on the angler's part will often produce a pattern of alternating quiet spells and periods of activity.

The first couple of months of the season are the only ones in which the boat fisherman may do as well or better at anchor than when drifting. This is because a static boat makes it possible to get a lure on a sinking line down to deep-lying fish.

Such use of a boat as a 'casting platform' should not be used as an excuse for the widespread but dangerous and counter-productive practice of standing up to fish – dangerous because it makes the angler unstable; counter-productive because it frightens fish; all for the possibility of adding no more than 3–5 yards to one's casting distance.

The tactics used from the bank are equally appropriate for the boat fisherman at this time of year. A black lure on a medium sinking line will often tempt the trout, and a white one may work if a black one fails.

Experiment with a variety of depths, timing the period between cast and retrieve, starting by allowing, say, ten seconds for a dozen or so casts and then increasing the pause to fifteen seconds, twenty seconds, and so on.

Vary the speed and style of retrieve from time to time, too, from a slow, smooth, steady 'figure-of-eight' through long, slow pulls, to short, sharp tugs and any variation on any of these themes. It is widely believed that lure fishing necessarily involves a rapid retrieve. It does not; indeed, you often find that slow, steady movement is more effective than a fast retrieve.

Takes very often come either during the first two or three pulls of the retrieve or as the lure, which will have been travelling roughly horizontally or even slightly downwards, turns upwards quite suddenly towards the end of the retrieve.

When fishing a buoyant lure on a quick-sinking line, it is tempting to presume that a 20 or 25 yards cast will enable you to fish along the bottom for 20 or 25 yards. In truth, of course, it will not – unless you pay out as much line as the water is deep immediately after casting. If you do not do this, with a 20 yard cast over 60 feet of water, the line will eventually hang straight down from the rod tip, its end barely touching the bottom.

Imitative fishing

Having gone on at some length about sinking lines and lure fishing, it should be said that even the first month or so of the season can offer welcome opportunities for imitative fishing with floating lines.

Many reservoirs produce hatches of their biggest black midges of the year in late March and early April, usually in the late afternoons on mild days. The pupae – which are of far greater interest to trout, and therefore to anglers, than the winged adults are – can be represented quite realistically on a size 10 hook. At such times, a team of two or three matching artificials can provide intensely exciting sport. The flies should be fished on a longish (12–16-foot) leader which has been carefully degreased. All that is required is to cast them across the wind and to allow them to be carried round by the weight of the breeze on the fly line.

As April progresses, the water and its inhabitants should begin to warm up and wake up, and the trout should begin to feed more predictably and consistently, chiefly in the mornings and through the middle of the day.

In addition to the aquatic creatures that help to make up the trout's menu at this time – shrimps, alder larvae and a growing assortment of midge pupae – an early season terrestrial, the hawthorn fly, may afford the first opportunities for some very good dry fly fishing. Because it hatches and hovers in clouds amongst trees and bushes, and is only blown onto the water by accident, trout feeding on it will usually be found close to the upwind shores of lakes and reservoirs, particularly where the wind blows onto the water from a coppice or spinney.

As an aside, it is useful to remember that the natural hawthorn fly subsides into the surface film and then sinks when it has been blown onto the water, and that the angler's fly should do likewise. Interestingly, that great fly fisher G. E. M. Skues, the father of modern nymph fishing, failed to notice this. He never understood why it was that trout took his sodden and submerged hawthorns with alacrity while ignoring similar artificials bobbing nicely on top of the water.

MAY AND JUNE

As is the case on all British trout waters, May and June provide the cream of the season's sport. At the beginning of May, we may realistically hope to find the fish feeding throughout the day. By the end of June, good fishing through the morning and in the evening will usually have become separated by a dead spell in the afternoon. The transition from the former 'daily profile' to the latter is gradual and imprecise, its progress being dictated by changes in the weather.

By the middle of May, sinking lines and lures will generally have become markedly less useful than they were earlier in the season, and most stillwater fly fishers will be using floating lines exclusively, usually with imitative or food suggesting patterns.

Midge pupae — in almost any of their many colours and sizes — remain bread and butter to the trout and artificials designed to match them are therefore at the forefront of the angler's armoury.

In addition, pond and lake olive nymphs making their ways to the surface to hatch, and rapidly growing damselfly nymphs, are likely to feature increasingly in the trout's diets. And, once we are safely into June, caddis flies (sedges) will become important to trout and anglers alike — as pupae in mid-water in the late afternoons and then either as hatching pupae or as winged adults in the evenings, offering spectacular sport either on an Invicta fished just beneath the surface, or on a floating sedge pattern skidded across the surface in a series of short, sharp pulls.

In the underwater periods of their lives, all of these creatures live amongst the weed which provides them with both food and shelter. Weed can only grow in water which is shallow enough for the sunlight to penetrate to the bottom. Obviously, this depth varies, depending upon the clarity or otherwise of the water. As a general rule, though, weed rarely grows on the lake bed in water more than about 20 feet deep. It follows that most aquatic insects will be found in relatively shallow water, that fish feeding on them will also be there, and that these are the areas upon which the angler should concentrate his attention — all of which is why the imbalance of opportunity between boat and bank anglers, so marked in March and April, becomes very much less so in May and June.

Reservoir boat fishing tactics during these most prolific months differ not at all from those so ably described by Peter O'Reilly in his chapter on *Lough and Loch Fishing*. I see no merit in repeating here what he has said there. Instead, I would simply commend his chapter to you.

But there is a need to make one or two points about bank fishing.

Just as there is a widespread tendency for people to stand up in boats, so do many bank anglers seem to find the temptation to go paddling and always to cast as long a line as possible quite irresistible. Indeed, there is a breed of reservoir fly fisher who seems to believe that he is not really fishing if the water is not lapping at his wader tops and if he is not double-hauling a heavy shooting head at the far bank.

Gratuitous wading is even more damaging to sport than standing up in boats is. Not only does it drive fish out from the banks but, done repeatedly by many people, as it tends to be in certain areas of some reservoirs, it tramples out of existence the marginal weed beds which support the insects trout feed on and thus removes from the trout any incentive at all to come close inshore.

Of course, there are circumstances of time

Rutland Water. There can be few sights more daunting to the fly fisher than a vast, featureless expanse of grey water

and place in which wading really is necessary, but they are much more occasional than one might guess from the picket line of anglers that so often marks out the 3-foot depth contour around our reservoirs. And it is worth remembering that to wade unnecessarily not only damages your own sport, but that it may also damage the sport of those around you and of future visitors to the reservoir.

Other characteristics of reservoir bank anglers are that they tend to look for open water, where they may cast and retrieve with the minimum risk of becoming caught in weed, and that they usually hope for a ripple, that their machinations may be concealed from the fish. While both of these factors can make for comfortable fishing, it is quite often the angler who has the courage to fish the holes amongst the weed beds, or who actually seeks out the trout feeding in a glass calm bay, who will eventually head homewards with the largest fish or the heaviest bag.

The balance of advantage in such circumstances always lies with the angler who

has learnt to watch for and to spot takes 'on the drop', as his fly — often a weighted nymph or corixa — simply sinks through the water having just been cast.

It is remarkable how few anglers realize just how many takes come 'on the drop' or how subtle such takes can be. Quite carefully conducted experiments on a gin-clear stillwater suggest to me that as many as 70 per cent of all takes come before the angler begins to retrieve, and I have watched a rainbow trout swim round in circles taking and ejecting a leaded nymph as many as three times, the floating part of the leader giving not the slightest indication of its interest.

Those fly fishers who believe the period between cast and retrieve to be 'dead time', using it to gaze round at the waterside wildlife and at the countryside in general, only beginning to think about their fishing again as they start to pull their flies back towards them, are placing themselves at an enormous disadvantage to those who watch the curve of the fly line on the water, its tip, or, best of all, the point at which the leader cuts down through the surface film for the slightest evidence of a fish's interest in their offerings.

JULY AND AUGUST

If May and June provide some of the season's best sport, July and August can offer some of the most difficult and testing fishing of the year. Aptly named 'the dog days', these hot, high summer months usually find brown trout skulking in deep water and wholly disinclined to feed. Even rainbows, with their higher temperature preference range, are likely to feed only spasmodically – usually early in the mornings and late in the evenings. To complicate matters further, fly hatches tend to be sparser at this time of year than they are in the preceding and following months and, when the trout are feeding, they are likely to do so on zooplankton.

Zooplankton is the generic name given to a whole range of minuscule aquatic animals. Amongst them, and of particular interest to trout, are some fifty species of tiny crustacea, daphnia (the water flea) probably being the best known of them.

Zooplankton depends for its food upon its vegetable counterpart, phytoplankton, and phytoplankton, in turn, is dependent upon warmth and sunlight for its well-being. In winter, when the water is cold and there is little sunlight, the phytoplankton dies back. As the water warms up and the light intensifies through the spring and summer, the phytoplankton reproduces increasingly rapidly (causing green opacity often referred to as 'algal blooming') and, inevitably, the zooplankton follows suit.

Two particular characteristics of zooplankton create problems for anglers. One is the creature's minute sizes. The other is caused by their daily vertical migration.

The size problem arises because creatures like daphnia are so small that they could not possibly be represented or suggested on a hook. It can often be resolved by going to the opposite extreme, by offering the trout quite a large, flashy lure fished quite quickly. The classic lure for this purpose is the Whiskey Fly, designed by Albert Whillock specifically with daphnia feeding rainbows in mind.

Resolution of the depth problem calls for rather more knowledge and experience.

During the night, the zooplankton may be found close to the water's surface but, as the sun comes up and begins to rise, so do they start to move downwards. By 6 or 7 a.m in the morning, they may be as much as 30 feet down, and they may have retreated to a depth of 70 feet or more by midday. They rise again slowly through the afternoon and evening, reaching the surface at about midnight, only to start the whole cycle once more.

The depth at which trout may be feeding on zooplankton can only be discovered by trial and error, tempered with an understanding of the plankton's behaviour and of the water itself. A medium or quick-sinking line will be needed and it pays to be methodical, trying one likely depth for a reasonable period before coming up in the water or going deeper.

Just because the best of the high summer, daytime fishing is likely to be found with lures and sinking lines, it should not be thought that they present the only opportunities for success. Early in the mornings, in the evenings, and on soft, cloudy days, the fish will often welcome an opportunity to come to the surface where they may well be found to be feeding on midge pupae. And, especially in August, a dry daddy-long-legs can provide spectacular sport, particularly if there is a bit of a breeze.

Daddy-long-legs are terrestrial creatures and tend to be blown on to the water from fields and meadows. Fish feeding on them are therefore likely to be found at the upwind end of a reservoir. A buoyant artificial on a fine, 10–12-foot leader, cast on to the ripple and either allowed to drift or twitched occasionally will often produce confident rises from larger than average trout. The tendency amongst those unused to dry fly fishing is to strike too quickly, pulling the fly out of the fish's mouth; the key to success is to discipline oneself to count slowly to three before lifting the rod, giving the fish time to turn down and close its mouth on the artificial.

KEEPING FISH FRESH

At this juncture, it is worth saying something about looking after the fish you catch.

Some years ago, when I was running a fishery of my own, one of our season rods rang me late one evening to say that there was something wrong with our trout. On cleaning some she had caught that day, she had found the flesh to be flaccid and coming away from the bone.

When I questioned her more closely, she told me that she had caught all the fish before eleven in the morning and that she had then kept them in a plastic bag on the bank beside her as she had fished on through a long, scorchingly hot summer's afternoon. Only reluctantly did she eventually accept that she could scarcely have cooked them more effectively at home in her oven.

Once they have been killed, trout must be kept as cool as possible. The ideal is to put them in an insulated cool-bag with several frozen ice-packs. Failing this, they should be kept in a hessian fish-bass, which should be immersed in water at frequent intervals and hung in such breeze as there may be. Perhaps surprisingly, hanging the bag in the water cools its contents less effectively than hanging it in the wind or even in the sun does — it all has to do with heat removal caused by evaporation.

SEPTEMBER AND OCTOBER

Although it is a less consistently good month than May, September offers welcome relief after the summer, with the trout often feeding from sunrise to sunset, building themselves up for the lean days ahead and for the spawning season. Any of the methods that have taken fish through the year so far may do so now, and bank anglers may once again expect to do at least as well as the boat fishermen.

Amongst the creatures to which the trout may turn their attentions at this time of year are pond or lake olive nymphs and corixae.

There is a tendency for reservoir fly fishers to use patterns much larger than those used by those who fish rivers, hook sizes 8, 10 and 12 being regarded almost as standard. This can be a mistake, especially towards the end of the season when the fish stocked earlier in the year have become naturalized and may well be concentrating their attentions on very small insects. The olive nymph is a case in point, being most realistically imitated on a size 14 or 16 hook, or even an 18.

Although many eminent anglers have gone to great lengths to produce accurate imitations of the nymphs of the various species of upwinged flies, the trout generally seem to be far less pedantic, and small Pheasant Tail or Grey Goose nymphs will usually serve the angler's purpose, the former being more consistently useful than the latter.

The natural corixa (or lesser water boatman) is an intriguing creature which breathes air, rather than absorbing oxygen from the water. It spends its life floating to the surface where it collects a coating of air on its slightly hairy underside and then swimming laboriously back down to the weed, amongst which it lives.

Weighted artificial corixae are very frequently taken by trout 'on the drop', as they are sinking, having just been cast, and are best fished around and between the weed beds in which the naturals are found. More realistic, though, is to use a buoyant artificial, made of ethafoam, and to fish it on a very fast-sinking, lead cored line and a longish (12–16-foot) leader, using very much the same technique that we discussed in relation to the Booby Nymph earlier in this chapter.

Towards the end of the season — from early to mid-September onwards — some of the most exciting fishing to be had is for trout feeding on coarse fish fry.

Far from living exclusively on genteel diets

of upwinged duns and nymphs, trout are voracious, carnivorous predators whose main gastronomic purpose it is to consume the maximum amount of protein for the least amount of effort. They will eat small fish at any time, provided that the quarry species is available in sufficient numbers and concentrations. In particular, they consume large numbers of recently hatched 'needle fry' when the shoals of these tiny fish are close to the surface in June and July, and they feed ferociously on shoals of larger coarse fish fry in the autumn.

Sometimes, fry feeding trout appear to herd shoals of fry together and then to charge them, wounding more of the small fish than they take, returning to pick off victims injured by the onslaught in a relatively leisurely manner. At other times, they seem to be more opportunistic, simply taking individual fry as and when it is easy to do so.

The more energetic fry feeders can quite often be located, either by the commotion they make or by the wheeling and stooping of gulls and terns attracted to the scene of the carnage by disabled or dying fry floating in the surface film.

Numerous artificials have been designed to suggest small fish, some of them very elaborate. My own experience suggests that matching sizes and colours of the species the trout are feeding on, and realistic presentation, are more important than is meticulous attention to the detail of the natural's appearance. The Jersey Herd, created by the late Tom Ivens, represents a perch fry as well as any other pattern I know; Bob Church's Appetizer, John Goddard's Persuader and my own White Marabou all serve well in various sizes to suggest bream and roach fry.

Shoals of fry tend to congregate in relatively shallow water at this time of year, often using weed beds or other obstructions for cover. When there is no evidence as to where they are or whether the trout are taking them, it is sound policy to keep moving, prospecting along the bank — or along the shore line from a boat — with a slow- or medium-sinking line and varying the depth and speed of retrieve.

Those who are tempted to strip their flies back would do well to find a shoal of coarse fish fry and to watch it for a few minutes. Although they may be able to swim quite quickly relative to their sizes when necessary, these little fish spend most of their time idling along very slowly, only putting on a burst of speed when frightened. Even when they do seek to dart out of danger's way, they can only sustain (relatively) high speeds for very brief periods. In practice, a smooth figure-of-eight retrieve usually proves to be the most effective one when fishing for unseen, fry feeding trout.

Rather different tactics are called for when the trout are visibly harrying shoals of small fish. Here, a floating line and a long (14—18 feet) leader will enable the angler to present his artificial accurately and to spot takes 'on the drop'. The trick is to wait until it looks as though a trout has just crashed through a shoal of fry to drop an artificial — either one of the standard ptterns listed above or, perhaps, a buoyant one — into the middle of the commotion and then simply to leave it. Whereas takes to an artificial retrieved on a sinking line can be quite fierce, those to a floating fry pattern can be quite leisurely, looking just like the rise to any other dry fly pattern, and those to a sinking lure are usually signalled only by a steady draw on the leader.

Another technique that can be used to great effect when rainbow trout are close to the surface in the autumn is the high speed skidding of a large, buoyant fly across a ripple or wave. Any pattern will do, provided that it is large and that it floats well — Hugh Falkus's Surface Lure or a well greased Muddler Minnow are two of the most effective. There is no need to use a long leader; 9 feet will do perfectly well. But, as this is one of the few instances in which long casting offers a distinct advantage, it does pay to attach it to a reasonably heavy (size 7 or 8) weight-forward line or shooting head.

Although it is possible to use the technique from the bank or from an anchored boat, it is far more effective from a boat drifted loch-style. You simply cast a long line out ahead of you and then strip it back as fast as you can, causing the lure to fizz across the water.

Nobody seems to be able to explain why this method works, but work it does, bringing the fish bow-waving after the fly and slashing at it furiously.

My own experience is that, exciting as this style of fishing can be, it produces far more follows than takes and far more snatchy tugs than fish firmly hooked and boated. But it is an intensely visual and entertaining method, and it can both set the adrenalin running and provide some vivid memories for us to savour during the chill, dark months ahead.

WINTER FISHING

I have a theory that winter reservoir trouting is more a pursuit dreamed up and promoted by angling journalists, who would otherwise have little to write about between November and March, than a serious pastime provided in response to an overwhelming demand by vast numbers of fly fishers. Be that as it may, increasing numbers of fisheries do now stay open for much of the winter or even throughout the year, and a number of factors must be taken into account by those who would go 'frost-biting'.

The first is one rarely recognized by reservoir anglers, most of whom have no idea of the extent to which opacity of the water conceals their dastardly designs from the fish. If we curse the algal blooms of summer for their ugliness, for the extent to which they conceal our flies and for their part in the chain which leads rainbows to become preoccupied with daphnia, we should thank them for much of the rest of the year for the extent to which they mask our intentions from the fish.

As soon as November's cold weather arrives, the residual algae die right back leaving the water quite extraordinarily clear, which allows fish to see lines, leaders and anglers from greater distances and far more clearly, and therefore makes them appear far shyer than they were in the summer. In order to cater for this, it will almost always be necessary to go down in point and fly sizes, except when fishing very deep.

The second factor has to do with the fish themselves. Much has been made of sexless 'triploid' rainbow trout over the past few years — fish which never reach sexual maturity and which therefore never take on the spawning livery that makes most rainbow trout so unattractive in the winter; the upturned kype and the dark, slab-sided drabness of the male who sprays milt around as soon as he is caught, and the dullness of both fight and flesh in the female, who sheds great streams of orange ova all over the bottom of the boat or into our fish-basses. However, triploids are relatively difficult, time-consuming and expensive to produce, and are only available in quite limited numbers. For this reason, they tend to be more commonly used in small stillwaters than in large reservoirs, the vast majority of which continue to be stocked with 'ordinary' rainbows. This means, of course, that the winter reservoir angler must continue to put up with all the problems that piscine sexual maturity presents — including the fishes' fruitless and frustrated preoccupation with each other to the exclusion of all else.

It will be noted that, as far as winter fishing is concerned, I have been talking specifically about rainbow trout. The reason, of course, is that the brown trout closed season — typically, from the middle of October to the beginning or middle of April, depending upon the area — is as applicable to reservoirs as it is to streams and rivers, even though it may be effectively impossible for the fish to spawn successfully in such waters. Any brown trout caught during the closed season must be released.

The third factor that should influence the way we approach winter fishing is the availability of food.

Every creature eaten by trout is part of a food chain which is eventually dependent upon the simplest vegetable food forms. We have already seen that algae suspended in the water die back in the winter, as do the weed beds. From this, it follows that the insects and other creatures upon which trout live must also die back or migrate to the lake bed and hibernate. If the creatures trout feed on are to be found at the lake bed in the winter, then it would seem logical to expect to find the trout there, too. And, indeed, it is. Not all the time, to be sure, but for a substantial part of it.

Although far fewer insect species elect to hatch in winter than in spring, summer or autumn, there are a few − chiefly midges − which will make the transition from larva to pupa and the upward migration to the surface to hatch even in January and February. On mild days, the trout may occasionally follow them up, taking them as they rise through the water or hang in the surface film waiting to hatch. I have seen trout rising to midge pupae in January in the only unfrozen bay of an otherwise completely iced-over lake.

But, by and large, the trout will remain at the bottom, torpid and inactive, feeding relatively little, and chiefly taking bottom dwelling midge and caddis larvae when they do choose to feed. And, of course, this is where we must fish for them, with a sinking line and, perhaps, a buoyant lure, to reduce the risk of constantly snagging the bottom.

Maybe it has something to do with comfort loving middle age, but I must confess that I would sooner spend the winter tying flies and toasting my toes in front of the fire than lead-lining for reluctant rainbows.

SMALL STILLWATERS

The growth of public interest in trout fishing over the past twenty years or so has encouraged the owners of countless lakes, reservoirs and gravel pits, all over the country, to stock them with trout and to open them to the public, either as day or season ticket fisheries or as club or syndicate waters. Often set in attractive surroundings and markedly smaller than most water supply reservoirs, such fisheries tend

Gravel workings put to good use. Many put-and-take fisheries have opened during the past twenty years, particularly in populous southern England

to be more intimate than their larger counterparts. And, because the numbers fishing them have to be strictly limited, even the day ticket ones usually develop something of a club atmosphere.

Stocking policies on small stillwaters vary enormously in relation to the fishing pressure on them. At one end of the scale, a 15 or 20 acre lake fished by a syndicate of ten or fifteen members may only need to be stocked before the season opens and then topped up at monthly or six weekly intervals thereafter. At the other, a 10 acre lake fished by fifteen or twenty day ticket anglers a day — as some are — may need to be re-stocked every morning. Whatever the policy, one of the advantages offered by small stillwaters over reservoirs is that the angler can be reasonably sure that he is covering fish for a high proportion of the time.

Tackle for small stillwaters

The tackle needed for fishing small stillwaters differs from that used on reservoirs only in terms of scale. A 9-foot, 6 or 7 rod will extend as much line as you are likely to need and will allow short, accurate casting when necessary. A double-tapered floating line will serve for, perhaps, 95 per cent of the time, but a neutral density or intermediate one may help to avoid scaring fish where the water is particularly clear, and a medium sinker can be useful during the first few weeks of the season or through the winter where winter fishing is allowed.

There can be no doubt that a long (14–18-foot) leader can help to avoid frightening trout in clear-water lakes. A 4X (about 4 lb) point will usually be found to be about right on small lakes, where the fish cannot run as far as they can in larger waters.

The flies used on reservoirs will do just as well on small lakes as will most of the rest of our reservoir tackle. The only major change that may be called for is in the landing net. Some small, commercially run fisheries put in a few truly monstrous rainbow trout — fish of 10, 12 or 15 lb or more — amongst their more modestly sized stock fish. It is essential to have a net that will accommodate the biggest fish you may expect to catch, so, if you plan to fish one of these jumbo-trout waters, it would be as well to have a jumbo-sized one with you.

A question of timing

Being relatively small and shallow, small stillwaters react markedly more quickly to changes in the weather than large reservoirs do, and choosing the right time to go fishing is almost as important as choosing where to go, particularly in the summer. No matter how carefully and conscientiously the manager of a small stillwater stocks his lakes, and no matter how artificial such waters may be, the seasons and the British weather are always there, making the fishing easy at certain times of the day and year and difficult at others.

In March and April, the trout may be expected to be feeding throughout most of the day. But if the water is cold, or if there is a northerly or north-easterly wind, the fish will almost certainly be deep down, sluggish and difficult to tempt with an imitative fly.

May and early June are usually as wonderfully productive on small lakes as they are on the reservoirs. But, as June gives way to the dog days of high summer, the water will warm up and the trout will feed only in the early mornings and (possibly) the late evenings, with a long, dead period through the middle of the day and the afternoons. Those who would head for the water after lunch at this time, and who are determined to be home in time for dinner, should not sally forth with any inflated ideas as to the numbers of fish they expect to catch. The wisest course in the summer is to set out as early in the morning as possible, to be prepared to take a long break through the afternoon and then, perhaps, to fish again just for the last hour or so before dark.

The 'evening rise' is an event to be cherished on streams and rivers and on large reservoirs, but it must be said that it is as remarkable for its rarity on many small stillwaters — especially heavily fished ones — as it is for the excitement it can cause in fish and fishermen alike when it does occur. Why this should be, I am not sure. But I have seen far too many fly fishers disappointed far too often ever to be sanguine about the willingness of trout in small lakes to co-operate in their own downfall as darkness shrouds the water.

In September, the fishing should once again become consistently good throughout the day. And, as the water cools down in October, and the weed starts to die back, the fishing will become increasingly like that to be found in March and April.

Waters, clear and coloured

Small stillwaters can be divided into those in which the water is clear, enabling the careful and observant fly fisher to see his quarry, and those that are turbid. Obviously, the former tend to offer more interesting fishing than the latter.

Coloured water fishing

The tactics used where the water is coloured and the trout cannot be seen except when surface feeding differ very little from those used on larger reservoirs. Deep fishing techniques with quick-sinking, lead cored lines will rarely be appropriate (although a Booby Nymph may well save a blank in very hot or cold weather) and, as was implied earlier, the fishes' reactions to changes in the weather are likely to be quicker than on larger, deeper lakes. But, generally speaking, the keys to success will be found in the application of logic and reasoning, in a developable ability to work out where the trout are and what they are likely to be doing. And, as always, the most successful angler will be he who can tailor his tactics to the dictates of the day.

Clear-water fishing

Clear-water lakes provide the fly fisher with the opportunity to stalk and catch individual trout, perhaps larger than average ones, rather than simply to go on fishing the water.

The first thing that must be understood about stillwater stalking is that it requires patience, determination and self-discipline. The angler who dashes to the water's edge and simply starts flogging away will almost inevitably catch an average number of average fish. He may take a large one occasionally but, when he does so, it will almost invariably be by chance. Even when he has acquired the ability to spot trout deep in the water and to put his fly to them delicately and accurately, he will have to learn to resist the temptation to cast to every fish he sees.

As must by now be obvious, successful stalking depends upon the angler's ability to see fish. This is a skill that can be developed and which will improve greatly with practice. The starting point is to give our eyes as much help as possible. A pair of polaroid sunglasses, which will remove the glare from the water's surface, is essential, as is a baseball or golfing cap, or a really broad-brimmed hat, with which to shade one's eyes from the sun.

Thus equipped, we must now learn to look *into* the water, rather than *at it*, and to identify the tell-tale signs that give a trout away – movement is the most obvious one, but shadows on the lake bed, regular shapes amongst irregular surroundings and the white 'blink' of a mouth opening and shutting can all provide clues.

It is important to remember that if the water is clear enough to enable us to see the fish it will also be clear enough for them to see us. Whatever people may say about 'stupid, stew-reared rainbows', trout are shy creatures, and large ones tend to be even shyer than small ones. So, we must do whatever we can to avoid scaring the fish if we are to stand any chance of success. Stealth is vital, and we must learn to move very slowly, to blend with our backgrounds and to use every available scrap of cover.

Once we have located a fish we particularly want to catch, it will almost always pay to watch it carefully and to establish what it is doing, rather than simply to start casting to it straight away. Most trout in small stillwaters, especially large trout, tend to cruise on remarkably precise and predictable paths, fol-

Stillwater stalking; Brian Clarke casting to a large rainbow trout at Zeals Fishery in Wiltshire

lowing exactly the same routes time after time. A fish may complete such a circuit in a couple of minutes, or it may take much longer — perhaps as much as ten minutes or more. Once its route has been established, we can be reasonably confident that it will return to the same spot again and again, and we can therefore plan and lay an ambush for it.

If a bare patch can be found on the lake bed somewhere along the trout's path, this will be a great help. Once the fish has passed it — *not* while it is approaching it — a well leaded nymph should be cast so that it sinks onto the clear patch.

Now comes the requirement for patience. The fly must be left, static, until our quarry comes round again. As the fish eventually approaches — or, better still, as it is just passing it — the fly should be retrieved quite quickly, so that it starts upwards through the water, perhaps producing a little puff of silt from the bottom as it leaves it. Quite often, but by no

means always, the trout will grab at the fly instinctively. If it doesn't, you will just have to try again.

Obviously, if there is no bare patch on the lake bed, we cannot simply drop the fly into the weed and hope that it will come up cleanly without a mass of vegetation trailing from it. The answer in this case is to change our floating line for an intermediate or a slow sinker (either of which will cast far less of a shadow and therefore be less likely to frighten fish) and to seek to intercept our chosen quarry in mid-water. This requires considerable practice; we must be able to judge the depth at which the fish is swimming accurately, and we must know how fast our fly will sink. Then, as the trout approaches, we must cast to a point that will enable us to pull the fly quite quickly right past his nose. This will sometimes have exactly the same effect as the fly being lifted from the bottom had. Just as often, the trout will either take no notice at all, or it may follow it for a while and then turn away. Once again, persistence seasoned with occasional changes of fly is the only possible answer.

FINALLY

Wherever we are fishing, and for whatever sizes and species of trout, let us resolve to treat our quarry with the respect that is due to it.

Leaders must be strong enough to cater for the heaviest and liveliest fish we may expect to hook, and knots should be well tested before use; there is no merit at all in letting ourselves be broken, allowing a fish to swim away with a hook in its mouth and, perhaps, with a length of nylon trailing behind it.

If fish are to be returned to the water, we should use strong leaders and barbless hooks, so that they may be subdued quickly and released with as little stress and trauma as possible.

And, if fish are to be killed for the table, they must be despatched as quickly and humanely as possible. There is no possible excuse for causing them to suffer more than is absolutely necessary.

Further reading

Brian Clarke, *The Pursuit of Stillwater Trout* (A. & C. Black, 1975).

John Goddard, *Stillwater Flies, How and When to Fish Them* (Ernest Benn, 1982).

Peter Lapsley, *Trout from Stillwaters* (A. & C. Black, 1981).

Christopher S. Ogborne, *Blagdon* (Laurels Publishing, 1987).

Kenneth Robson, *Robson's Guide* (Beekay Publishers, 1985).

Ronald Broughton

Born in 1920, Ronald Broughton qualified in Manchester and has a large, single-handed practice in Salford. He is also an anaesthetist.

His early fishing with jam-jars in the ponds of the ancient village of Flixton developed into an abiding interest in the life of streams and stillwaters.

His first fishing with rod and line was for pike in Japan, when, as a Royal Air Force officer, he was surgeon to the Commonwealth Occupation Air Forces.

Dr Broughton is Chairman of the Lancashire Fly Fishers' Association; Chairman of the Ribble Fisheries Association, which represents all fishery interests within the Ribble watershed; and he was a founder member and first Chairman of the Grayling Society – a position he still holds. He serves on the Fishery Advisory Committee of the National Rivers Authority in the North West, is a committee member of the Lancashire branch of the Salmon and Trout Association, and is on the committee of the Lune and Wyre Association. He also represents the Ribble Fisheries' Association and the Grayling Society at the National Angler's Council AGM, and the Ribble and Lune on the Standing Committee of Consultatives.

Ron Broughton fishes mainly in the Yorkshire Dales, particularly on his beloved River Hodder. He contributes regularly to *The Flyfishers' Journal* and the journals of The Fly Dressers' Guild and the Grayling Society.

His book, *Grayling: The Fourth Game Fish*, has been widely acclaimed and, for the first time, shows this fish within the totality of its distribution throughout the northern hemisphere.

SALMON FLIES

tied by Irene Ross

1. Black Doctor   2. Dusty Miller   3. Green Highlander   4. Jock Scott
5. Mar Lodge   6. Silver Grey   7. Torrish   8. Thunder
9. Black and Orange Tube   10. Member   11. General Practitioner

SALMON FLIES

Flies tied by Peter Deane, tubes by Brenda Elphick

1. Munro Killer   2. Logie   3. Stoats Tail Silver and Red   4. Hairy Mary   5. Heather Moth
6. Gunna's Special   7. Sweep   8. March Brown   9. Blue Charm   10. Lady Caroline   11. Silver Doctor
12. Willie Gunn   13. Silver Stoat   14. Tadpole   15. Garry Dog   16. Black and Yellow
17. Red Black Eyed Prawn Fly   18. Collie Dog

SEA-TROUT FLIES

tied by Moc Morgan

1. Alexander   2. Black and Orange   3. Peter Ross   4. P.D.'s Invicta   5. Blackie (Sunk Lure)
6. P.D.'s Worm Fly   7. P.D.'s Soldier Palmer   8. Moc's Beauty   9. P.D.'s Wet Winged Greenwell
10. Teal Black and Silver   11. Muddler   12. Hairy Tom   13. Red Mackerel   14. Dai Ben
15. Teifi Terror   16. Bumble   17. Pryf Coch   18. Moc's Cert   19. Haslam
20. P.D.'s Black Pennell   21. P.D.'s Loch Ordie   22. P.D.'s Camasunary Killer

DRY FLIES

tied by Mike Weaver

1. B.W.O. (Day)   2. Dark Olive   3. Grey Duster   4. Pale Watery
5. Jassid   6. Rusty Spinner   7. Deer Hair Beetle
8. Hairwing Sedge   9. Yellow Humpy   10. Adams
11. Black Midge   12. Eric's Beetle   13. Black Gnat   14. Coch-y-bondhu
15. March Brown   16. Iron Blue   17. Olive Upright   18. B.W.O. (Evening)

DRY FLIES

tied by Peter Deane

1. G.R.H. Ear   2. Beacon Beige   3. Deane's Sherry Spinner   4. Blue Upright
5. Pheasant Tail   6. Dry Winged Ginger Quill   7. Kites Imperial
8. Mike Weaver's Spent May   9. M.W. Mayfly   10. Deerstalker
11. Lunn's Particular   12. Terry's Terror   13. Houghton Ruby
14. P.L.'s Hawthorn   15. P.L.'s Palmered Sedge   16. P.L.'s Daddy   17. P.L.'s Grannom
18. Grey Wulff   19. Hackled Greenwell   20. Caperer

IRISH LOUGH FLIES

tied by Peter Deane

1. Dunkeld   2. Connemara Black   3. Medicine   4. Cock Robin   5. Kingsmill
6. Leonard's Duck Fly   7. Orange Pupa   8. Ringrose Pupa
9. Golden Olive   10. O'Reilly's Grasshopper   11. Green Peter
12. Yellow Mayfly   13. Two Feather Mayfly   14. Shadow Mayfly
15. Dry Buzzer   16. Daddy   17. Fiery Brown Dry Fly
18. Sooty Olive   19. Murrough   20. Gosling   21. Fiery Brown
22. Bibio   23. Paisley   24. Golden Olive Bumble

STILLWATER NYMPHS AND LURES
tied by Peter Lapsley

1. Olive Midge Pupa   2. Black Midge Pupa   3. Claret Midge Pupa   4. Shrimp   5. Corixa
6. Montana   7. Stick Fly   8. Jersey Herd
9. Grey Goose Nymph   10. G.R.H. Ear Nymph   11. P.T. Nymph
12. See-thru Damsel Nymph   13. Dick Walker's Mayfly Nymph
14. White Marabou   15. Appetiser   16. Black Marabou
17. Whiskey Fly   18. Persuader   19. Sweeney Todd

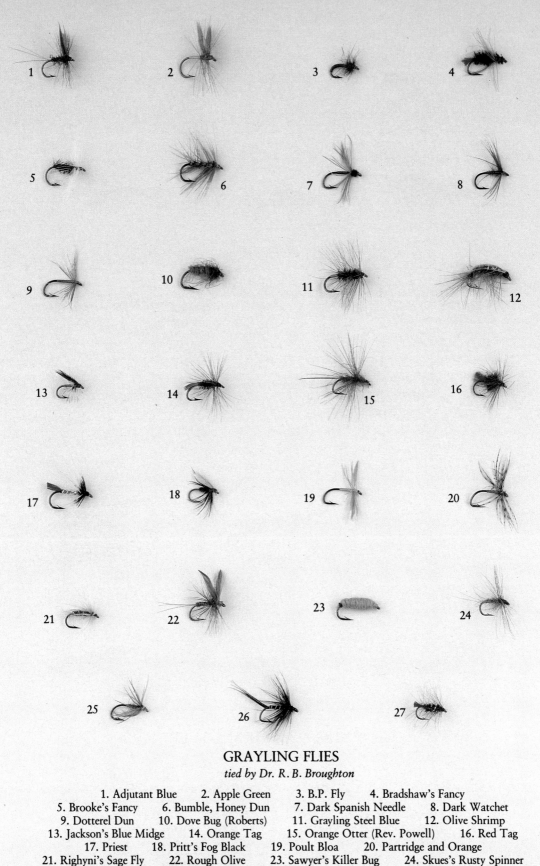

GRAYLING FLIES

tied by Dr. R. B. Broughton

1. Adjutant Blue   2. Apple Green   3. B.P. Fly   4. Bradshaw's Fancy
5. Brooke's Fancy   6. Bumble, Honey Dun   7. Dark Spanish Needle   8. Dark Watchet
9. Dotterel Dun   10. Dove Bug (Roberts)   11. Grayling Steel Blue   12. Olive Shrimp
13. Jackson's Blue Midge   14. Orange Tag   15. Orange Otter (Rev. Powell)   16. Red Tag
17. Priest   18. Pritt's Fog Black   19. Poult Bloa   20. Partridge and Orange
21. Righyni's Sage Fly   22. Rough Olive   23. Sawyer's Killer Bug   24. Skues's Rusty Spinner
25. Water Hen Bloa   26. Williams's Favourite   27. Grayling Witch

7

GRAYLING

Dr R. B. Broughton

This grey shadow, this bar of silver crested with orange flame, this jolly fish that will rise to fly long after trout have gone to spawn, this strong fish that tests the finest tackle that is needed to tempt it to the hook, this worthy quarry, this Ombre.

It is a fish of cold water and clear streams, far more intolerant of pollution than the rest of the Salmonid family. Its history is ancient, and its home is throughout the northern hemisphere from the Arctic Sea to as far south as the limestone rivers of Yugoslavia.

Its appearance is curious but elegant, when compared with its cousins, the trout and the salmon, the sea-trout and white fish of the Arctic. It is a large-scaled, greyish-silver fish, with darkened back, pointed eye, large dorsal fin and the family mark, the adipose fin. Its shape is smoother than the trout as the depth of the body at the anal fin is greater, and its head is smaller. The flanks exhibit black spots. These are but fleeting in the juveniles, but as it matures in its third year, the spots become permanent. Work, with careful observation and photographic record of tagged fish in Italy, suggests that the adult spots in their number and distribution above and below the lateral line, near and further from the head, are personal to individual fish, and also distinguish one population from another. Fish in the British Isles are often poorly marked and the spots are faint compared with other European and with Arctic grayling.

The fins are quite beautiful, the tail being markedly forked, and the pelvic fins having the most delicate markings between the cartilaginous rays. The adipose fin proclaims its family, being one of the Salmonidae, but it is the dorsal fin that is the most remarkable. It is a sexual attribute, being much larger and more flowing in the male. As the fish reaches maturity, the colouring of this fin becomes more pronounced. Sometimes it is a deep red, sometimes a flamboyant orange. There are rows of dark markings between the rays which branch out into two secondary rays along the margin of the fin. Sometimes the fin ends in a pointed shape, sometimes the trailing edge is rounded, and it appears to signify, in its different shapes, its relationship to different tribes of fish, as do the spots on the flank.

Figure 36 *The grayling*

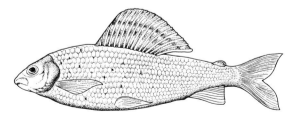

pear shaped pupil
maxilla anterior of eye
large dorsal fin – trailing and larger in the male
adipose fin
deeply forked tail
spots on body and between rays on dorsal fin

There remain two highly interesting attributes. One is the decidedly pear-shaped pupil with the iris cut-out on the forward side. Other fish such as trout, have this in a minor degree, but a more pronounced cut-out is to be found in the three-spined sticklebacks and in sea fish such as blennies and groupers that live on the bottom or under rocks. This shape is often backed by an increase in sight cells, suggesting a better binocular vision than with a normal pupil.

The lower jaw tends to be smaller than that of the trout, and the lower lip is slightly behind the upper, so that the mouth opens more in a downward direction than straight forward, and as the angle of the jaw finishes well forward of the eye, it gives the appearance of a much smaller mouth. Eye and mouth configuration may well explain the acute angle at which the grayling rises from the river bed to take surface or sub-surface food.

The grayling is distributed throughout the northern areas of the northern hemisphere in North America, Europe and Northern Asia. It first appears as fossil remains in Europe some 20 million years old, but after the last ice age wiped the rivers clean of their fish stocks, it spread through river connections now long gone. From the Danube to the Rhône and Rhine and on to the North Sea river that still exists, in its bends and swathes of pebble beaches in the drowned land between the British Isles and the Continent. Through ancient channels, its spread through the Thames and east coast rivers to the Severn, the Welsh Dee and possibly the Ribble, was assured.

Figure 37 *The rise of the grayling. The white gape is noticeable because of the more vertical rise than the trout*

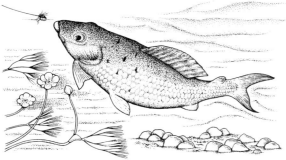

Whether the monks of the Middle Ages took to spreading the grayling's original habitat or not is probably irrelevant. It is a delightfully romantic notion and may possibly have some truth in it, but it is more likely that trout and grayling were already there by natural progression from Eastern Europe long before Norman monks found Yorkshire streams good to live by. That they, monk and grayling, inhabited the same countryside is due more to a mutual liking for the same waters than to pisciculture. What is not in doubt, is the Victorians' love of grayling and their successful seeding of waters virgin to this fish, whatever the recent generations of fishermen in southern streams may feel and have often said about grayling. It was the first Freshwater Fishery Act of 1878 that separated it from the rest of the Salmonidae in a manner that was not evident before, mainly, I believe, on the score that its spawning season was at the opposite end of the winter. These days we know that *Salmo Gairdneri*, the rainbow trout, spawns in the British Isles at much the same time as the grayling, but nobody that I know of has ever suggested that the rainbow should be classified as other than a game fish. Halford encouraged the grayling's presence in trout streams, protesting that by the end of September the best of the trout fishing was over, and the danger of taking female trout in spawn was so great that, after August, the only worthy quarry for a fisherman was the grayling.

The first recorded introduction of this fish into new waters was in 1816 into the Test, and, within a couple of years, into the Itchen as well. The Clyde followed in 1855 and then the Nith. The Tweed took its first grayling through an overflow of an enclosed water producing an accidental discharge of fish into the main river in 1880. So delightful did the Scots find them, that south of the Border, the Eden, as the Ribble with its newly-introduced barbel in more recent times, was subjected to a clandestine stocking via the churchyard at Musgrove. The Thames has been restocked on several occasions, both in the 1860s and more recently. The original population was probably as old as the colonization of the east coast rivers from the North Sea river some ten thousand years ago. The recent introduction into the chalk and limestone rivers to the west have been successful, but those to the east less so. The Darent has been the best of these. The Lea valley survivors, so it is reported, inhabited for a time the tidal reaches of the Thames. This, though a pale reflection of the grayling of the northern Arctic coasts of Russia, which migrate to and from the estuaries as the sea-trout do, speaks well of an attempt to clean a river from the Augean-like pollution of previous years.

The great coarse fishing rivers of the Anglian Water Authority have had until recently but a frail hold on any grayling introduced into them. Recent stocking has met with success, with populations breeding well in some six rivers.

There are now successful attempts at the artificial rearing of grayling. These have been introduced by the Fishery Departments of Water Authorities such as Yorkshire and Anglia, because of the fear of importing disease in fish from other areas. For this reason alone, the surplus and often unwanted stocks in the chalk streams have not been used to supplement rivers in other areas. Furthermore,

now that there is a greater knowledge of the many genetic strains in any one species of fish, each particular to its own river system, there is a greater caution shown to the introduction of grayling from other rivers. Anglers have long known that grayling vary in appearance from area to area. The shape of the mouth, the general configuration, the flank spots, whether the dorsal fin ends in a long sweep or is markedly lobule in shape, the colour in its shades of blue or of red, darkness and lightness, all these we have known as variables subject to whatever river system the fish lives in. Now we know scientifically that it is so.

It is possible that the failure to thrive of any introduced stock may be due as much to the genetic incompatibility of the fish with its new surroundings as to any fault in the environment.

What is amazing is how widespread they are. The late Reg Righyni, the moving spirit in the formation of the Grayling Society in 1977, fished and took grayling from 142 rivers within

The late Reg Righyni on the Anton, a tributary of the Test

the British Isles, and there are undoubtedly more. The most northern is the Tay and its tributaries, and the most southerly and westerly the Tamar. In between there are grayling rivers in Wales and the Borders, southern Britain, Norfolk, Lincolnshire, Derbyshire and the Yorkshire Dales, Lancashire, Vale of Eden, Northumberland and Durham and the lowlands of Scotland.

We know that an enclosed water is no bar to survival, and also that rivers that once had a thriving population hold them no more, so why do they exist contentedly in one situation and not in another? Perhaps it is easiest to define the conditions under which they do flourish.

What appears to be most necessary is clean cool water of moderate flow. Lack of pollution is crucial, grayling being more sensitive to this than any of the other Salmonids. Moderate average summer temperatures of less than 18°C with a maximum 24°C are necessary for their survival and spawning. Hence they do better at a higher elevation the further south they are. It is a myth that grayling like slow, chubb holding water. A river of 20 metres width with a gradient of 2−6 metres per kilometre gives a good steady flow and allows the collection of a mixture of gravel and loam to form its bed, allowing a good growth of weed and insects.

The size of a river is also a factor, larger ones producing bigger faster growing fish which live longer; and alkalinity with a high calcium level helps better crustacean production.

The tendency to form a shoal, a coalescence of family groups of grayling, has long been noted. It happens in rivers and stillwaters. It does not necessarily need deep water or the sharp cold of winter. Shoaling in chalk streams can take place in quite shallow water, especially where it is open and free of weeds, but let the sun go off the water or the chill of winter enter into the valleys and the fish make for deeper water. The hatch pools hold the biggest, oldest fish, riding out the swirling depths, but the little pots on the lee of a carrier, or off a fallen tree, or the tail of an island, or where the weed has been cleared by swans will hold whole families of grayling.

In the deeper waters of the wide spate rivers, shoaling is not so easily seen unless feeding is visible at or just under the surface. This sudden feeding activity of a whole flock of fish all at the one time is an interesting phenomenon and is probably due to several factors. A change of temperature, a prolonged shaft of sunlight, the last rays before the sun dips below the hills, all seem to be potent forces of feeding energy. The water may have been quiet all day with but small fish showing, but wait until the last of the day's sunlight is about to leave the water and all of a sudden there are groups of rings on the surface as a shoal of grayling starts to feed. However desperate the day has been, even if the water is beginning to rise and is becoming coloured, even if one is fishing for no better reason than that one has travelled far and is by the river with rod tackled up, there is no point in going home before those magic moments that come even in the depth of winter round about an hour or so before the sun sets. Even if the sky is entirely clouded over, there still comes a change in the light, and it is that that produces activity and feeding in the fish towards the end of the day. Earlier the opposite is true. Of a day, in the couple of months either side of Christmas, and any time after eleven o'clock in the morning, a sudden clearing of the sky, or a prolonged shaft of sunlight warming a patch of water, and the fish start to feed. This is true even if they are feeding at the bottom of a deep pool, and it is the man trotting a worm or fishing a deep and probably weighted fly that will be most likely to find out when the activity really starts. The fish may become active without ever disturbing the surface, especially if the wind is keen and the air immediately above the water cold, and he who is looking for feeding fish in the area immediately below the surface may never *see* it happen at all. The spate rivers are easier to fish deep down without lead on the fly than the chalk streams. The latter, because of the clarity of the water and the keen sight of the grayling, have less space upstream of the fish to sink a fly to a suitable depth, so that increasing the weight of the fly is necessary. The hatch pools give more scope for the spate river techniques

Cyril Beardsworth grayling fishing on the lower reaches of the River Hodder

of sinking the fly. It is the frequent heading of a pool in a spate river with obstructive rocks, and a quick drop in levels, that produces the underwater currents that sweep backwards and down and that can take a 'slow-sink' line to the very depths in a short space of time. Where this is most marked, the fish can sometimes be seen lying with their heads pointing downstream. It is not that they have gone mad and are trying to suffocate themselves, but that they have found a current flowing upstream well below the surface. It behoves the dry fly man to study the knowledge and tactics of his coarse fishing brother if he is to appreciate the actual flows and their action on the fish.

There is a curious phenomenon that anyone who fishes for grayling soon comes to experience, and that is that in any one day's fishing, all fish are usually of one sex. Sometimes they all have the long sweeping dorsal fin of the male; sometimes they are all females with their shorter prettier heads and dorsal fins less tall and less long in the trailing edge. Why this should be nobody has yet been able to tell me, but it is so.

The grayling's stillwater habitat is the one that surprises fishermen most. It has frequented Lake Bala, or Llyn Tegid in the vernacular, in North Wales from time immemorial. If you wish to fish there through the courtesy of the Bala Fishing Association you will learn from them that you will find the fish more often congregated around the mouths of the small rivers that fill this great lake. As in Gouthwaite in North Yorkshire, they require the presence of good streams with gravel beds for their spawning, in order to continue their success as a self-reproducing species of stillwaters.

Here in Tegid the grayling frequent the relatively shallow areas of the margins of the lake, particularly in the northern and southern extremities of the water. There they find the bed of pebble and loam to their liking and the supply of aquatic food is plentiful. There is a tendency to migrate into the upper reaches of the Dee and up the smaller side rivers in summer and to return to the lake margins in the autumn. Rarely do they ever frequent the depths.

Gouthwaite on the other hand is the result of damming the river Nidd above Pateley Bridge on the eastern side of the Pennines; and by good fortune contains the original river grayling within its confined waters. The lucky thing is that there are good spawning streams, as well as the upper reaches of the main river; and much to the detriment of the trout fishing in these streams, the grayling enter into them in great numbers to spawn in the late spring.

Both these lakes show an effect very much like that produced by rainbow trout in large

A fine fish. Brian Clarke with a 17 inch, 2 lb 14 oz grayling from the River Test

enclosed waters, a tendency to form a slowly travelling shoal, following the shallower contours of the lake and feeding as they go. Taking large quantities of chironomids, they require flies of a dark colour and of small size, cast by an angler who knows how to keep himself invisible to the fish and who is capable of handling one of a pound's weight on the finest nylon he has the courage to use.

It is the rate of growth of grayling that makes it surprising that so little has been made of their capabilities in enclosed waters. As they tend to grow as fast as rainbow trout in their first three years, and will live three times as long, if allowed to do so, growing steadily if more slowly as age increases, it is indeed curious that they have been so neglected. They will take fly, both natural and artificial, long after brown and rainbow trout have ceased to do so, and so they prolong the fly fishing season by several months, without recourse to the feathured lure.

The Loudsmill Fishery near the River Frome below Dorchester, where grayling taken from the river were placed among resident coarse fish, has made its mark by producing monsters. Fed by an inlet from the River Frome, this small fishery of 3 acres set in chalk has produced fish of over 3 lb, one being the 1988 record grayling. Because here the grayling has been treated as a coarse fish and returned to the water after capture, the possibility of a monster specimen was always there. The present record is held by a fish of 4 lb 3 oz, also taken from the River Frome. But it is probably more as a wild fish than as a specimen fish that grayling prove most attractive, and it is interesting that large, outsize grayling tend to be caught by bait or weighted lure rather than by traditional artificial flies.

If in a river you are catching brown trout in water that holds both kinds of fish, then usually you should fish lower down the pool to find the grayling, the trout being either nearer to or in the fast water in the neck of the pool or right down on the lip before the water breaks, where often the small trout are.

The sea-trout angler in such rivers as the Earn, the Ribble or the Hodder and the Welsh

Dr Ron Broughton into a good grayling on the River Hodder

Dee, will have noticed another phenomenon, and one not necessarily to his liking. In the late summer months the large grayling inhabit the same water as the nocturnal feeding sea-trout and are bold takers of large flies in the darkness. Indeed, throughout the season, grayling and sea-trout cohabit quite easily in the same flows of water. It is this good even flow with a bit of depth to it that grayling love. Where trees line the bank on the deep side of a river, they tend to leave that to the trout, both brown and sea. Often too the salmon, spawning in the autumn, keep to the most shaded depths. Here the grayling prefer the more open waters toward the shallower side of the stream.

There is a delightful stretch on the upper Hodder where this is very evident. I have sat on the bank of a late summer's evening, watching the stream as it flows down below close-growing trees on the other bank, waiting for the evening rise. It is a slow quiet process, waiting for the rise of a fish to a spinner, changing as the evening advances from Red Spinner to Rusty Spinner and then to Orange Quill, and later, after the river has settled and the light begins to fade, to an Olive Sedge, and last of all, in darkness, to a black bumble-like dry fly or a Mallard and Claret under the surface.

On the near side of the stream it will be grayling sipping down spinners; within the stream and on its further side the brown trout will be active. In among the jumble of rocks at the foot of the trees the sea-trout will on occasion rise fiercely to the dry fly. On a good evening, with a suitable light and a magnificent hatch of fly, I have taken my fill of all three fish before the light has failed and the evening rise has died away.

This of course, like all fishing logic, has its exceptions. During summer or prolonged fine weather in the autumn, you will no doubt find large grayling apparently working and feeding in the fast streams at the head of the pool. If you watch carefully and can observe through the clear water without disturbing the fish, you will see that the grayling is not in the fast water, but just alongside it. All fish conserve their energy whilst feeding. Trout tend to ride the water, having their food more or less delivered to their mouths with the minimum of change in their position. Grayling however rest closer to the bottom and have to rise faster and more vertically to the passing morsel of encapsulated fat. It is a matter of swings and roundabouts as to how the fish conserves its energy. Grayling do bottom-feed to a greater extent than the trout. When trout grow over a certain size, which in a good limestone river will be about a foot long, they become cannibal to some degree, but I have never found fish remains in grayling. Often enough the stomach contains small bits of stone, which have been ingested either accidentally in their search for river bottom organisms or from the breakdown of caddis cases. It may be that they take in enough protein from caddis and shrimp that they do not need to eat small fish.

The rooting about in the bottom of the stream in order to disturb and fetch out shrimp from beneath small stones on the river-bed witnessed, photographed and described by Roy Shaw in the magazine *Trout and Salmon* is good reason for the success of the Sawyer Grayling Bug in chalk streams, and of the darker-coloured shrimp look-alikes in limestone rivers. Sometimes other animals disturb the bottom for them, and when this happens regularly they are quick to learn how to feast with very little effort.

The day following a Grayling Society annual general meeting, when it is usual for the local anglers to arrange fishing for all those attending, found me fishing the River Onney above Ludlow. It was the first week of a frosty

November with high pale blue skies, and I approached this, to me new, small river with great respect. The beck, for such it is at this point, takes a slow bend under trees in a length of about 100 yards. There were brown and rainbow trout to be caught on fly in the first 30 yards. Under the trees in the deeps on the far side of the pool below all this activity were two very red salmon keeping company. Small sipping rises towards the shallow side of the river, before the bed of the river rose to meet the convex curve of the meadow, betrayed the presence of grayling. After this the river suddenly flattened itself out, losing the opposite high bank in a wide shallow ford some 1 foot 6 inches in depth. The lip was occupied by voraciously feeding small brown trout and salmon parr, but it was the broad shallowing expanse of the ford above it that held the better part of the grayling.

As I arrived and stood looking and trying to take stock of the complex patterns of the little river, the cows came down a short steep hill from the milking parlour, and slowly and with many a pause as they took their fill of water, they crossed the ford into the meadow. The disturbance was considerable, and my original thought was that it would be a complete waste of time to bother about this lower quarter of the stretch. How wrong I was! While the cows slowly wended their way to the pastures, trying to keep beyond their sphere of interest, fishing up just under the surface, and keeping out of sight, I concentrated on the stream on the opposite side from the trees. There was nothing very large on the surface, the occasional pale watery, and presumably a large number of reed smut or small midge pupae. Apart from the occasional jolly rainbow and the rarer brown trout, I was wasting my time.

It was then that I bothered to look at the ford. Its surface was dimpled with rises. I put on a size 18 Blue Midge and started to fish with more applied technique than with hope. In the end I took half a dozen grayling of various sizes, the biggest being about a foot long, and carefully returned them to the water. It had now become obvious what was happening. Unlike the chalk stream fish, which have to turn the gravel over for themselves in order to find the shrimp they want, these grayling had it done for them, and they had learnt that there was abundant small fly to be had after the cattle had disturbed the bed of the river.

The problems of capturing grayling are not those that confine one to dry fly or to wet fly, but are concerned with what level they are feeding at at any particular time, and on what they are feeding. They are the most particular feeders, and I have found myself changing from surface to sub-surface and deeper levels, not once but several times in a day's fishing, as necessity dictated.

There is one thing it is vital to note in

changing from trout to grayling fishing. The grayling lies at a greater depth, and thus not only rises to the fly with a more vertical movement, but also has a wider window of vision than the trout. It is also possible that the forward extension of the pupil and its backing of extra retinal cells increase its acuity of vision. It is much more likely to refuse at the last moment than the trout, and is quicker to eject a distasteful object. Even when the whole action is visible it is far easier to miss on the strike. But, having missed, it is a mistake to leave the fish for another time. Two or three casts more and the take may be firm and the outcome more satisfactory, provided that all care has been taken not to disturb the water or expose oneself to the fish's view.

Drag must be attended to, for the grayling does not like abnormal movements in its prey.

Derek Bradley grayling fishing on the River Wye, Chatsworth Estate, Derbyshire

I have found that the induced take can be used but once on any particular fish.

There is a form of terminal induced take that is possible with both wet fly and bait fishing. In water of 1½–2 foot in depth the fly may well slow to a point where it is hovering just above the bed of the river. It sometimes happens that a fish has been following, and if the beginning of the lift of the line for the next cast is confined to but a slight movement of the wrist the grayling may suddenly make up its mind to take firmly. A similar effect is produced with bait below a float, when at the end of a 'trot' the line is stopped preparatory to winding in. The gentle lift of the bait thus induced is often enough to provoke a firm take by a following fish.

Having set the hook, the next difficulty is what to expect of the fish and how to play it into the waiting net. In this country at least the grayling does not leap on being confined by the pull of the line. Indeed they often do the opposite. They will run on first feeling the pressure of the rod but not as far or as fast as the trout, nor do they often leave the pool. On the few occasions that I have found them to do this, it was more as a result of the fish using its weight rather than its speed. Usually, on feeling the fast water at the lip of the pool, they fight their way back into its depths, there to anchor themselves with raised dorsal fin against the pull of the line or the current. Salmon can stick on the bottom in the same way, especially when very large, as can sea-trout, but grayling can remain immovable for what seems an eternity. I have never slid a garland of tobacco down the line, as I have read as good advice when dealing with recalcitrant salmon, but sometimes I have been tempted. The tactic of a loose line, as for a weeded trout, sometimes works, but the pull of the water on the drowned line is often enough to remind them that safety is in stillness. Walking upstream to exert pressure from a different angle may work, but it may pull out the hook. Usually the only thing to do is to stand with the point of the rod raised and to keep a steady pressure until a tremor along the line tells you that the fish is beginning to tire. As soon as that happens it is time to change the direction of the pull a little; just changing the position of the rod tip is often enough to unbalance the fish. This sort of contest can go on so long that the angler becomes convinced that it is a rock or half-buried branch that he is attached to. A savage pull is the worst thing one can do, even when the fish gives an indication at last that it is about to move. Patience, a belief in one's knowledge of what has gone before and a steady pressure are what are needed.

In winter, bait fishing comes into its own. It is used for deep-lying fish that are not feeding in the upper layers of the river. It should not be thought of as a gross matter of vast lugworms on large hooks, anchored on the river-bed with heavy weights. If delicacy is needed for the best of fly fishing, then so it is with bait fishing. The rods are long and responsive, the line is 3 lb and the terminal tackle no more than 2 lb. The worm is a small 2 inch long gilt-tail, caught through the head by a size 16 hook. The float is a slim balsa cylinder and the weight no more than is required to cock it. Fish are invariably lip-hooked with this tackle which can trot a bait at any desired depth to a hundred yards downstream of the angler.

Those experienced in these techniques can also pole fish with rods of incredible lengths. There is no reel and the line is encompassed within the rod. The float will be fishing some 35 feet from the angler, the line clear of the water and the bait being presented directly over the shoal.

But whether trotting or fly fishing, the mark of the winter fisherman is his ability to suck the ice from the top ring of his rod when the winds bite, the snow crunches underfoot and the ice cracks around the edges of the pool. I have caught fish on fly in the Dales in these conditions, using size 18 pupae and Blue Midge, though often enough deep-lying flies are required. The first leaded flies to be described were Rolt's Witches. In order to reach the fish lying in the deep runs and pools, this sort of fly was probably always used, and the practice has continued to the present day, with artificials such as Roberts's and Sawyer's Grayling Bugs and copper wire weighted nymphs.

Flies for grayling fall into two groups, the Imitative and the Fancy. The former are all those that represent nymph, imago or spinner that one usually uses for trout, together with representations of those that will be in season throughout the autumn, winter and early spring. The Fancy group contains several flies that represent whole groups of naturals, such as Greenwell's Glory and the Apple Green, as well as artificials that have no recognizable natural equivalents. It is these last that cause most confusion. It is well to remember that the famous Red Tag was created to catch trout in low water summer conditions and was originally known as the Worcester Gem, and that all Fancies are equally successful with trout as with grayling. What it is necessary to know is that they must be very small when used on the surface, from size 16 right down to 20. Those used as a wet fly can be much larger. Size 14 is a common size, and size 12 is often used in the Bumbles, Witches, Shrimp and Grayling Bugs. It is possible that these dark-bodied flies, when used for dry fly fishing, are taken for smut or midge that have escaped the pull of the surface film, and these small sizes can well be used as wet flies for the sub-surface imitation of these naturals.

All the Fancies have ostrich or peacock herl somewhere in their construction, and some have what Carter Platts called 'flame tails'. Of all the Fancies, the most ancient and the most useful are the palmered flies, the modern variants being the Witches and the Derbyshire Bumbles. Cotton's Black Palmers have always been extraordinarily useful and still are so today. They are used dry or wet, and like shrimp imitations lend themselves to leaded bodies, as they can absorb the extra bulk.

The grayling is not averse to taking the dry fly; indeed he can give great pleasure when truly on the take for imago or spinner. As the season advances and the autumn chill descends on river and field, probably the most useful dry fly is the Ginger Quill. It intrigues me that a hackle of ginger seems an absolute necessity in a representation of the pale watery in the autumn. The Apple Green, that can also pass for a small olive, has a ginger hackle, as has the

Whirling Blue Dun, and the Greenwell's Glory has a feather that varies from pale ginger to deep red according to what sort of olive is being imitated. Grayling fishing leads the angler into realms of fly imitation that the trout angler does not know, for from October to March there are insects present that do not enter the list for anglers in the fairer months.

The large dark olive is one of these, and is seen by those whose quarry is salmon or grayling in the early spring before the first hatch of trout anglers appears. Then there is the dark midge of the limestone rivers that forms a large bulk of the winter grayling's insectivorous food. This winter midge is not confined solely to limestone rivers, but seems to be more abundant there than on waters that flow over free stone acidic rocks. Its immature form is a pupa that often gets trapped under the surface film and the grayling take great delight in sipping it down, forming quiet little rings, and ignoring the large quantity of imago on the surface. It is this pupa, of an olive brownish colour, that I attempted many years ago to imitate with a variation on the buzzer patterns of the still waters, to my own mind, most successfully.

Smutting trout have always been a problem to the angler, but grayling throughout the season smut more, and the fisherman who would take one or two must bend his mind to the difficulty. Those great anglers of the last century, Pritt, Jackson, Theakston and Ronalds, used much ingenuity in finding and creating artificials to try to overcome this problem, and have left us several good weapons to hand. The terms midge and gnat as used by them may not have any scientific meaning, but there is no doubt what they intended, and their imitations are several and ingenious. John Jackson has seven separate dressings, including the Blue Midge. Pritt can add the simplest Black Gnat of all − but a few twists of ostrich herl caught with black silk on an otherwise bare hook − and the famous Fog Black. Ronalds has his own variations and adds a Golden Dun Midge. The odd thing is that the Black Gnat is neither black nor necessarily a gnat, which may explain why purple silk dubbed with grey-blue fur or herl is so often effective when the reed smuts are up and the dark midge pupae are trapped under the surface film. My own stand-bys are Jackson's Blue Midge, Pritt's Fog Black and my own BP Fly.

Beyond these diminutive flies are the autumn forms of the early season flies, the Whirling Blue Dun, the Little Pale Blue and the Cinnamon Fly, and of course the true winter flies such as the Willow Fly and the February Red. Ask any angler what are his favourite grayling flies and his reply will depend to some degree on where he fishes. Generally the mild darkness of purple silk and the attractive qualities of peacock herl will be present. Rough streams tend to cock hackles in the wet fly for 'kick' and liveliness. Northern rivers will have a preponderance of spider-type flies, slim short bodies with soft mobile hackle, that were used as nymphs long before Skues's arguments with Halford. Indeed his original experiments were with northern flies and led to his sparsely hackled nymphs for the chalk streams. The Welsh and Border rivers have what I am told are white flies, where the dark body is offset by a pale hackle and which can be used either as a floater or allowed to sink under the surface of the water.

I have made, with much effort and the use of great discipline a reduced list of thirty flies that I know to be appreciated by grayling, and I have grouped them according to the naturals that they appear to imitate. I know of at least 130 more, and I have not the slightest doubt that that number could be doubled, especially if one takes the trouble to see what fishermen outside this country use to catch their grayling!

Part of the pleasure of fishing for this wild fish is to become aware, season by season, of what may attract it, and to try and find the reason for its choice. I have concluded with my irreducible dozen — from at least the time of Walbran it seems to be the magic number. What I am absolutely certain about is that it will promote a long and erudite argument as to what flies should really be put into such a list.

General list of thirty flies

Iron Blue	Snipe and Purple	
	Dark Watchet	
	Adjutant Blue	
Olives	Rough Olive	Water Hen Bloa
	Greenwell's Glory	Gold-Ribbed Hare's Ear
	Apple Green	Grey Duster
Pale Wateries	Dotterel Dun	
	Poult Bloa	
	Ginger Quill	
Spinners	Skues's Rusty Spinner	
	Righyni's Sage Fly	
Gnats and Midges	BP Fly	
	Jackson's Blue Midge	
	Pritt's Fog Black	
Perlidae, Needle and Willow Flies	Partridge and Orange	
	Dark Spanish Needle	
Shrimp	Olive Shrimp	
	Robert's Dove Bug	
	Sawyer's Grayling Bug	
Fancy	Grayling Steel Blue	Brookes's Fancy
	Bumble Honey Dun	Bradshaw's Fancy
	Grayling Witch	Priest
	Red Tag	Orange Tag
	Orange Otter	

The irreducible dozen

Wet		
	Water Hen Bloa	Poult Bloa
	Snipe and Purple	Blue Midge
	Grayling Steel Blue	Partridge and Orange
Dry	Brookes's Fancy	Red Tag
	Ginger Quill	Grey Duster
	Apple Green	Skues's Rusty Spinner

Further reading

Ronald Broughton, *Grayling; The Fourth Game Fish* (Crowood Press, 1989).

John Jackson, *The Practical Fly-Fisher, particularly for Grayling or Umber* (John Slack, 1853).

W. Carter Platts, *Grayling Fishing* (A. & C. Black, 1939).

T.E. Pritt, *North Country Flies* (Sampson Low, Marston, Searle & Rivington, 1886).

R.V. Righyni, *Grayling* (Macdonald, 1968).

John Roberts, *The Grayling Angler* (H.F. & G. Witherby, 1982).

Charles Jardine

Charles Jardine was born in Canterbury in 1953 and came to fly fishing early, through the enthusiasm of his father, the late wildlife artist, Alex Jardine. Having contested the issue with a perch three years previously, he caught his first trout on a fly at the age of six.

Fishing of all sorts played a large part in Charles's life during his formative years, primarily in Kent and particularly on the Little Stour, where he 'pottered about, weed cutting and generally undoing father's hard stream maintenance work'. All this produced in him a deep love of trout and of the environment in which they live.

Later, Charles continued to fish whilst at art college at Thanet, Canterbury and Medway, where he discovered his other passion – painting the creatures he was fishing for.

It was an invitation to join Dermot Wilson at Nether Wallop Mill in Hampshire that pitched Charles headlong into fulltime fishing. Here, with Jim Hadrell, he gave fly casting tuition and guided anglers on the Test and Itchen for four years, obtaining the Association of Professional Game Angling Instructors' qualification in 1979.

On the company's demise in 1982, Charles returned to Kent, took up a position teaching art to handicapped children and started fishing for pleasure again.

He began to write articles for *Trout Fisherman* magazine (which he continues to do), for *Trout and Salmon* and for *Gamefisher*, and he became angling correspondent for *The Daily Telegraph* for a period. He has illustrated many books on angling and, with Bob Church, was coauthor of *Stillwater Trout Tactics*. As a painter, he has exhibited in a number of exhibitions in England and abroad, and he is a member of the prestigious Society of Wildlife Artists, his main subjects being fish in all their forms.

Throughout the summer months, Charles, who has added the NAC qualification to his APGAI one, is to be found demonstrating fly casting techniques at numerous game fairs and country shows. His long-suffering wife Carole and children Annabelle and Alexander have capitulated to his obsessions for angling and painting with stoicism and forbearance. As he says, it's a good job he doesn't play golf as well!

8

CASTING A FLY

Charles Jardine

I am constantly surprised by the diversity of casting styles I see as I walk the banks of our rivers and reservoirs or bob across the waves. People will tell you that there is no right or wrong way to cast a fly. They may be right, but what I am sure of is that there are efficient and inefficient ways.

Where casting is concerned, 'efficiency' may be defined as achieving distance and accuracy without undue effort. My aim in this chapter is to explain how such efficiency may be attained and then to add to the basic principles some wrinkles and ruses to enable the reader to cope in tricky circumstances or conditions. Before I do this, I think it important to make a few points about tackle.

ROD ACTIONS

Although the other contributors to this book have discussed the fly rods and fly lines best suited to their particular styles of fishing, a rod's action and the way in which it is balanced by its reel and line have a considerable influence on the way in which it performs as a casting tool.

Essentially, there are three types of rod action: tip or fast, producing a tight line loop which facilitates distance casting; middle to butt, with what used to be called a 'wet fly action' – slow and producing a wide loop, this action can be useful for 'short lining' from a boat on reservoirs and lochs; and 'compound', 'progressive' or 'parabolic', which has a middle to tip action.

Personally, I find a middle to tip action most pleasant both to cast and to fish with. It is very biddable and therefore copes easily with an overhead cast, a roll cast, a double haul or a Spey cast. The real advantage it offers is control; you can actually feel the rod's performance through the handle, which, in turn, allows line loops and speeds to be tailored to the needs of the moment – to cast a tight, downward loop to pierce a headwind, for example, or to create a rolling loop for the presentation of a team of flies on a high density, ultra-fast sinking line.

Whatever a rod's action, we must never forget that its performance simply reflects our casting style and prowess. While there are certainly good and bad rods, bad casting is caused chiefly by the caster giving the rod inefficient or erroneous messages. Conversely, the competent caster can perform well with almost any rod, even with a broomstick or a garden cane!

REELS AND BALANCE

Master that he was, I believe the late Richard Walker did angling one disservice. He advocated the use of small, light-weight reels to harmonize with the ultra-light carbon fibre rods that came into use during the 1970s. In truth, a lightweight rod actually feels lighter if it is matched with a reel of significant weight. Indeed, it can almost give the impression that the rod butt and the reel seat are 'kicking up' into the forearm during casting, which is to be welcomed, especially when a rod of 10 feet or more is to be used single-handed. In my opinion, the new carbon fibre and magnesium-based reels offer no advantages over their heavier and more traditionally built counterparts.

It is also important that a reel should be large enough to accommodate both the fly line and a reasonable amount of backing. This is less vital for fishing on rivers, where trout rarely head for the setting sun, but it matters a great deal on large lakes and reservoirs where 100 or even 150 yards of backing can boost one's confidence enormously.

In any event, a reel should have a minimum of 40 yards of backing on it because this can actually help casting, especially if the spool has a wide and/or deep drum. The 'memory coils' caused by a line being wound on to too small a spool defeat distance and destroy accuracy.

FLY LINES

There is now a baffling array of fly lines on the market at an extraordinary range of prices. The one thing that is certain is that poor quality and 'mill end' lines ruin both rod rings and casting style, and should be avoided at all costs. With fly lines particularly, 'you get what you pay for'. Always buy the best you can afford; you will be repaid a thousand times over by clean, effortless shooting and handling qualities.

Similarly, fly lines do not last for ever, although careful, regular washing in soapy water can help. A worn, cracked or otherwise damaged fly line makes good casting impossible; discard it. If you do not, it will only frustrate you.

The types and sizes of the lines you buy will depend upon the kind of fishing you plan to do, but tapers do play a major role in the development of good casting technique. The tapers available are as follows.

Level

Mercifully, as far as I am aware, nobody uses level lines any more. They have no contribution whatever to make to good casting technique.

Double tapered

People will tell you that the benefit of a double tapered line is that its life can be extended by turning it around on the reel once one end has become worn and cracked. Sadly, this is misleading. The chances are that if the line is worn it will be the belly section that is damaged and that reversing the line will do little or nothing to remove the problems thus caused.

However, there can be few better lines with which to learn one's trade, the ability to load a rod with sufficient power with various lengths of line extended being a considerable advantage. The elongated belly section enables a double tapered line to be extended well beyond the critical first 30 feet, which makes both long casting and delicate presentation possible and allows the competent caster to lift as much as three-quarters of the line off the water for re-delivery at another angle − the weight and taper nullifying the line sag that can occur with weight-forward lines and shooting heads.

Because so much of a double tapered line can be aerialized, it is advisable to use a line size *lower* than that designated for the rod if long casting is likely to be a frequent objective.

Weight-forward

Nowadays, weight-forward lines are popular with stillwater fly fishers, primarily because of their excellent shooting and handling properties. Indeed, growing numbers of stream fishers now choose weight-forward lines. And there seems little point in having a sinking line in any other format unless one is salmon fishing.

However, many people ask too much of weight-forward lines. You simply cannot aerialize as much of a weight-forward as you can of a double taper. This is because the belly of a weight-forward is all in the front 30 feet of the line, the back 60 feet being fine, level running line. If you false cast with the belly beyond the tip ring, a hinging effect will occur on both back and forward casts, reducing power and shooting ability and destroying the fly line's coating quite quickly. Maximum efficiency with weight-forward lines is achieved by casting with the back end of the belly just within the tip ring.

Shooting heads

The same considerations apply to shooting heads. Those bought from tackle shops are generally 30 feet long. I cut mine from double tapered lines, to lengths of between 33 and 40 feet, which offers me greater power and the opportunity to aerialize more line.

Where shooting heads are concerned, the choice of running lines is important, some materials being better suited to certain tactics than others. Monofilament is still popular with lure anglers. Braided monofilament reduces shooting distances and sinking rates but offers a pleasantly tangle-free system for figure-of-eight retrieves and for lure fishing. The relatively new braided monofilament and terylene mixes can be a little harsh on rod rings but shoot and handle well.

Incidentally, it is as well to be aware that fine running lines can inflict quite nasty cuts, especially on hard, fast takes from trout. A bandage of some sort around the index finger of the rod hand can help prevent them.

Before closing on fly lines, I should add that there is much work yet to be done on the development of tapers. One recent innovation, the Wulff Triangle taper, has an extended belly, a long back taper and an ultra-thin running line. It has proved excellent for long lining from reservoir banks. New materials for fly lines are coming into use, too, solid monofilament (Monocore) being just one of them. There must be much more to come.

LINE JOINS AND STRETCHING

The last aspects of our tackle that will affect its casting capabilities are line joins and memory coils.

Joining a fly line to braided monofilament is easy. Simply insert the fly lines into the braid for about 2 inches and secure the join with superglue. Where braided terylene is to be attached to a fly line, I would use a nail knot coated with Gudbrod 'Speed Coat', which provides a smooth and very strong join.

For shooting heads, I strip a couple of inches of the coating from the core at the heavy end of the line and whip the core into a small loop. This makes it easy to change line types when necessary, the shooting line being blood- or grinner-knotted to the loop.

I mentioned memory coils briefly under *Reels and balance*. They occur when a line is wound tightly around the drum of a reel. Although padding the drum out with backing line will reduce the problem, it will not solve it altogether. The coils can be removed, however, by stretching the line immediately before use. If you are fishing with a friend, pull the whole of the fly line from the reel, hold on to one end and get him to pull quite hard and steadily on the other. If you are alone, run the fly line round a tree or fence post (checking first that it has no sharp or rough surfaces) and pull on both ends at once.

THE GRIP

One's grip on a fly rod can make all the difference between exasperation and comfortable harmony. Beginners often seem terrified of their first encounter with 9 feet or so of carbon with a placid cork handle. Their 'fear of the unknown' causes them to take an almost boa-constrictor-like grip, effectively keeping the instrument at a safe arm's distance. It is then that one has to point out that the risen veins in the wrist, the glowing white of the knuckles and the 'locked' feeling along the whole arm do not bode well for the establishment of a happy relationship with the fly rod. The best advice is to treat a fly rod rather as you would the steering wheel of a car; the tighter you grip it, the less will you feel from the road or the engine; by holding it gently, you can readily pass messages to it and interpret what it is doing.

There are three basic styles of grip to choose from: the first with the thumb along the top of the rod handle, the second with the forefinger along the top and the third, the 'handshake' grip.

The thumb uppermost method is the least used of the three. It leads to inflexibility and to the wrist breaking back, which is an anathema, as we shall see.

Many British fly fishing instructors counsel against using the forefinger uppermost grip. I might, too, had I not seen the great Austrian fly fisher, Roman Moser, using it to great effect with a casting style that has much to commend it. But, and it is a big *but*, it would appear that the forefinger-uppermost grip is best applied to Moser's 'oval hoop' style of casting (of which, more anon) than to our more familiar overhead technique. So, with this in mind, we shall explore the 'handshake' style, which I and most other instructors tend to favour.

Allow the rod handle to fall across the palm of the hand. You will note that the weight of the rod will counter-lever the butt cosily up into the forearm. Only when this happens should one place the thumb either to one side or partly on top of the rod and grip the handle

The thumb uppermost grip leads to inflexibility and to the wrist breaking back

The forefinger uppermost grip is of value only for a very specific and limited range of casts

The handshake grip, favoured by most professional casting instructors

lightly with the fingers. This sequence should lock the rod and the forearm comfortably together and place a certain amount of restriction on wrist movement, which helps efficient casting. If you grasp the rod handle like the handle of a hammer, as most beginners do, an angle will develop between the rod handle and the forearm. This is the first phase of 'wrist break', which causes great problems and should be avoided.

STANCE

Good stance is essential to successful casting. If you are right-handed, the right foot should be placed slightly forward of the left one, so that you are standing obliquely, facing at about 45 degrees to the left of the point you mean to cast to, and your balance should be biased towards your right foot. (If you are left-handed, of course, the greater part of your weight should be over your left foot, which should be placed slightly forward of the right one).

If you stand too square to your target, virtually facing it, the temptation will be to go into a throwing stance, resulting in the cast being made from the shoulder, which is disastrous.

THE OVERHEAD CAST

Almost inevitably, the beginner finds him or herself in something of a 'Catch 22' situation when it comes to actually casting. You cannot work a fly rod properly unless you have a reasonable amount of line out beyond the rod tip, and it is difficult to get line out unless you can cast. The answer is to cheat – to lay the rod on the ground with the fly reel handle uppermost and to pull out the leader and about two rod lengths (20 feet, say) of line by hand. As walking on water is beset with problems, and as water seems to present many novices with a sort of mental barrier anyway, it is sensible to do one's initial practice on grass.

Incidentally, a proper fly should never be used for casting practice sessions as it can cause injury. The place of the fly should be taken by a tuft of wool tied to the point of the leader with a figure-of-eight knot.

So, with the correct grip, the rod butt snugly resting against the underside of the forearm and the line running out straight in front of you, the fly line trapped by the index finger of the rod hand, and with the correct stance, the serious business of casting can begin.

The overhead cast begins with an upward movement of the rod, which is critical. It is so important that I would go so far as to say that it determines the success or failure of a cast.

Beginners tend to rely on sheer muscular effort to get the line airborne, producing a vicious hissing of water and a ponderous ascent of the fly line which eventually falls in a tangle around their ears and may produce a stream of bluish oaths to long-suffering gods. The mistake is caused by the urge to throw.

One of the most poignant illustrations I offer when teaching beginners or demonstrating is to attempt, with all my might, literally to throw a fly away from me – winding up and levering back from the shoulder and, again from the shoulder, pitching the fly line as far as I can. It usually falls in a crumpled heap at my feet. The whole episode is utterly futile in terms of fly casting. And yet this same movement is re-created (usually instinctively) by beginners and, indeed, by many seasoned fly fishers when striving for distance. The vital flaw is quite simply that the fly fisher is trying to use his own muscle power rather than the tackle that was designed to do the job for him.

So, how can we get away from this throwing action?

Firstly, the line must be *straight* in front and trapped against the cork handle by the forefinger of the rod hand. These points are important as you need a reaction from the fly line the moment the rod tip starts to move upwards; curves and slack areas between rod point and fly prevent this from happening.

The upward movement of the rod is made by lifting and bending of the *elbow — not* with the wrist or with a towering of the shoulder — and should initially be done slowly, almost as though you were stroking the line off the grass or water with a feather. As the rod tip gradually accelerates upwards to 10.00 or 10.30 on the 'casting clock', the line follows it. Then the acceleration is made *upwards, not* backwards.

It is worth looking at this crucial stage in some detail.

During the 'lift-off', the rod will have been gradually easing the line clear of the water's surface. Now we must load the rod with the power it needs to make the forward cast — hence the need to accelerate at the 10.00—10.30 position. It is a precise area; if you leave the 'power stroke' too late, the wrist (or, indeed, the arm) may be forced back beyond the vertical, stopping at 2.00 or, worse still, 3.00 at the back.

By starting the power stroke at 10.00—10.30, the elevation is upward, making it much easier to stop in the vertical, 12.00 position, or only just beyond it.

But why should we want to stop at the vertical? Because that is by far the most efficient point at which to load the rod with the power it will need in order to deliver the forward cast. A fly rod is essentially a spring, loaded by the weight of the fly line. The further it is allowed

Figure 38   *The caster's clock face*

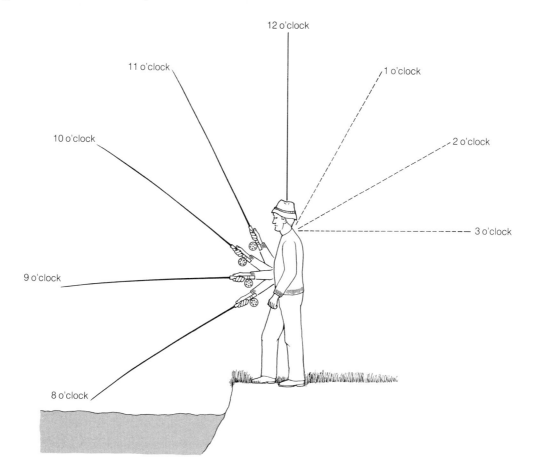

to drift back beyond the vertical, the less energy will the fly line be able to load it with, until, eventually, if the rod is allowed to drift back to 3.00, the line will be unable to load it at all, and the only option you will be left with is the throwing one, which, as we have already seen, is hopelessly inefficient.

So, you accelerate the rod briskly from 10.00 to about 11.00 and then allow it to drift up to between 12.00 and 1.00, but no further. I say 'drift' because I find that allowing the elbow to 'drift' upwards with the accelerating rod creates a relaxed, rhythmic and efficient action, rather than the 'stuttering' cast you tend to get if the rod is stopped suddenly at 12.00. I cannot emphasize too strongly, though, that all this is primarily an elbow movement, rather than a wrist or shoulder one.

With the rod and forearm in perfect line with each other, increased flexing of the elbow during the up-cast should bring the wrist up close to the shoulder. In fact, some anglers (and some good ones, too) actually hold their elbows slightly out to the side, their forearms angled slightly inwards, their hands coming up to their faces at the top of the up-cast. This is, perhaps, the ultimate action, but most fly fishers – and most professional instructors – prefer a straighter movement.

There are two options available to the beginner.

Firstly, with the forearm and rod moving straight up until the base of the caster's thumb is in line with the bridge of his nose. This action is not dissimilar to that used by darts players, and it enables great accuracy to be achieved which can often be used to advantage in practical fly fishing situations.

Secondly, the rod hand can be brought up to a point midway between the ear and shoulder. Although this makes the serious error of wrist break a little more likely, it is the one I favour, especially for beginners. It is more relaxed and it frees the caster from the (unfounded) fear of being hit in the face by the fly or fly line. (In truth, this is very unlikely to happen, but the illusion exists.)

All this detail may seem excessive, but it really is not. Master this movement and you will have made a good up-cast (I abhor the phrase 'back-cast', which smacks of flies caught in the grass or on barbed wire fences). Moreover, a good up-cast is *the* key to a good forward cast. A good up-cast loads the rod with the power needed to enable *it* – not *you* – to project the line forward in a good forward cast. This is, of course, entirely contrary to the practice seen so often around our trout fisheries, where almost all the emphasis is placed on the forward cast, the backward movement apparently being regarded as almost incidental.

The initial movement completed, what now?

If the up-cast has been properly executed, the effect should be what Charles Ritz described as 'high speed, high line', which is just what we want. In fact, a good up-cast should cause the line almost to pull the hand upwards as the rod drifts to the 12.00 or 1.00 position. It may be allowed to do so a little, but the rod hand should never go higher than the top of the head. If it does, the shoulder will come into play, which disrupts good casting.

Now, having spent much time looking at what happens in front of us, let us turn our attention to what is going on behind us – which has much to do with gravity.

After its acceleration upwards and behind us, the line will, of course, start to fall earthwards. Once it falls below the upright tip of the rod, the power will dissipate and be lost, and the angler will be left with no alternative but to go into a shoulder throwing movement, widening the loop and setting up a series of insoluble problems.

The time for action is indicated by the tugging of the fly line on the rod tip – the 'fully loaded rod' message – and *this* is the time to make the forward cast.

I am not averse to a sideways glance over the shoulder to see whether the fly line is 'on the up', but I resist a full-blooded turn of the head, which results in shoulder casting and swivelling of the body, both of which can undo a lot of good work.

In a perfect world, there should be no need to put any more effort into the forward cast other than that needed to tell it where to go.

The line flowing upwards and behind us, loading the rod, should be sufficient. Needless to say, this is not a perfect world, and we casters do need to exert a little effort.

Imagine you are looking at a wall at eye level in front of you. If you use the action you would use to 'tap a nail' into the wall, this will produce the correct movement for redirecting the fly line forwards. It is honestly as simple as that.

I could wax lyrical about feeling that the rod is fully loaded, easing the tip over and wafting the line out in front, but this sounds vague and is open to misinterpretation; instead I would much rather dwell on the 'hammer tap' — I like it; it is descriptive and accurate.

So, from the vertical position — where the hand ends up at the final stage of the up-cast —

you merely tap a smallish nail with an average hammer (not a 6 inch nail and a sledge hammer!) into the imaginary wall in front of you.

If I was being strictly honest about this, I would have to confess that this is, in fact, a slightly 'wristy' movement, not extremely so, but it does involve some flexibility of the wrist. The Americans call it a 'snap'. The 'power snap' is not a bad description.

This snap or hammer tap is usually sufficient to put the line out in front of you to where you will be fishing. It is not over yet, though. Like all good strokes which maximize the power stored in implements like golf clubs, cricket bats or tennis rackets, a follow through is essential to make the delivery clean, controlled and precise. Essentially, this only requires the

The overhead cast: *start in the 8 o'clock position with the rod tip close to the water*

Lift steadily into the up-cast, accelerating from 10.00 or 10.30 to 12.00 and allow the rod to drift back no further than 1.00

angler to allow the rod to drift down to about the 8.00 position after the forward tap, the fly line speeding out across the water as he does so. The basic overhead cast has been achieved.

I may appear to have laboured the point and to have devoted too much attention to what is, after all, just one particular cast. I make no apology for having done so. Get the discipline right for this cast and all other casts become straightforward; they are, after all, simply variations of it.

FAULTS AND CURES

What happens if things go wrong?

Problem. The fly line merely folds towards you, failing to get into the air.

Remedy. You are coming up too slowly or all at one speed, and have forgotten to accelerate towards the top of the up-cast.

Problem. You lift off too quickly, ripping the fly line from water with gusto, usually with great upheavals at the surface, the line often leaping up in the air, crumpling in front of you or festooning you with loose coils.

Remedy: Strangely, this movement generally stops abruptly at the point you should have

PAUSE, *to allow the line to extend upwards and behind you, tap forward . . .*

. . . and follow through

accelerated from (10.30). The remedy is to start slowly, building up to the point of acceleration.

Problem. You notice: (a) you are having to go into a throwing action to get the fly out in front; (b) there is a tugging from behind you as you cast and you find bits of grass impaled on your fly, or you catch a barbed wire fence or some such; or (d) you lodge the fly in the back of your coat (or worse).

Remedy. All these mean one thing — your wrist has 'broken'. Instead of stopping the rod at or near the vertical to enable the line to load it, with the wrist kept as stiff as possible, your wrist has flexed backwards, taking the rod with it to the 2.00 or 3.00 position where it *cannot* be loaded by the line, and gravity has added to your problems. The remedy is simple. Keep the wrist under control and as stiff as possible at the top of the cast. If you find this very difficult, a good ploy is to pop into a sports store and buy one of the velcro-fastened 'ties' used by footballers to hold their socks up. Strap this around the wrist and the lower part of the rod handle (by the reel fitting). It will help to keep the rod butt close to the forearm while, at the same time, allowing a certain amount of natural flexing.

Problem. You are casting into a slight head-wind. All seems to be going well behind you but, on the forward cast, the line appears to be going out in a wide, rounded loop which catches on the wind and collapses.

Remedy. Once more, wrist-break is likely to be the culprit. The wrist and rod drop back, perhaps almost to the horizontal, the throwing action you are then forced to use propels the line upwards and almost 'bowls' it out in a rounded loop. This wide loop has much greater wind resistance and far less penetrating power than a tight one. Once again, the answer is to keep your wrist stiff.

Problem. Although you are sure that you kept your wrist stiff and that the back-cast was near perfect, you are still putting the line out in front of you in a wide, wind resistant loop.

Remedy. This happens when your 'hammer tap' is aimed too high. The line sets off on an upward trajectory. When it reaches the point at which it loses its impetus, it comes back down along the path along which it was sent. To overcome this, always make sure that the 'hammer tap' is made on an horizontal plane in the basic over-head cast. (There are circumstances in which higher or lower trajectories are needed. These specialized casts will be dealt with later.)

Problem. The most audible problem is the one where you find yourself looking over your shoulder to see who is taking pot shots at you with a rifle.

Remedy. This is known as 'whipcrack' and, oddly, seems to be less prevalent that it once was, although I cannot tell you why. It occurs when you do not allow time for the line and leader to straighten behind you on the up-cast. As you tap the rod forward, you crack the line just like a bull whip, quite often cracking the fly off the leader. In the words of the legendary Lionel Sweet of Usk, the remedy is, 'wait for it; wait for it!'

Problem. You catch the fly on the rod tip during casting.

Remedy. This is more annoying than disastrous and is quickly sorted out. It is caused by moving the rod through too tight an arc, perhaps starting to accelerate at 11.00 instead of 10.00 or 10.30. All you need to do is to widen the casting arc slightly. If this fails, you are probably being too jerky in the various casting movements, so try to make everything smoother — which is how it should be anyway.

Problem. Your fly catches on the fly line or leader during the forward cast.

Remedy. This usually happens either when you are striving for a bit more distance or when you are casting hurriedly, to cover a rising fish, for instance. It is generally caused by pushing forwards with the rod arm. Good casting relies on having a fixed base or platform (an effectively static elbow) for the rod (spring) to be loaded and to work from. If this fixed base is suddenly removed (by moving the elbow forward), the leader and tip of the fly line, unfurling above the main body of the fly line, are bound to fall and are likely to become caught up.

SHOOTING LINE

The purpose of 'shooting' line is to make the weight of the line beyond the rod tip pull out loose line through the rod rings. It is simply a development from all the hard work you have already done, and is the product of a good up-cast. It requires little or no extra effort, the necessary power having been stored in the rod during the up-cast.

Instead of trapping the line with the index finger of the rod hand, hold it in the non-rod hand *and hold that hand still. Do not allow it to move up and down with the rod while you are casting.*

All you have to do is to release the loose line immediately after the forward tap and, lo and behold, the line will shoot out through the rings and carry on moving until the power is dissipated and it comes to rest.

The timing of the release is important. Release the line too soon and the power stored in the rod will be dissipated too quickly and the line will collapse in a heap. Release it too late and the rod's power will already have been used, leaving none with which to pull the line out.

It may be thought that aiming higher on the forward cast will enable more line to be shot. What happens in reality, though, is that the whole casting arc tends to be angled backwards, the line going out horizontally behind you (or worse) instead of upwards, and you get caught in the grass or whatever.

FALSE CASTING

To extend line, you simply do a normal up-cast, tap the rod forward, shoot some of the loose line from your non-rod hand, trap the line again as you go into another up-cast (*before* the line touches the water), tap the rod forward and release more line. This is called 'false casting'.

If two or three false casts are required to extend all the loose line you have, the casting arc should be between about 11.00 and 1.00 or 1.30. Lift into the up-cast, tap forward to about 11.00 and extend line, trap the line and tap back and up to 1.00 or 1.30, tap forward and extend line again.

You can only release line on successive forward casts, not on the up-casts. If you try to release line on an up-cast, it will fall in a terrible tangle around your ears.

It should also be noted that any rod will become soggy and unresponsive if you extend more line than it can handle. As an example, where a rod is rated for a size 6 line, it will perform at its best with 30 feet of DT6 line extended. Forty feet will overload it. If you expect to be extending 40 feet regularly, then you should load the rod with a weight one lower than that for which it is rated, that is to say, in this case, with a DT5. If you are using a weight-forward line, you can only extend 30−35 feet, regardless of the line's weight. Beyond this, with the belly and some of the fine shooting line out beyond the tip ring, the line will develop a will of its own and become unmanageable.

Many fly fishers do far too much false casting, frightening a good many trout in the process. Such anglers seem to become mesmerized by fly lines travelling back and forth through the air in graceful (or ungraceful!) loops. Fish cannot be caught unless the fly is in the water − and yet the hypnotism continues. I have seen people making ten or more false casts that culminate in a final cast that looked like bedspring coils. The chief reason for so much false casting seems to be the search for distance. But, under normal circumstances, three (or, at most, four) false casts should suffice, whether you wish to shoot 20 yards of line or 50. The key to getting extra distance is to be found in the double haul − which we shall consider later − rather than in repetitive false casting.

THE ROLL CAST

The roll cast has numerous uses but is often overlooked. It can help you to put your fly to trout in otherwise almost completely inaccessible places; it can overcome the potentially rod fracturing resistance of a sunk line under water; and, it makes short line, loch-style fishing a relaxing pleasure. It can also get you out of some fearful messes.

It is a simple cast to master, if taken slowly. Some people say that it is splashy on touchdown. In fact, it should be just as delicate as an overhead cast if performed properly.

Let us assume that you already have 10–15 yards of line on the water in front of you with the rod angled downwards, its tip almost touching the water. It helps if the line is reasonably straight, but this is not essential.

From this 8.00 position, the rod arm — once again only bending at the elbow and with the wrist reasonably stiff — is moved steadily upwards and slightly to the right. The speed with which you do this will depend upon the effect you wish to create. It is done quickly if you wish to shoot line, slowly if you are looking for delicacy of presentation.

At the top of the upward movement, the rod should be angled back to about the 1.00 position with the line hanging down and curving forward, making a half moon or orange segment shape.

The roll cast: *move the rod slowly upwards and to right or left, depending upon the wind*

Pause when the rod is in the 1.00 position, to allow the line to fall into a curve and behind it

From this point, the rod arm is brought slightly into the body and punched outwards and downwards simultaneously, using the elbow, in a hammer blow that normally stops at the 9.00 position.

By adjusting the trajectory, you can determine how the fly will be presented. If you finish higher, at 10.00, say, you will create the wide loop that suits a team of flies when drifting broadside; finish at 8.00 and you will create a tight loop which will punch into a headwind or enable you to 'inject' your flies into a tight space.

It is important that the fly line should hang away from your body during the initial movement, to prevent the line or flies from hitting you when you punch the rod forward. Another safety problem can arise when the wind is blowing from the right (for a right-hander; from the left for a left-hander). It can be overcome quite simply by bringing the rod over to the left shoulder *so that the loop of line falls to the left hand side*, the cast being made from that side. If a 'wrong sided' cast like this lacks power, aim it to the right and then repeat it from the right hand side once the fly line has settled.

When learning to roll cast, it can pay to look over your shoulder and watch the loop of line develop, making the forward cast when it is in the 'half moon' configuration.

To get the feel of the cast, start by doing it almost in slow motion, gradually increasing line speed as your confidence grows. But it is important to make the forward tap smartly, however languid the rest of the movement.

With the wind from the right, the rod should be angled over to the left and the curve of the line should form beyond the angler's left shoulder

Snap the rod down and forwards, rolling the line out over the water

THE DOUBLE HAUL

Newcomers to stillwater fly fishing could be forgiven for presuming that the more demented efforts of some anglers striving for distance has something to do with the 'double haul'. In fact, it very rarely bears any resemblance to it at all.

Sooner or later, most fly fishers become besotted with distance, constantly urging their flies towards the far bank of a river or making Herculean efforts to reach the other side of the reservoir – probably half a mile or more away.

The truth of the matter is that a well executed, delicately controlled cast delivered at comfortable range will almost always be more useful than a bad one touching down like a jumbo jet further afield. However, and although this holds true for most of the time, there are occasions – when fish are rising just beyond normal casting range, when we have to contend with a strong headwind, or when, for a variety of reasons, we may wish to project a tight, piercing loop while fishing a river – when the double haul can be an invaluable addition to our repertoire.

It is important to understand from the outset that the double haul, like all casting techniques, has little to do with strength or exertion on the angler's part but a great deal to do with applied power, harmony between the angler and his tackle, and style. It is also worth making the point that the double haul and its infant, the single haul, has as many applications on small brooks, chalk streams, lakes and lochs as it does on reservoirs, and that it matters little whether you use a size 4 or 5 weight system or a size 9 or 10 weight one. It is the angler making the cast who is either efficient or inefficient, not the weight of the tackle. And it is perfectly possible for a good caster to cast a great deal further with a DT5 than a poor one can with a size 9 shooting head.

Like all good stories, the cast has to start somewhere. For this one, we are looking for a sound, 'accelerated lift-off' or 'single haul' to form a base to build on. There is nothing difficult about this, but we must get the line hand to do most the work, rather than overburden the rod hand.

This single haul is a useful cast in its own right and is particularly useful in a wind when a swift change of direction is needed, enabling

The double haul: *pull down on the line with the left hand as the right accelerates the rod into the up-cast*

The haul should be completed as the rod drifts back to the 1.00 position

Allow the upward and backward velocity of the line to 'pull' the left hand up towards the rod during the pause at the top of the up-cast

us to cover trout cruising at a fair rate of knots when hunting pupae in the surface film or fish ploughing through the waves in front of us when we are drifting broadside. It gives us the increased line speed we need to create a tight loop. This is the essence both of the single haul and of the double haul – increased line speed, compressing the fly rod more positively over a shorter distance and thus injecting more power into the forward cast.

A correct stance is essential, and do not be hoodwinked by the inexpert. The often seen 'tournament' stance or open stance, with the left foot stridently ahead of the right, does little for all-day casting comfort, and yet so many people adopt this wide-legged posture. It has to be understood that tournament casters may only cast in this position for five to fifteen minutes in a day. We mere anglers may be out there for twelve hours at a time and, to fish effectively, we must be almost as fresh late in the evening as we were during the first few adrenalin-charged hours.

It is therefore better to opt for a closed stance, with the left foot pointing towards the water, in the direction of the cast, and the right foot at right angles behind it (or vice versa, if you are left handed). The principle advantage

of this stance is that it restricts body sway and excessive movement from the trunk, which can prove ruinous to the task in hand.

So, with the feet correctly positioned, it is time to begin.

With some 20 or 30 feet of fly line straight out in front of you and with the rod tip in the familiar 8.00 position, grasp the line close to the butt ring with the line hand. As the rod is raised in the usual manner, slowly to begin with, the line hand pulls down steadily on the opposite side of the body. This pull should end as the rod accelerates up to the vertical, the line hand finishing at waist level or a shade lower. A long draw or haul is the essence of this manoeuvre, generating line speed, and it should not be hurried. You are seeking to achieve a gradual build-up of power. Try it almost in slow motion; you will feel it loading the rod and accelerating the line high and fast behind you.

For the single haul the forward cast is made exactly as it is in an ordinary overhead cast. Do not try to add yet more power at this stage. You will already have loaded the rod with a great deal of power. If you try to add more with the rod hand, you will cause a problem, the line being sent out so quickly and forcefully

At the end of the pause, the left hand should be close to the right

Haul down with the left again as the rod is tapped into the forward cast

Release the line from the left hand and follow through with the right

that it is likely to recoil on itself, setting up shock waves and instability and producing a less than satisfactory landing.

Once the single haul has been mastered, it is time to look at the double haul. I liken this manoeuvre to rubbing the top of your head in a circular motion while patting your stomach. The movements necessary for this cast, and their timing, are a maze through which there are no short cuts. Only time and practice will provide mastery.

In essence, the sequence of the double haul runs thus. Starting from the 8.00 position, the line is grasped by the line hand at the butt ring. As the rod is raised through that familiar arc, the line is pulled smoothly downwards to the hip. Do not forget the 'natural drift' at the top of the up-cast, which helps so much with this and many other casts.

The line should now be travelling upwards and back from the rod tip, accelerated by the single haul. Indeed, the line should move upwards so determinedly that the line hand is almost pulled up to the butt ring by the momentum. Rather than keep the line hand at the hip, allow it to float back up to the butt ring of the rod, the rod by now having assumed the usual 1.00 pause position.

The timing required to affect a downward single haul followed by a smooth drift of the hand back up to the butt ring is precise, unhurried and smooth, and requires a good deal of practice. Any jerking, with either the line- or rod-hand, will simply set up a vibration along the line, causing a significant loss of power just when the rod should be being loaded to its maximum.

The increased line speed will cause the line to straighten more quickly above and behind you than it did with an ordinary, overhead cast. So, as soon as the line hand has reached the level of your nose it will be time for the conclusion — the strong, steady downward haul in conjunction with the rod's forward movement.

At this point, the rod hand should add no more power but simply act as it does for all other casts, tapping the rod forward and finishing with a gentle follow through.

The line hand, however, should move in conjunction with this movement, hauling the line smoothly but forcefully down to hip level. The point of release should harmonize with the power tap. The line hand should reach the hip just as the tap forward is made, and the line should be released at this point if the sequence is not to be repeated.

All casting is difficult to describe in words, so do, please, read this in conjunction with the photographs.

AWKWARD WINDS

The wind can present we fly fishers with some of our most difficult problems — either real or imagined. I wonder just how often we avoid or forsake good fish holding areas because of it. I know that I have succumbed to the charms of frequently almost barren lee shores simply to escape the effects of an adverse breeze elsewhere. And every river fly fisher knows the torment of having a delicate dry fly, pitched elegantly upstream, dumped some feet off target or wafted back towards him, fly and leader landing in a heap at the tip of the fly line.

In truth, though, defeating the wind is surprisingly easy once the principles of casting are properly understood and a sound technique has been developed. All you need to do is to bring the line forward rather faster than usual and to aim slightly lower than normal on the forward cast. It really *is* that simple.

Let us go to the windswept bank of a reservoir or, indeed, to an early April day on a river, with the wind 'tunnelling' downstream towards us.

The first thing that will become apparent with a normal overhead cast is just how quickly the line is swept out behind us by the wind flexing the rod faster and imparting more power to it than on normal days. This can be used to advantage, provided you remember that everything happens quicker, so there is much less time in which to make the forward tap. Because considerable line speed will have been generated during the up-cast, you need to use *less* effort than usual as you tap forward, rather than more. I know it sounds implausible, but I promise you it is true.

Having made the back-cast, and knowing that you must tap forward a little sooner than usual, look straight ahead and drop your line of sight to the wave tops. Now, instead of tapping the rod forward to 11.00 or 10.30, aim for 10.00 or 9.30. In a really fierce wind, you may even have to come down to 9.00.

This will have the effect of aiming the trajectory of the loop slightly downwards. Even in the strongest of winds, there is always an area of slack air just above the water's surface. If you can project your line into this space, cutting in beneath the wind, you will be able to make good and surprisingly effortless casts.

So, rather than forcing the issue with a head-on wind, you are actually able to use less effort to greater effect. While Hurricane 'Flora' may pose a problem or two, this technique, possibly supported with a slightly heavier line than usual, should enable you to master most difficult conditions.

Oddly, a wind coming from behind presents more problems than a headwind. Although the forward cast can sail out flatteringly in front, it is the up-cast – and therefore the power source for the forward cast – that is at risk.

It is at such times that a thorough working knowledge of the up-cast movement is required, perhaps in conjunction with a single or double haul. The key to defeating a wind blowing from behind is to drive the line up and back with sufficient force to make it straighten and load the rod. This can only be done with high line speed.

The problems this will overcome are chiefly those associated with loose line resulting from an insecure power base.

Firstly, inconsistent or wide loops formed on the up-cast will be caught by the wind, which will cause the light leader and fly line tip to become enmeshed with the heavier belly of the line, creating so-called 'wind knots'.

Secondly, an unstraightened line propelled forward while still unfurling from the up-cast movement may drop, clipping the rod tip or even catching the angler on the way forward.

Thirdly, if the line is driven back with insufficient force, it will 'back up' against the wind, producing a concertina effect and failing to load the rod for the forward cast.

To overcome all these difficulties, line speed should be increased on the up-cast so that the line straightens into the wind above and behind you. Again, it is vital to keep the wrist stiff, with the rod as an extension of the forearm, rather than to allow the wrist to break.

Side winds can also pose problems. The world is not a perfect place. If it was, I would always fish from a reservoir bank with the wind blowing on to my left shoulder, enabling my early season nymphs or summer pupae to be despatched comparatively easily towards the mouths of waiting trout. I would be comfortable, the wind would carry the flies away from my body (bearing in mind that leaders 20 or more feet long are not uncommon in my armoury), the fly line would travel high and fast behind me on the up-cast, flexing the rod fully, and the forward tap, perhaps aimed a little higher than usual, say, to 10.30 would allow the wind to 'coast' the tight loop out across the rolling wavelets. Bliss.

But what happens if, in this imperfect world, the wind is blowing from the right? Don't worry. The cure is actually quite painless, effective and easy to master. The simple solution is to cast across the body, over the left shoulder, the right hand coming up to the left ear (or vice versa, if you are left handed). The only variation from the norm is a slight angling of the casting plane, a simple tilting of the rod to accommodate the sideways movement.

The initial movement is the same as usual, starting with the rod tip at water level. The up-cast is made across the body in *exactly* the same manner as it is with a wind from the left, with exactly the same acceleration points. It is even possible to use a single or double haul while doing this.

I certainly find this way of casting very useful, especially when fishing rivers, although I confess to altering the technique when distance casting on reservoirs. Here I opt for what I call the 'trailing loop'.

THE TRAILING LOOP

The trailing loop is a development of a style called the 'oval loop', which has been evolved on rivers in Germany and Austria. It calls for the line to be accelerated *under the rod tip* on the up-cast and *over the tip* on the forward tap. This is not a textbook cast but one born of necessity to overcome particular weather conditions when striving for distance with long leaders and heavy, weighted flies.

Serried ranks of anglers casting manfully into fields and dam walls, all with their backs to the water, are quite common sights in adverse wind conditions. The trailing oval loop enables the angler to fish the same areas while offering the distinct advantage of allowing him to see where he is about to cast to, watching for fish movement, and to use greater line speed to shoot line out where it counts, over the water.

The 'back to the water' method produces excellent casts across the land (where there are few fish) while the back-cast − intended to land on the water where the fish are, has a nasty habit of running out of steam, the power loss leading to crumpled lines and tangled leaders, offering little in the way of clean turnover. Rather like a car in reverse, it goes, but not very quickly.

Mastery of the 'oval loop' requires practice. But once it has been learnt, you will literally feel the cast's power develop through the rod and into your hand. It is one of the most pleasing casts to get right.

Timing is the essence of success and it is also important to have a working knowledge of the double haul. The success of this cast depends upon maintaining line speed and tautness with the line hand, allowing the rod hand to steer the rod and to create a well-formed loop without sacrificing power.

With the line held taut with the line hand, the first movement is a fast, diagonal one to the side with the rod and rod hand. The resistance of the length of fly line already on the water will cause this high speed, diagonal movement to drive the line under the moving rod and to accelerate upwards. As the rod hand reaches the area opposite the shoulder, it is allowed to drift a little higher to the 1.00 position.

If you glance at the loop's configuration at this point, you will see that it is still climbing upwards.

Just as the leader and the point of the fly line are about to unfurl, the elbow of the casting arm is brought into the body, the line hand hauls on the line and the forward tap is made in the usual way. All this will bring the rod and fly line into a single, harmonized plane, propelling the fly on its long leader safely across the water, well above the rod tip.

If the rod is loaded properly to begin with, it is possible to shoot the full length of a fly line in one movement with this cast. But it does require practice − ideally on a playing field or some such, with a piece of wool substituting for a fly, rather than on trout-filled waters.

ODD CURRENTS, NYMPH PITCHES AND TIGHT CORNERS

One of the most frustrating aspects of river fly fishing is the difficulty of presenting a fly without 'drag'. How often, at that critical moment when a dry fly is just about to drift down across a rising trout, is it whisked away, leaving fish-frightening furrows in its wake? This is usually caused by the angler failing to allow

for variations in the current between himself and his quarry. The problem does not arise if the river is benign enough to be moving at an even pace across its width. But rarely do such conditions arise. And the fly fisher must constantly remember that most natural insects − apart from the occasional skittering sedge − drift down on the surface not moving at all in relation to it.

A tendency for a fly to drag can usually be overcome by presenting it on a slack or wavy line. Once the basic principles of casting have been mastered and practice has established a comfortable relationship with one's fly rod, the presentation of a slack line becomes quite easy.

The simplest technique to use is the 'slack line pitch'. The cast is made in the normal way, the only variation coming *just after* the forward tap. At this point, as the line speeds towards its destination, the rod hand pulls back on the handle just a little, momentarily causing the rod tip to pause and move backwards. This will cause a series of shock waves to ripple along the length of the line, waves which will remain until the line lands on the water. Here, they will allow the fly a longer drift until they are gathered up by the current.

Sometimes, especially where the current is very fast, it may be necessary to put an even more dramatic series of curves into the line. Still using the method outlined above, the line hand must now be brought into play.

Make a normal overhead up-cast but, at the top of it, allow the line to drop *just a fraction*. This will cause a slightly wider loop and a slightly higher trajectory when you tap into the forward cast.

Instead of aiming the forward tap horizontally, project it upwards to about 10.00 and pull down with the line hand just as you execute the 'tap', before releasing the line. This will send the line on a slightly upward trajectory, straightening it just beyond the chosen target area, and it will gently slide back down the path along which you sent it. This, of course, sets up a calculated concertina in the line which will be translated into quite pronounced waves in the line when it lands on the water.

While this cast can be immensely useful when casting upstream, especially on fast water, it becomes almost essential to success when downstream dry fly fishing, a technique much used in continental Europe and in America. Although downstream dry fly fishing is considered unethical on most British waters, the requirement for drag-free presentation it places

upon the angler makes it a difficult 'art form'.

Another useful drag defeating, cross-current cast is the 'reach mend'.

The expertise of the American fly fisher, Gary Borgens, is well known, and it was he who first showed me this cast. Essentially, it is a slack line cast with a difference. The difference is that it delivers the fly very accurately to its target while creating a large, slack bend across the water, but without the water disturbance caused by normal mending procedures. Instead of making the upstream or downstream mend once the line is on the water, the mend is made while the line is still in the air.

This is one of those casts that looks alarmingly difficult but which, with practice, can become almost second nature quite quickly.

The standard, high line up-cast and forward tap are made in the usual manner. Immediately after the tap, though, the rod is folded over to the left or right hand side by tilting the elbow up into a horizontal plane in the line with the chest. It is then brought back straight away to the 8.00 start/finish position.

This lateral movement will be duplicated in the line, causing it to curve to one side or the other. But, just as important as this is the fact that the forward tap will have projected the fine leader and fly line tip towards their destination and that they will continue to go there while a bow is put into the heavier belly of the fly line.

Finally, let us look at ways of 'reaching the parts that other casts cannot reach'.

It has to be said that trout seem to delight in making life intolerable for the fly fisher. I have hung upside down in trees like a beleaguered Amazonian sloth; crept, disenchanted, through nettles, cowpats and thorns; argued the toss with bees, wasps and the occasional bull, just to get my fly to where I believe a trout may want to see it.

Trees are amongst the most persistent villains in the river fly fisher's utopia, which is just as well, really, or fly dressers might go out of business. Inevitably, trout like tree cover. The challenge must be met head-on − or, rather, sideways on.

Consider for a moment; it may be impossible to achieve a high line up-cast because of branches. The remedy is simple. You merely cast in exactly the same manner, applying the same acceleration, loading points and forward movement as for the overhead cast, but in a horizontal plane. Do not forget that the rod has to stop in order to flex and to be loaded for the forward cast. And remember that the cast requires a firm, fixed base if it is to be successful, so do not use too much body sway or movement when side-casting.

SALMON FLY CASTING

I am not qualified as a salmon casting instructor. Therefore, and because I know him to have been closely associated with the late Capt. T. L. Edwards – perhaps the finest casting tutor of all time – I have based what follows upon Eric Horsfall Turner's contribution on the same subject to the original editions of *The Complete Fly-Fisher*.

Salmon fly rods vary in length from 12 to 16 feet. Many of them are too heavy and cumbersome to be used single-handed. So, while the principles of casting with them are exactly the same as those that apply to single-handed rods, the actual techniques used are a little different.

The overhead, double-handed cast

This is really no more than an ordinary, overhead cast with the lower hand supporting a rod that cannot be used single-handed.

As we saw when we were considering the single-handed overhead cast, the rod must have a secure, static base upon which to work. If no such base is created, it will either be impossible to load the rod to its full potential, or the power loaded into it by the line will be dissipated, rather than applied to its correct task, the projection of the line out over the water. For exactly this same reason, it is essential when fishing double handed that the lower hand, which supports the rod, should be kept still at all times, the upper one doing the work. If you have difficulty with this, you may find the late Capt. Tommy Edward's trick of hooking the thumb of the lower hand into the trouser waistband helpful.

Beyond this, the principles of rod loading and timing are exactly the same with a double-handed rod as with a single-handed one. If you concentrate on the upper hand, imagining the rod to be single-handed, you should have no difficulty.

With 20 or 25 feet of line straight out in front of you and trapping the loose line beneath the index finger of the upper hand, start with the rod in the 8.00 position. Lift the rod steadily up, accelerating into a high, fast up-cast from about 10.00 to 12.00 and then pause, allowing the rod to drift gently back to 1.00 while the line straightens in the air. A tap forward followed by the immediate release of the line should send the line zinging out across the water.

Once you have mastered this with the lower hand held determinedly still, you should be able to improve upon it slightly by allowing the lower hand to drift naturally upwards to the base of your rib cage at the top of the up-cast. But it must never be allowed to move more than a few inches up or down, and it must never push forwards or to right or left at all. Sideways movement of the lower hand causes what is called 'cutting', the rod tip prescribing a circular movement, rather than moving back and forth on a single axis, which causes loss of line speed.

The Spey cast

The Spey cast, which strikes such terror into the hearts of those who have not learnt how to do it, is really no more than a variation on the roll cast theme.

Before we start, it is important to say that a Spey cast can only be executed with the right hand up when fishing from the left bank of a river, or with the left hand up when fishing from the right bank, and that the forward foot must correspond to the 'up' hand.

Let us imagine that you have fished a cast

out and that the line is lying almost straight downstream of you. If it is deeply sunk, perform an ordinary downstream roll cast to lay it out on the surface.

Bring the rod up to the 10.30 position, pointing halfway between the line's present position and the point at which you want it to land at the end of the cast. Now, starting slowly and accelerating as you progress, sweep the rod tip in a downward and upstream curve across the front of your body, the lowest (9.00) point of the curve being in line with the target area and the rod coming up to the 1.00 position from which you would start a normal roll cast. This should whisk the line into a position in which its point is roughly in line with the target, the rest of it hanging in the half-moon or orange segment roll cast position. All you now have to do is to execute an ordinary roll cast; it is as easy as that.

The double Spey cast

There may be occasions when a downstream wind is so strong as to make it impossible to put enough power into the cross-body sweep to get the line into a position from which it can be roll cast forward without catching the angler's body. Such conditions call for a 'double Spey' cast.

The starting point is to reverse the positions of your hands and feet so that the right hand is up and the right foot forward when fishing from the right bank, and vice versa.

Now draw the line steadily upstream until the rod tip is well upstream of you. Lift the rod to the 10.30 position, sweep it downstream across your body, then upwards to the 12.00−1.00 position above your downstream shoulder and you are poised to put an ordinary roll cast out towards your target.

The double Spey cast: *preparing to lift*

The lift begins

The U movement before the roll

The start of the final roll

The final roll

CLIMATIC EFFECTS ON CASTING

It would, perhaps, be remiss of me to close without saying something about the effects that certain climatic conditions can have on casting. I remember, years ago, the late Dick Walker outlining the difficulties of getting line to shoot, especially in the evenings. I have experienced this myself in grey, overcast, muggy weather, as well as late in the day. I do not believe that lack of wind is the real cause (although it certainly doesn't help). The real culprit, I am convinced, is the density and humidity of the atmosphere itself.

Whatever the cause, its effects can be deeply frustrating. As the forward cast is made, the line is shot across the water, unfurling as it goes. As it tries to penetrate the heavy air, I believe that tiny molecules of water cling to the surface of the fly line, adding weight to it, causing it to sag and eventually dissipating its momentum.

The only antidote to this that I have yet come up with — the use of a heavier line — is, in some ways, self-defeating. The problems it poses are obvious; it offers less delicacy of presentation and a larger surface area for the molecules to adhere to. Perhaps the answer lies in improved line profiles. New ones are being developed all the time, so maybe we shall see one soon that actually overcomes this difficulty.

FINALLY

There is no easy route to casting prowess. As with all disciplines requiring precise timing and technique, real understanding and proficiency can only be developed through practice and through time spent analysing mistakes and 'good uns'. Even this approach is not without its problems. How do you know, for instance, that you are not teaching yourself bad habits, or that the 'expert' friend who tries to teach you is not passing on *his* bad habits? You don't.

So, here I can only reiterate what Peter Lapsley has said about casting instruction in the Preface to this book. An hour or so's tuition from an instructor qualified either by the Association of Professional Game Angling Instructors (APGAI) or the National Angler's Council (NAC) can make all the difference between success and abject failure, and can speed the learning process enormously. After all, if you were a golfer, who would you turn to for guidance? The professional, of course. The APGAI or NAC coach is his counterpart in the game fishing world, and I would urge any beginner or improver or, indeed, the experienced angler with 'a little problem' to seek his assistance.

The written word is by no means the ideal medium through which to teach casting, either. (Even video manufacturers have fought shy of this particular subject.) But I hope that I have conveyed the *principles* reasonably clearly and comprehensibly in this chapter, and that they may help you to improve your style and effectiveness with a fly rod. And if I have helped you to catch just one more trout, salmon, sea-trout or grayling than you would otherwise have thought possible, then my words will not have been wasted.

Tight lines and singing reels!

Neil Patterson

Quite simply, Neil Patterson has never grown up. He may look like an adult, but this fronts a child-like curiosity which fidgets furiously inside him when he's in the vicinity of a river or lake containing trout.

This often happens because, fifteen years ago, he moved to Berkshire where he converted a derelict stable, a mere tournament cast from one of the last remaining unspoilt stretches of chalk stream in the south of England. This is now a fly fishing labora-tory, a watering hole for fishing friends and visitors from all over the world, and the home he shares with his long-suffering wife, Doris.

Situated in this enviable position, he spends his time snooping on his neighbours (the trout), study-ing everything and anything to do with the art of telling them lies with fur and feather: to catch them, to return them, to try for them again – when they're that bit harder to catch.

Over the years, as a columnist and regular con-tributor, Neil has had his findings published in all the leading British fly fishing journals. Many of his ideas and fly patterns have been written up by authors, both in this country and, more notably, in the United States. His fly rod has taken him to France, Switzerland, Alaska, Florida and Argentina.

When he grows up, Neil's ambition is to write a book, although several publishers have given up waiting. This is the first time his writing has ap-peared between hard book covers, rather than soft magazine ones.

9

THE ANGLER AND THE INSECT

Neil Patterson

On rivers and lakes there's one noticeable difference in the approach of the skilled fly fisherman who is consistently successful and the unskilled fly fisherman who is forever frustrated.

The former knots an imitation of *something* on to the end of his line while the latter ties on *anything*.

There's a Latin name for the skill required to knot on that something. It's called *entomology*.

If you could eat your words, odds are you'd choke on this one. The study of insects is not a subject that's easy to digest. However, even though Latin nomenclature and insect physiology may stick in your throat, entomology and everything it stands for glides blissfully in one end of a hungry trout and out the other; no bother.

The truth is, trout thrive on the study of insects — even if you don't. If they take their mind off it for even a minute they miss their next meal. For this reason, the fly fisherman needs to have a working knowledge of the subject and it warrants a section in this book.

But how much do you need to know? And what? And exactly how can it help?

As a fly fisherman who feels more at home at the water-side with a fly rod and landing net than a jam-jar and a butterfly net, my approach to compiling this chapter was guided by the following discipline:

(a) Do I really *want* to know about this?
(b) Do I really *need* to know about this?

So how did I go about arriving at a low fat approach to the study of aquatic insects that would eventually prove distinctly unhealthy to the gourmet trout?

LOOK, NO LATIN

I always thought that you had to be a scientist or scholar in ancient languages to be able to tell one fly from another.

The fact is, you can become a dab hand a good deal quicker without being either.

Of course, the scientific grouping of insects into *orders*, *families*, *genera* and *species* does help by sorting out insects and putting them into boxes. But nature already was ordered, long before the Romans (and university lecturers) roamed the earth and gave them funny names.

All you need do is use your eyes and spot the *physical* characteristics insects have in common. This is what I've relied on to produce this 'Slimmer's Guide to Entomology'. It's no less authoritative as a result.

The whole project took off when I hit upon

the one physical similarity all the aquatic insects I *wanted* to know about had in common. They all had *wings*. At some time in their lives — normally in their final stages — they *flew*. Some flew to escape the river where they spent most of their lives. On the other hand, others take to the air and find themselves water-borne, and therefore trout-bound, courtesy of a gust of wind or poor navigation — discovering very quickly why they ask if flying is one of your hobbies on insurance forms.

It was therefore *wings* that provided me with the first step in identifying the fly I held in the palm of my hand. I group flies under five headings:

1. Flies with upright wings.
2. Flies with roof-shaped wings.
3. Flies with hard wings.
4. Flies with flat wings.
5. Lastly, other flying objects you need to identify.

Having sorted them, I singled out the key players that I *needed* to know about in each of the five groups. These are flies that make themselves available to trout in enough quantity to interest them in a stomach-rumbling way, and are therefore of interest to the fly fisherman.

Once I'd got these insects to step forward, I stripped them down and noted visible physical characteristics that would make identification simpler. I then interrogated them to discover any interesting behavioural idiosyncracies that might be used for recognition and fly fishing purposes.

These I have included in a short section called 'Assassin's notes'.

Most books on the subject of fly fishing entomology only give dry information about how to identify trout food. This section on assassination highlights moments in the life of individual insects, or in some cases, group of insects, when they are available to the trout and therefore most vulnerable to assassination. This should give deadly clues to the preying fisherman who, in turn, is out to assassinate the trout.

THE UPS AND DOWNS OF THE UPWING FLIES

Almost all of our popular fly patterns have been developed to imitate the various members of the upwing fly group.

In recent years, these elegant flies with their sail-like wings have started to mean new things to fly fishermen. They can't tolerate pollution or changes in the water. As a result, this delicate insect has become an *indicator species*, a barometer of our rivers and stillwaters.

If there's something wrong, they will be the first to know about it and for this reason, they should be the first flies we should know about.

They were once only considered to be of real interest to the river fly fisherman. However, in the last few years, a new generation of lake and stillwater anglers have shifted the emphasis and now upwing flies are contributing more to their sport.

In total, there are forty-seven different flies. The practical river fly fisherman need only concern himself with a maximum of twenty. The devoted stillwater fly fisherman, even less.

Like most things in nature that end up flapping a set of wings, the life-cycle of the upwing fly begins with an *egg*. Unlike a chicken, the adult female upwing fly doesn't lay her eggs in twos and threes, she lays them in thousands. An estimated five to six thousand; all in one sitting.

Only a handful of these microscopic specks reach the next stage, which, depending on temperature water conditions and the type of fly, can happen within days. This next stage is the *nymph*.

Munching its way through the mulch it finds on the river-bed where it hatched out, the nymph grows very rapidly and soon starts

Figure 39 *Upwing fly lifecycle*

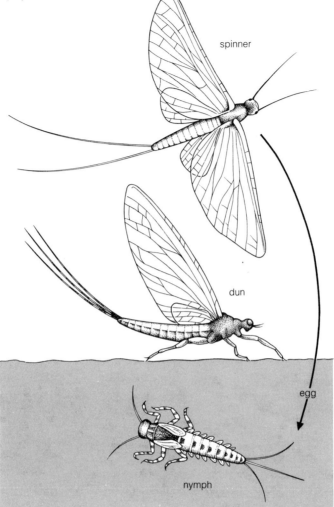

bursting out of its clothes. In its lifetime, it sheds its skin many times.

Most nymphs complete their underwater development in a single year. For some, it's shorter. For others, like the mayfly, they are sentenced to a diet of detritus and water for two years.

Different species of nymphs occupy different parts of the water and behave in very different ways. This helps to control the flow of fly traffic in our waterways and prevents all these nymphs bumping into one another.

The *burrowers*, as the name suggests, live in underground dugouts and are fully equipped with earth moving apparatus in the shape of

Nymph of upwing fly

two large shovels up front and large gill plates on the side of their body to fan what little oxygen there is their way.

The *crawlers* haunt the river-bed, scavenging on what they can find on moss, or beneath leaves and stones. As you would expect their legs are strong and shaped rather like a shot-putter's.

Clingers are broad and flat and live under stones in fast water. All the aerodynamic features needed to ensure that the water slip-streams over them are fitted as standard. Under magnification you will see that at the end of each leg they have a little clinger, or claw, conveniently positioned.

They are powerful swimmers and can go like the devil when it's time to move. No wonder, one false move and they're washed downriver and out to sea.

Slow-swimmers are built for clinging and swimming, but they don't excel at either. Strong and stocky, they are built like torpedoes, just in case they need to swim. When they do, they cross their fingers.

Swimmers, or agile darters, are the most common nymph of the upwing fly group. These slender, streamlined nymphs are the GTI model in the range with tails fringed with hairs for jet propulsion.

These nippy little operators have no intention of crawling or clinging anywhere. Perched on a frond of weed, they bob up and down like athletes in starter blocks waiting to make their next move.

Disturbed, these nymphs dart away quickly for a short distance, slam on the brakes and remain motionless to confuse any predator.

When all five of these teams of nymphs

Figure 40   *Upwing nymph types*

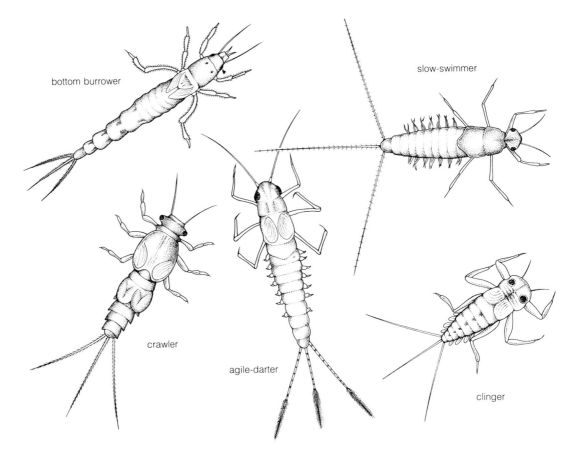

begin to mature, the wing pads behind the head darken and swell. They are now ready to hatch out into the next stage — the most exciting — for now they are about to leave one element and move into another.

Days before this event, they quit their respective perches or hidey-holes and become uncharacteristically restless and excitable, like dogs hearing the word 'walkies'.

Even the introspective burrowers start going through the motions of preparing to shed their watery coils for earthly ones and will spend several mornings doing test-runs to the surface.

When this final moment arrives, some nymphs hoist themselves skywards on weed stalks. But most bob to the surface aided by a tiny bag of gas or air they have stored in their nymphal case in their warm-up before the event.

At the surface, the nymphal case splits and a fully winged *dun* climbs out of the shuck. It drifts down on top of the water until its wings are dry enough for it to take off into the nearest bush where it will hide away tucked under a leaf or blade of grass.

Above: *Large Dark Olive Dun* (Baetis rhodani)

Below: *Blagdon — a large, fertile stillwater*

Needless to say, on dry days this happens faster than on cold, wet days. The dun is exactly as the name suggests. It's drab and matt.

This is not the case with the final stage in the life of the upwing fly. For the male and female, the next stage is charged with romance, and there's no time to lose.

Dressing up for this occasion can take as little as two hours. Normally it takes a day.

Pale Evening spinner (Procloeon pseudorufulum)

Female B-WO spinner with egg sac
Upwing spinner crawling underwater

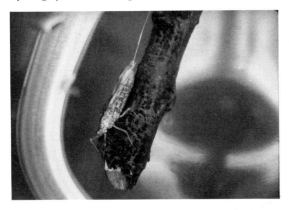

But if the weather is wet, cold or windy, it can take several days. Even weeks. However long it takes, it's worth it, for when the dun sheds its outer skin for the last time and emerges from the dressing room transformed into a *spinner* its wing and body are bright and glassy, its legs long and elegant; in the air sweeping tails fan out to give it a rhythmic, waltzing pattern. It is super-sexy and ready to mate.

The males crowd the dance-floor near the river. They glide up and down, dancing on the spot — unless the wind moves them on.

Sometimes the females keep the males waiting for several days before appearing. When they finally join them, the male wastes no time picking a mate and they make love, mid-air.

With this over and done with, the male returns to the bushes. The female returns to the water to deposit her eggs, which is a private occasion, and different female spinners have different ways of going about it.

Some fly low over the water and let the water wash the eggs from their tail ends. Others fall on the water spread-eagled and dip their bodies into the surface film and lay them into the current. Members of the largest team in the upwing fly group do it in a totally different way. They crawl under-water and deposit their eggs exactly where they want them to be.

Whatever method they choose, most females spend their last moments glued to the surface, crucified; their fate decided.

How to use the 'vital statistics' charts

You're standing by the waterside with an upwing fly you've picked up off the water standing to attention on the back of your hand. You can tell whether it's a dun or a spinner — but what's its name?

The answer is at the top. You look at the *vital statistics* chart at the beginning of each fly's curriculum vitae. Then you start at the bottom, the fly's, that is. Ask your fly: *how many tails does it have*? The answer will be two, or three, indicated in the first box.

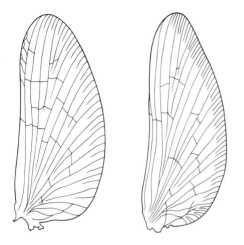

Figure 41 *Forewing detail*

In the second box there is a forewing. Every upwing fly has a pair of these. Some are more heavily veined than others. This is noted in the box. On closer inspection, some have parallel veins on the trailing edge of the forewing. In between these veins is either one, or two, shorter veins. This can be a key identification feature and where appropriate it is indicated in the magnified circle.

The next question to ask your fly is: *how many wings does it have*? The answer will be two, or four.

If the answer if four, move on to the next box. This indicates what type of small hindwing your fly has tucked alongside the larger forewing. It will either be oval-shaped, or standing upright, with or without a little bump on the trailing edge (noted in the box).

Alternatively, it will have a tiny spur-shaped wing that lies parallel to the body. Check the magnified circle in the forewing box. Oval-shaped hindwing owners have two short veins. Spur-shaped wing owners have one. Now you're ready. Ask your fly: *what shape of hindwing does it have?*

In the next box there is an indication to the size of the fly: *is your fly Extra-Large, Large, Medium or Small*?

Size can only be used as a general guide. To start talking in millimetres is ridiculous. For this reason, I have put my faith in depending on practical features rather than size to determine what fly I have in my hand.

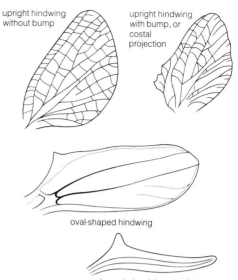

oval-shaped hindwing

spur-shaped wing, lying parallel to body

Figure 42 *Hindwing types*

In the sixth box there's an emergence chart. This will put you right if you think your fly is a March Brown but it's September.

The last box tells you the nymph type your fly has just hatched from.

One thing I haven't boxed, but you'll still want to know: *is it a boy or a girl?*

Female spinners approach a swarm of males spinners from above. To keep a look out for them, the eyes of the male upwing fly pop out of the top of his head. The female's eyes are not so prominent.

And if you're still in doubt about the sex of your specimen, the male has a small pair of claspers underneath its body, behind the tail. As a general rule, the male is smaller than the female of the same species.

Figure 43 *Eyes of male upwing spinner*

Figure 44 *Claspers of male upwing spinner*

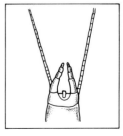

Collecting without the clutter

Identifying upwing flies is fun, but you need to do a little work to begin with. But not a lot, if you do it my way.

You certainly don't have to hulk a mini space-lab down to the river with you. Armed with my *vital statistics* chart, you only have to take four other pieces of equipment with you — none of them technical or bulky.

The first is a hat, to catch your fly. The second is the smallest of Swiss Army knives, which I hang around my neck on a leather bootlace. This tiny knife is the manicure model.

Use the little tweezers to hold the fly by the head and the toothpick to separate the wings to inspect them.

Third, you need a low-powered magnifying glass. My one is a little larger than a matchbox. It's flat and slips back into a leather sleeve. (Some of the larger Swiss Army knives incorporate a magnifying glass along with the tweezers and toothpick. This will do fine, if you don't mind carrying it around.)

Lastly, and this is optional, it's a good idea to carry an empty film canister with you in case you want to take a specimen home to check, double check; or treble check.

The bug-hunting angler's collecting equipment

Opposite: *A typical chalk stream — the River Kennet*

NOW MEET THE GANG

The Mayfly

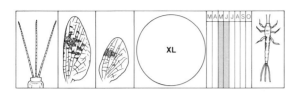

Life-style

This is the insect that features most heavily in fly fishermen's dreams, the fly trout herneate to gobble up when it hatches out in chalk and lime rivers and lakes for two to three weeks at the end of May and the end of June. Early hatches start after lunch. But as the days go by, hatches and spinner falls begin earlier and earlier until they fuse into one huge entomological explosion which has resulted in Mayfly-time being called 'Duffers' Fortnight'.

Family features

The mayfly nymph is a burrower. It lives in warrens that it digs into the soft silt. It has a pair of large diggers up front to help it tunnel.

On both sides of the nymph there are gills that fan a steady flow of oxygen along its body. This conveyor belt also brings with it particles of food.

The dun has large, greyish-yellow wings laced with light brown veins. The body is butter-coloured with brown blotches, becoming more evident at the tail-end.

The male spinner is considerably smaller than the female. The wings are matted with veins. The thorax, legs and tail are black; the body ivory.

The female spinner's wings have a blue hue with brown veins. The thorax, legs and tails are a paler brown; the body, a pale cream.

Assassin's notes

During a mayfly hatch, you will find large numbers of small, immature nymphs still digging down into the mud, rather than making their way up to the surface.

This has led to speculation, indeed for some, including myself, confirmation, that the nymph is available to the trout for a two-year span, not just one. This may be why they burrow: they'd need to if they're to survive two long, nervous years living in a river filled with ravenous trout.

Unlike most male spinners, after mating the male mayfly spinner falls on the water to die alongside his mate.

Blue-Winged Olive

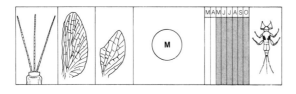

Life-style

Without demeaning it, the B-WO (as it's respectfully known by fly fishermen) is one of the most common upwing flies. It is found throughout the country, in rivers alkaline and rain-fed; in lakes, lochs and loughs (even canals).

They are most likely to appear in the early summer through to the late season, but I have spotted them in every month of the year. I've seen grayling rising to them on Christmas day.

In the early and late part of the summer they are largely an evening fly, and continue to hatch well after dark.

Family features

The nymph is a crawler that hugs on to anything that can give a little grip in the fast flowing water; moss, for example.

Apart from rivers, the B-WO is equally at home in big lakes where you'll find it battling the swell of wind-blown water as it pounds the stony shallows.

The female dun has a distinctive, slate-coloured wing. The body is small in comparison. Arched in shape, it is greengage-olive in colour. The body of the male is rusty, orange-brown. His eyes are red.

The female spinner has been dubbed the 'sherry spinner'. In actual fact, by the time she has courted, mated and dumped her eggs in the river, the female is more the colour of a freshly boiled lobster.

When the female releases the sticky egg ball from the vent, she curls her tail around it and presses it against the last two segments of her body. This is done with so much pressure it actually dents her body. The eggs are dropped from the air.

The male spinner is smaller and has a set of distinctive claspers in place of the female's green shopping bag or pitted tail. He has bright red eyes compared to the female's greenish brown.

Assassin's note

The B-WO dun can be spotted at some distance. It is the dun with the forewing sloping lazily back over its arched body.

Unlike other upwing fly spinners, female B-WO's form a women's guild. Together they travel some distance upriver assembling in their hundreds at a favoured spot; a bridge or some other feature by the river. This behaviour makes great sense and may account for the fact that the B-WO is one of the most abundant of the upwing flies.

By migrating upriver, the female spinner makes up for lost ground. After the current has carried the egg, and later the dun downstream, the spinner may well have moved at least a quarter of a mile from the initial egg-laying site. Her action ensures the survival of the species by preventing it from being washed downriver and into the Channel.

Caenis

Life-style

Although small in size, the *Caenis* is big trouble and has earned itself the name 'Angler's Curse'.

They hatch out in great numbers, and drive the angler and the trout to total distraction. If this wasn't bad enough, *Caenis* are widespread, from one end of the country to the other. And, wait for it, in rivers *and* lakes; from May to August, in the early morning and late evening.

Watch out.

Family features

The short, stubby *Caenis* nymph is a shallow burrower. It inches its sinister way around the river or lake bottom with just enough silt covering it to conceal its creepy-crawlings.

The most distinctive features of both the female and the male dun and spinner are their short broad wings (caenis were once known as 'the Broadwing'), and dull cream, stumpy body.

The only real distinguishing feature between both the male and the female dun and spinner is that the tails of the spinner are slightly longer.

Assassin's notes

As mentioned earlier *Caenis* explode, they don't hatch.

Suddenly, they're there in their thousands. They tend to concentrate themselves in localized areas and have an immediate impact on the trout in the region.

In an equally unexpected fashion the dun transforms into spinner. This can happen within minutes of hatching, as soon as the dun comes into contact with an obstacle in the water that it can clamber on to – a post, a reed, an wading angler's boot.

The females land spread-eagled on the surface. Fanned out in this position, she extrudes her eggs in a straight stream to the uncontrollable delight of every trout, who proceed to hoover these little flies in one after another as if they were soup.

Claret and Sepia Dun

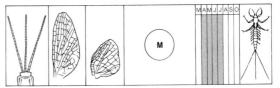

Life-style

I've grouped these two three-tailed upwing flies together. They are of more interest to the stillwater fly fisherman than the river angler although they are both found in sluggish, peaty, acid streams.

The Sepia Dun appears in early April until mid-May. The Claret takes over about this time and continues to appear until mid-June. The latter is the most common of the two species.

Family features

The nymphs are swimmers, but despite their long, whippy tails, which they like to spread out on permanent display, they're not built for speed. Instead, they slouch around the stones and peat on the river-bed.

When their laboured swimming gets too strenuous, their dark brown body provides them with perfect camouflage. As they lie doggo, a set of long, leaf-shaped gills create a substantial current along both sides of their bodies supplying them with essential oxygen.

The Claret Dun has smokey-grey forewings with a paler buff hindwing. This is a useful identification feature. Its body is a dark brown colour compared to the dark sepia of its counterpart. The wings of the Sepia Dun are fawn-coloured, with dark brown veins.

Telling the two spinners apart is strictly for the specialist. Both have brown bodies with a claret shade. However, there is one feature which separates the Claret Dun from the Sepia Dun. On closer inspection, the sepia spinner has a hazy black area on the top of the forewing.

Assassin's notes

To hatch, the nymph of the Sepia Dun crawls on to the bank, or up a weed-stem sticking out of the water. On the water, it rides the current with its three tails forked apart, which makes it easy to spot, from above — and below.

March Brown

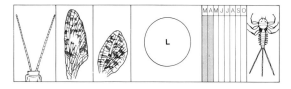

Life-style

The March Brown is probably the one upwing fly that you'd heard of before you got interested in fly fishing.

None of your cushy chalk streams for this rough and tumble guy. It makes its home in the large, pounding, acid rain-fed rivers of the west and the north of England and Scotland.

Although it is called the March Brown, the nymph lets go of its tenuous grip on the river-bed, hatching out in April and May, although a few can be spotted in March.

If you're not on the river at the right time, you stand a good chance of missing the hatch. This is fast and furious and normally happens from midday to lunchtime (or through lunchtime, because the clocks are normally changed and put back at this time of year).

The hatch starts as if someone has pulled a switch. You look at the river and there's not a fly on the water. You blink and when you open your eyes the river is fluttering with March Brown duns celebrating their arrival into a spring morning.

It is worth mentioning here that you may see March Browns hatching out as late as mid to the end of May. This will probably be a fly called, rather unimaginatively, the Late March Brown, which is a member of a different family, genus and species.

As a nymph, this Late (or False, to give it its other name) March Brown lives amongst the stones next to the regular March Brown. The only difference is that it hangs on a little bit longer.

The best trick for distinguishing the two insects is to examine the forewings of your specimen which, fortunately, because of the size of the fly, is not a job for an ophthalmic surgeon.

The regular March Brown has a pale area in the centre of the wing. This area is heavily criss-crossed with veins on the wing of the Late March Brown.

Family features

The March Brown is built like the sole of a deep-sea diver's boot. It is flat and broad in proportion to its length to help it hug the bottom as if its life depended on it, which, in fact, it does.

The nymph is sometimes called a 'stone-creeper'. This name is only accurate when the nymph is motionless. When it comes to moving around, the March Brown nymph shifts rather smartly, and if necessary across rocks in 4-wheel drive.

It is dark brown, with blotches of yellow-brown. Its gill plates and three long, spikey tails, which it holds forked apart, are pro-

River Usk (rain-fed stream)

minent identification features.

The male and female March Brown dun are simple to recognize. Their pale fawn, mottled wings with a distinctive light patch in the centre of the forewing and dull brown bodies make them very easy to identify. The male's thorax and abdomen are normally darker than the female.

It is well to note that the March Brown has a distinguishing birthmark, a dark streak at the top of each leg.

The spinner is correctly called the 'Great Red Spinner'. The body of both sexes are dark, reddy-brown ringed with straw.

Assassin's notes

March Brown hatches are localized, normally being found just below rapid shallows.

Yellow May Dun

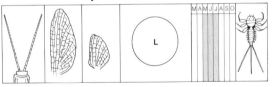

I have included this fly, not because it is of great interest to the trout, but because its chrome-yellow colour make it the easiest to recognize and, if not mentioned here, you'll see it and wonder why it is not in the section.

I also mention it because when you see one you may as well know that trout rarely feed on them. I have yet to find one in an autopsy; and I'm not the first angler/entomologist to discover this.

They are very common and flit past your nose in May and June, on chalk and rain-fed streams. The male and female duns have a brilliant sulphur hue with dark metallic eyes.

Autumn Dun

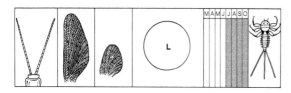

Life-style

As the name suggests, this large fly with heavily veined wings is at its most prolific at the end of the summer, in August and September; on rushing rain-fed streams, in Wales and the West of England.

The Autumn Dun is also found at this time along the shores of some of Britain's larger acid lakes.

Family features

The nymph is a large stone-clinger with the same flat, rock blending features as the March Brown. The dun shares the same criss-cross vein pattern and only size distinguishes the spinner, male and female, from the March Brown.

Assassin's notes

If you see a March Brown in August, it is almost sure to be an Autumn Dun. If this March Brown is on a lake, it is certainly an Autumn Dun.

Large Dark Olive

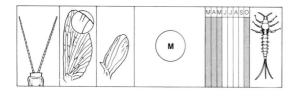

Life-style

This large, upright fly marks the start of the fly fisherman's season giving the trout the first taste of what tit-bits he can expect to find on the surface in the season ahead.

The intense hatches of Large Dark Olive begin to waft off chalk and rain-fed rivers (it is not common in lakes) in March and April, reappearing in October, with sparse hatches through to Christmas. This second edition of the fly is smaller and lighter in colour.

At the beginning of the season, the hatch starts late morning.

Family features

The nymphs are veritable Nijinskys in comparison to the burrowers, clingers and crawlers mentioned previously, who share the same river with them. They are swimmers, swinging from one weed stem to the next when the current allows.

When it doesn't, they leap from stone to stone and sit like coiled springs between leaps planning their next, sudden move.

For aquatic creatures, they are aerodynamically built, with bullet precision. Their bodies, in shape and colour, correspond very closely to the dun they hatch out into, but, unlike the dun, the nymph has three tails; the two outer tails are longer than the one in the middle.

At a distance, the male and female dun look like they've been moulded out of gunmetal. The wings are a flat, dark grey; the body, a dark green. To tell them apart, I look at the eyes. The female has light green eyes, the male's eyes are the colour of a house-brick.

Both spinners have transparent wings. The male has a distinctive dark thorax and olive-grey body with a brown bottom, although in time this turns to red. The female's body colour is more consistent, starting as a yellow brown and slowly changing to a mahogany in the latter stage of its life.

Assassin's notes

The Large Dark Olive pokes its head out of the river at a mean time of year. This directly affects its behaviour.

To begin with, unlike a dun hatching out into the hot July sun, it takes the Large Dark Olive longer to dry its huge expanse of wings. For this reason, on a cold day, the dun will travel some distance before it is able to part its damp wings and launch itself to the safety of the bankside bushes.

During this time, gusts of March wind often have a greater influence on the dun's journey than the current. Instead of a serene, well-composed picture of entomological elegance, the Large Dark Olive can become highly animated, skittering across the surface, tossing and turning on the ripple like a sailboat about to be wrecked.

Another feature that should not escape any assassin's notice is the way the female spinner lays her eggs.

Like the B-WO, to ensure the survival of her species, and to make sure her eggs don't get washed away, she doesn't delegate the responsibility of depositing her eggs on the river-bed to the vagaries of the current. Instead, she crawls underwater and deposits them exactly on the site of her dreams, preferably on a weed stem, well away from marauding larvae.

Females favour specific areas of the river for this method of egg laying. A bridge support, wood piling or rock protruding out of the water is prefered to reeds, sedges or other herbage.

The spinner will normally alight on the post, head facing skywards, egg-end turned downwards to the water. She then turns and begins to crawl down the post. As she pushes her way through the film, using her tails as pressure levers, she traps an air bubble beneath the wings to act as an oxygen tank and a lifebuoy when she releases her grip on the post or the river-bed. By this means she can bob up to the surface again like a ping-pong ball.

Depending on the force of the current and difficulties in egg laying, at the surface her wings either open up like an umbrella and she flies away or, exhausted, she spreads them on the surface in the spent position, lies down and dies.

Medium Olive

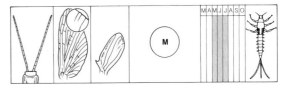

Life-style

The Medium Olive can be found from one end of the country to the other; no midway position here. And it hatches out in rivers, fast and slow moving, from the beginning to the end of the season. To give this upwing fly its due, it is the fly fisherman's sheet-anchor; the river trout's bread and butter.

Family features

As the archetypal olive, it displays all the common features. The nymph is a swimmer, and is smaller than the Large Dark Olive. The dun was once called the Yellow Dun. This may be due to the fact that when in flight, the Medium Olive is a creamy colour compared to other, darker greyer-coloured olives. Study it on the end of your finger and you can see why. The wings look as through they've been spread with butter. The body is tinged with a yellow hue. The legs are grey-olive; the tail is the standard light grey.

The spinner is very similar to its large dark brother, only smaller. The male has red eyes; the female, green.

Assassin's notes

The Medium Olive hatches out all season long so that the nymph can be found actively moving around the weeds and the stones all season. As swimmers, they often throw their cares to the current and are swept away from the protection of the weed or rock cluster.

Whereas some families of upwing flies mate and swarm near the water, the Medium Olive will collect together over land, sometimes several hundred yards from the river. Because of this, male Medium Olive spinners are rarely found lying spent on the river.

Female spinners crawl beneath the surface to lay their eggs.

Small Dark Olive

Life-style

Unlike other members of the olive family, given the choice, these tiny olives prefer to be up some thundering mountain stream rather than slouching around a stately chalk stream.

But this tearaway is not really that fussy and makes its home on all types of river – just as long as it can get up late in the morning to hatch around midday, on July and August mornings. It normally breaks off late afternoon. By evening it's gone altogether.

Family features

The nymph is another nippy, agile little darter.

The dun has small dark grey wings in distinct contrast to the olive body that yellows at the tail. It wears yellow stockings and its two tails are grey.

The male spinner has cellophane wings, a dark brown thorax and a translucent yellow body with an orange-brown bottom. His eyes are a reddy-coloured brown, while the female has black eyes. Her body is dark brown tinged with olive, with a yellowish bottom.

Assassin's notes

Like the Large and Medium Olive, the female

Small Dark Olive takes the plunge when it comes to laying her eggs.

When she pops back to the surface after egg laying, she finds two things. Firstly, unlike her big brother, she doesn't have the bulk that's needed to penetrate the surface.

Secondly, because late in the season, in the warm, balmy evenings, for instance, the surface tension is greater and the surface stickier, she can often be found just under the surface film, not always lying in or on top of it.

Pale Watery

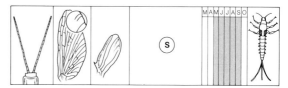

Life-style

This fly is not as widely spread as many other olives. By and large it is a southern fly, appearing to be most at home in the soft chalk streams of the south of England.

It is also a fair weather fly, not casting a shuck until May is out, but it does continue to hatch until October, when it makes a showing in the evening.

Family features

The nymph is another agile darter and this is all the fly fisherman need know.

The recognition features of the dun are more prominent in the male than the female. The male has lemon yellow eyes.

Both sexes have pale, grey-olive bodies and watery-grey wings. The female is the Small Dark Olive's big sister in appearance, but is marginally lighter in colour.

The lemon eyes of the male spinner make him easy to pick out in a crowd of females or other olive spinners. Like the female, his wings look like they've been cut out of glass, but whereas the male has a creamy see-through body and an orange-brown bottom, the female is a golden brown, the colour of butterscotch. For this reason it is sometimes known as the 'Golden Spinner'.

Assassin's notes

The Pale Watery hatches out in short, furious bursts and tends to get mating and egg laying done early on in the evening.

For this reason they are a 'day fly', in the true sense of the word, and act as a consistent drip-feed throughout the summer days, arriving on the water at times you wouldn't expect olives to appear.

One easy way to distinguish the female spinners from the female Small Dark Olive spinners is to get down on your knees if you think you see Pale Watery spinners by a bridge or obstacle in the river.

If the small spinners are crawling underwater, the Pale Wateries you thought you'd recognized are, in fact, Small Dark Olives.

Pale Watery spinners lay their eggs by dropping them on the surface of the water and letting the current do the rest.

Iron blue

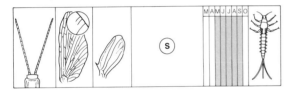

Life-style

Fly fishing folklore will have you believe that these little dark specks scattered on the water are like caviar on toast to the trout.

If this is true, then the trout are very lucky, for at certain times of the year the Iron Blue is common on rivers, both rain-fed and chalk.

Moreover the trout get two helpings; one in May and early June, a second at the end of the season during September and October.

I confess, I once pooh-poohed the notion that these highly rated trout-risers only poked their heads out of their nymphal shucks and

hatched on grim, wet and windy days.

Certainly hatches can be local and sparse, this I have never disputed, but surely they weren't *this* fussy?

I can only report that there's more truth in this theory than one would think. And I am not the only fly fisherman of my generation, wary of theories handed down to me, who has had a day of foul weather brightened up by the solid, stubborn appearance of these sooty little flies, who boldly go where no olives have gone before.

The arrival on the water of the Iron Blue hatch is prolonged and not abrupt, building slowly to a climax.

Family features

The nymph is another swimmer. The dun, both male and female, have dull grey-blue wings, a dark olive body and dark grey thorax, shades that blend together to make the Iron Blue the colour of a rain cloud.

The male spinner is known (strangely) as the 'Jenny Spinner'. It has glassy wings, a translucent body with a brown bottom, and red-brown eyes. He wears white socks to match his tails.

The female has a dark, red-brown body, pale yellow legs with black feet and a jet-black thorax.

And just to prove she picked a rough day to hatch out, two black eyes.

Assassin's notes

As a true member of the olive family, and a fly that likes to rough it, the female spinner crawls beneath the surface to lay her eggs.

Like the Small Dark Olive, you will often find this delicate adventurer trapped beneath the surface film or encased in it, having attempted to re-enter the atmosphere. The male spinner is often found on the water accompanying his mate. This is because Iron Blues tend to couple-up over open water. To keep warm perhaps?

Small Spurwing

Life-style

After studying this fly, angler-entomologists have always ended their research by giving it a different name.

For my money, the name above is the best as it highlights the most distinctive difference between it and other flies in the olive family to the casual observer, with a low-powered magnifying glass. This feature, a small spur-shaped hindwing, is illustrated in the third box.

The Small Spurwing is found in rivers and streams of all kinds and, occasionally, on lakes.

They make their first appearance at the beginning of May and continue through to the end of the season, but June is the prime time for this prolific little hatcher when it pops out of the shuck all day long.

Matinée performances get fewer as the season progresses. In the final stages of the season, late afternoon and early evening produce the crowds.

Family features

The nymph is an agile darter. It can easily be distinguished from other olive nymphs mentioned earlier because all three tails are the same length. However, the key recognition point of this dun and spinner, male and female, is the little hindwing.

Male spinners have bright red eyes. The female spinner is known as the 'Little Amber Spinner'. She has a beautifully coloured body, the upper part being a pale amber colour with faint cream rings. The underside is a creamy yellow with a light amber bottom.

Assassin's notes

Like iron blues, small spurwings make love in public, preferring not to disappear into the woods. And together they fall, the spent male dying on the river in almost as many numbers as the females.

Pond Olive

Life-style

The name is very nearly a hundred per cent accurate. But apart from ponds, Pond Olives can also be found on large lakes and can't resist a sluggish stretch of chalk stream. This takes them all over the country, but you'll only get to see them in the summer months, June and July being the most likely time. A second brood has been known to hatch out, but I only mention this in case you spot one in September.

Family features

The nymph is a streamlined agile darter, with long tails fringed with hairs for extra propulsion and a double pair of gills running along its side, to make living in stillwater with a low oxygen content bearable.

Like the small spurwing, the nymph's tails are of equal length and have a distinct downward turn when viewed in a tank.

Colours vary, but the end result is always a darker body shade than other swimmers you are likely to scoop out in your net.

But be careful. This dusky hue mustn't be confused with other species of nymphs primed to hatch out that have dark, almost black, thorax buds.

The dun is not easy to recognize out of context, which is a pond or lake, and the best way to perform a bankside identification is to give the wings your full attention.

To begin with, there is only one set. The base of these wings are broad and are tattooed with a series of small cross-veins along the top of the leading edge. These are highly visible and are the most reliable feature you'll find.

Both duns have a dark brownish-olive body. The male spinner has orange-red eyes, a red-brown bottom and pale grey tails loosely whipped around with brown rings.

The female spinner is one of the most feminine of all the olive spinners. This has earned her an equally enchanting name, the Apricot Spinner.

It's hard not to break into poetry when describing her. The key identification feature is the broad yellow band on the leading edge of the wing. The body, as her name suggests, is the colour of a blood apricot (if there is such a thing). It's apricot streaked with red. The legs are a bright olive green and the tails are buff ringed with red.

Want a date?

Assassin's notes

You don't often see duns taxi-ing around the surface on lakes or ponds waiting for the breeze to give them permission to take off. They have as acute a survival sense as any other newly hatched dun and leave the area as quickly as possible.

The nymph and the female spinner are therefore of the greatest interest to the fly fisherman.

Lake Olive

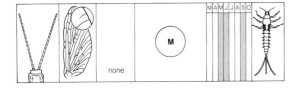

Life-style

The Lake Olive is a fair weather fly, preferring to lounge in the shallow, sheltered bay of a lake. They prefer chalk to acid lakes, and the bottom should be cushioned with moss. The plant life mustn't be scanty and should be easy to scale.

The Lake Olive makes its first appearance in April and May and its last at the end of the summer. A hatch can occur any time from midday to early evening, depending on the weather. The better the day, the later the hatch.

Family features

This speckled lounge lizard's legs suggest that the name 'agile darter' given to the Pond Olive nymph may well contravene the Trade Descriptions Act.

They are short and stumpy, and if it has to move it climbs rather than launching itself nimbly from weed frond to weed frond like the other nymphs in the swimmer category.

The general appearance of the duns is more green than olive, although later in the year this green turns to brown in the autumn.

The key identification feature is that Lake Olives don't have hindwings and you can clearly spot a yellow tinge on the leading edge and on the roots of the smoky-grey wings. The female spinner is a medium brown colour with none of the film-star qualities of the Pond Olive.

To differentiate the two olives with certainty, you need a low-powered magnifying glass to compare the two flies' tattoos. Whereas the Pond Olive has from three to five small cross-veins along the top of the leading edge, the Lake Olive has considerably more, from nine to eleven.

Figure 45 *Detail of forewing leading edge*

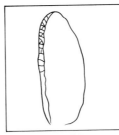
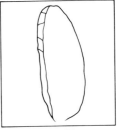

Lake Olive   Pond Olive

Assassin's notes

Unlike other nymphs of the same family, these medium-large nymphs are to be found in relatively deep water where weed does not surface. From my research, everything points to this particular nymph not opting for a particularly active or energetic life, which should be of great interest to the assassin.

Pale Evening Dun

Life-style

As the name suggests, you needn't bother getting up early in the morning to get a glimpse of this straw-coloured dun.

Pale in complexion, as a result of all the late nights, its prime time is July and August, although the official emergence time is May through to October.

It is widely distributed, making its bed in the more sleepy stretches of river, both acid and alkaline. For this reason, it is strange that on the southern chalk streams it is not plentiful. Hatches appear to be very localized. But where it is in evidence, it boasts quite a reputation with those not in too much of a hurry to go home at night.

Family features

The nymphs of the Pale Evening Dun are agile darters and resemble those of the Pond and Lake Olive, apart from one distinct feature: the gills are single. As it is predominantly a river dweller, there is no need for an auxiliary set of oxygen fans.

The male dun has yellow eyes, pale yellow legs and pale grey wings, with a hint of green at the roots. The body of both sexes is a pale straw with a honey-coloured thorax. The male spinner has lemon yellow eyes. The female has an ochre thorax, dissolving down to an amber tail-end.

If in doubt, check the wings. It has only one set, making it one of the easiest flies to identify confidently on a summer's evening when many different species of similar size and colour are out on the town.

Assassin's notes

Getting the time of year, the day and the exact location correct are not enough if you want to spot this fly. Indeed, instead of polaroids you may be better off wearing ultra-violet spectacles.

The Pale Evening Dun leaves it to the last moment before poking its head out from under the sheets. Often it waits until all the colour in the sky has bled out before making an appearance, although you may see spinners that have emerged from duns the night before.

More often than not, the mating and egg laying happen after dark, when most anglers have gone home. This may well explain why, historically, this fly has not been rated as highly as it might. But those eye-witnesses who have not been in a hurry to leave the water insist that it commands greater interest than B-WO hatching out at the same time.

ROOF-SHAPED WINGED (CADDIS) FLIES

The scientific name for this group of flies is Trichoptera, or 'hairy wings'.

Since upwing flies also have hairs on the trailing edges of each of their wings, I have chosen to group them all under the name that best describes their physical appearance.

In the British Isles, generations of fly fishermen have called these flies 'sedges'. In the USA they call them 'caddis'.

Over the last twenty years it has been our fellow fly fishers across the Atlantic that have done the most research and study on this group of flies. Because of this, many British fly fishers have broken with tradition and followed the American example. From this point on I also will refer to them as 'caddis'.

If they resemble anything, caddis look like moths. And like moths, many of the larger caddis come in the late evening, or as night approaches, flying many miles if attracted by light.

Unlike moths, their two sets of strong, hairy wings fold back over their body in the shape of a roof or a tent, extending the length of the body by a third. They also have two long antennae that are often several times the body length. They don't have a tail.

In total there are 189 different types of caddis in the British Isles. (Consider yourself lucky. In the USA, there are 1200.)

Fortunately trout are rarely pernickety when a caddis flops in front of their nose. Whatever the scientific name, the time of the year, or location, they will grab it regardless, for good reasons.

Firstly, because caddis are loners. They don't hatch out in unison, in great numbers, at a given time of day.

Secondly, when they do hatch out in numbers it's usually in the evening when the sun is low in the sky, and the light doesn't allow the trout to be too particular about colour and small details. Thirdly, and lastly, the caddis is an acrobat, and a tease.

When the adult hatches out it makes an ungainly and highly conspicuous spectacle of itself when it makes a break for the bank. It paddles and flaps as if the Devil was after it, which, on a trout-infested water, has the result you would expect. The trout snaps at this entomological exhibitionist almost involuntarily, its movement having put it on the menu.

Life-style

As a group, caddis are more widespread than upwing flies. They are to be found the length and breadth of the British Isles − in rain-fed rivers and chalk streams; lakes and ponds. Nearly every type of freshwater habitat has its corresponding caddis.

They prefer shallow, rather than deep water, deep being anything over 10 feet. Most species are found near aquatic vegetation.

The immature stages of caddis, with the exception of only one in the British Isles, are aquatic. The caddis lays her eggs in a dark-green goo, in a string, a ring or a spiral. She hangs them on aquatic plants, or on the leaves just above or below the surface, or she deposits them directly on to stones or rocks underneath the water like some of the female upwing fly spinners.

As soon as the small, naked grub crawls out of the jelly, it seems to realize that without camouflage its days are numbered. It immediately starts to cover its body with grains of sand, sticks, twigs and bits of weed for protection. This bric-à-brac is glued together by a sticky silk web which is secreted from a gland at the end of its tiny mouth.

As the grub grows, it continually adds on more scraps of aquatic jumble as it bursts out of its patchwork caravan. Each type of caddis has its own style of case, its own uniform. Some use sand grains, others pebbles. Some use only twigs; others twigs and stones. Discarded shells are also used. Some cases are spiral-shaped, others conical. Some are square; others don't bother to make one at all. Caddis grubs in the last category are in a minority, which seems to prove that this curious habit of transforming yourself into a mobile single-storey building with legs may have more going for it than simply giving the caddis larva something to amuse itself with during the long summer days.

Caddis in case

Figure 46   *Caddis fly lifecycle*

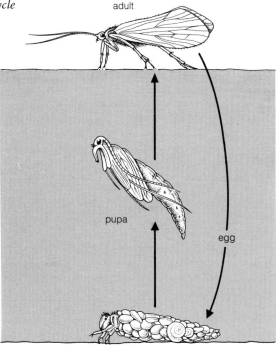

When he's not cowering in his homespun bungalow, this happy homemaker sticks his head and six legs out the front door and heads off in search of food, dragging his house along with him in case a mugger jumps out.

By and large, caddis are vegeterians, but many are meat-eaters and are partial to small aquatic creatures.

After about a year, the caddis grub's architectural career comes to an end. He hangs up his home by gluing it to a weed stem or stone, locks up the front and back door with bits of whatever is at hand and goes into retirement. He now enters into the pupation stage.

During this time, the grub hordes gas bubbles and spins a pupal skin around himself. Inside this skin, wing cases are formed and antennae appear in pre-packed form. Legs develop and are stored under his body. The middle two of these legs remain free to propel the caddis capsule skyward.

When the pupa is fully formed, the larva chews his way out through the front door and starts his ascent. Some prefer to take the stairs and climb their way up a weed stem to the

Caddis pupa

surface. Others take the lift. They fling themselves into the current and let the air trapped underneath their skin whisk them upwards, legs paddling furiously.

When they reach the surface, the flimsy pupal skin bursts open under pressure (or is it excitement?) and the fully formed adult abandons all caution and heads for land.

Although some caddis take off with some grace and elegance, others claw their clumsy way across the water, the back edges of the wings tipped down on the water surface in the

Adult caddis (caperer)

folded position. This is as tempting to the trout as a water-skier wobbling over the nose of a great white shark.

Once safe on land, the adult caddis keeps a remarkably low profile. He tucks himself away into cracks on the bark of trees, under bridges and in between stones, avoiding light with the same determination as Count Dracula.

Caddis can drink, but they can't eat. However, they are still able to survive for up to a month before leaving their secret hidey-holes to mate, lay their eggs on the water and die. A few caddis crawl under the water to lay their eggs.

Assassin's notes

A caddis in a case is to the trout what chicken in the basket is to the hungry angler.

This slow-moving, crunchy stage in the life of the caddis is of great culinary interest.

The pupa's two strong paddles make its ascent to the surface a high-speed event breaking all fast-food speed records.

But once hatched, the adult caddis motoring towards the bank in an attempt to take off, presents the trout with the perfect meal-on-wheels.

Caddis Calculator

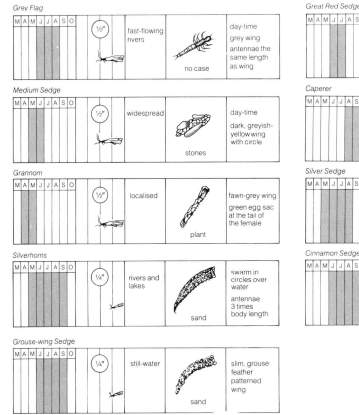

Grey Flag

| M A M J J A S O | ½" | fast-flowing rivers | no case | day-time grey wing antennae the same length as wing |

Medium Sedge

| M A M J J A S O | ½" | widespread | stones | day-time dark, greyish-yellow wing with circle |

Grannom

| M A M J J A S O | ½" | localised | plant | fawn-grey wing green egg sac at the tail of the female |

Silverhorns

| M A M J J A S O | ¼" | rivers and lakes | sand | swarm in circles over water antennae 3 times body length |

Grouse-wing Sedge

| M A M J J A S O | ¼" | still-water | sand | slim, grouse feather patterned wing |

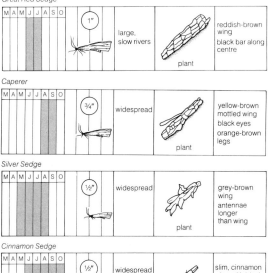

Great Red Sedge

| M A M J J A S O | 1" | large, slow rivers | plant | reddish-brown wing black bar along centre |

Caperer

| M A M J J A S O | ¾" | widespread | plant | yellow-brown mottled wing black eyes orange-brown legs |

Silver Sedge

| M A M J J A S O | ½" | widespread | plant | grey-brown wing antennae longer than wing |

Cinnamon Sedge

| M A M J J A S O | ½" | widespread | plant | slim, cinnamon wing with black markings fast-flowing rivers |

FLAT-WINGED FLIES

We may be digging new ponds and reservoirs but one thing is certain, we're not making rivers any more. If anything, we're killing them.

With increased pollution, use of agricultural nitrates and abstraction, the water in rivers and lakes isn't getting any cleaner or more pleasant to live in, especially if you're a struggling aquatic insect.

With this grim outlook in mind, the next group of flies should perhaps head our list as the most important flies to the fly fisher — in the long term. Called Diptera, this group include the midges and mosquitoes that live in our stagnant, oxygen-free water butts where other aquatic insects we've mentioned wouldn't last two minutes. Flat-winged flies are survivors.

Nearly all this group are terrestrials — land-born insects whose life-cycle doesn't take them anywhere near water so their life doesn't depend on it. The housefly is one, the daddy-long-legs another.

This order is highly adapted to what the future might bring. In all, it has over 3000 members. Let's start with the aquatic team, the most important members of this order to the angler. They're called *chironomids*.

Chironomids

This isn't a name I would have chosen, but it's the one most anglers seem happy to bandy around the bankside, so be prepared.

Otherwise known as *non-biting midges* (to make them fisherman friendly), or *buzzers* (so you don't confuse them with light flying aircraft approaching you at ear level), in total there are 400 different chironomids to choose from. Thankfully, most of them are too minuscule for even a trout with a microscope to bother about. But the bigger ones form the largest part of the trout's diet in lakes and, ever-increasingly, in rivers, although the average river angler hasn't cottoned on to this as yet.

In terms of their distribution, chironomids are everywhere, nationwide. Even if you're sitting in the centre of Birmingham, in a flat on the tenth floor, you can bet that there's one near you right now.

During the season, barely a day passes without some midge or other hatching out sometime, morning, noon or night. Just as long as there's no ice on the water.

Life-style

For some chironomids, life starts at the top. The adult female lays her eggs gently on the surface in one dollop and there it stays until the little larva hatches out and plummets to the bottom. There most of the worm-like larvae either make dugouts in the mud, build tubes of sand which they stick to themselves, or dash around freely using sinuous whip-lash movements.

The colours of the larvae vary widely and depend by and large on the type of water they live in. High oxygen, alkaline water produces green or brown-coloured larvae. Low oxygen, acid water contains more reddish and purple-shaded larvae.

The most predominant colour is red. Known as bloodworms, these larvae are full of haemoglobin to help them store oxygen and live in parts of a pond that oxygen and other aquatic insects cannot reach.

Midges can emerge at any time of year and at any time of the day, depending on three factors: firstly, the species; secondly, the temperature; and thirdly, the length of daylight hours. The longer the daylight hours, the larger the number of midges that hatch and the more varied the kinds of midges.

The midge pupa resembles the larva in many ways, but a closer microscopic look will reveal wings and legs tucked away like a parachute at the thorax. You will also see little, white breathing filaments at the head, fins and tail.

Figure 47 *Flatwing fly lifecycle*

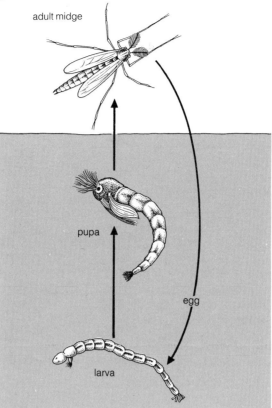

adult midge

pupa

egg

larva

Fully equipped with the most up-to-date means to accumulate oxygen, before hatching, midge pupae make regular trips from their homes, building up their oxygen store so they can break out their skin-stockings and rocket back up to the top again.

At the surface, they either attach their respiratory tubes and hang horizontally in the surface with their thorax piercing the surface; or they rove, wriggling, just beneath the surface. When the time is right, the thorax of the pupa splits and the adult crawls out on to the surface and flies off to the bankside vegetation.

These adults are easy to recognize. In design, they are all much the same and only the colour varies. Viewed on the end of your finger on six stilt-like legs, they are the entomological equivalent of the Hunchback of Notre-Dame, with two V-shaped wings that look like a cape thrown over their shoulders.

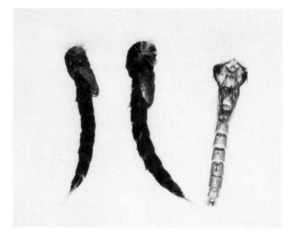

Midge pupa

The male has a bald head veiled with tiny white antennae. He has only one thing left to do, to ensure that there will be more midges to

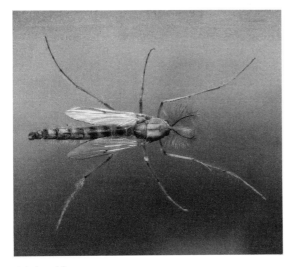

Adult midge

take his place when he's gone. To this end males gather in swarms and are joined later by the females, who select a mate and disappear with him behind the bushes. The females return to the water with their eggs carefully stored under a hook-shaped body, held in place by a set of trailing legs.

In size they range from ⅛ to ¼ inch. In coloration, they vary from black, green, red, orange, olive and grey.

Assassin's notes

Since the larvae bury themselves away in the mud, they are of little interest to the angler. However, prior to hatching, when they have sprouted their respiratory equipment and leave their holes, they are a big attraction to the trout. But even then not as much as they are when they reach the surface as pupa and find the surface thick and gluey on calm, hot days.

Hawthorn fly

The hawthorn is more than an insect. To the trout it's manna from heaven.

Its name is a sensible one. It appears for a period of about three weeks at the start of the season, when the hawthorn bushes flower. Although the hawthorn is not widely distributed, in the areas where it is found, they congregate in great numbers.

On the back of the hand they look like large houseflies (⅜–½ inch) but slimmer. The females are bigger than the males. They are black and shiny, with transparent wings. They gather together out of the wind behind bushes and trees by the waterside, about 6–10 feet above the ground.

On the wing, they can't be mistaken for they dangle a large pair of black, hairy legs beneath them for all to see.

Hawthorn

Assassin's notes

When the wind changes, a hawthorn inevitably finds itself waterborne, and almost certainly trout-bound. The trout never see the larva and pupa.

Black Gnat

There are several species of black gnat. All are terrestrial and are dark brown in colour with flat, shiny wings. The males are slim; the females fat. You can fit two, head touching the back end of the other, across the nail of your little finger.

Black gnats are common and widespread. One species makes an appearance in the spring, another in the late summer, early autumn. Like their big brother, the hawthorn, black gnats only appear at the waterside in their adult form to mate, forming large groups in whichever side of the bush or tree is protected from the wind.

One false move, one gust of wind, and the black gnat is out of one element and glued to another as trout food.

Reed Smut

Reach for your magnifying glass. Twenty of these tiny aquatic insects resembling minute houseflies can stand on the nail of your little finger without overcrowding. Fortunately for them the trout have to squint to be able to see one of them.

On the other hand, reed smuts — or 'the black curse' as they're collectively and perhaps more accurately named — hatch out in great numbers during the summer months. En masse, neither you nor the trout can ignore them because they come down in one, continuous black, spooky sheet.

At times like this — often once a day — all the trout has to do is close its eyes and steer an open mouth to the surface and suck them in.

The larvae attach themselves to weed stems in well-oxygenated water and therefore reed smuts are mainly found on rivers.

HARD-WINGED FLIES

This type are more commonly known as stoneflies. This is not because their flat, highly polished steel wings are as hard as stone, but because they are to be found clinging to stones in the cold, boulder strewn rivers of the north, where life is hard.

I have kept them until last because, despite their toughness and armoured plating, they are not as abundant as some of the more delicate aquatic insects we've mentioned.

Only a little over thirty species have found their way into the recorder's books. The vast majority are river dwellers. Stillwaters fall short on one essential element dear to the rugged stone-fly's heart of steel: rough and tumble.

In case one should suddenly creep out of the water and catch you unawares, or biff you on the back of the head, here's a description and introduction to the life-cycle of what hit you.

Life-style

Female stone-flies lay their eggs on the surface in a variety of different ways, depending on the species. When they've hatched out (this can take days, or weeks) the nymph has a year (some have three years) to prepare itself for its landward migration.

The nymph is built to take knocks and bangs. It has long antennae to stop it bumping into things, two weight-lifter's legs with a set of nut-crackers at the end of each of them so it can keep its grip and squeeze the last breath out of any small aquatic creature that would make a good meal. (Stone-flies are carnivorous.) Its legs are especially handy when the nymph reaches maturity and it is time to hike two large heavy wing pads across the river-bed to the shore under the cover of darkness.

Once ashore, the stone-flies hatch from the nymph into fully developed adults and are ready to mate, about which they don't have any airs and graces. They don't even take to the air. Mating is done there and then, on the ground. No courtship or flights of fancy. Indeed, the male hatches out with only short, stubby pretend wings that don't work. The female is better equipped, but she has to return to the water to deposit her eggs.

Stone-flies have four wings. The hindwings are broader than the forewings and curve slightly, hugging the contour of the body. Up

Large stone-fly

front, they have two long antennae with two spiky tails at the rear. In general, stone-flies are a yellow-brown colour.

The largest stone-fly measures a little over 2 inches and spreads her yellow-green wings from the Midlands northwards over streams from April to August.

The *February Red*, measuring a little under a quarter of an inch, appears in slower, weedier water at the start of the season. It has rusty red wings with two dark bands.

The *Willow Fly*, which is about the same size as the February red, makes an appearance at the end of the season. It's a slip of a fly with brown wings and is one of the few stone-flies that is happy to drop its macho image and put its feet up in the more cosy southern chalk streams.

Finally, the tiny dark *Needle Fly*, barely the length of your little fingernail, has followed this trend and has weaved its way into streams from the top to the bottom of the country. There are two species of Needle Fly. One appears early on in the season, the other at the end.

Assassin's notes

The stone-fly is at its most vulnerable during its slow migration across the river to the land. It is a poor swimmer and a clumsy flier. It's not an insect that's commonly imitated by the fly fisher at any stage of its development.

OTHER FLYING OBJECTS

There are several forms of winged trout food that the fly fisher needs to be able to recognize, but aren't grouped together under one specific heading. I call them UFO's, but by the time you've read through this section you'll be qualified to identify them and understand exactly what their mission is on planet earth, or rather, planet *water*.

For although all the insects I am about to describe *fly*, without exception it's their life underwater that is of the most interest to the trout and fly fisher alike.

Water-boatman

For some reason, instead of keeping the name we gave this insect as children, fly fishers have decided to exalt it and give it a latin name.

The simple water-boatman of our childhood has now been dubbed the latin family name *Corixa*. Goodness knows why, because although this family comes in a couple of dozen different designs, they all look and behave in a very similar, barely indistinguishable fashion. For simplicity's sake, I am going to refer to them as good old *water-boatmen*.

Water-boatmen are lake insects, appearing in the early summer — April, May and June — and early autumn. They are oval-shaped, and about five-sixteenths long. In front they are a pale yellow colour; their back is hard and

Water-boatman or corixa

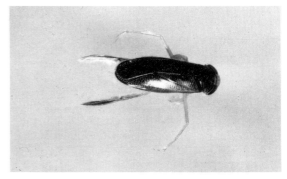

shiny and dark brown in colour; underneath they are cream.

Up front, the water-boatman has two pairs of legs. Between them is another pair. These two hairy legs rest at right angles to the body and leave you in no doubt whatsoever of the reason for the name 'water-boatman'. They're oars. And they can propel this insect at high speeds.

The water-boatman hatches out of an egg into a mini-version of the adult just described. Like whales, life for the water-boatman consists of regular trips to the surface to gulp at the air. This is stored away in bubbles between their hindlegs.

By now you may be wondering why the water-boatman open up a section dedicated to *flying* objects. Read on.

Water-boatmen (and boatwomen) don't mate in the water. Instead, their backs open out into wings and they both fly ashore. On their return from land, they re-enter the aquatic atmosphere by hitting the surface with a bang, to break the surface tension. Once back in the water, the female lays her eggs.

Dragonflies and Damselflies

These two summer insects are the most dramatic and elegant insects you are likely to spot on a river or lake.

Flitting gracefully from lily pad to weed stem to sedge stalk, their two sets of irridescent blue or green wings sparkle like pieces of glass. These four wings each operate independently, giving the adult the ability to weave an intriguing spell as they dart forwards, sideways and backwards in the sunlight.

The adults of both species are meat-eaters. Their manoeuvrability plus a set of eyes that take up almost the entire surface area of their head allows them to see in all directions. This gives little hope of survival for any small gnat or mosquito that crosses their line of vision.

Both nymphs are aquatic, living amongst the weed in lakes and slow-moving rivers. Once they've hatched from the egg, the nymphs very quickly start to act in an adult fashion, that is, they start tucking into all the other young

Adult damselfly

insects and small invertebrates they can lay their jaws on.

To help them do this, both the dragonfly and damselfly nymphs carry a very special piece of apparatus around with them. Their lower lip can open out like a drawer to grab its prey. Having done this, it slides back into the mouth with the contents.

As the nymphs get larger, nothing is safe. Not even small fish and tadpoles. Luckily, for their neighbours their underwater stay lasts only a year and when they leave they are not sorely missed. When the nymph reaches full development, it crawls out of the water. Once ashore, its skin splits down the back and the adult emerges to reap havoc once more among the insects smaller than itself − only this time in the air.

As adults, dragonflies are larger and bulkier than the more delicate and slender damselflies. When stationary, dragonflies hold their wings at right angles to their body, like an aeroplane. Damselflies hold them parallel to their bodies when at rest.

Although the foraging trout flop hungrily at these adults, it's the nymphs that offer the biggest opportunity for both the trout and the fly fishing assassin.

Assassin's notes: the damselfly

Of the two, the damselfly is the most important. It appears in great numbers and continues to show up more frequently in autopsies that I've conducted in the last fifteen years.

The nymph is slimmer than the dragonfly

and sports three distinctive leaf-like append-ages at the tail-end of its body. These are gills that take oxygen out of the water. They also double as paddles.

When it comes to swimming, these gills are only part of the act of swimming. A much more important part of the thrust comes from the damselfly wiggling their bodies backwards.

The wings of the adult damselfly are narrow. They are not strong fliers. From observation, they appear to prefer to fly around with a little help from a friend. Males and females couple up and fly around in tandem, mating as they go.

The female lays her eggs underwater, crawling down the stem of a plant. I have noted that the male very often accompanies the female on this journey, hanging on to her for dear life. When he prefers not to take a dip, he often doesn't let go of his grasp. I have see the male stand clear of the water clinging on to a weed stem and clutching on to the female who is under the water laying her eggs.

When the eggs have been laid, the male flaps his wings and starts to take off, lifting the submerged female out of the water and carrying her off to another egg-laying site.

Assassin's notes: the dragonfly

The dragonfly is not easy to assassinate.

The nearest the female adult gets to the water is to dip her tail gingerly just below the surface to lay her eggs in the tissues of aquatic plants.

The large, flat nymphs are masters of disguise, blending perfectly with their surroundings. If they look like anything at all, they look like small sticks. They prowl the lake bed, marauding. Their tactic is to creep up behind their prey at a snail's pace, and pounce.

On rare occasions when they need to swim, the dragonfly pulls off the strangest stunt. It draws in water through an opening it has at the back-end. It then spurts the water out again by contracting its muscles. Jet propulsion in its simplest form.

Alder fly

The alder is of more interest to the lake fisher than to the river fly fisher. In May and June it is plentiful on both types of water.

Truly speaking the alder is a terrestrial insect. In only one of its four stages of development does it actually wet its feet.

The adult is a fat fly, shaped like a condensed sedge. Its nicotine-stained, net-like wings are heavily veined and shiny and look like leaded windows. It has a black body, black legs and a black head.

Unlike sedges, once they decide to land on you, they are difficult to shift and behave in a more friendly, less neurotic fashion. This is basically because they are feeble fliers.

Also, unlike a sedge, the female adult alder lays her eggs on land – on leaves or grass stems, not too far away from the water. The newly hatched larva wriggles its way to the water and buries itself under the leaves, mud and silt on the bottom of the lake or river.

Dug away in the murk, the ochre-coloured, pearshaped alder larva, fringed with small pointed gills either side of its body, makes few friends. In fact, it eats almost everything it meets on its travels, shaking hands with one

Alder larva

Adult alder

of its claw-like mandibles to introduce itself and not letting go until it's devoured its new acquaintance.

After a year, to the relief of most of aquatic insect life, the alder larva heads back to the land where it digs itself away again, pupates and hatches out into an adult which, instead of making war, makes love with a mate, and dies.

Assassin's notes

During the migration period in April and May, the larva creep slowly along the river or lake bed towards the shore.

Ants, beetles and moths

Ants come in three colours: red, brown and black. In late summer, they come to the water in swarms, with wings. One gust of wind and they come to the attention of any trout in the vicinity.

Beetles come in two forms: terrestrial and aquatic. Of the former, Scotland and Wales's coch-y-bonddu and cockchafer beetles need to be noted. Both are jet black with brown or red wings which lead to their downfall when they fail to produce the power required to prevent them being blown on to the river.

The aquatic beetle's larva is worthy of attention. Some are so round and fat that creeping — their normal mode of transport — is hard work. The more common aquatic beetle larvae have six legs and a tiny head with a large, squirming, heavily segmented grey-olive body tapering down to two spikes, or tails.

To close this section on entomology — and to prove that I have left no stone in the river unturned, lest hidden underneath may be an important item on the trout's menu that I haven't mentioned, I end with the moth.

All that needs to be mentioned here is that there are, believe it or not, several species of moths that spend a large part of their lives underwater. The most common is called the Brown China Mark moth.

A fat moth pattern skated between the reflections of a sinking sun and a rising moon sums up all the practical fly fisherman need know about the life-cycle of the moth that is of any use.

Personally, you wouldn't get me to change from a sedge pattern at this time of day, or night. Not for all the moths in China.

FLY FISHER'S ENGLISH—LATIN DICTIONARY

Upwing flies	Ephemeroptera
Mayfly	*Ephemera danica, vulgata*
Blue-winged olive	*Ephemerella ignita*
Caenis	*Caenis robusta, horaria*
Claret dun	*Leptophlebia vespertina*
Sepia dun	*Leptophlebia marginata*
March brown	*Rhithrogena haarupi*
Autumn dun	*Ecdyonurus dispar*
Yellow may dun	*Heptagenia sulphurea*
Large dark olive	*Baetis rhodani*
Medium olive	*Baetis vernus, tenax*
Small dark olive	*Baetis scambus*
Pale watery	*Baetis bioculatus*
Iron blue	*Baetis pumilus, niger*
Small spurwing	*Centroptilum luteolum*

Pond olive	*Cloeon dipterum*
Lake olive	*Cloeon simile*
Pale evening dun	*Procloeon pseudorufulum*
Roof-shaped winged flies	Trichoptera
Great red sedge	*Phryganea grandis, striata*
Caperer	*Halesus radiatus*
Grey or silver sedge	*Odontocerum albicorne*
Cinnamon sedge	*Limnephilus lunatus*
Grey flag	*Hydropsyche pellucidula, instabilis*
Medium sedge	*Goera pilosa*
Grannom	*Brachycentrus subnubilus*

Brown silverhorn	*Athripsodes cinereus*	UFOs	Hemiptera—heteroptera
Black silverhorn	*Mystacides, nigra, A. aterrimus*	Water-boatman	*Corixa*
Grouse wing	*Mystacides longicornis*		Odonata
		Dragonfly	Anisoptera
Flat-winged flies	Diptera	Damselfly	Zygotera
Midges, buzzers	Chironomidae		Megaloptera
Hawthorn	*Bibio marci*		
Black gnat	*Bibio johannis*	Alder fly	Sialis
Reed smut	*Simulium*	Ants	Hymenoptera
Hard-winged flies	Plecoptera	Beetles	Coleoptera
Large stone-flies	Perlidae	Moths	Lepidoptera
February red	*Taeniopteryx nebulosa*		
Willow fly	*Leuctra geniculata*		
Needle fly	*Leuctra fusca, hippopus*		

Further reading

John Goddard, *Trout Flies of Stillwater* (A. & C. Black, 1969).

——, *Trout Fly Recognition* (A. & C. Black, 1966).

——, *Waterside Guide* (Unwin Hyman, 1988).

J.R. Harris, *An Angler's Entomology* (Collins, 1952).

Martin E. Mosely, *Dry Fly Fisherman's Entomology* (Routledge, 1920).

C.F. Walker, *Chalk Stream Flies* (A. & C. Black, 1953).

——, *Lake Flies and Their Imitation* (Herbert Jenkins, 1960).

Peter Deane

Peter Deane went into his family's business in the City on 1 January 1936. He joined the Honourable Artillery Company and was commissioned in the Somerset Light Infantry a month or two after the outbreak of the Second World War. He joined the 1st Battalion of his regiment in India in 1941 but contracted polio in 1943 and was invalided home, confined to a wheelchair.

On his return to England, Peter settled in the West Country, living at Hemyock on the river Culm, teaching himself to tie flies and then to fly fish (in that order), and joining the Culm Flyfishers' Club. He quickly built up a clientele for his flies and has tied for several members of the Royal Family, including the Queen, the Queen Mother and the Prince of Wales, as well as for many notable rods at home and abroad. He pioneered the use of hair-winged salmon flies in the United Kingdom, starting with the river Beauly in Scotland in 1950.

Peter fishes the Test and the Itchen, but his favourite river is the Bybrook in Wiltshire which he sees as the nearest thing possible to an angler's paradise.

Peter moved to Eastbourne in Sussex in 1955, expanding his fly tying business and, in 1963, opening a wildlife picture gallery specializing in sporting and natural history pictures, which he ran successfully for eleven years.

His abiding passion is decoy ducks (he bought his first one on 10 March 1948, the day before he tied his first fly). His other interests include bird watching, nineteenth-century French art and the sculptures of Les Animaliers.

In addition to the fly dressing chapter he contributed to the original editions of *The Complete Fly-Fisher*, Peter has written occasional articles for *The Field* and for all the major angling periodicals. He retired in September 1988, having been a professional fly dresser for forty years.

10

FLY DRESSING

Peter Deane

When the Editor of this edition of *The Complete Fly Fisher* approached me regarding bringing my chapter on fly dressing in the original edition, published in 1963, up to date, the natural reaction was to reflect as to what had happened over the past twenty-five years as far as developments of salmon and trout flies were concerned and the immediate answer, much to my surprise, was not a great deal.

Having said that, it is only fair to add that the standard of fly tying in this country now could not be higher and, moreover, that the number of fly fishermen who tie their own artificials is legion. When I first started tying in 1948, this certainly was not the case and comparatively few did. Even so, over such a long period, a quarter of a century no less, one would have imagined that some revolutionary ideas should have manifested themselves. But except perhaps in one sector (stillwater fishing) there have been precious few as far as I can recall. Here's an absolute paradox therefore − vast numbers of fly fishermen tying flies and tying very well at that, reading everything on the subject that comes to hand, but genuinely new approaches very sparse on the ground.

In the case of trout flies for rivers and streams, I can only think of two for which the style and method of tying was to say the least 'different' when I began as a professional fly dresser; which were very successful from their inception, are equally so today, and are still being used consistently up and down the country. They are Frank Sawyer's Pheasant Tail Nymph and its variations and Lee Wulff's Grey Wulff and its many variations, both to my mind quite exceptional and in a class on their own.

The Swisher and Richards approach through their excellent book *Selective Trout*, first published in 1971, with its many fundamental changes, did not have the impact I thought it might have over here and I was asked to dress comparatively few of their artificials. But I am inclined to think their Paradun dressing has been responsible for the popularity enjoyed by the parachute-type fly over the past decade and today. Mark you, Doug Swisher and Carl Richards said in their book 'tradition is something handed down from the past − an inherited culture, belief, practice or attitude and very few fields of endeavour have more tradition associated with it than the sport of fly fishing', which is very true. They were of course in this particular instance referring to flies and not fly fishing equipment, which has advanced out of all recognition over the past twenty-five years. We have naturally produced several patterns of our own which have an edge and become standards but the method of dressing them is quite orthodox.

The thing which has surprised me most as far as floating flies are concerned is why the late Vincent Marinaro's *A Modern Dry Fly Code*, first published in 1950, then again in 1970, has not influenced our fly dressers, both professional and amateur, more than it has. It will come, of course, and the divided tail on dry fly artificials will become as commonplace here as it is in America. And the great Marinaro's designs, the thorax tie to mention one other, will be universally used and appreciated.

There is one trend I feel sure will be in fairly common use in the very near future. I have noticed, especially over the past two seasons, a tendency to go down in hook size. When I began dressing flies, there were still numerous hook manufacturers and they produced many shapes which included intermediate sizes. For example, the Redditch Scale included 17, 15, 13, etc. with the even numbers in between. The smallest was usually size 18 although sizes 20 and 22 were available from some manufacturers.

Today, as leaders improve, the smaller sizes, especially in the United States, are in universal use. John Goddard, in an article published in *Trout and Salmon* in 1989, fished Herbert Wellington's water in Montana and was surprised by the use of such small flies as sizes 18, 20 and 22 (dressed probably by Craig and Jackie Matthews or their assistants of Blue Ribbon Flies fame) and by their ability to hold such large strong active fish. I suppose in 1988, my last season as a fly dresser, I tied more flies on size 18 and 20 hooks than I had done over the past thirty-nine years! Incidentally, there is nothing difficult in tying on small hooks — it's on big hooks, especially the very big ones that the gaps and mistakes stick out like sore thumbs, so take heart!

In the case of salmon flies, the hair wing had almost completely ousted feather by the end of the 1960s and justifiably so. Why it didn't happen before is the only surprising thing about it as far as I am concerned. Hair gives better movement under the surface than feather ever did, stands up to wear and tear exceptionally well and because one bunch of hair does not mask another, everything in the wing is seen by the fish and works accordingly.

Moreover, hair wings are far easier to dress. But despite all this, the beauty of a fully dressed mixed or built feather wing salmon fly was quite something, if dare I say it, not nearly so attractive to salmon.

The most killing salmon flies on many rivers today are not only hair winged but also extremely simple to tie into the bargain. Such patterns as Tosh, The Munro Killer, Old Charlie, Willie Gunn, the Hairy and Black Marys. The last two named possibly began it all in Britain.

The one sector of fly fishing I referred to earlier on which has grown and developed out of all proportion to others is, of course, that on reservoirs and lakes — a veritable explosion with new waters opening almost daily. Small fisheries abound everywhere and there cannot be a town in this country these days which does not offer fly fishing adjacent to it or as near to it as 'damn it' is to swearing.

Coupled with the inception and growth of The Fly Dressers Guild, stillwater fishing is responsible as much as anything for the extremely high level of fly tying in the country today. Stillwaters cater for everybody; all you have to do is to buy some tackle, catch some fish and the usual progression thereafter is to start tying your own flies. The object of this chapter is to show you how to start doing that — nothing more.

The principles are exactly the same whether the materials you use have been recently introduced or not. As there has been such an extraordinary interest in fly tying, some of the introductory flies I will be teaching you to dress may be a fraction less orthodox than in the original chapter but they are simple to tie nevertheless.

After forty years as a professional fly dresser with clients who have fished not only waters in the British Isles but on rivers in France, Spain, Africa, Iceland, Norway, the United States, South America and New Zealand, I believe it is generally true to say that the simpler the pattern used, the more successful does it tend to be.

GETTING STARTED

As I said before, fly dressing is a comparatively easy business. Any fly fisher can tie flies for salmon, sea-trout, brown trout, rainbows or grayling. It is rather like handwriting, which we take for granted; of course, some do it far better than others. Many write naturally well and a few develop their writing to such a pitch it becomes an art in itself, known as calligraphy, much in the same way as well-known fly dressers develop their skill.

On occasions the perfectly dressed fly can fail as miserably as the crude one; so apart from the personal satisfaction of tying well, the less impressive efforts of enthusiastic amateurs can and often do hold their own. The real satisfaction comes from taking a fish on something you have tied yourself and not from the extent to which your skill is admired by fellow fly fishers, though it would be smug to suggest that one is indifferent to such admiration.

My aim is to show the beginner how to dress a series of flies selected for their simplicity in construction, the availability of materials, and attractiveness to fish, involving the basic techniques from which more complicated flies can eventually be tied. The order in which I have arranged the instructions is important. The first lesson is a hackled dry fly, which I consider the easiest for a beginner to try his hand at. This does not mean I consider dry fly fishing more or less important than any other kind; it's just an ideal starting point where fly dressing is concerned.

The object of each lesson is to give the simplest step by step instruction, so that the first finished fly can be used to catch fish irrespective of what it may look like. Each lesson is complete in its own sphere and the basis for other patterns to come. Stress is put on the instruction, the easiest way to use the materials, advice, the amount of material required and how and from where to select it. Many refinements are omitted on purpose. If the reader wants to progress he will do so regardless of this. Before starting on the lessons however, it is necessary to say something of the tools and materials that will be required.

MATERIALS

There is such a vast range of materials available today that one could spend any amount of time building up a collection, so I offer the same advice as practically everyone else who has written on the subject: buy the minimum and add to it as required. Fly dressers take almost as much pride in their materials as they do in the flies they make with them. With economy in mind and the prior knowledge that the beginner will, through trial and error, be bound to waste a certain amount, I have adopted the following course. At the beginning of each instruction in tying a particular fly, I give the dressing and the materials required to make them. Some materials used in one pattern can be used in another and in such cases this will be referred to at the time. The sooner one becomes familiar with the types of hooks, silks, furs, feathers and equipment available, the better. The following firms specialize in supplying materials for the fly dresser: E. Veniard Ltd, who now do so through all retail tackle shops; Tom C. Saville of Nottingham; Rare Feathers Ltd of Worcester; and Sportsfish of Hereford. All three issue excellent catalogue. Their addresses are in the appendix. I can vouch for the quality of materials of all of them, Veniards being my main source of supply since the day I started and their service always matched the quality of materials.

I have no intention of discussing materials to any great extent, as the subject is too big to be included here. A perfunctory survey with each lesson accompanied by an added comment where essential will suffice for practical purposes. I must, however, say something about hackles.

Hackles

Every fly fisher knows the importance of a hackle on a fly, whether it be a floating or sunk pattern. Good cock hackles make a dry fly float better, give 'kick' or life to wet flies (others are tied with hen hackles) and act as an 'attractor' when dyed a bright colour and used on salmon flies. Their importance cannot be overestimated.

In 1963 when the original edition of *The Complete Fly-Fisher* was published, good cock capes, from which individual hackles could be selected, were in very short supply and to get a first class cape was an achievement. The position has now changed completely and they are readily available, in fact two American firms, possibly more now, specialize in producing cock capes solely for fly dressers — they are Metz (The Metz Hatchery of Belleville, Pennsylvania) and C.Q.H. (Colorado Quality Hackles of Fort Collins, Colorado), both well known by all fly fishers today. There is also a British firm which produces the highest quality Grizzle (Plymouth Rock) cock capes, called the D.J. Hackle Farm; and Rare Feathers, whilst producing quality capes, are now really renowned for their jungle cock capes and other rare feathers.

Each cape is individually packed in a self seal polybag, stapled on a card, graded 1, 2 or 3 and named (breed and/or colour). The Metz and C.Q.H. capes are expensive, Rare Feathers and the D.J. Hackle Farm less so. At the time of writing Metz or C.Q.H Grade 1 capes sell for £40−£45 each, Grade 2s sell for £27 and Grade 3s £20. These figures are approximate.

If you can afford to indulge yourself in such a cape or capes, a lot of worry and time wasting will be overcome from the start. The hackles on these capes are not only beautifully shaped, the fibres (barbs as the breeders call them) on each side of the stalk are equal in size for almost the full length of the hackle, and, in Grades 1 and 2, some individual hackles are so long that it is not uncommon to be able to dress two flies with one hackle. The greatest boon with such capes are the small and very small hackles — not only plentiful but beautifully shaped. The problem, and what a problem it was at times, in finding suitable hackles for size 16, 18 or 20 hooks, has been erased; they now abound!

The colours, including most of the shades of natural blue, are available for the first time to everyone; so are grizzles, reds, gingers, whites and blacks. In some cases it can be positively economic to use such capes but, as I have said, they are not cheap. The difference in grades is that 1 is fuller (more hackles) than 2 and 3 less than 2, but in all cases the quality is all too apparent. All these capes are sold at some retail outlets, and you can buy them direct from Saville, Sportfish, Rare Feathers and D.J. Hackle.

If I were a beginner, though, I would start at the other end of the market, with the cheaper, less specialist copes. I used these capes for many years and never had a single complaint about the hackle quality of my flies. I had some excellent capes from these sources — a few from the home market but the majority from China or India. Such capes are packed in cellophane envelopes and retail at between £3 and £6 each. You will get good blacks (usually dyed), dark reds, fox reds, rarely bi-coloured (furnace and coch-y-bondhu) and ginger but seldom badger or grizzle capes. It is remarkable how soon one's eye learns to spot a good cape amongst a lot of not so good ones. Again it's a case of buying what you can afford.

So the beginner can take heart as the supply of cock capes continues to improve. Much has been written about cock hackles and I have shouted the odds about them in the preceding paragraphs, but the cock hackle which makes a fly float best of all in my opinion has a quality which past fly dressers called 'spring'. Any cock hackle has spring when its barbs have a pronounced curve. By holding it by its tip and running the finger and thumb of the other hand down the stalk so the fibres stand out at right angles, you will notice that the tip of each fibre curls so as to form what looks like a little 'foot'. Such hackles, which may appear ugly, actually make splendid floaters, and the so-called 'feet' make them sit well on the water and float far longer than any hackle with stiff, super-pointed fibres. Dark red cock hackles (Indian game) have a pronounced tendency to be well 'sprung' but are not so readily available as they used to be. It's only fair to add that they also have a tendency to be lacking in graduation – sometimes the fibres at the tip

are longer than those at the base. Irrespective of this, for making your fly float, they have no equal.

Lastly, always buy your hackles, cock or hen, on a skin and never loose in a packet. There are a number of reasons for this but the most important are that an individual hackle of a certain size is so much easier and quicker to select from a skin (cape/neck) and that capes are easy to store, which becomes an important consideration all too soon.

TOOLS, HOOKS AND ACCESSORIES

Fly tying vice

There are so many vices on the market these days, ranging in price from a few pounds to £200 plus, that it is not easy to know what to recommend; it depends upon what you are prepared to pay. I started with a British Eclipse at £1.50 or less, changed to a French Tissot and finally graduated to the American Thompson which I have used for the past thirty-four years and cannot praise too highly. It can hold a size 2/0 trout hook or a size 10/0 standard salmon double without any ill effects on the jaws.

My choice is an inexpensive vice called 'The Croydon' which costs about £16 and is ideal for the beginner. Its jaws are operated by a lever giving instantaneous grip or release and will hold very small trout hooks and salmon hooks up to size 2 (Figure 48). Moreover, the lever which operates the jaws will be found to be extremely helpful to the beginner as a hand rest during operations. It is held on the workbench or table by a clamp and its pillar is, of course, adjustable for height.

Catch

Some vice clamps have a small rubber button or washer on the front or the side, the idea of which is to hold the fly tying silk during operations. In truth it is worse than useless and the beginner should ignore it as it will hinder rather than assist.

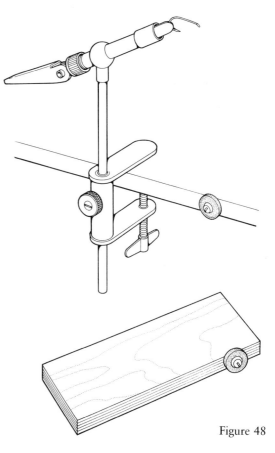

Figure 48

If you are fortunate enough to have a workbench or table specifically for fly tying, you can easily make yourself a catch by slipping a small metal washer over the point of a screw so it slips down to the head. Then drive the screw through the centre of a tap washer (Figure 48).

Screw this into the edge of the workbench about 4 inches to the right of your vice clamp. This device will hold the tying silk on your hook taut at appropriate times between the washer and the bench. I cannot overstress the importance of this catch. If you cannot get a permanent work table, I recommend the Deane/Elphick Vice Clamp Adaptor (D/EVC), a ridiculously pompous name for such a simple piece of equipment. All it consists of is a piece of wood ½ inch thick, 8½ inches long and 3 inches wide with the tap washer etc. screwed in about 1 inch from the right edge (Figure 48). You place your clamp adaptor along the edge of your table, put the vice clamp on top of it then tighten up the clamp screw. Apart from its usefulness, it protects your table from being marked by the clamp.

Cup screw

If you have a permanent workbench, drive a cup hook into its edge, well out of the way but within reach of your right hand. The idea of this is to hang your lengths of waxed silk on it to prevent them tangling. If you do not have a permanent bench, extend your 'D/EVC Adaptor' and put the cup hook in that.

Hackle pliers

The jaws of these pliers are opened by pressing the shoulders between the finger and thumb and closed automatically when the pressure is released. Their main purpose is to hold a hackle whilst it's being wound round the hook shank. Two pairs are required – medium sized.

Scissors

Curved slender blades are ideal; buy the best quality you can afford.

Dubbing needle

This can be made from any large darning needle driven eye first into a wooden or cork handle. Also sold at all tackle shops.

Penknife and razor blade

The former with a blunt blade, the latter sharp.

Sable hair watercolour brush

Size 00 is ideal – rather expensive but do not economize on this by buying a cheap substitute for sable. It's for applying varnish to heads of all flies and is in constant use. The brush is cleaned with acetone after each application of varnish and the hair in the cheap ones just falls out in no time. A sable brush will last years if cared for.

The Peter Deane fly tyer's bottle stand

Not essential but very useful. The varnishes you need are in standard size bottles but if necessary you can all too soon make one yourself to hold three bottles or more.

My first efforts at dubbing – a half dozen dry flies for one of my clients took me ages to dress and the struggle nearly killed me. I finally finished them only to ruin them all by knocking a bottle of varnish over the lot. That evening I made a rough bottle stand and sent it to Veniards the following day, and they have sold their interpretation of it ever since to hold three or six bottles. In these stands there are also three recesses to hold your brush or brushes.

Acetone

A bottle from the chemist costs about 40 pence. This is used to clean your varnish brush and the hands.

Varnishes

A small bottle each of black, red and clear Cellire Varnish No. 1 plus a similar sized bottle of spirit varnish.

Cotton wool

A packet of cheap cotton wool for cleaning fingers with acetone – this removes all varnish stains from the hands. It is also used for cleaning brushes.

Apron

Another essential. Apart from keeping pieces of feather and fluff off one's clothing, it saves much time when you knock things off the table which fall into your lap instead of on the floor, especially trout hooks. A white one is best.

Fly tyer's wax

A piece of prepared wax will be required from the beginning and is available from all shops selling materials.

Tying silks

Pearsall's Gossamer Brand sold in small reels. You will need the following colours: one each of black, yellow, red and hot orange.

Floss

Mirabou Floss sold on identical reels to the silk; you want the same colours as above plus a reel of white.

Tinsels

Six types of tinsel are used by fly dressers; wires, flats, ovals, embossed, rounds and lace. We are only concerned with the first three and, possibly later on, with embossed, but rounds and lace need not concern us. I have always abhorred rounds and only once in my life used lace on some gigantic double salmon flies I was tying for Norway. All tinsels are sized; flats, for instance, go from 1 to 11, wires 25 to 27 and ovals 14 to 19.

Buy only small reels and remember ovals are expensive; to prevent tarnishing, store in a box. If you can wrap them in black paper, so much the better.

Hooks

No problems here. British are best and always have been, and they are recognized throughout the fly dressing world as such. Buy either Partridge's or Sprite's. I suggest the following trout hooks as a start. Twenty-five each down eyed, wide gape, in the following sizes: 16, 14, 12, 10 and 8 (Redditch Scale). In the case of trout flies, I have always used down eye hooks though up eyed are usually associated with dry fly patterns. I soon noticed in the early days some of the notable dry fly fishers I tied for used down eyed hooks and if they were good enough for them, they were good enough for me. Subsequently I only tied on up eyes if requested.

Salmon hooks

Ten each size 4 and 6, standard single. Ten each size 8 and 10 low water singles.

Storage

For storing feathers there is nothing like old cigar boxes as the cedar from which they were made is moth repellent. Other types of containers should be sprinkled with naphtha flake which may be obtained from a chemist.

BASIC OUTFIT

The following list is what you will require as a basic outfit to make a start on the opening lessons. The only extravagance is a golden pheasant crest and frill; again, like cock hackles, always buy on the skin as they are easier to store and select and far less expensive to obtain that way. Choose one with bright golden crests and equally bright orange and black tippets. The majority of salmon flies have a tail made of topping and, in the old days, had a crest over a feather wing. Golden pheasant crests and topping are also used extensively these days as tails on sea-trout flies and lake and stillwater patterns.

Croydon fly tying vice.

Pair of scissors with curved blades.

2 pairs of medium size hackle pliers.

Dubbing needle.

Piece of fly tyer's wax.

Small bottle of clear Cellire Varnish No. 1.

Small bottle black Cellire No. 7.

Small bottle red Cellire No. 6.

Small bottle spirit varnish.

Bottle stand (optional).

Sable watercolour brush size 00.

Bottle of acetone from chemist.

1 reel of gossamer tying silk in black, yellow, red and hot orange.

1 reel of Mirabou Floss in black, yellow, red, hot orange and white.

One small reel of silver and gold Tinsel in the following sizes only.

Wire   size 17
Flat   size 3
Oval   size 15

25 each down eyed, wide gape trout hooks in sizes 16, 14, 12, 10 and 8.

10 each standard salmon single hooks size 4 and 6.

10 each low water single hooks size 6 and 8.

1 black cock cape (dyed).

1 fox red cock cape.

1 dyed blue dun cock cape.

1 black calf tail.

1 piece of ostrich herl dyed black.

1 large peacock eye for stripping with herl.

1 golden pheasant crest and collar (topping and tippets).

1 linen apron from Millett's Stores or similar.

Some readers who have watched friends tying may wonder why I have not included a bobbin holder. I am convinced that in the initial stages a bobbin holder is more of a hindrance than a help and complicates movements rather than assists them. I only use them on very large salmon hooks and do so with some reluctance. I must add though, that without exception, all the girls I trained and who worked for me, eventually took to a bobbin holder. To the best of my knowledge, nobody I have ever taught has ever used a whip finishing tool!

Finally, nylon as opposed to gossamer silk for tying; the American fly dressers were using it in 1948 but I don't personally like it because it has a little 'give' and with gossamer you soon learn to know what tension you can put on the silk. Again, try it in the future if you want to and, if you prefer it, all well and good.

GETTING STARTED

Before making an actual start on a trout fly, there are two operations which must be learned — those of starting and finishing a fly. It is much easier to learn them on a bare shank and it will save endless time in future if they are mastered at the outset; they consist of: (1) winding waxed silk round the shank from eye to the bend of the hook and back again; (2) the whip finish. When you can carry out these two simple operations your first attempt at tying an actual fly should take under fifteen minutes.

FIRST LESSON: ATTACHING SILK TO HOOK

To simplify this and subsequent lessons I am numbering each successive step. Proceed as follows.

1. Set up your vice on a table or bench by screwing the clamp firmly on the edge, making sure it is 4 or 5 inches to the left of the rubber catch irrespective of whether the catch is screwed into your worktable or you are using a clamp adaptor.

2. Place the following materials within easy reach; a piece of wax, a reel of black silk, acetone, a small piece of cotton wool, a penknife and some size 14 trout hooks.

3. With your penknife cut or dig off a small

piece of wax about the size of a pea and hold it between the lips (not in the mouth). This softens the wax quickly. If you have warm hands, just hold it in the fingers.

4. Still holding the wax between the lips, cut off a length of black tying silk about 1 foot 6 inches long and hold it in the middle between the finger and thumb of the right hand. Take the wax with the finger and thumb of your left hand and mould it as flat as possible. When it is soft, pull first one end of the silk and then the other through the wax so the complete length is covered. Hang your waxed silk over the cup screw on the table edge. Wax five more pieces of about the same length and put the soft piece of wax on top of your reel of silk so it sticks to it, then you won't lose it. Finally clean your fingers with a piece of cotton wool and a little acetone.

5. Take a hook — I suggest a size 14 down eye — and inspect the barb, point and eye. Always make a point of doing this. There is nothing more annoying than tying a fly only to discard it when you have discovered your hook is faulty.

6. Lift the lever of your vice so the jaws open slightly and place a hook in between them. The point of the hook should be covered by the jaws. Failure to cover the hook point results in a tendency to rupture the silk against the point in winding it round the shank, which is all too easily done in the early stages. Then tighten up the jaws. Try, if you can, to adjust your vice jaws so that, when they are tightened to hold hooks between size 14 and size 10, the clamp lever is a continuation of the jaws. At some stages this is a useful aid as you can rest your left hand on it during tying operations.

7. Test your hook for temper by flicking it up and down with the thumbnail on the eye. If the temper is correct, it will spring back to its original position; if it is too soft it will not do this; if it is too hard it may even snap. Make sure the hook is held firmly by the jaws. The hook shank should always be parallel with the top of the bench; nothing is more frustrating than having the shank of the hook dip down and point to the floor when you start to wind on your silk. If this happens, re-align the hook

at once and make sure it is held firmly. If it is not, re-adjust the jaws.

8. Take a piece of waxed silk and pull it through the fingers to clean off any surplus wax. Hold one end between the finger and thumb of the left hand and 3 inches up with the finger and thumb of the right hand, keeping the silk taut between the hands.

9. Place the taut silk against the hook shank with the right hand uppermost, about the length of a hyphen to the left of the eye.

10. Still keeping the silk taut between the hands, wind it with the right hand three or four close touching turns round the shank, working towards the bend of the hook. If the silk has been kept taut, the turns made by the right hand will not only have gone round the shank but also round the length of silk held by the end in the left hand. Continue to wind towards the bend for three more turns.

11. Let go of the silk with the left hand and place the still taut long end in the catch (Figure 49).

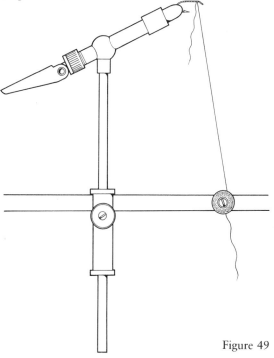

Figure 49

12. If this has been done correctly the silk will hold firm on the shank. Cut off the waste silk.

13. Take the silk out of the catch and hold it in the finger and thumb of the right hand about 2−3 inches below the hook shank. If you work with too long a piece of silk, manipulation will be just that much more difficult. In other words, work with a comparatively short length and just slide your fingers down the silk as you need more. Now wind slowly in close even turns towards the bend of the hook, keeping the silk taut the whole time. Remember, the shorter the piece of silk you work with, the more control you have over it.

14. On reaching the bend (do not take the silk beyond the straight part of the shank) wind back in slow, even turns, each turn touching but not overlapping its neighbour. Stop about ⅛ inch short of the eye and place the silk in the catch. The work is now ready for the next lesson.

Comment: This may seem an extremely long winded way to explain such a simple operation, but it is important and a good foundation always simplifies the rest of the work. After a few tries the beginner will manage it in a second or two and carry it out automatically.

SECOND LESSON: THE WHIP FINISH

This is another simple operation which may be learned at the first attempt or in some cases after a little practice. The fact remains that until the beginner can do this with confidence, he or she cannot finish any fly securely, no matter how expertly they have dressed it. For this purpose we must imagine the whole fly is completely tied and only needs a whip finish to make it secure.

1. Take the silk out of the catch and hold with the forefinger and thumb of the right hand about 3 inches below the eye of the hook with the *forefinger on top of the silk, thumb underneath*. The elbow should be pointing to the right and approximately parallel with the edge of the table.

2. Without moving the arm, rotate the forefinger and thumb (turning away from your body) so that the thumb now comes on top and the forefinger underneath. Do not release your grip, and keep the silk taut between the hook and the fingers. The loose end of silk should fall automatically across the length held in the right hand making an approximate letter 'D' (Figure 50).

3. Keep the silk taut with the right hand, and now take hold of it with the forefinger and thumb of the left hand, this time the left forefinger uppermost at the point where it was gripped with the forefinger and thumb of the right hand. If you can, anchor the loose end of

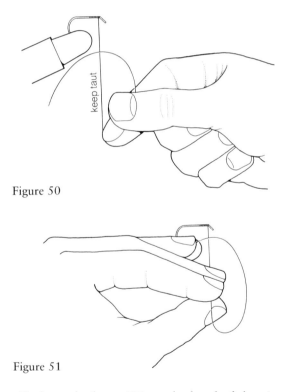

Figure 50

Figure 51

silk from the letter 'D' on the head of the vice with the fourth finger of the left hand (Figure 51). Take the right hand away.

4. Still keeping the silk taut between the left hand and the hook, with the free right hand slide the loose end of silk (one end of which is anchored with the fourth finger) up the taut

silk to the eye of the hook, virtually the top bit of the 'D'. This is made easier if the left hand holding the silk is raised up towards the chin, still keeping the silk taut.

5. Now bring the left hand straight up so it's above the hook and slightly beyond the top of the vice, but the silk is still taut. The taut silk should have squeezed the top of the 'D' tight against the shank. Once you have achieved this, move the free right hand to take the silk from the left hand, remembering to keep it taut, and repeat this operation three more times, working towards the eye (Figure 52).

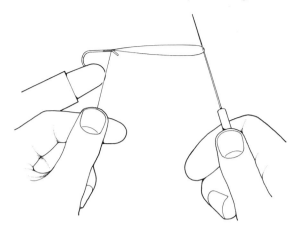

Figure 53

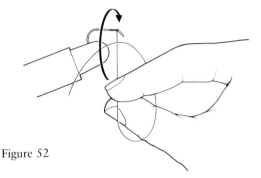

Figure 52

Practice will soon show the most convenient time and position to change hands. It will be seen that the short, taut length of silk has not only been wrapped round the end of the hook but also around the bight of silk formed when the position of the fingers was rotated at step 3 – making a letter 'D'.

6. With the right hand, insert the dubbing needle in the loop and pull on the loose end with the left hand (Figure 53). The binding will tighten on the head of the fly and you can slip

the dubbing needle out just before the final tightening.

7. Pull the loose end tight and snip off the end of the silk with the scissors, leaving a fraction of silk showing. If you cut off too close, the whipping could possibly work loose. Practice the whip finish until you have absolute confidence.

Comment: Once you can attach silk to a hook shank and execute a whip finish two very important hurdles have been surmounted. Friends of mine in the past, having watched me tie flies have often asked me to let them try. In many cases the flies they tied were good, considering they were not familiar with handling the materials, but in every instance they came unstuck at the whip finish. For this reason, among others, I stress the importance of learning it first.

THIRD LESSON: A HACKLED DRY FLY AND VARIATIONS WITH BLACK COCK HACKLES

It is now time to start tying and to give the beginner some confidence. Naturally, we will start with easy patterns. All those in this lesson are uncomplicated and are as simple as any I know. And not only will they catch trout, but

they also involve many of the basic movements and techniques used in fly tying generally, whether for trout or salmon flies. Mastering them will therefore assist you in the lessons that follow. All these flies are black in colour, and the amount of materials used in each pattern is economical to say the least. The tie or dressing of a fly is written down in much the same way as a cooking recipe and usually in the order in which you tie in your materials.

I have divided this lesson into ten phases, the first is a dry fly, the Black Gnat. This particular dressing could not be easier but the fact remains that it will take fish on occasions just as well as the more complicated black gnat patterns. So here we go.

Phase one: Black Gnat — dry

Hook: Size 14 down eyed wide gape.
Tying silk: Black gossamer tying silk.
Body: Black silk.
Hackle: Black cock cape.

After you have equipped yourself with the above materials, proceed as follows:

1. Wax a few lengths of black silk and hang them over the cup screw.

2. Put the hook in the vice having inspected and tested it first, and make sure it is not only held firmly but that the shank is also parallel with the top of your workbench.

3. Take a length of silk, pull it through the fingers to remove any surplus wax and then wind it on to the hook shank, starting just short of the eye and working towards the bend. Don't forget that the distance between the finger and thumb of the left hand and right hand should only be some 3 inches or less; it is so much easier to work with. Once the silk is holding, put it in the catch and cut off the surplus.

4. Take the silk out of the catch and work in close even turns until you have covered the shank, stopping at the bend. The present fashion is to stop just above the barb with trout flies and the point with salmon flies. Then take the silk back in close even touching turns to where you started. Put the silk in the catch.

5. Pick up your black cock cape and select a hackle for the size of the hook. As a general guide, the length of the fibres of the hackle should be a fraction longer than the shank of the hook. Tear off all the soft fibres around the base of the stalk.

6. Hold the prepared hackle between the finger and thumb of the left hand, the best side of the hackle (the brightest) facing you. Never pick up a hackle by its tip when tying in as it will wobble about. Always hold it as far up the stem as you can. It is so much easier to control like this.

Holding the hackle well up the stem, push all the bare stalk of the hackle under the hook shank and over the silk still in the catch (Figure 54). Take the silk out of the catch with the right hand holding it short (about 3 inches) and take three close turns round the hackle stalk and hook. Then place silk in the catch.

7. Cut off the surplus hackle stalk just short of the eye, not beyond it. To do this, insert scissors over the silk and under the eye of the hook. This prevents us from cutting the silk inadvertently, which is all too easily done at first. Take another turn of silk around the head of the fly (insurance) and put the silk in the catch.

Figure 54

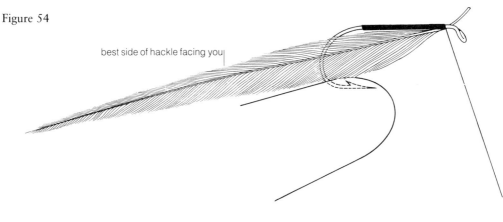

best side of hackle facing you

8. Attach the hackle pliers to the tip of the hackle, taking a fair amount of tip in the pliers, and wind the hackle in a clockwise direction round the shank, between the end of the body and the eye of the hook. Keep the hackle tight whilst winding as it makes it far easier. The first two turns should be taken towards the left, that is, as close as possible to the body, the next turn in front of the first two or even through them, then three or four more close turns in front of these, remembering to leave enough space for the whip finish. Leave the hackle pliers attached to the hackle tip and let them hang.

Wind two tight turns of silk *under* the hackle tip with the pliers attached. Keep the silk taut and put in the catch.

9. Cut off the hackle tip with the scissors, again taking care not to cut the silk. The safest way to do this is to insert the scissors, curves uppermost, to the right of the silk in the catch and under the eye of the hook. Extend the hackle pliers attached to the hackle tip to the right of the vice and snip off the hackle point. This method gives a clear view of what and where you are cutting.

10. Take the silk out of the catch and with the forefinger and thumb of the left hand stroke back any hackle fibres sticking out in front of the eye; then wind one tight turn in front of the hackle making this turn slightly towards the left rather than encroaching over the actual eye.

11. Whip finish your fly (Figure 55).

Figure 55

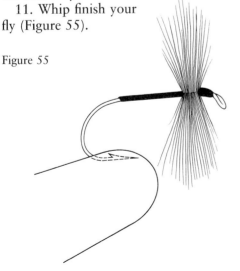

12. All that remains is to varnish the head, but rather than do it at this stage, I always wait until I have finished all the flies in a particular session and then varnish them all together. Incidentally, I always varnish my trout fly heads, with one or two exceptions, even on very small flies, with black varnish. It looks and wears better. Lastly, if there is still the odd hackle fibre sticking out, just snip it off. Don't be afraid of using your scissors.

Comment: This may sound a very laborious method of instruction to dress such a simple dry fly, but these instructions become automatic after a little practice even though they may seem difficult in the initial stages. The commonest fault at the beginning is to leave too little space to form the whip finish. Then you go to the other extreme and leave too much. But you soon learn exactly how much space you need.

Phase two: Silver Ribbed Black Gnat

Hook: Size 14 down eyed wide gape.
Tying silk: Black.
Body: Black silk.
Rib: Silver wire size 27.
Hackle: Black cock.

We can now take a further step by tying the same fly with a silver ribbed body. Again, I will start with the dressing.

1. Begin tying with your waxed black silk in exactly the same way as you did with the previous pattern and wind the silk in close even turns to the bend. Put the silk in the catch.

2. Take your reel of silver wire, cut off a 6 inch length and tie it in at the bend where your last turn of silk has stopped. I find that the best way to do this is to hold one end of the wire fairly short again because it is easier to control that way, and to poke about half an inch of it under the hook shank and over the taut silk still in the catch. Take the silk out of the catch, holding it short, and tie in with two close touching turns of silk. Do *not* cut off any surplus wire pointing towards the eye or

beyond it at this stage. The ideal of course is for the amount of wire to be the same as the length of the body of the fly.

3. Continue to wind the silk in close, even turns up the shank. They will form the body, and bind down the surplus wire at the same time. If you have managed close touching turns of silk, none of the surplus wire underneath will show through. Stop at the place you consider will leave enough room to tie in the cock hackle. Put the silk in the catch.

4. If you have carried out this operation carefully, there could still be a bit of silver wire protruding beyond the eye. Cut this off where the black silk body stops.

5. Take hold of the wire with the left hand and make four (no more) equidistant clockwise turns, slightly slanting, up the body. To wind any type of tinsel, you use the 'change hands' procedure, starting with one hand and taking over with the other at the most comfortable or convenient point. Having done this, attach your hackle pliers to the silver wire and tie it off with three turns of silk. Put the silk in the catch.

6. Snip off your wire and put it carefully aside for use with the next pattern.

7. Prepare and tie in your black hackle; wind it round and whip finish (Figure 56).

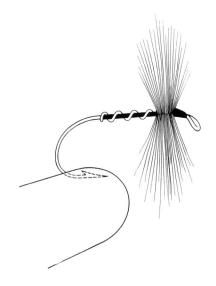

Figure 56

Comment: This is as simple a form of tinselling as you can get. It is also the basis of all tinselling whether you are using it to dress a 5/0 salmon fly or a size 18 trout fly. The aim is to judge the amount of surplus tinsel for your fly body, irrespective of whether you are using one type of tinsel, two or even three on the same fly. Naturally it is better to overestimate than to underestimate as this enables you to cut off any surplus.

The reason is fairly obvious. If you tie in tinsel at the start of making a fly body and then cut off the surplus half way along the body's length, the first half of the body is going to be fatter than the second. You will therefore have to compensate with tying silk or other body material, building up the second half, which is time consuming. A good body of any material always makes the rest of the tying easier and, of course, improves the look of the fly.

Phase three: Williams' Favourite

Hook: Size 14 down eyed.
Tying silk: Black.
Whisks: Four or five black cock fibres.
Body: Black silk.
Rib: Silver wire size 27.
Hackle: Black cock.

A continued development of the same dry fly, this time with tail whisks and a shaped body, again ribbed with silver wire. The natural Black Gnat has no tails but this does not deter the trout as they take the pattern with confidence. The official name of this fly is Williams' Favourite.

1. Proceed as before taking the black silk to the bend and put the silk in the catch.

2. Pick up your cock neck and select a large, stiff hackle for the tails or whisks of the fly. These will generally be found on the extreme left or right side of the cape, about halfway up. The fibres on these hackles usually have a pronounced curve and are ideal for the purpose.

3. Irrespective of which side of the cape you have taken this hackle from, with the best

(shiny) side facing you, tear off four or five fibres from the left hand side of the hackle. Again, the left hand fibres for some reason or other seem to sit better on top of a hook.

Holding the fibres between the finger and thumb of the left hand and taking advantage of their natural curve, place them on top of the hook shank just above where the silk has stopped at the bend. Take two close turns of silk around the base of the whisks and one turn underneath them. This will make the whisks cock up and splay out. Finally take one more turn round the base. Place the silk in the catch (Figure 57).

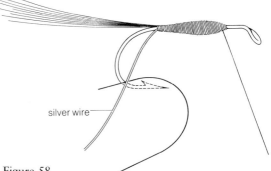

silver wire

Figure 58

6. Take four turns of silver wire up the body — not more; there is a great tendency in the early days to over-tinsel flies. Tie off the wire, put silk in the catch and cut off surplus wire.

7. Tie in and wind the hackle. Whip finish.

Comment: The shaping of most trout fly bodies and some salmon fly bodies is no more than a refinement; it serves no practical or logical purpose, except to give the impression of a better finished article. It certainly won't impress trout whether the artificial is dry or wet; all it does it to show the dresser has taken a little more trouble with the work.

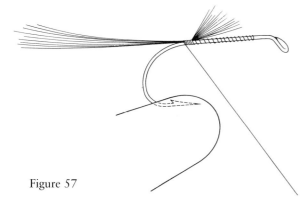

Figure 57

4. Take a 6 inch length of silver wire and tie it in with two turns of silk. Continue winding in close even turns as you did in the previous pattern, stopping when you reach the identical place. Place the silk in the catch and cut off any surplus wire if need be. It's more than likely that the butts or thicker ends of the whisks will not reach the front end of the fly body. Don't bother about it. The lump formed by the ends will scarcely show when they are bound down.

5. Take the silk out of the catch again and wind it back to just under halfway down the shank, then back again to the front of the body. Now wind the silk approximately a quarter of the way down the body and then back to the front of it. The idea is to shape the body a trifle — a carrot shape is the ideal — slender at the tail end and a little thicker at the eye end (Figure 58).

Phase four: Merry Widow

Hook: Size 12 down eye.
Silk: Black gossamer.
Tails: Black calf tail tied in short.
Body: Black gossamer.
Hackle: Black cock.
Wings: Black calf tail. A small bunch sloping over the eye a fraction and never split.

This pattern was created by my assistant, Brenda Elphick, of Eastbourne, and is considered by many to be one of the best floaters for stillwaters.

1. Attach silk to your hook in exactly the same way as in the other three patterns but do not take it down the shank more than six turns. Take it back again right up to the eye and return to where you started. Put the silk in

the catch and cut off the surplus end. The reason for going right up to the eye and back is to lay a foundation for the next step.

2. Pick up your calf tail and snip out a small bunch of short hair — the tip of a calf tail has long hair and the base short ones. Grip the tips of these short hairs quite tightly in the finger and thumb of the left hand and, with the finger and thumb of the other hand, pull out any under fur or weak hair in the bunch. In order to achieve this you may have to relax your grip with the left hand a trifle.

You are now left with a bunch of strong hairs. Re-arrange it so the tips are level and hold the bunch just above the base with the finger and thumb of the left hand, tips pointing to the right. This is going to be the hair wing of the fly.

3. Place the finger and thumb of your left hand on top of the hook shank so the base of the hair wing is in the vicinity of the silk foundation you have already made. Keep your finger and thumb there, slightly to either side of the shank (Figure 59).

Figure 60

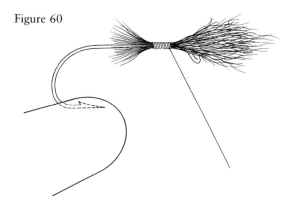

holding the base. This small bunch of hair should now look like (Figure 60).

This method of putting on a hair wing or a feather one for that matter is called 'pinch and loop' and, once you get used to it, is extraordinarily simple and comes quite automatically.

5. Take another couple of turns over the base, pull the wing almost upright, take four tight turns in front of it and then one complete turn round the base again. Put silk in the catch. The wing should now look like Figure 61.

Figure 59

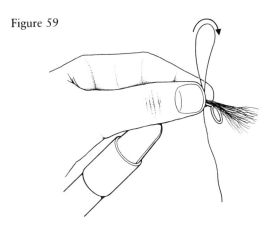

4. With the right hand, take the silk out of the catch holding it fairly short and taut, and bring it up inside the thumb holding the hair, loosely over the top of the hair and down inside the ball of the forefinger without pulling it tight. Bring the silk down below the shank without relaxing the finger and thumb and pull tight. Without letting go of the hair, do this again and then take two more tight turns without the finger and thumb over it but still

Figure 61

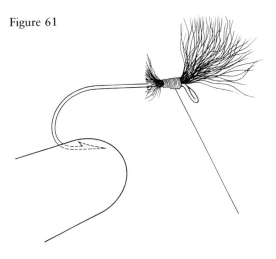

6. If the bases of the wing sticking out towards the bend of the hook are very long, cut them off about one-third of the way along the shank, bind them down and then take the silk back to the wing and put it in the catch.

7. Select a hackle, remembering you are tying on a slightly bigger hook. Take off any weak fibres and tie the hackle in with three

Figure 62

turns just to the left of the wing. This time the *worst* side of the hackle should be facing you. Put the silk in the catch.

8. Cut off the stem of the hackle stalk just beyond the end of the hair base. You can imagine now that when all is bound down, the fly body will be taking on a carrot shape (Figure 62). Take silk to the bend and put it in the catch.

9. Pick up your calf tail again and snip off a bunch of hair about one-third the size of the wing bunch. This will form the tail.

10. Tie in at the bend with three turns of silk and cut off the surplus hair about where it meets the tied-in wing bases and hackle stem. Bind the surplus down. Take the silk up to the wing and take one turn in front of it. Put the silk in the catch (Figure 63).

11. Wind five to six tight turns of hackle directly behind the wing and about two in front, making sure the best side of the hackle is facing forwards all the time. This usually happens automatically when the first turn is made. Tie off in the usual manner.

Comment: If you have not already done so, varnish all your dry fly heads with your brush and black varnish. Do not forget to clean the brush tip in acetone frequently and to clear the hook eyes with your dubbing needle if need be. Put flies away in a box and cut down any of those that are too frightful so you can use the hook again. This completes the dry flies in this exercise.

Figure 63

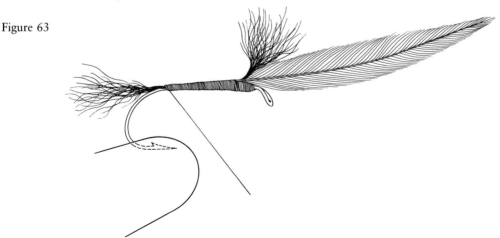

Phase five: Black Gnat — Wet

Hook: Size 12.
Silk: Black.
Tails: Black cock fibres — short.
Rib: Silver oval size 15.
Body: Black silk.
Hackle: Black cock.

We now start on the sunk patterns, again all easy and very effective, beginning with a wet Black Gnat, the counterpart to the dry one in phase one.

1. Place the hook in the vice and proceed in the normal way, winding the silk down to the bend and then putting it in the catch.

2. Take a large hackle from the side of the cape for the whisks. Select three or four fibres and tie in, rather short this time, on top of the shank, in the normal place. Do not cut off the surplus. Put the silk in the catch.

3. Cut off about a 4 inch length of silver oval. Holding the oval near one end, with the finger and thumb nails of the other hand, pull out about ¼ inch of silver and you will see this particular type of tinsel has a core of cotton. Expose for ¼ inch or a fraction more.

4. Tie in the silver oval where the silver ends and the core is exposed under the short whisks with two turns of silk. Put the silk in the catch.

5. Bind down the surplus whisk ends and the core of the oval tinsel in close even turns, stopping at the point where you tie in your hackle. Cut off any surplus whisk fibres and oval core, shape body slightly and put the silk in the catch.

6. Wind four turns of oval tinsel up body in equidistant turns. Attach the hackle pliers to the oval tinsel and tie the tinsel off with three turns of silk.

7. You can use one of two methods to cut off the surplus tinsel. Either just cut it away at the end of body, or expose a trifle more core, snip off tinsel covering and bind down with three turns of silk. This is a more thorough way which will prevent the rib from ever pulling out. Whichever way you adopt, put silk in the catch. All that remains now is to put on your wet hackle. The procedure is somewhat different from tying in and winding on a dry hackle.

In the old days most wet trout fly hackles were taken from hen's capes and were therefore much softer in texture. They were often wound round either by the tip or by the base in the normal manner. For many years now, cock hackles have been used for most wet flies and the procedure we use for preparing them is called 'doubling'. The reason for doubling is that it helps to give the fly a good entry rather than hover about at the surface — in other words to sink as fast as possible. I think the best way to explain this process is by diagrams (Figures 64—67).

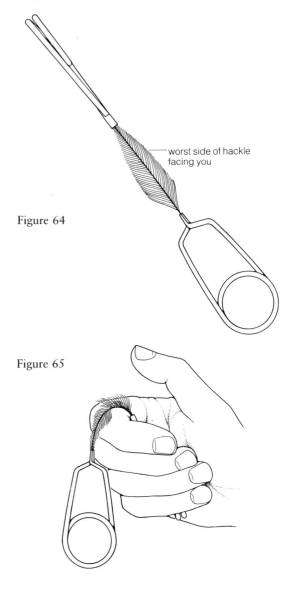

Figure 64

worst side of hackle
facing you

Figure 65

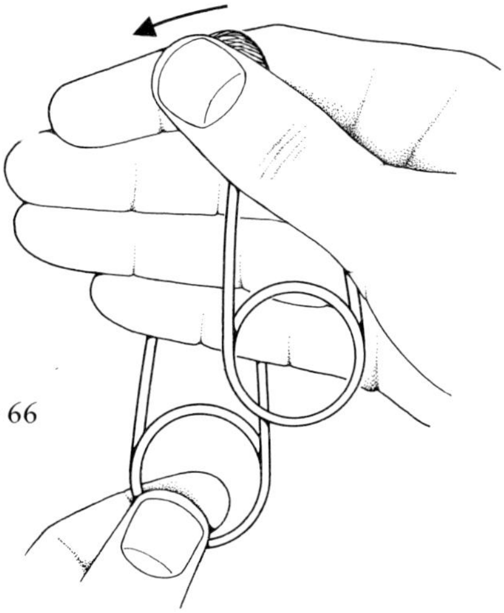

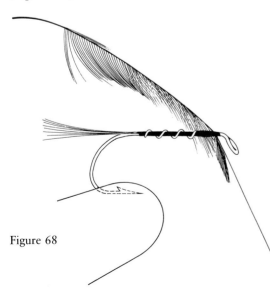

Figure 66

Figure 67

Figure 68

8. Tie in the doubled hackle by the tip, where the double ends and the tip begins (Figure 68).

9. Grip the hackle stalk with hackle pliers and wind the first turn as near to the end of the body as you can. With a doubled hackle you cannot go to and fro as with a dry fly. Each turn must go just in front of the previous one. Put on a maximum of three turns and leave hackle pliers attached to the stem. Take three turns of silk around the stem to secure it. Place the silk in the catch and cut off the surplus hackle.

10. Whip finish.

Figure 69

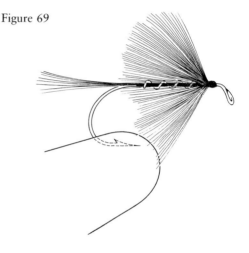

Comment: The flies should look like Figure 69, with the turns of hackle close together and angled back towards the bend. Use the minimum number of turns; the more you have the longer the fly will take to sink.

Phase six: Black and Peacock Spider

Hook: Size 12.
Silk: Black.
Body: Peacock herl.
Hackle: Black cock – long in the fibre.

Another wet fly and this time a famous one.

1. Secure a size 12 down eye hook in the vice and carry out the normal procedure, attaching waxed black silk just short of the eye – but this time leave the bit of surplus silk held in the left hand somewhat longer.

2. Wind the silk down the shank to just short of the bend but this time do *not* cut off the surplus. Put the silk in the catch.

3. Pick up your peacock eye with its best side towards you and select one strand, known as a herl, from the bottom left hand corner of the eye. A single strand of herl has a 'flue' on it, longer on one side than on the other and it is the longer flue which makes the body. Hold the herl between the finger and thumb of the left hand and place the thick end against the point where the silk stops with about ¼ inch surplus pointing towards the eye of the hook — in other words using exactly the same method as when tying in a silver rib.

4. Secure with two or three turns of silk and continue to wind silk up the shank, stopping at the end of your body-to-be. Put the silk in the catch and cut off any surplus herl if need be.

5. Wind on your peacock herl body with the quill edge leading (not the side with the flue) and you will soon notice a quite fluffy body forming. Keep each turn touching the one behind it as you proceed and stop at the appropriate place where the hackle is to be tied in. Attach your hackle pliers to the surplus herl and secure it with three turns of silk, but do not cut off the surplus. Put the silk in the catch.

6. If all has gone to plan your fly should look like Figure 70.

Figure 70

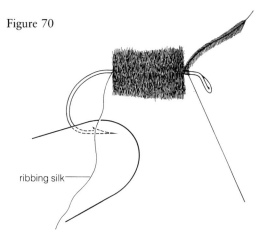

ribbing silk

7. With the spare bit of black waxed silk at the rear end of your herl body, rib the body with four turns of silk and attach your second

pair of hackle pliers to the end of this ribbing silk. Secure the ribbing with two turns of tying silk, place the tying silk in the catch and cut off the spare bit of ribbing silk and the surplus peacock herl. The reason for ribbing the peacock herl is that herl bodies, whilst very attractive to trout, are liable to get broken or torn in a fish's mouth, so they need a little protection.

8. Double a hackle with longish fibres and put two or three complete turns (no more) round the head. Secure and whip finish (Figure 71).

Figure 71

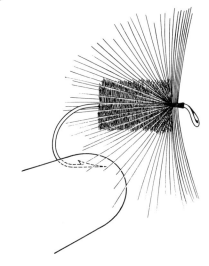

Phase seven: Black Pennell

Hook: Size 10.
Silk: Black.
Tails: Golden pheasant tippets.
Body: Black silk.
Rib: Silver oval size 15.
Hackle: Black cock — long in fibre.

I have advised you to buy golden pheasant with toppings (crests) attached as one uses such a lot of this material. This fly is a long established favourite, with a small splash of colour for a treat. Proceed as follows:

1. Put your hook in the vice and take your black tying silk down in touching even turns just short of the bend of the hook and put the silk in the catch. Pennells have two character-

istics; short, slender bodies and long fibred cock hackles.

2. Pick up your tippet frill and pluck out a well marked feather. The black on the tips and further up each fibre should be bright, and the orange colour likewise. Do not accept faded material.

3. With the points of your scissors, cut out a section of five or six fibres. You can tie them in either by taking advantage of any natural curl or by rolling them between the forefinger and thumb. Irrespective of which method you adopt, *always* tie in on the second black bar so little or none of it is showing when the body is made (Figures 72a and 72b). Tie in on top of the shank with three turns of silk, and put the silk in the catch.

Figure 72a

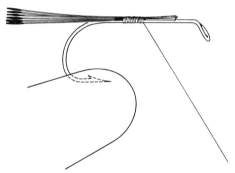

Figure 72b

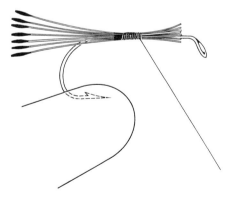

It has always been most noticeable to me, even to this day, that many fly dressers tie in tippets too long, sometimes well past the second black band. Apart from looking out of balance, this makes them very vulnerable during casting.

4. Just under your tippets, now tied in, add a short length of silver oval tinsel. Needless to say, neither the surplus tippet fibres nor the oval tinsel has been cut off at this stage. Wind silk up the hook shank in close even turns binding down neatly so that nothing underneath shows through. You can very slightly shape the body if you want to, but some people believe that all Pennell bodies should be level. Put the silk in the catch and remove any surplus tippet butts and silver oval.

5. Wind four or five turns of oval tinsel up body, tie off and cut away the surplus.

6. Select a long, strong fibred black cock hackle. Remove the soft fibres and double it. Tie it in by its tip and wind on three to three and a half turns. Tie off and whip finish (Figure 73).

Figure 73

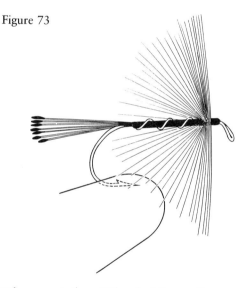

Phase eight: Black Nymph

Hook: Size 12.
Silk: Black.
Whisks: Black cock – very short.
Body: First half black silk.
Rib: Silver wire size 27 over first half only.
Thorax: Black ostrich.
Wing cases: Black rook – primary or secondary feathers.
Legs: Four black cock hackle fibres (optional).
Additional: 1 pair of rook's wings.

Everyone has an assortment of nymphs in his fly box these days. Here is a very simple tie, more representative of style rather than of any particular insect. Even so, trout take it with confidence. Although there are eight items in the dressing of this fly, it really is the easiest you have attempted apart from your first effort. It's all common sense, requiring a minimum of skill. Note the addition of the rook's wings, not on the basic list. From now on such items will be listed as 'Additional', so that you can see what you have to buy.

1. Place the hook in the vice as usual. Attach the silk and wind it back along the shank to the bend. Put the silk in the catch.

2. Select a longish hackle for the tail whisks or take some more fibres from the one you used before. You want three or four very short whisks on top of the hook. Tie in and put the silk in the catch.

3. Tie in a length of size 27 silver wire — a remnant if you have one. This time the body will be only half the length of the shank, so try and judge your surplus wire to be that length or thereabouts.

4. Wind silk up shank and stop when half shank is covered. Put the silk in the catch and cut off the surplus wire and tail whisk butts if need be.

5. Wind the silver wire up the shank about three turns; secure and cut off the surplus. Put the silk in the catch.

6. Select a large, long rook feather from the wing and cut a section about ½ inch wide. Fold in two, with the best sides outwards. This will be the roof which goes over the thorax. When cutting out this section, do so from the middle of the feather downwards, not upwards, as the fibres are coarser the nearer they are to the tip. We want our section fairly supple.

7. With the best sides of the wing section outward, tie them in by their base with two turns of silk where the body ends. This is quite easy to do. Hold the section by its tips with the forefinger and thumb of the left hand and, with the tying silk in the right, take two tight turns around the base. Cut off roof section base short of the eye and bind it down. Put the silk in the catch (Figure 74).

Figure 74

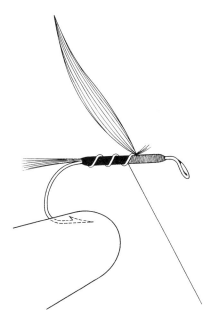

8. Take your piece of dyed black ostrich herl. You will notice that it is constructed in exactly the same way as the peacock herl used on the Black and Peacock Spider. Pull off a single herl, not too long in the flue, and tie it in on top of the folded wing section base with a turn of silk. Continue winding towards the eye, stopping just short of it. Put the silk in the catch and cut off any surplus roof section and herl not covered by the silk.

9. Wind on the ostrich herl with close even turns, so that each turn contributes towards an overall fluffy appearance. The first two turns should have started and covered where the roof section was tied in. Continue to wind on, stopping just short of the eye. Tie off with two turns of silk and put the silk in the catch.

10. The next step is optional; the legs. Some think them necessary, some a waste of time. If you want to put them in, take four or five black cock hackle fibres holding them by their bases just under the eye of the hook with the finger and thumb of the right hand. When they are in position, transfer them to the forefinger and thumb of the left hand and tie them in with three turns of silk. That is what is called a

'false throat' and it is in constant use today, not only on trout flies but on salmon flies as well. Put the silk in the catch and cut off any hackle surplus from the throat.

11. Lastly, grip the roof section firmly with the forefinger and thumb of the right hand and, exerting a little pressure, pull it flat over the top of your ostrich thorax and hold it there. Take the silk out of the catch with the left hand and take two tight turns over the folded roof section, just by the eye, and then two more. Put the silk in the catch and cut off the remainder just short of the eye itself. Take another turn round and then whip finish (Figure 75).

the shank parallel to the top of your work table. Put the silk in the catch.

2. Cut off a small section of silver wire and tie it in where the silk stops. The spare end should come to the middle of the shank. Wind the silk over the wire in close even turns, so that no wire is left exposed. Put the silk in the catch.

3. Wind the wire round shank for about five turns, stopping at the end of the body. Put the silk in the catch and cut off the surplus wire.

4. A single piece of black ostrich herl is tied in where the body stops and wound up to the eye. Tie off with two turns of silk, cut off the surplus herl and whip finish (Figure 76).

Figure 75

Figure 76

Comment: You have now tied a fly on a reasonably small trout hook and should not have had any trouble. Had we started on size 16, it would not have surprised me if you had found it difficult.

Phase nine: Black Midge Pupa

Hook: Size 16 down eyed.
Tying silk: Black gossamer.
Body: Black silk taken well round bend of hook.
Rib: Silver wire.
Thorax: Black ostrich.

1. Put a size 16 hook in the vice, attach the silk and take it in even touching turns right down the shank and as far round the bend of the hook as you can. You can simplify this by only placing the point of the hook in the vice, no deeper than the top of the barb, still keeping

Phase ten: Black Buzzer

Hook: Size 8 down eyed.
Tying silk: Black.
Body: Black wool.
Rib: Silver oval size 15.
Breathing tubes: White wool.
Additional: A hank each of black and white wool. Buy Anchor Tapestry Wool if possible as it is less expensive and sold in smaller hanks − it is a first class material.

1. Put the hook in the vice as you did for the previous fly and, again, when you attach your silk take it right round the bend of the hook. Place the silk in the catch.

2. Cut off a length of silver oval and tie it in at the bend with three turns of silk. Wind it 'on' in even turns right up to the eye or just short of it. Put the silk in the catch.

3. Cut off a 4 inch length of black wool. You will notice that the wool is made up of four strands (known as four-ply). Separate two of the strands from the other two and put the piece you are not using aside for another fly. Tie the wool in *at the shoulder*, just behind the eye, with two turns of silk (Figure 77). The surplus end of wool should be about a quarter of the length of the shank and it should point towards the bend. Place the silk in the catch. It should be noted that wool, like floss, should always be tied in at the shoulder.

Figure 77

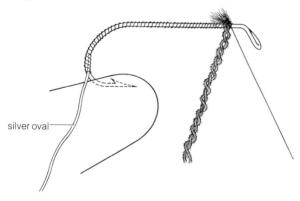

silver oval

4. Wind your two strands of wool, twisted together if need be, down the body and right round the bend and back to the eye. Tie them off with three turns of silk. Put the silk in the catch and cut off the surplus wool.

5. Wind the silver oval rib up body for about seven turns and tie it off short of the eye. Put the silk in the catch and cut off the surplus tinsel.

6. Cut off a small section of white wool. Do not separate it, but place it on top of the eye. Tie it in with three or four turns of silk and then trim off the surplus. Whip finish leaving a small tuft of white wool sloping towards the rear of the hook (Figure 78).

Figure 78

Comment: These last two types of flies, much favoured by lake and reservoir fishermen, complete our introductory phases. Should you have managed these, you have accomplished many of the basic techniques used in fly tying; there is only dubbing, the making of flat tinsel bodies, palmering and some winging to come. If you now feel like some muscle flexing, we will proceed. If you need a little more practice on what we have done, take your time, otherwise we will go on to the next step.

FOURTH LESSON: MOLLY SWEET NYMPH

Hook: Size 8 down eye wide gape.
Silk: Yellow.
Tails: Four or five oak turkey fibres.
Body: Yellow seal's fur or seal's fur substitute.

Rib: Two unwaxed lengths of yellow tying silk.
Wing cases: Oak turkey fibres.
Thorax: Dun coloured seal's fur or substitute.
Head: Black varnish.

Additional: Small packet of yellow seal's fur or substitute.

Small packet of dun coloured seal's fur or substitute.

1 oak turkey feather.

An excellent pattern for lakes and reservoirs created by Molly Sweet, the widow of the late Lionel Sweet of Usk fame.

1. Put your hook in the vice and wind waxed yellow silk to the bend of the hook.

2. Tie in four or five oak turkey fibres to extend for about a ¼ inch beyond bend.

3. Tie in two pieces of unwaxed yellow silk, each about 6 inches long, with two turns of silk, then cut off the surplus from the unwaxed silk ends and oak turkey fibres. Put the silk in the catch.

4. The body of this pattern is yellow seal's fur or seal's fur substitute. When any type of fur is spun on to a hook, the process is known as dubbing. Some tyers find it quite difficult at first, others take it in their stride.

Take a pinch of seal's fur with the finger and thumb of the right hand and put it in the palm of the left and tease out the fur fibres a little. Moisten the tips of the forefinger and middle finger of the right hand with your tongue or with a little water and roll the fur fibres back and forth so the fur is formed into a spindle just over an inch in length; it should be slightly thicker in the middle, tapering off at each end. You will find that moistening your fingertips will assist you greatly and that it prevents the dubbing from separating. The seal's fur spindle should look like Figure 79. The spindle should be slightly on the loose side but not so loose that when you pick it up by one end it falls apart.

Figure 79

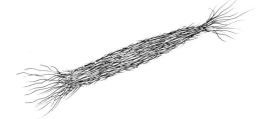

The main pitfall with one's first attempt is to start with too much fur, then too little, but practice will soon set you right. Having tried several methods of spinning on fur, I find that the one I have adopted is the easiest and quickest and that it does not require the silk to be re-waxed.

5. Take the silk out of the catch, holding it quite short with the forefinger and thumb, and pick up your dubbing by one end with the left hand. Lay the tip of the other end, even if it's only two or three fibres, on the shank and take one turn of silk round these fibres. Then bring the silk up vertical and keep it taut.

6. With the forefinger of the left hand gently push the spindle up against the taut silk so it's touching the upright silk along its whole length (Figure 80).

Figure 80

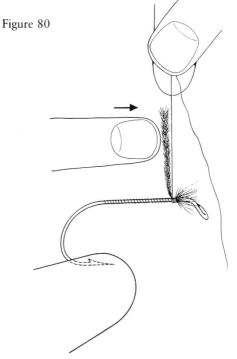

7. Still keeping the silk taut and upright, with the right hand (or with the left if it suits you better), twist the spindle and silk together in a clockwise direction and go on twisting until all the seal's fur is around the silk. This should take only four or five twists.

8. With only half of the shank to cover, wind the dubbing and silk up the shank to the desired

length; try to get a carrot shape, even if this means winding an additional turn or two over the front end. If you have slightly over-dubbed the body, do not worry but tie off with two or three turns of silk and put it in the catch. If the whole thing does not unravel, heave a sigh of relief and raise your eyes to the ceiling.

9. Rib the body with two lengths of un-waxed yellow silk twisted together, about three or four turns. Tie off the silk and cut off the surplus ribbing silk. Put the silk in the catch. If your body looks untidy or there is little sign of tapering towards the tail, remember that scissors are meant for cutting; make slight adjustments to the body if you need to.

10. Cut off a section of oak turkey fibres for the roof of the thorax, about ¾ inch wide. Fold their best sides outwards and tie in where your body ends, by the base of the wing section. Cut off the surplus section of 'roof', bind down these ends and take the silk back to the end of the 'roof'. Put the silk in the catch.

11. Now you have to make the thorax with dun coloured seal's fur or substitute. Naturally, as you have less of the hook to cover, the amount of seal's fur needed will not be as much as that required for the body, and the

spiral will be shorter. Remember, the thorax must be as thick as the thickest part of the body you have just done but not carrot shaped. Proceed in exactly the same way and shape with the scissors if you need to.

12. Take the oak turkey roof section firmly over the thorax, tie it down and cut off the surplus, then whip finish in the normal manner (Figure 81). With this pattern, it is not necessary to tease out the body with the dubbing needle, but use the scissors to cut out any odd wisps of hair if necessary.

Figure 81

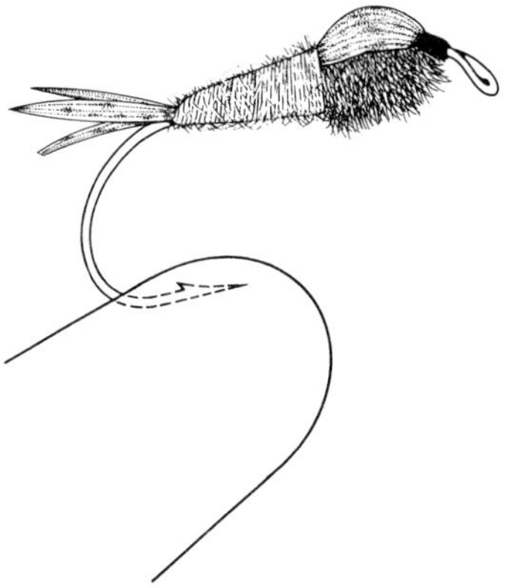

FIFTH LESSON: WET WINGED BLUE DUN

Hook: Size 12 down eye.
Tying silk: Yellow.
Whisks: Blue dun cock fibres.
Body: Stripped peacock eye quill.
Rib: Gold wire size 27.
Hackle: Blue dun cock.
Wing: Teal primary wing feather.
Additional: Pair of teal wings.

Before you begin tying this pattern you have to prepare the body material — in this case stripped peacock eye quill — which is an easy operation but time consuming, so do a number at the time and keep a quantity in a box for future use.

Pick up your peacock eye, best side towards

you. You will find the best quills for stripping are just below the purple and brilliant blue markings, down to where they become some-what thicker. Reverse the eye and select six quills from the left hand side making sure they are above the thicker coloured herls — you now have to strip these quills.

You will have noticed that an individual quill has a pronounced curve. Place an old magazine or catalogue — preferably with a glossy cover — on your bench or table and place one herl on top of it with the butt end pointing towards you. Hold the butt end down with the left thumb and the upper part with the index finger so there is a space between finger and thumb of about 2—3 inches. Take your blunt penknife (a sharp blade could easily cut the quill) and starting an inch below your index finger, gently scrape off the flue on this side of the herl in short downward strokes. Do not press too hard or you may cut the quill. Continue to work down towards the butt. Reverse the herl and carry out the same procedure, turning the quill several times if necessary. You will note that the stripped quill has two colours running up and down its length, almost white and darkish brown – the better the contrast between them, the better the quill. As I have said, strip a number of quills and don't worry if you spoil a few before you find how much pressure to put on the blade. The trick is to use a blunt blade and to work in short lengths.

1. Wind your waxed yellow silk in even turns towards the bend, cut off the surplus silk and put the silk in the catch.

2. Take a large hackle from your blue dun cape. Take four fibres and tie in at the bend about ½ inch long, no more.

3. Take a 6 inch length of gold wire and tie it in at the bend with two turns of silk. Now, to save any waste, gently pull the wire until the surplus is approximately the same length as your intended body. Here we have saved both an operation and wastage.

4. Saving another operation, keep the tension on the silk with the tying hand, pick up a stripped quill and tie it in with the darker colour uppermost. Place the silk in the catch (Figure 82).

5. The whisks, gold wire and quill are now tied in. The surplus end of the wire is the correct length so the waste ends of the whisks and quill can be tied down and the body slightly shaped. If any waste ends still protrude from where you have stopped winding the silk, trim them off. Put the silk in the catch.

6. Wind the quill in even turns to the end of the body and tie off with two turns of silk but do not cut off the end of the quill. Put the silk in the catch. If you have wound your quill correctly it should show equal parts of light and dark which give the impression of the segments on the body of a natural fly.

7. Wind the gold wire round the quill body for about four turns, no more. Secure the wire with two tight turns of silk and another turn for good measure. A tip is that, after the two turns, should you have a fraction of wire over, turn it back towards the body with the point of your scissors and bind it down with the third turn of silk. As you develop your fly tying, such refinements become routine.

8. Select a blue dun hackle, prepare and double it, tie it in by the tip and wind on two or three turns. Tie off with three turns of silk, place the silk in the catch and cut off the surplus hackle.

9. Now gently ease the hackle fibres above the shank down each side with the forefinger and thumb and make a platform of silk with one or two turns to take your wing. Should you by any chance have over-hackled the fly, there is an easy remedy – lay your scissors curve downwards across the shank and cut off all hackle fibres above it. I invariably do this on low water salmon flies rather than 'false throat' them. It looks and answers very well.

Figure 82

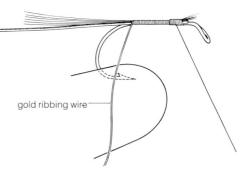

gold ribbing wire

10. The wet feather wings I use on flies of this type are very easy to make although the approach is a trifle unorthodox; it is very successful nevertheless. The usual drill is to take an equal section of primary feather from a left and right wing, in this case teal, and match them together. I only use one primary feather, either a left or right, it does not matter which, and use it as follows.

Hold the bottom of the quill of your feather with the long fibres facing left. Decide how broad you want your section to be and, with the point of your dubbing needle, separate the fibres above and below the section as in Figure 83. (For this pattern, the section should be about ½ inch wide.) When you have done this, grip the end of the section you require and pull it slightly towards the left; then without relaxing your grip pull again, this time slightly downwards. You will find that instead of the tips curling upwards, the whole section is now quite level. Cut out the section with the scissors at the base (Figure 84). Fold the section in

two, best sides inwards. It is important that each side should have an identical number of fibres in it; if one side has more than the other, comb the surplus out with a dubbing needle point.

11. Hold the folded section with the finger and thumb of the left hand around the base. Put it on the hook in the appropriate place and, using the pinch and loop method, tie it in. Cut off the surplus base of the wing level with the eye and whip finish (Figure 85). If, by chance, your wing is too long, trim it with scissors; if it needs a severe cut, do this as in Figure 86.

Figure 85

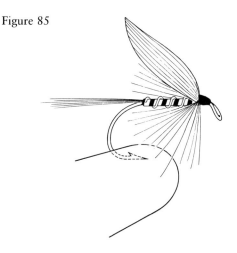

Figure 83

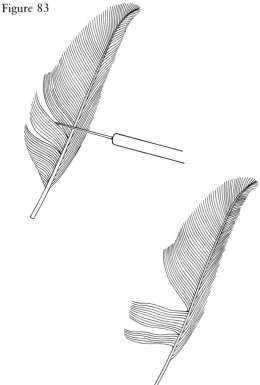

Figure 84

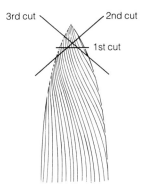

Figure 86

You can wing a lot of flies in this way but never try on any account to trim bronze mallard, teal or pintail flank feathers with scissors. Beginners find winging with bronze mallard difficult, their wings thus formed tending to 'splinter'. The remedy is simple. You can still use one feather but you need to double the width. Fold the double width section in half and then in half again, with the best sides outwards, but do not attempt to re-align the shape of the wing as you may have done with a teal wing primary. Instead, you will find the tips can easily be levelled by adjusting with the ball of the finger and thumb while holding the wing and sliding to and fro. The same applies with teal and pintail. It works extremely well without making the wing too heavy.

One other point with all winged wet flies is that I always varnish the head with spirit varnish first which requires a moderate time to dry quite hard (a matter of hours rather than minutes); then I varnish them again with black which makes them look very well and gives the fly longer life.

SIXTH LESSON: TERRY'S TERROR
(orange and yellow tag)

Hook: Size 14 down eye.
Tying silk: Yellow.
Tag: Orange and yellow goat hair in equal parts.
Body: Single strand of peacock herl.
Rib: Copper flat size 2. Gold flat if copper is unavailable.
Hackle: Fox red cock.
Additional: 1 packet each of orange and yellow goat hair.
1 reel of copper flat size 2. Lurex will answer, but I bought a huge reel of copper flat many years ago in a local shop selling materials for electricians! The original dressing called for a flat copper rib but I feel sure that gold flat would answer just as well.

This fly was devised by the late Cecil Terry, the Bath surgeon, and the late Ernest Lock of Andover, a well known professional river keeper and fly dresser. The pattern was given to me by Cecil Terry a couple of weeks after I started tying, and I have been associated with it ever since. For my money, it is the best all round trout fly ever; it is taken both for the iron blue dun and its spinner in the small sizes, and for all stages of the hatching olive nymphs, duns and spinners. It also makes a good sedge. It is, of course, a river fly but I know of no better on lakes and large stillwaters. Salmon take it, and a client of mine hooked seven salmon at Waterville, Co. Kerry, with one, grassing four of them. It's my first choice if I am in doubt but, naturally, it can fail as miserably as any other on occasions. Unlike many other patterns, it does not adapt easily into a sunk pattern. The late Harry Plunkett Green, author of the classic *Where the Bright Waters Meet*, when asked what it represented, said, 'The lights of Piccadilly Circus'. I think he had it about right!

1. Select about ten fibres of orange goat hair and ten fibres of yellow; put them together but do not mix them. The tag should be of two equal sections of orange and yellow tied on together with the orange colour nearest you. When you have put the two sections together, trim each end a fraction so they are equal in length. Tie in with three turns of silk. The ends nearest the eye should be the length of the fly's body. Do *not* cut off the long end at this stage.

2. Tie in the copper or gold rib and one peacock herl from just below the eye. Take the silk up to the end of the body. Put the silk in the catch and cut off any material beyond the

Figure 87

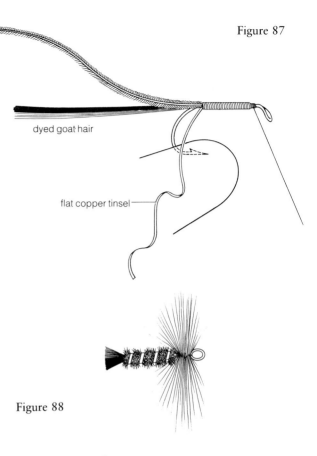

end of the body; the fly should now look like Figure 87.

3. Wind the herl up the body and tie it off with two or three turns of silk, but do not cut off surplus herl.

4. Rib the body with three or four turns of copper or gold tinsel. Tie off the tinsel. Put the silk in the catch and cut off surplus herl and ribbing.

5. Select a hackle, tie it in and complete the fly with about six turns of hackle.

6. Cut off goat hair tag to about ¼ inch or a fraction less. Put your goat hair down carefully so you won't upset it accidentally and have it ready for tying the next one. Flare out the tag by putting the scissors or dubbing needle under it where it joins the hook. This makes it look better (Figure 88).

Comment: This fly is always worth tying, especially when one is in doubt about what to select.

Figure 88

———— SEVENTH LESSON: MAGGS MAYFLY ————

Hook: Size 8 down eye wide gape.
Tying silk: Yellow.
Whisks: Four cock pheasant tail fibres.
Body: Yellow raffia
Rib: 1. Gold oval size 15.
    2. Two unwaxed strands of red silk.
Ribbing hackle: Black cock — one side of
    hackle only and trimmed.
Hackle: Fox red cock.
Wings: Two large Blue dun (dyed or natural)
    — shaped with scissors.
Additional: Hank of yellow raffia — *not*
    Raffine.
    1 pair cock pheasant tail centres.

I mentioned earlier on that a fly dressing is usually given in the order in which the materials are tied in. In the case of winged dry flies you always tie in the wings first, though the dressing is given in the usual manner.

1. Select a pair of moderate sized blue dun hackles, pulling them out by the stalk base. Remove all fibres until the points are just a trifle longer than the length you require for the wings. Hold each hackle in turn by the stalk and cut three or four fibres very short on each side of the stalk (Figure 89). This is a precaution to stop the wing pulling out or coming adrift.

2. Attach yellow silk to the hook and make a foundation for the hackle point wings.

3. Tie in the first wing with its best side towards you and with the wing pointing well out over the eye. Bind down with three turns of

Figure 89

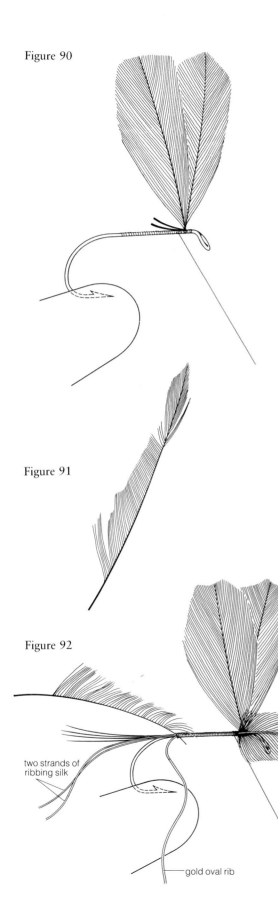

Figure 90

Figure 91

Figure 92

two strands of
ribbing silk

gold oval rib

silk over the short cut fibre stumps. Pull the hackle point backwards so it stands upright and put three turns of silk in front of this wing.

4. Do the same with the other hackle point but this time with the worst side of the hackle facing you.

5. Separate the two hackle wings with a turn or two of silk and take the silk behind wing and put it in the catch (Figure 90).

6. Tie in a longish fox red hackle with its worst side facing you and take the silk a few turns down the shank. Cut off all three hackle stalks to slightly different lengths. Bind down with silk and take it to the bend of the hook. Put the silk in the catch.

7. Tie in four cock pheasant fibres as a tail at the bend and put the silk in catch.

8. Tie in the following materials at the bend, in this order − on the principle that what you tie in first, you wind on last. Black ribbing hackle, two pieces of unwaxed red silk and a piece of gold oval tinsel. Then put the silk in the catch.

Before you tie in the ribbing hackle, you must prepare it. Select a moderate size black cock hackle, remove all weak fibres and, with the best side facing you, hold the tip of the hackle between the finger and thumb of the left hand and remove all fibres below the hackle stalk by tearing them off. Then, gently pulling the fibres above the stalk so they stand upright, trim with scissors; the fibres at the tip end are short and graduate in length towards the butt (Figure 91). Tie the hackle in by the point at which the short trimmed fibres start; then tie in the red ribbing silk and oval tinsel. Put the silk in the catch. Cut off the surplus from the materials you have just tied in at the place where you trimmed off the main hackle stalk. Take the silk up body and put it in the catch (Figure 92).

9. The next step is to tie in a length of raffia which, like floss and wool, is tied in at the shoulder. Again, you have to prepare this material for use. Cut off a 6 inch length of yellow raffia and put it on a hard surface such as the back of a wooden tea tray or on your workbench, if it does not matter if it gets slightly scratched. Unfold the raffia. When it is flattened out, it may be ½ inch or more wide. Hold it down near one end and score this end with your dubbing needle point at intervals of about $^1/_{16}$ inch. Pull away one at a time to obtain individual lengths of 6 inches or more $^1/_{16}$ inch wide, an ideal width to work with on this sized hook. For smaller hooks the width can be even narrower. If your length of raffia is too wide, the body will be fat, lumpy, and unsightly.

Tie the raffia in and wind it down towards the bend of the hook and then back again to the shoulder. The raffia body should be quite smooth and nicely tapered without any unsightly lumps. Tie it off with three turns of silk which is then put in the catch.

10. Wind on about four turns of oral tinsel at even intervals.

11. Twist the two lengths of red silk together and wind them up the body, in between the gold oval tinsel. Tie them off and cut off the surplus raffia, oval tinsel and silk.

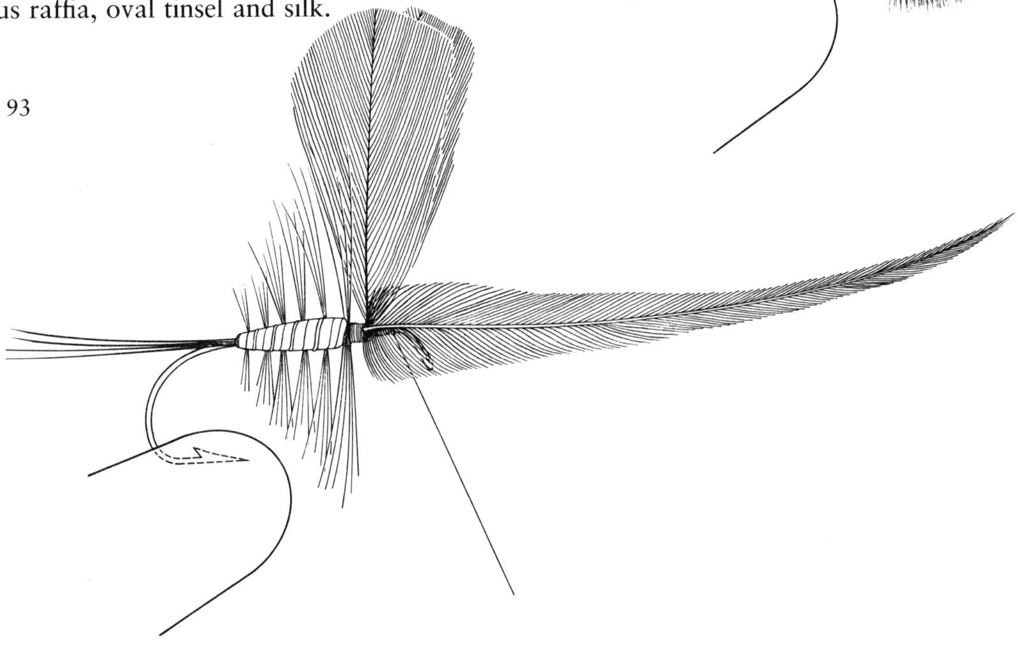

Figure 93

12. Take the black ribbing hackle stalk in the hackle pliers and it wind up the body hard against the gold oval tinsel, winding on any remaining turns of hackle at shoulder. Tie off the hackle and remove surplus stalk. I recommend using the hackle pliers as the stalk of the ribbing hackle has to be right up against the tinsel. And you should make sure that the hackle is wound in such a way that the bright side is always to the front (Figure 93).

13. Finally wind on main hackle with as many turns as you can behind reserving one and a half to two turns in front. Whip finish in the usual way (Figure 94).

Figure 94

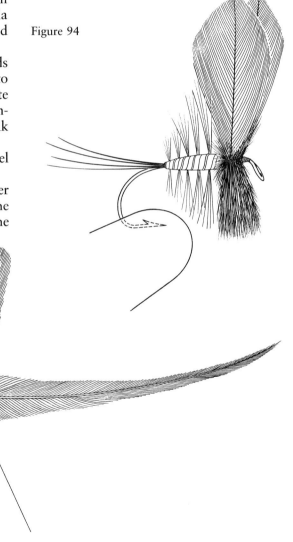

14. If your hackle point wings are too long, trim them down to size with scissors in the manner I have suggested.

Comment: This is one of the best general pattern mayflies I have come across for any water as it is an excellent floater. Strangely enough, it is the first artificial mayfly I ever dressed. If you have managed this pattern and the result is passing fair, you have done very well. Although it is quite straightforward, you have a lot of material to put on the hook.

EIGHTH LESSON: HAIR WING SILVER DOCTOR

Hook: Size 6 low water single salmon iron.
Tying silk: Yellow.
Tag: Silver wire size 27.
Tail: Small topping with dyed blue hackle point on top.
Butts: Red DFM wool.
Body: Silver flat size 3.
Rib: Silver oval size 15.
Hackle: Dyed blue cock hackle followed by false throat of grey mallard fibres.
Wing: Grey squirrel tail.
  Blue calf tail fibres.
  Yellow calf tail fibres.
Head: Black and red varnish.
Additional: 1 packet (cape if you can afford it) of dyed blue cock hackles.
  1 Yellow calf tail.
  1 Blue calf tail.
  Packet of grey mallard flank.

1. Place the hook in the vice; the point does not have to be covered but make sure the shank is level with the top of the bench. Attach the waxed silk in the usual manner and work the silk down to just above the point. When you are about ³⁄₁₆ inch away from it, make sure the rest of the turns are touching. Put the silk in the catch.

2. Cut off a small length of silver wire and tie it in where the silk has stopped above the point. Bind it down in even touching turns for about ⅛ inch. Put the silk in the catch and cut off any surplus wire.

3. Wind the silver wire in touching even turns for about ⅛ inch. Hold the wire in your left hand and tie it off with two turns of silk with the right hand. Put the silk in the catch and cut off the remaining wire.

4. Select a small topping from the beak end of your golden pheasant crest and tie it in on top of the shank with two turns of silk where the silver tag ends. Put the silk in the catch but do not cut off the surplus end of the topping.

5. Select a small blue hackle from your packet or cape. Pinch or cut off the point about ⁵⁄₁₆ inch in length and tie it in on top of your crest so it covers about one third of the crest and no more. Put the silk in the catch but do not cut off the surplus.

6. Cut off a small length of red DFM wool about 3 inches long. Again, this is four ply and you need one strand. Tie in the wool and wrap it round the hook about five or six turns, until you have a compact little ball that has covered some of the surplus golden pheasant crest and blue hackle tip. Tie the wool off with three turns of silk — this is what is called a butt and it is a characteristic of all three 'Doctors', silver, black and blue. Put the silk in the catch and cut off any surplus golden pheasant crest and blue hackle tip (Figure 95).

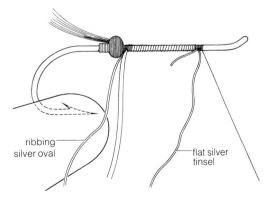

Figure 95

7. Tie in a length of silver oval so that the surplus reaches the estimated end of the body, making allowance, of course, for the hackle and wing to come. Follow this by a length of flat silver tinsel, again with the surplus reaching the end of the estimated length of the body. Bind both these down with close turns of silk. Put the silk in the catch.

8. Tie in a separated length of white floss at the shoulder and wind it down the shank in wide even turns to the red butt and then back again, covering the entire body. Tie the floss off and put the silk in the catch. This white floss underbody is of the greatest assistance in making a long level tinsel body. American fly dressers have used this method in body tinselling for years.

9. Now take the flat silver tinsel in close touching turns up the body, making sure there are no gaps and no lumps. Tie it off with three turns of silk, put the silk in the catch but do not cut off the surplus flat tinsel. If your flat tinsel is slightly tarnished you can buff it up at this stage with a small length of chamois leather about ¼ inch wide and 3 inches long.

10. Rib the body with silver oval tinsel in equidistant turns. Do not overdo the ribbing; five or six turns is ample. Tie off the rib and cut off any surplus flat and oval tinsel. Put the silk in the catch.

11. Now the shoulder hackle — dyed blue. If you have bought a cape, select a suitable sized hackle, double it and tie it in in the usual way. I recommend cutting off all the fibres above the shank as already described. If you have bought a packet of hackles, select the largest you can find, remove all weak fibres and then pull off a small bunch of fibres and tie the hackle in under the throat in the usual way. Do not make the hackle too long. It should come about a third of the way down the shank.

The head hackle is normally of wigeon but grey mallard fibres will do just as well. Tie in a false throat of this under the blue, a trifle longer this time. Tie off, put the silk in the catch.

12. Lastly, winging — all done with hair and quite easy. Firstly, make sure that the area you have left to tie your wing on and covered with tying silk is coated with spirit varnish. This is essential with all hair wing patterns. Cut out a section of grey squirrel tail, hold it by the tip and, with your fingers, comb out all underfur and shorter fibres. Level the tips and tie the bunch in with the pinch and loop method on top of the shank. The end of the squirrel fibres should come just, and only just, beyond the end of your golden pheasant topping. Tie the hair wing down with at least six turns of silk, trim the surplus ends at a slight angle and continue to bind down making the last turn of silk at the base of the hair fibres, rather than at the eye of the hook. Put the silk in the catch and apply another coat of varnish (Figure 96).

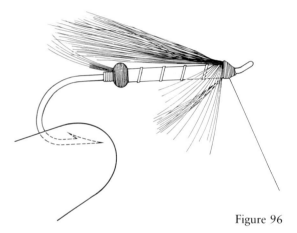

Figure 96

13. Now for the blue calf tail. Take a bunch similar in length but not as thick and tie it in using the same method. Put the silk in the catch and varnish again.

14. Finally, tie in the yellow calf tail; but this time only use about six or seven fibres as this is the counterpart of the golden pheasant crest used on most feather wing salmon flies.

15. Whip finish and coat the shaped head with varnish.

16. When the spirit varnish is dry (and this may take several hours), apply a coat of black varnish. When this is dry, make a ring round the head with red varnish, but do not cover the head completely. The fly should look something like the one in the colour plate.

NINTH LESSON: ROSEMARY

Tube: 1 inch plastic tube size 4.
  ¼ inch tube extension.
Tying silk: Black.
Body: Black floss.
Rib: Silver oval size 15.
Hackle: Blue cock hackle fibres as used on
  Silver Doctor.
Wing: Red calf tail.
Head: Black varnish.
Additional: Length of plastic tubing size 4
  available from Tom Saville.
  Length of extension plastic tubing also from
    Tom Saville.
  Calf tail dyed red.
  1 size 2 forged straight bronze hook.

This tube fly is a variation on the Hairy Mary which, whether on a hook or a tube, must account for a fair proportion of all salmon taken on fly in the UK. The Hairy Mary was almost immediately followed by the Black Mary (the same fly but with a black hair wing) so here is a third which I have called the Rosemary and which should work quite well.

As salmon fishermen know, tubes come in various materials, copper, aluminium and plastic. Plastic tubes are usually sold prepared and sized, some with recess for trebles. I recommend you to buy a length of hard nylon tubing from Tom Saville. It is sold by the foot. You should also buy a length of translucent PVC extension tubing, again sold by the foot. Both of these tubes are inexpensive and you can cut them into any desired length. The hard nylon PVC is sold in packets of one foot and naturally takes up a curve in the packet. To straighten it, soak it in a bowl of hot water for a minute or two, run a straight wire or a thin knitting needle up its length and put it in the freezer for ten minutes. It will come out straight and can then be cut into the required lengths, in this case 1 inch.

You will require one more item, a forged, straight bronzed size 2 hook. All you have to do is to cut off the eye with pliers and you are ready for tying. For larger bored tubes, Sportsfish sell an excellent adapted hook very cheaply.

1. Put the prepared hook in vice, slide ¼ inch of PVC extension over one end of your tube and then push the whole thing over the eyeless hook shank. To stop the tube twisting during tying, push a darning needle up the end of the extension and tube so that it fits tightly.

2. Bind three or four turns of black waxed silk over the extension, whip finish, cut off the silk and varnish (Figure 97).

3. Wind on black silk at end of tube and take right down to where the extension joins the tube. Put the silk in the catch.

4. Tie in a length of size 15 silver oval tinsel in the usual manner and take the tying silk back up your tube to where the body will end, making an allowance for hair wing to follow. Put the silk in the catch.

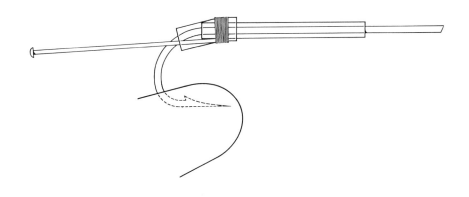

Figure 97

5. Cut off a moderate length of black floss, separate it and tie one length in at the wing end of the tube.

6. Take the floss back to the extension end of the tube and wind it back again to the wing end making every effort to get a smooth body. If the needle works loose during the process, just push it back again. Tie off your floss with three turns of silk and cut off any surplus floss.

7. Wind the tinsel up the body about four or five turns, tie it off and do a whip finish as a precaution at this stage. Cut off the surplus oval tinsel and put the silk in the catch.

8. Spirit varnish the area of silk ready for the wings.

9. Cut off a section of red calf tail, comb out the short hairs and fluff, level the tips and put it on top of tube only. Tie the bunch of hair down with the silk and cut off the butts dead level with end of tube, not slanted. Put the silk in the catch and varnish the head again.

10. Tie in the same amount of calf tail under the tube; cut off the butts — again, dead level with the eye. You now have two sections of red calf tail one above and one below the hook shank, the ends of the hair coming past the end of the extension so that when the treble is inserted, the tips of the hair wing just mask the treble (Figure 98).

11. All that is required now is a bunch of dyed blue hackle fibres or each side, about half the length of the tube and tied in as if you were

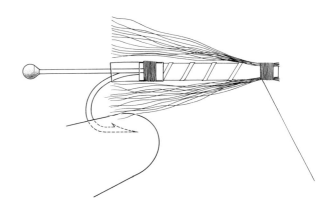

Figure 98

putting on a false throat. These hackle fibres are tied between the top and the bottom of the hair wing.

12. Bind these fibres down neatly, cut off any extending beyond the head of the tube, whip finish and varnish the whipping with spirit.

13. When spirit varnish is dry, re-coat with black varnish. See illustration on coloured plate.

14. Should you be tying several tubes, find a flat piece of cork (old table mats are ideal) and cut it into 1 inch strips with a sharp knife. Stick ordinary dressmaker's pins through each strip. You can now place each tube fly on a pin while its head dries. Simple but effective.

CONCLUSION

Should any of your patterns be somewhat disappointing in appearance, don't worry. I have no doubt they will take fish just as well, but do strive for neatness nevertheless.

The most important thing about fly tying is that you should enjoy it. I still do so after all these years, and find it relaxing into the bargain.

Further reading

John Buckland, *The Pocket Guide to Trout and Salmon Flies* (Mitchell Beazley, 1986).

Mike Dawes, *The Fly Tier's Manual* (Collins, 1985).

Jacqueline Wakeford, *Fly Tying Techniques* (Ernest Benn, 1980).

Jean-Paul Pequegnot, *French Fishing Flies*, trans. Robert A. Chino (Nick Lyons Books, 1987; available through H.F. & G. Witherby Ltd).

Datus C. Proper, *What the Trout Said* (Knopf, 1982).

A. Courtney Williams, *A Dictionary of Trout Flies*, 6th edition (A. & C. Black, 1986).

Ron Holloway

Ron Holloway was born at Stockbridge on the River Test in 1936. During the war, he explored almost every yard of the Test between Redbridge and Stockbridge – usually with a rod and line and not always with the owner's permission. These boyhood days by the river led Ron into a lifelong love of Hampshire's chalk streams.

After service in the army and a few years in the pharmaceutical industry, Ron returned to the chalk streams, this time to Martyr Worthy, where he has remained for the past twenty years, maintaining a beat on the Upper Itchen, a superb stretch of classic chalk stream which is still able, under his skilful management, to be sustained as a wild brown trout fishery.

Ron Holloway's expertise in river fisheries management has been recognized by both the Canadian and the United States governments. He has been invited to tour problem rivers in both countries on several occasions, to advise and to demonstrate practical river rehabilitation techniques and techniques for brown trout fisheries management.

A passionate fly fisher for trout and salmon as well as an immensely experienced fishery manager, Ron is a member of the Association of Professional Game Angling Instructors. His fishing schools in England and Scotland are always well attended. The Hampshire College of Agriculture at Sparsholt, near Winchester, also uses his knowledge and expertise in their training of young river keepers and fishery managers.

11

RIVER FISHERIES MANAGEMENT

Ron Holloway

INTRODUCTION

The purpose of river fishery management is to provide quality sport fishing for the angler. We shall be discussing the whole subject as seen through the eyes of a river keeper as it is the river keeper who actually carries out the work in and on the river. All the work discussed here relates to the chalk streams of southern England but the principles and methods employed can be used on rivers throughout the country or, in fact, the world, as the basic principles of wild brown trout management are the same the whole world over.

REASONS FOR RIVER FISHERY MANAGEMENT

Of all the streams and rivers which have historically carried stocks of wild brown trout, few, if any, have survived without suffering the ravages of man's intervention at some time. To the thinking river keeper the need for improvement is painfully obvious in many instances. The task of the river keeper is to improve the fishing quality for the angler and to begin to achieve this the keeper himself has to be an experienced person who has a feeling for moving water and understands the whole life-cycle of the wild brown trout. To think like a brown trout and then to think like a fisherman must be the aim.

Over the years, streams and rivers have been degraded in many ways, pollution, changes in agricultural practices, changes in forestry methods and urbanization of the catchment area being among the main contributory factors. Unfortunately, the river keeper is not responsible for, and has little or no control over, what goes on in the catchment area of the river. If streams and rivers are to survive in the future, the entire management of the watershed must be considered.

The most frightening assault on our rivers and streams does not come from over-fishing or the introduction of self-destructing hatchery fish. The assault on our fisheries pours down from the heavens in the form of acid rain; it is belched out from industrial effluents and municipal sewers; it is to be seen in the form of soil eroded from farmland, loaded with nutrients, along with fish farm effluents and a wide variety of other habitat destroying, non-point source, pollutants. Of course, there is more – abstraction, channelization, land drainage, wet land destruction, afforestation, de-forestation – and so on. The impact of the multiple use of all the land in the river catchment area must be fully understood before any major fishery management decisions are made.

Most river keepers are in positions that call for management of fish or the water in which the fish live, but they are not responsible for the management of the whole landscape. Someone else decides how many cows and sheep graze in a given watershed; where and how many trees are cut or planted; what sort of roads are built and where; where buildings are placed and sewage effluent is discharged; where slurry pits are sited and silage clamps built. All these decisions are crucial in the maintenance of production in a trout stream. The maintenance of the trout population cannot be diassociated from the management of the watershed. With all the pressures rivers and streams are being subjected to, it is essential to look before you leap, and to establish a round management policy from the outset.

___IDENTIFY THE RIVER AND ITS PROBLEMS___

Before any management policy can be established, a thorough examination of the river has to be undertaken to establish as accurately as possible what the resource consists of and what the river was like in the past. During this examination, a diagnosis of the problems is made, and the problems are noted in order. Water quality and all flow rate information can be obtained from the local National Rivers Authority office. A bio-mass study has to be undertaken to establish how many of the various species of fish live in the river. An electro fishing sweep through the river will give a good idea of the stocks of the various species of fish. This operation will also be arranged by the local NRA office on request. Any past records and reliable local knowledge must be taken into consideration in establishing a complete status report and not until all this information is compiled can a constructive management policy be formulated. Whenever possible, the keeper must walk the bed of the river in chest waders to establish the various forms and type of substrate, to establish the accumulations of silt deposits and all sub-surface obstructions, and make a mental note of the natural cover for fish, that is, aquatic weeds, rocks and stones, undercut banks and so on.

Where bank erosion has taken place, the original line of the bank has to be established and marked for reinstatement. Bankside vegetation has to be surveyed with a view to increasing or decreasing the shade on the river. Mature trees can be pollarded to reduce the risk of them falling into the river and to increase the light. In places, correct planting will increase shade and stabilize soft banks.

Pinpointing the limiting factors controlling the population of wild brown trout is the next step. Here, knowledge of the whole life-cycle of the brown trout is important as it enables the keeper to look at each stage of the trout's life from egg to three year-old and to identify the areas or periods in the life-cycle where assistance will improve and increase survival.

Having established that the river is relatively free from pollution and severe fluctuations in flows, and that the temperature ranges are tolerable for brown trout, the next key to survival of the trout is to see that there is sufficient cover or hiding places for them. The cover will enable the trout to hide from predators, reduce territorial competitions and restrict cannabilism.

The fertility of the river has to be looked at to establish that the water will support all the necessary aquatic vegetation which will, in turn, provide cover and support sufficient invertebrate life to enable the fish to feed and grow.

BASIC MANAGEMENT AIMS AND PLANNING

Having identified the characteristics of the river and pinpointed all the problems, a management policy can now be laid down and an overall plan developed to tackle the problems in the correct order.

As no two rivers are alike and each has its own character, it follows that each river will have its own special problems. Although there may be some basic similarities between rivers, and problems may be similar, all general recommendations must be tempered with the thought that each individual river should have its own tailored management plan.

Where rivers have been neglected but still maintain small stocks of wild brown trout, a knowledge of the brown trout's life-cycle and of what is required at every stage of its life will be of great value. Start by looking at the spawning areas. If the area of spawning gravel is limited then thought must be given to increasing it. It is pointless to truck in tons of gravel and simply to dump it in the water, expecting the trout to climb over themselves to spawn in it; it just doesn't work that easily.

Firstly, carefully plot all the areas where the resident stock attempts to spawn. In the chalk streams of Hampshire the spawning times usually run from the middle of November through to the beginning of March, with the peak activity during the last two weeks of December and the first two weeks of January. These peak times do vary depending on the geographical area. It will be noticed that the spawning trout seem to prefer some areas of gravel to others where, to the human eye, the two appear identical. It is a characteristic of the southern chalk streams, which are mainly spring-fed, that many of the feeder springs well up in the bed of the river. It is to these up-welling springs that the hen trout gravitate to lay their eggs. In rivers which have few or no up-welling springs, the hen fish will seek the next best alternative — areas of good gravel, of the right size, which are kept clean by good

quality water flowing over them at the right speed.

It is the areas in which the resident trout spawn that must be enhanced in the summer. If there is a lack of gravel, bring some in to enlarge the spawning area. It is essential that this imported gravel should be the same size as the natural gravel. Summer is the best time to lay the gravel as, by this time, the alevins from the previous winter's eggs will have hatched and swum away to the nearest cover. Laying the gravel in the summer allows time for it to 'weather' for a few months and to mix and blend with the natural gravel.

To obtain the best advantage from the enlarged spawning areas, experience has taught me to create spawning channels approximately 4 feet wide and no more than 25 yards long. It is quite simple to produce these channels in a chalk stream by cutting the aquatic weed correctly in the autumn weed cut (Figure 99). Due to the high pH of the chalk streams, calcification of the gravel occurs rapidly. To obtain the best returns from a spawning channel, and to encourage the trout to use it, a good scarification of the gravel is required just prior to spawning time. This breaks up the crust which will have formed on the gravel, enabling the

Figure 99 *Prepared spawning channels in a chalk stream*

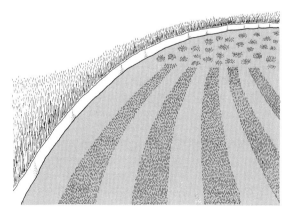

hen fish to dig their redds more easily and to inflict less damage on themselves as they do. The less damage inflicted on the hens during spawning the better, as this decreases the incidence of post-spawning fungus, which can severely reduce their survival rates.

Another advantage of creating spawning channels is that the walls of the channels restrict the lateral movement of fish. And, as a cock fish cannot see through the channel wall he will be unable to see other cock fish in the neighbouring channel, which reduces inter-cock fighting to a minimum. This, in turn, can reduce damage to the fish and, again, increase spawning survival.

In areas where there is good spawning gravel, but no weed to create channels, it will aid survival if some artificial cover is created, adjacent to the redds. This will provide bolt-holes for the spawning fish close to their redds, so that they can hide from predators which prey on them when they are at their most vulnerable.

After spawning has finished, it is a good idea to note the numbers and positions of redds for future comparison. As the weeks go by, the mounds of gravel in which the eggs are incubating will weather and become harder to see as algal growths return to the recently disturbed gravel. Care must be taken not to disturb the spawning beds until the fry have swum up from the gravel. The first fry usually show in the margins of the stream during the first week in April, so, if an early spring weed cut is carried out during this month, great care must be taken not to disturb any spawning areas at least until the end of May.

The fry, as they emerge from the gravel, are at one of their most vulnerable stages. I am convinced that it is at this stage at which the greatest mortality occurs. Not only have I watched kingfishers feeding themselves and their young on trout fry but other birds feeding freely that one would not expect to predate on fry. Blackbirds and wrens have been seen eating fry, and coots, moorhens and ducks are also partial to them, to say nothing of the mature brown trout and yearlings, which will scour the edges of the stream to devour their own

young. Eels can also predate heavily on swim up fry. So, how can we protect these minute trout from over-predation?

As the fry emerge from the gravel, the current tends to wash them some considerable distance downstream until they find slower flowing water in the margins of the stream. Although the fry do not shoal up, there can be quite an accumulation of them in these quieter shallow areas. Where there is little natural cover in the form of banks of weed or overhanging vegetation, it will pay to put some in.

One very simple but effective method of creating instant fry cover is to cut some longish fronds from a spruce tree, or an alder or a willow, or from any tree which is really 'twiggy', push the butts into the bank and allow the fronds to trail in the water almost parallel to it. After a few days, the twigs will have collected debris which will float down on the stream and, very soon, the fry will find and hide themselves in this, safe from predation.

Algae and plankton abound in such circumstances, creating a larder for the fry to live on.

After a few months, the fry will have grown bigger and stronger and will be able to cope with the faster water in the main stream. Now they will disappear into the luxurious growth of summer aquatic weed, hardly to be seen again until the late autumn, when the heavy weed cuts open up larger areas of gravel. By this time, the year's offspring will be healthy fingerlings 3 to 4 inches long. The growth rate of fingerlings and one year plus trout in the chalk streams is phenomenal.

Generally speaking, brown trout of 5–9 inches tend to prefer shallows and fast riffles to the deeper, slower flowing areas of a river. Many side streams and carriers which have

Figure 100　*Man made fry cover*

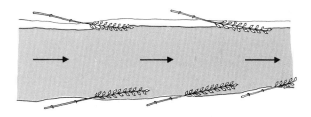

these swift flowing riffles have, naturally, become very efficient nursery streams. In times past, even before the art of breeding trout in hatcheries, these nursery streams were netted and the yearling trout planted out into the main stream to replace mature fish caught the previous year by the anglers. This transplanting of trout was the forerunner of today's modern stocking technique. For the good of every fishery, it is essential that all side streams and carriers are kept clean and clear, and that they are treated with just as much care as the main river fishery. Although the side streams are small and sometimes not seriously fished, it is folly to neglect them as they play an essential part in the life-cycle of the wild brown trout.

Mature trout of 10 inches plus are about two years old. Their survival in the river in any numbers will indicate a healthy brown trout environment.

The good keeper will now try and disperse these two-year-old fish evenly throughout the river. Before doing this, sparsely stocked areas must be looked at critically with a view to improving their holding capacities. This can be done by increasing feeding lies; creating extra cover; clearing silt beds; and generally improving and making the whole area attractive to trout. A good keeper is always looking at the river with a view to improvements and to how he can possibly increase the wild trout production and survival.

AQUATIC WEED MANAGEMENT

In a river fishery this is the hardest and most time-consuming work a river keeper does during the whole year. On the chalk streams of Hampshire, aquatic weed is cut during agreed periods of time each month from April through to October with minor variations in between. This regular cutting is essential for the maintenance of the river and the trout fisheries. Southern chalk streams are, by their very nature, fertile rivers and this fertility manifests itself in prodigious growths of aquatic weed life during the growing season, from March to October. There are several types of weed that have to be taken into consideration when a weed management policy is set up. Firstly, each species of weed has to be identified and given a priority rating as to its benefit to the river. The main species we expect to find are as follows:

Water buttercup (*Rununculus*): This is the best type of aquatic weed found in the chalk streams. It is deep rooted and an excellent oxygenator. It affords habitat for many types of invertebrates. It creates excellent hiding cover for trout during the summer months, and it does not usually filter out silt.

Water celery (Apium nodiflorum): This also is well rooted weed. Although it does not create so much cover for trout, it does hold excellent varieties of invertebrates and, like rununculus, it does not filter out large quantities of silt.

Starwort (Callitriche stagnalis): Although an excellent carrier of invertebrates, starwort is not deep rooted and it is easily washed away in high water. It also filters out large quantities of silt and is therefore far less beneficial than the previous two weeds.

These are the main beneficial weeds found in chalk streams. There are other types such as mare's tail, carrot weed, ribbon weed and Canadian pond weed, all of which afford little benefit to a river where wild trout production is the aim — but bad weed is better than no weed at all. Other types of aquatic plant life can be found but rarely in large quantities.

Experience has taught us that the merits of each type of weed come readily to the fore after a few years of weed cutting on a particular stretch of river. Personally I have found concentrating on rununculus as the prime species has helped to improve the weed pattern. Rununculus can be transplanted quite easily and can be used to cover bare areas of river bed which have been cleared of the lesser types of weed. Having said that rununculus is the best weed and should be encouraged, its spread and growth does have to be controlled rigidly each weed cutting time because if it is allowed to spread it will rapidly choke the river, bank to bank. If this is allowed to happen, the effects can be many. Firstly the vast growths will restrict the flow of water downstream and may well create flood conditions upstream. This, in turn, can keep the river banks underwater and encourage even more erosion of the already soft banks. Also, fish will have restricted space to live in and, if there was a good stock of trout before the weed growth got out of hand, then the trout may well move out to roomier surroundings – usually your neighbour's fishery! Lastly, opportunities for dry fly fishing are severely restricted in a weed-choked river, which will not endear the keeper to the dry fly angler!

To avoid these situations, the weed has to be cut regularly. The easiest and most efficient method is to get into the river and cut the weed with a scythe. Although this is an old fashioned method, experience has shown that, in the hands of an expert, the scythe is still the most effective tool to use in cutting and managing prolific weed growths.

The first weed cut of the year is undertaken in April as by this time in a normal year the springs will have broken, the winter bournes will be flowing well, the daylight is increasing and the weed is growing fast. This first cut will establish the pattern for the whole season to come.

A chequer board effect is the usual pattern adopted in the chalk streams (Figure 101) but other patterns can be used if water conditions are changing. In low water years, the bar system can be used to hold up the water levels.

Weed cutting on the River Itchen

This is achieved by cutting weed to leave bars of weed from bank to bank to create a series of weirs up and down the river (Figure 102). By using correct weed cutting methods, the level of the river can be controlled quite effectively.

There are other benefits which can accrue from efficient weed cutting. The chequer board effect spreads out the water flow from bank to bank. This in turn distributes the fish over a larger area by creating many good lies for feeding trout. And, of course, each clump of weed becomes a potential 'bolt-hole' for the trout. Good and efficient weed cutting is essential for the maintenance and improvement of all chalk stream trout fisheries.

Where rivers are too deep to cut by hand, then other methods must be used, such as motorized weed cutting boats and chain scythes. The use of both of these implements can be very effective if the aim is just to reduce

the volume of weed in order to drop the level of the river. Unfortunately, both methods are totally non-selective and cut all weed in their path. It is now becoming acknowledged that as more and more owners use weed cutting boats to cut weed, even in the shallow stretches, the character of some parts of the chalk stream is being seriously altered.

Large growths of the 'wrong' weed and increased accumulations of silt can be characteristic of stretches of chalk stream in which weed cutting boats are used regularly.

Accumulations of silt are, and always have been, a major headache to river keepers. The aim must be to keep silt on the move rather than to let it build up on the bed of the river. Here again, correct weed cutting methods, especially when using hand scythes, can usually keep on top of the problem. Weed can be cut in such a way as to use the current of the stream to wash away any accumulated banks of silt and, with a little agitation, even large banks of can be moved. In some areas of more persistent silt deposits other, more permanent methods have to be used, such as sheep hurdles and corrugated iron sheets staked in the bed of the river to divert stream flows. But care must be taken when these constructions are put in permanently that they are covered by water at all times. Sheets of rusty tin sticking out of the water are ugly.

On most trout rivers, bank maintenance is an on-going job year in and year out. Over the years, river keepers have struggled to maintain river banks and it is only since the arrival of JCBs and Hi-Mac machines that any real help has been available. Previously, the pick, shovel and wheelbarrow were all that was available and if a large length of bank had to be reinstated or repaired it took a great deal of hard work and time. Nowadays, with tipper lorries and JCBs, large bank works are usually relatively easy to carry out. Even so, there are areas of river bank which are inaccessible to heavy plant and here the keeper still has to rely on the time-honoured pick, shovel, wheelbarrow and a punt.

Wherever bank work is to be carried out, a good deal of thought and planning is necessary;

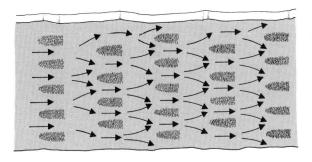

Figure 101　*Chequer board effect weed cutting*

Figure 102　*Bar cutting pattern*

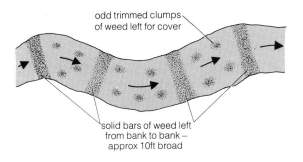

odd trimmed clumps of weed left for cover

solid bars of weed left from bank to bank – approx 10ft broad

Above: Figure 103   *Shutting in a stream with tree trunks, the banks to be stabilized with good backfill*

Above right: Figure 104   *Tree trunks used to patch an eroding bank, suitably pegged and backfilled*

Right: Figure 105   *Large tree trunks used to stabilize eroding banks*

more damage can be done by bad planning than by shoddy work. Where a river bank is to be reinstated, several points have to be considered before work can begin.

Firstly, stake out the line of the intended new bank, taking care to follow the line of the old one, that is to say, observing all the bends and curves of the original. Never straighten river banks as this creates channelization of the stream, which can totally change the nature of the meandering flow and create havoc with the rest of the river. Wherever work is carried out on the bank, great care must be taken not to shut in the stream too much as this will speed the flow, which can cause even more erosion of the other bank and may even erode the new bank more quickly. Shut in the stream by all means, as this will speed up the flow and keep the bed of the stream free from silt, but the happy medium must be attained and this can be done by trial and error over the first few yards.

Thought must also be given to the nature of

the 'fill' being used. Soil is useless as it will quickly be washed away and create silt deposits lower down the stream. Any natural material such as chalk, stone or heavy gravel can be used, but care must be taken if building rubble is used; it must be covered with natural material so that the chalk and rubble weather and vegetation grows to achieve a completely natural looking bank. Rubble and concrete on their own will never weather down and look natural. Waste road making materials, which are tar based, must never be used on river banks, for obvious reasons.

Timber from windblown trees can be used very successfully in bank repairs and whole tree trunks, staked into the bed of the river, give a firm base on which to build a bank. A backfill of logged wood and chalk will soon establish natural growth (Figures 104 and 105).

There are many methods which can be used to carry out bank repairs and it pays to repair a bank as quickly as possible. An eroding bank, if left neglected, can entail large and expensive

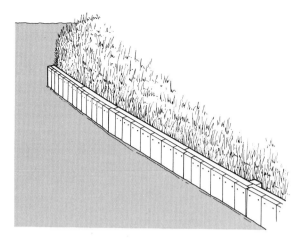

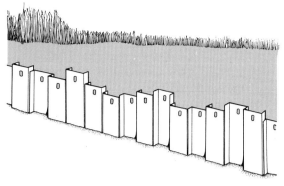

8ft x 12in x 1in oak planks | 3in x 3in oak posts
back fill
bed of river

Above left: Figure 106   *Oak buck piling used in awkward situations*

Above: Figure 107   *Steel piling can be used on major problems*

Left: Figure 108   *Camp sheathing to protect shallow banks*

Below: Figure 109   *Gabion baskets*

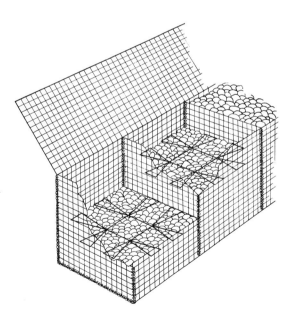

civil engineering works to repair. A log, pegged in good time, and backfilled, will soon solve the problem – a stitch in time saves nine.

In some areas, buck piling has to be used to stabilize a badly eroding bank. In mild cases, oak buck piling can be used, but in deep and extreme instances, steel piles may be necessary. Where shallow banks are to be protected, camp sheathing is an excellent method to adopt (Figures 106, 107 and 108).

Where continued erosion of a river bank is a problem and steel piling is not practical, then the use of Gabion baskets should be considered. These devices come in various sizes, but the most useful is 3 feet by 6 feet. The baskets are constructed with very tough, plastic-coated, 3 inch square steel mesh. When sited correctly and filled carefully with stone, flint or rock, the fully packed and sealed basket weighs many hundredweights and will make a firm base for any river bank restoration work. Gabion baskets can be adapted for use in many situations.

PREDATORS

Having established the right conditions for trout to thrive, it will inevitably be found that other creatures will be attracted to the stream, as good wild trout conditions also afford ideal habitat for numbers of nature's less lovable beings: pike, herons, dab chicks, sea gulls and cormorants; all will gravitate to a well stocked trout stream. All are beautiful animals in their own right, yet too many of any one species can have dramatic effects on a chalk stream, and a happy balance has to be achieved somewhere along the line.

Pike have their part to play in the life of a stream and I don't worry if I see the odd pike about, as they do deal with weak and sickly fish. Too many, however, can soon make significant inroads into the trout stock, so regular and efficient electro fishing sweeps along with good 'river keeping skills' will keep the numbers under control. Whilst electro fishing for pike, other species of unwanted fish can be removed — grayling and coarse fish can be tanked to other fisheries which welcome such species. It is wasteful to clear and kill unwanted fish when they can be given to others who will appreciate them for their particular sport, and this can create goodwill between the game angler and his coarse fishing counterpart.

Fish eating birds are all protected by law, so to defend a valuable trout fishery, the river keeper's 'dissuasion skills' are all put to the test. The odd pair of swans and Canada geese can be a pleasant feature on any fishery, but flocks of 50−100 are certainly not welcome, and swans and geese in these numbers can do very serious damage to aquatic weed growth and the insects it supports. Heavy grazing by these birds leaves large areas of gravel shallows completely bare. Trout will not live on such areas and tend to move off to deeper water for protection. This concentrates the fish, severely restricting fishing opportunities and reducing the feeding areas for the trout. Another problem posed by large concentrations of swans and geese is that their droppings can severely foul the river banks.

Geese can be shot during the wildfowling season but swans are protected by law. They can, however, be transported to other areas in which they will be more welcome, provided that their removal is first negotiated and agreed with the Ministry of Agriculture.

Another troublesome predator is the human poacher. Poaching has always been a problem on game fisheries, and it probably always will be. The only effective means of combating poaching is constant and consistent policing of the water. There are many anti-poaching techniques; indeed, a whole book could be written on the subject.

STOCKING

Having discussed the management of rivers with self-sustaining populations of wild brown trout, thought must be given to fisheries that have to rely on stocking with farm reared fish. Not all river fisheries can support the fishing pressures required by the owners, with wild trout as the sole source of stock, especially when market forces and profits are all part of the management policy.

Heavy fishing pressure can be sustained on a wild brown trout fishery if a catch-and-release policy is adopted. Provided that barbless hooks and correct fish handling techniques are used, such a policy can be a useful management tool. Not all trout fishermen are easily satisfied with a catch-and-release policy, though, preferring to kill their quarry and take it home. So, to satisfy this need, some fisheries resort to a put-and-take system in which sizeable trout are planted in the stream at the beginning of the season and again at intervals thereafter as the anglers reduce the stock.

In situations where hundreds of 2–10 lb trout are caught each season, then so be it; the daily or weekly stocking of fish of these sizes will have to be undertaken. No river system, however good, can meet such a demand naturally. To the thinking angler, fish of such sizes are alien to the whole river. A well managed put-and-take river fishery will be stocked with sufficient numbers of fish of sizes that have always been natural to it, and create a 'wild river feel' for any visiting angler. Tackle restrictions can be used to increase the challenge to the angler – dry fly only, for example, restrictions on hook sizes – anything, in fact, that will increase the challenge and re-introduce 'wildness' into the angling experience.

On rivers which do not naturally sustain good heads of wild trout but appear to be able to grow trout, the stocking of fry and fingerlings can be considered. These juvenile trout are allowed to grow on and, hopefully, to become of good catchable size in ensuing years. Again, this adds a further dimension to the impression of 'wildness'. To the thinking sport angler, an 8 oz wild trout caught on a dry black gnat on a small Welsh mountain stream is at least as great a prize as a fat, stocked 5 lb brown trout caught on a Lunns Particular on the River Test. To create the feeling of wildness on a fishery should be the aim of every keeper and fishery manager where stock fish are used.

One of the unwritten laws in artificial fish rearing is the time honoured saying that, 'if you want disease in your own stock, then buy it in'. In other words, if you are stocking your own water with fish bought from a fish farmer, then be sure you buy from a certificated, disease-free fish farm. The local NRA fishery officer will gladly assist you in selecting disease-free stock from reliable sources.

The law requires permission to be obtained before each and every movement of fish from one water to another and especially between fish farms and fisheries. Far from being a bureaucratic nuisance, this serves to help limit the spread of fish diseases, and it is essential that all fish movement order forms should be correctly filled in and passed to the NRA fishery

officer in good time. If in doubt, do not hesitate to ask his advice.

The almost perfect form of stocking is to rear one's own stock fish on one's own water, using the resident wild trout as brood stock. If suitable facilities and experienced staff are available, then half a dozen pairs of wild fish can be netted from the natural redds in autumn, the hens stripped of ova, and the males stripped of milt and the resultant fertile eggs incubated in a hatchery. The resultant fry can be reared to the required size to be planted back into one's own river. The benefit of this method is the increased survival rate of each age group compared with their relatively poor survival rates in the wild. The other important benefit is that, by this method, the genetic integrity of the wild fish is not disturbed to any great extent.

Unfortunately, to avoid the risk of bringing in diseases, some stock fish farms have bred from their own stocks of fish for many generations. In some cases, this has led to them inadvertently selecting an inbred strain of trout which will grow well in a stew pond environment, but which has virtually lost all the natural characteristics of a wild trout. So often does one hear that stock fish are too easy to catch when released into the wild. It has also been shown that inbred stock fish are often unable to reproduce successfully. These are important facts to take into consideration if the policy is to re-establish a self-sustaining stock of trout. If, on the other hand, the aim is simply to create a commercial put-and-take fishery, then triploid rainbow trout should be considered. These are specially bred, sexless fish – neither male or female. They do not go through the stresses of maturation. They therefore feed all the year round and are always in good catchable condition. By using triploid stock, a fishery can offer quality fish throughout the year. Gone are the days of catching gravid hen fish and black cock fish dripping in milt.

Finally, as a general recommendation to any river keeper or fishery manager, I would say, 'Constant vigilance', and, 'Think like a wild brown trout', because aquatic eco-systems, essential for healthy fish communities, continue to be impaired due to the growing demands for alternative uses of water.

Particularly for sport fishermen, high environmental quality is in itself an objective, a benefit and something to be desired as part of the fishing experience. In the past, we gave little thought to restricting the use of water as there were not the competitive pressures on its use. Nowadays, we must all realize that water for fisheries and for human consumption are two of the most sensitive uses. The public must be made aware that healthy fish communities and aquatic eco-systems serve as a barometer for human health and well-being. The newly formed National Rivers Authority must be able to deal with environmental issues within watersheds to safeguard fish stock and fishing opportunities. From now on, I believe, the NRA must recognize a broader objective than simply the provision of fishing. It must acknowledge a responsibility to maintain a healthy aquatic environment which will then serve as a quality indicator for the human environment. As river keepers, we have a vital part to play in all of this.

Further reading

W. Carter-Platts, *Trout Streams, Their Management and Improvement* (1927).

Lancelot Peart, *Trout and Trout Waters* (1956).

Col. R.H. Pease, *The River Keeper* (1982).

Frank Sawyer, *Keeper of the Stream* (1952).

Richard Seymour, *Fishery Management and Keepering* (1970).

John Parkman

John Parkman's entry into the world of stillwater trout fishery management was entirely due to the third-world urge for self-determination. Until 1973, he had pursued a happy and successful career in property and marketing on behalf of multinational oil companies. When the Arab nations nationalized their crude oil resources, much of the fun went out of the job, and when he found his employers viewing his room with greater favour than his company he took early retirement cheerfully and set about doing what he feels he should have done in early youth — water keeping and fishery management.

Since then, he has developed his fishery — Bayham Lake at Lamberhurst, near Tunbridge Wells in Kent — from an overgrown and derelict marsh into one of the most prolific and respected fisheries in the country.

Always in the vanguard of progressive thinking, John's professional abilities have been widely recognized by his peers who, in 1984, elected him Chairman of the newly formed Association of Stillwater Game Fishery Managers — a position he still holds and in which he has gained a reputation for forthrightness, determination and farsightedness.

John's lifelong commitment to the countryside and to country sports is demonstrated through his membership of the Country Landowners' Association, the Salmon and Trout Association and the British Field Sports Society. A lifelong and dedicated fly fisher, he is also passionately devoted to all other country sports, finding equal enjoyment in fox hunting, pheasant shooting, wildfowling, beagling, coursing and ferreting. He has caught almost every variety of British freshwater fish and, if asked for his fishing preferences, will put early morning tench fishing very close behind an evening on a chalk stream.

John Parkman has contributed to most of the British field sports magazines, his first article having appeared in *The Fishing Gazette* when he was thirteen years old. Recently, he wrote a penetrating analysis of the future for reservoir fisheries for *Trout and Salmon*.

12
STILLWATER FISHERIES MANAGEMENT

John Parkman

In recent years, with the massive advances made in fish culture and with the almost universal need for re-stocking, the twin sciences of river and stillwater fishery management have come much closer together than they were previously and it is now widely acknowledged that the problems and rewards of both branches have more in common than ever before.

Nevertheless, and notwithstanding the common issues, stillwater fly fisheries present a very special challenge to those who manage them in their efforts to achieve the very best results of which their particular water is capable. This brings us to the first and most vital consideration in the establishment of such a fishery.

LOCATION

Almost any body of standing water is capable of providing fly fishing of some sort but its prospects of long term success depend mainly upon three factors – water quality, depth and size. It is generally accepted, almost as an axiom, that the fisheries with the best potential are those with alkaline water from a chalk or limestone source. Many will argue that, because alkaline water is generally clear, highly productive and visually attractive, it represents the best possible medium for lake fishing, but it is as well to remember that the agricultural practices of the last three decades, coupled with industrial and domestic pollutants, have rendered almost all ground water over-fertile and that the clearer the water in any lake may be, the greater will be the risk of eutrophication, resulting from excessive light penetration, producing algal blooms and heavy weed growth.

It can therefore be said, and should be borne in mind by all who are planning to establish a stillwater fishery, that clear water from an alkaline source will require a much higher degree of day-to-day management than will a lake in which the water is less clear and rather more acidic. If time and labour are limited, as is so often the case, the ideal water is one which is clear but which carries sufficient stain to prevent light penetration much beyond 3–4 feet. The acid/alkaline balance (technically known as the pH) should be just above even, lying anywhere between 7 and 8 on the pH scale.

Other factors important in the consideration of water quality are the normal level of dissolved oxygen carried by the water (DO) and the biological or biochemical oxygen demand (BOD), arising mainly from decaying vegetable

Ashmere Fishery in Middlesex — a beautifully run, members-only fishery

matter. These latter factors will be greatly influenced, at the appropriate times of year, by the growth of water weed and its subsequent decay and by leaf fall into the water. It is therefore important to consider the size and quantity of trees surrounding the lake and their location in relation to the prevailing wind. Excessive weed growth must also be controlled, preferably by hand or mechanical cutting but, if necessary, by the use of the appropriate chemicals. If chemicals must be used, caution should always be the watchword, with a close eye kept on the weather and strict adherence to the manufacturer's recommendations as to application.

Almost as important as the quality of the water is the question of its quantity. Too much or too little water, arising from flood or drought, can severely disrupt the fishing for weeks at a time and close attention should therefore be paid to the exact source of the water which is to fill the lake. Ideally, a lake used for stillwater fly fishing will have, as its main source of water, a governable intake from a stream or river which is itself spring-fed. It will have its own springs beneath the bed of the lake and may also be fed by secondary springs emanating from the surrounding watershed. With the exception of gravel pits, any lake which is entirely land-locked, which has no inflow of any kind and which relies entirely upon rainfall for its replenishment should be regarded with suspicion. Such a water is likely to face severe problems arising from high summer water temperatures and may also find itself facing rapid depletion in times of drought. Equally strong reservations apply to those lakes into which the inflow from feeder streams cannot be controlled or diverted when heavy rainfall produces flood conditions.

It is important always to remember that the trout, in all its varieties, is essentially a fish of cold water. While those fisheries which are lucky enough to possess an abundance of cold spring water may not be too concerned about temperature, the majority of stillwater fisheries

Even small lakes can provide fine sport − a corner of Rockbourne Trout Fishery in Hampshire

Bayham Lake, John Parkman's Trout Fishery − early in the season, before the bankside vegetation has started to grow

do not have such good fortune, nor is there, in most cases, an entirely reliable supply of cool water from the inflow. These fisheries must therefore rely upon depth if a sanctuary is to be provided for the fish during spells of extreme weather. It is difficult to generalize because many factors play their part in the determination of water temperature but, as a rule of thumb, no lake should be considered for stocking with trout unless it can provide, over at least 20 per cent of its area, a minimum depth between 3 and 4 metres. Greater depth is nearly always desirable but anything over 8 metres can be counter-productive in that it may encourage a considerable proportion of the fish — particularly brown trout — to spend much of their time in water so deep that normal fly fishing is neither practical nor pleasurable.

Consideration of the size of a fly fishing water is very often a matter which is highly subjective. Very small lakes, of half an acre or thereabouts, can be enjoyable and very challenging to fish but, of course, the number of rods which can be accommodated on such waters is very small indeed, and the majority of stillwater fly fishers (other than reservoir anglers) prefer to find their sport on lakes in the 2–20 acre range. From the fishery manager's point of view, the most important consideration, perhaps, is the extent to which the size of a water will relate to variations in temperature. Obviously, smaller waters tend to heat up more quickly and to reach higher top temperatures than the larger areas. In all cases, regardless of size, the wise fishery manager will also pay attention to the shape of the water, bearing in mind that a varied water line, with islands, promontories, bays and inlets will accommodate greater rod numbers and will be infinitely more pleasing aesthetically than will a water which is regular in shape. Straight banks without features, contours or vegetation are offensive to the soul of the thinking angler and have the incidental effect of making bank angling ultimately more difficult.

At this point it may be as well to comment briefly upon the question of tenure and upon the consents necessary for the construction of new lakes. Dealing first with tenure, the primary objective must always be freehold ownership of the lake and of adequate surrounding land to provide seclusion, protection against intrusion and space for the construction of supporting facilities such as car parks, fishing huts and rearing pools. If freehold acquisition is impossible, then it is essential that a properly constituted leasehold be established and any such lease should be for a substantial number of years so that capital invested may be recovered and so that a long term policy of management may be drawn up. It is equally desirable that any lease agreed upon should contain adequate provision for renewal and should be drawn in terms which permit the leaseholder, within reasonable limitations, to sell the leasehold interest if he should choose to do so.

Whatever form of tenure may ultimately be adopted, it is essential that there be a written, detailed contract between the owner and the user. Only too frequently, naive fishery managers have allowed themselves to be talked into accepting the responsibility for stocking and maintaining a piece of water on the strength of the so-called 'gentlemen's agreement'. From bitter experience, most have learned that gentlemen remain gentlemen only so long as they are not upset. Almost inevitably some dispute will arise between owner and user and the user, lacking any legal definition of his rights, will be powerless to protect his position.

Regarding the construction of new lakes, planning consent will nearly always be necessary, and it is wise to have discussions with the local planning authority at as early a stage as possible. It is also necessary to consult with the appropriate officials of the National Rivers Authority (NRA), bearing in mind that licences will be required if there is to be any impoundment of flowing water or if any abstraction of ground water is contemplated.

Three points are important when considering the construction of a new lake. Firstly, it is vital to check the credentials, knowledge, experience and financial stability of any civil engineering contractor who may be involved in the work. The average groundwork contractor, used to working on building sites and local authority sports grounds, is quite useless when working with, in or around water. Using the maxim that time spent in reconnaissance is seldom wasted, always insist upon seeing other relevant work which your proposed contractor has already carried out and upon speaking to at least three customers with whom he has had previous dealings.

Secondly, never, never construct a new lake without installing overflow facilities capable of dealing with a 'once in a hundred years' flood and never be tempted to omit the installation of adequate, efficient and *lasting* facilities which will permit the lake to be drained completely.

Thirdly, be careful to plan the whole layout with the task of mowing constantly in mind. Easy slopes, level ground and thoughtful siting of trees and bushes (*no* tree stumps) will save countless hours in the years to come.

MAINTENANCE

Having dealt with the siting, acquisition and/or construction of a suitable body of water, maintenance must be the next consideration. If any single aspect of fishery management is under-valued, under-estimated and under-executed it is that of adequate day-to-day maintenance. Even among professional fishery

Bankside vegetation properly trimmed, at Zeals Fishery in Wiltshire

managers, it is common to see widespread evidence of neglect and ignorance of the basic principles of water keeping. It is amusingly anomalous that, for satisfactory fly fishing in stillwater, the maintenance of the banks and of bankside vegetation is of primary importance. This means that there must be adequate room for the back-cast, that the grass on the banks must be regularly mown to prevent the fly from constantly catching in vegetation, and

that the marginal plant growth must be regularly trimmed so that it provides adequate cover for bank fishermen but does not interfere with the playing and landing of fish or with the recovery of the fly in the latter stages of the retrieve after each cast.

It must also be remembered that, where weed growth in the water is either limited or non-existent, the marginal vegetation will provide almost the only means by which the larger water-borne nymphs may leave the water in order to carry out their final metamorphosis. A healthy, but controlled, bankside growth serves the best interests of both the fisherman and the major fly life and it is therefore a grave mistake to trim out all bankside vegetation and run the grass banks straight into the water. Aesthetically speaking, the existence of a properly controlled bankside 'hedge' of vegetation is infinitely more attractive than the rather dead, park-like atmosphere created by trimmed-out banks. Nevertheless, in the autumn, when the plants begin to wilt and fall into the water, it is best to give the whole lake a 'short back and sides', thus encouraging strong new growth in the following spring and preventing excessive marginal silting.

Most lakes, even those relatively newly established, will naturally develop a wide, interesting and very beautiful variety of bankside vegetation, but if this does not occur it is a simple matter to transform an uninteresting piece of water by importing attractive marginal

Reed-mace

plants culled from the banks of other, nearby rivers, lakes and streams (preferably with the riparian owner's permission!).

The same can be said of weed growth in the water but here the balance between adequate and excessive weed growth can be much more difficult to achieve. As described earlier, the eutrophic, over-fertile nature of almost all today's ground water means that wherever the water clarity is sufficient to allow sunlight to penetrate to the bottom of the lake there will be excessive weed growth. Chemical controls, although effective, need careful handling and can have disastrous side-effects. Broadly speaking, they are also non-selective and the total destruction of water weed will also inevitably mean the destruction of the habitat of a large percentage of the fly and insect life upon which the trout will seek to feed. It is therefore greatly preferable to control weed growth by hand or by machine if this is at all possible. The labour element is greatly increased, of course, but the selectivity and precision of control by these methods will bring its own reward.

It is not practical, in this context, to embark upon an exhaustive survey of the desirable and undesirable water plants but two varieties deserve special mention — each equally notorious in its own way. On the bank the most undesirable of all the reeds and rushes is the giant reed-mace, often wrongly called the bullrush. If left to its own devices, reed-mace will multiply from its original bridgehead at an alarming rate, spreading furiously through root development and through wind action upon the massive seed heads it produces. The main stem is intensely fibrous and the plant is capable of growing in up to 2 metres (6 feet) of water. Unchecked, the dense root formation and fibrous over-burden will rapidly consolidate into a marsh-like platform, extending outwards and side-ways by a minimum of one and a half metres (4 feet 6 inches) per annum, thus diminishing the available fishing area by a compound factor of its own initial area each year. No other marginal water plant is capable of surviving in competition with reed-mace and, although it can be chemically controlled, by far the best method of eradication is by constant pulling of the emergent plant. This is best done about mid-June when the plant is halfway to maturity. It is imperative that all emergent plants be lifted before the end of the summer in order to prevent the seed heads from blooming.

In the water, the bad news is that the fly fisher's greatest enemy is Canadian pond weed and the worse news is that this plant is exceptionally prolific, is almost useless as a habitat for underwater life, cannot be pulled and thrives upon cutting. Once established, the only practical method of control is the use of chemicals but the profusion and density of the plant, when in full growth, mean that it is often impossible to treat the whole of the infestation at one time because of the risk that the dying vegetation will de-oxygenate the water and cause mortality among the fish. If the growth is heavy, no more than 20 per cent should be treated at any one time and this often means that total elimination becomes impossible. If therefore behoves fishery managers to learn to recognize this plant readily and to keep an eagle eye out for its first appearance. If spotted early enough, its development can be prevented by cutting the emerged growth and by heavily raking the bottom in the immediate area. If possible, the scene of work should be surrounded by a fine mesh net to contain the cut tendrils and care should be taken to see that none of the cut weed escapes to re-root elsewhere in the lake.

None of the other plant life likely to be encountered in or around a stillwater trout fishery presents the same threat as the two I have singled out and almost all the others are capable of control by the intelligent use of scythes, mechanical cutters and selective ground sprays. Only one other plant deserves passing mention and that is giant hogweed. This plant, a close relative of the common meadowsweet, is instantly recognizable by its size (8–10 feet at maturity) and is exceptionally beautiful and valuable in a water garden environment. On a fishery however, it should be allowed to grow, if at all, only where there is no possibility that the rods will come into contact with it. During the growing season

Giant hogweed

(May–July) the plant is capable of rendering any naked skin with which it comes into contact photo-sensitive, resulting in very painful and unpleasant blistering.

Needless to say, brambles, stinging nettles and docks should be ruthlessly eliminated from the environs of the fishing water, but all are easily capable of control through careful use of selective ground sprays. In the same context, a close watch needs to be kept on the growth of seedling trees and bushes around the banks. Unchecked growth can rapidly interfere with access to the banks and with room for the back-cast.

Among fishery managers, opinions regarding the desirability of water fowl and wading birds are sharply divided. There is no doubt that, in excessive numbers, ducks and geese can foul both the water and the banks and offer a greatly increased risk of an infestation of eye fluke among the fish. Nevertheless, reasonable numbers of various varieties of wild fowl are unquestionably an added visual amenity, as is the odd swan. As every fly fisher knows, moorhens and coots have the infuriating characteristic of fluttering, panic-stricken across the surface of the water just as one is settling to cast to a rising fish but each of these birds, together with kingfishers, rails and grebes, has its place in the ecology of a lake and should be encouraged but not allowed to multiply to the point at which they may become a positive nuisance. Incidentally, any rapid decline in the population of coots and moorhens on the water is almost always attributable to the presence of mink but this will be dealt with in more detail later under the subject of vermin control.

On most fisheries, where the stock fish average 1½ lb or more, herons do little or no harm, feeding mainly on frogs, newts and small coarse fish. Generally speaking only one of the birds likely to be encountered on the average stillwater fishery gives any real cause for concern and this is the Canada goose. These birds are large, prolific and noisy. During the mating and nesting period they conduct their sex lives with an astonishing and irritating vigour, accompanied by a cacophony sufficient to blow both the mind and the eardrum. As an accompaniment to the gentle art of fly fishing their behaviour presents an entirely undesirable sideshow and it is therefore wise to control the

Canada goose

numbers of these birds present on the fishery, keeping the population down to no more than two or three per acre. It is worth remembering, however, that, like all geese, these birds are heavy grazers and if the banks of the lake are well grassed they will often make a substantial contribution to the task of mowing.

On the physical and practical side of matters, the thoughtful fishery manager will always see that bridges, wide enough for two people to pass, are provided wherever necessary, and he will cover his bridges with chicken wire so that his rods do not slip on the algal slime which will inevitably develop on the boards in the spring and autumn. He will also examine his fishery to see where fishing platforms and stages may be established to give access to water which would otherwise be inaccessible. Last but not least he will provide board walks across those areas of the bank liable to be marshy. All such constructions, together with any boat landing stages, must be inspected constantly and maintained thoroughly if they are not to present an unacceptable danger to the rods, especially to those more aged or infirm.

Within the definition of the word 'maintenance', it is also wise to include the establishment, development and proliferation of fly life in particular and of the whole ecological food chain in general. Given reasonable water quality, even the most newly established lake will rapidly populate itself with a huge variety of midges but, unless there is a substantial inflow from a stream or river, many of the other species may need to be introduced artificially. If this is to be done, remember that it is not necessary, normally, to introduce large numbers of each of the required species. A small breeding population, introduced at the right time and usually at the larval stage will quickly multiply if the environment is favourable, and if it is not then you are wasting your time in seeking to introduce that particular species in any case.

In any established water, it is a fair assumption that any species not already present does not find the environment suitable and that attempts to introduce it will probably fail. Nevertheless, if greater variety in the fly life is required, it is surprising how quickly a number of larvae can be gathered from a neighbouring water and transferred into the fishery. It is also worth recalling that previous generations of water keepers placed great faith in the use of floating 'fly boards' for the propagation of fly life. These consist of two or three thin planks joined in a flat rectangle roughly 1 metre by half a metre (3 feet by 1 foot 6 inches). A staple is inserted at one end to which is attached a length of binder twine or nylon sufficient to reach comfortably to the bottom of the lake. At the far end of the string

is a weight heavy enough to prevent excessive drifting. A number of these boards are then distributed around the surface of the water from which it is desired to import extra fly life. This is best done, obviously enough, during the period through which the desired varieties will be hatching. After a few days the boards should be lifted and, with the eggs on their undersides, should be kept wet while being transported to their new home where they are simply introduced into the water in the same way thus allowing the eggs to hatch and the larvae to populate the water.

STOCKING

Now that we have a water which is held on a reasonable form of tenure, is a sensible size, depth and shape with adequate aquatic life in all its forms and with the banks properly maintained, we are free to consider the object of the exercise, which is stocking with trout. At this point it would be well for all fishery managers − existing and potential − to offer a heartfelt vote of thanks to those earnest and hard-working pisciculturalists who first of all imported the rainbow trout into this country and who subsequently made possible the production of diploid and triploid fish for the greater benefit of the fishery manager. There is no doubt that, for the purpose of stocking a lowland stillwater trout fishery, the rainbow trout is incomparably superior to his native cousin, the brown trout. Rainbows are hardier, have a better food conversion ratio, a faster growth rate, are more resistant to disease, are less subject to the consequences of stress during grading and transportation, feed more readily and fight harder and more spectacularly when hooked. The economics of stocking with rainbows versus brown trout speak for themselves − most smaller fisheries report a recovery rate in excess of 90 per cent of all rainbows stocked against a figure of 30 per cent or less for brown trout. Considering that brown trout command a premium of about 40 per cent pound for pound above the price for rainbows, it is not hard to calculate that for either commercial,

syndicate or private fisheries the rainbow represents a dramatically better investment. Very few commercial fishery managers now stock with any significant numbers of brown trout and there are relatively few fish farmers who still rear them in any quantity. Despite all this, most lifetime fly fishers still hold the brown trout in high esteem and if one small brown figures in a bag of eight while the others are rainbows then, regardless of size, it is the brown which will excite comment at the end of the day. Thus, many of the more discerning fishery managers continue to slip in a few browns each year, more from affection than from practicality.

Recent experience with triploid (neutered/sexless) fish has demonstrated that they overwinter superbly and offer the rods first-class sport in late autumn, winter and early spring. As spring progresses, most fisheries, these days, turn to diploid (all-female) fish which are then used for all re-stocking purposes right through the summer and into the early autumn. This pattern of stocking offers the best possible insurance that the rods will catch handsome, fit and healthy-looking fish throughout the year. For the benefit of those who may be surprised at the use of the phrase 'throughout the year' it should be explained that, at intervals up to the mid-1980s, all the Water Authorities successively eliminated the closed season for rainbow trout in enclosed waters, thus permitting year-round fly fishing. Unfortunately, as was the way of Water Authorities, no standard form of words was used for the amended by-laws and confusion still exists in those areas (e.g. Wessex, the southern counties and Yorkshire) where ambiguous phraseology has allowed uncertainty and misinterpretation to creep in. Nevertheless, the majority of fishery managers now feel free to choose their own seasons and an increasing number stay open throughout the twelve months.

While the decision over species virtually makes itself, the decisions on size and source are not nearly so easily resolved. For the non-commercial fishery manager the decision on size is merely a matter of personal and/or syndicate-collective preference but where the fishery is operated on a business basis the size of the stock fish relates closely to the type of clientele sought and to the specific niche, within the market, that the fishery manager is seeking to occupy. For instance, some fisheries, aimed at the specimen hunter, stock exclusively with fish in the weight range upwards from 4 or 5 lb. These fisheries, while commanding a high permit price, are rather vulnerable in that fish may not always be available in the sizes and quantities they require and that any deterioration of the rearing conditions for these large fish while still at the fish farm can result in a very serious decline in the quality and condition of the fish.

The majority of the more successful commercial fisheries stock with fish averaging around 1¼–1½ lb with the higher priced waters, mainly in the south, often using 2 lb plus fish as their basic stock. Most fly fishers like variety in their bag and it is therefore common practice, among the more successful fisheries, for a wide range of sizes and weights to be introduced to the water, up to and including fish of 10 lb and more. It is important to remember that in any fishery, be it private, syndicate or commercial, where the fishing pressure is high there will be little or no opportunity for natural growth among the stock fish once released into the lake. Therefore if big fish are required, big fish must be introduced.

The frequency with which any trout water will need to be re-stocked depends almost entirely upon the fishing pressure to which it is subjected. Some private and syndicate waters, lightly fished, can survive adequately on a single stocking for the season but in most cases regular re-stocking will be necessary and here a good general rule can be to top up the water when the catch record shows that the stock has been depleted by 20 per cent or more. The more frequent the stocking, generally speaking, the easier the fishing.

Although it seems abundantly obvious to anyone who knows anything at all about still-water fishery management, it is also necessary to point out, for the benefit of those who are newcomers in this field, that the possibility of natural reproduction can be almost totally discounted and that, where normally sexed fish are used for stocking a stillwater, there will often be very high winter mortality if the fish are large enough to be sexually mature.

Since, in recent years, the reliable producer of high quality stock fish has become an endangered species, it is vitally important, in the interests of the continuity of the fishery, to locate a source of fish which produces to the required levels of size and quality, with a trustworthy proprietor who is operating a business which is economically sound and may therefore be expected to continue trading in this market for the foreseeable future. Some years ago it was possible to rely upon the acquisition of fish, load by load, on the open market, but the steady rise in the price of trout of Billingsgate fish market has syphoned off, into the table trade, all but the most resolute of re-stocking farmers and anyone now running a stillwater fishery and requiring substantial numbers of fish from year to year is best advised to form a sound and business-like relationship with two or more reliable suppliers and to have year to year contracts with each of his suppliers upon which both parties can rely.

It is wise also to bear in mind that, while fish from a given farm may be of good size and high quality, they may not necessarily take as readily to their new environment as fish from another farm. It pays to experiment widely among the re-stocking farms until connections are established with those farms from which the fish are not only of the required quality but have also demonstrated ready compatibility with the water into which they are to be stocked.

When negotiating with fish farmers, the shrewd manager will enquire in detail into the methods used by the farmer to extract, grade, store, load, transport and unload the fish. All of these factors have a heavy bearing on the stress the fish will undergo during these operations and on the rapidity with which they will thereafter settle down in their new home, begin to feed and become catchable. Fish which are held overnight in cages prior to loading or which have been crammed into an inadequate transporter, over- or under-oxygenated, subjected to over-heating while the lorry driver stops for lunch or have been roughly or carelessly loaded or unloaded, will show the signs of this accumulated stress for many days and may actually lose considerable weight before they regain sufficient self-confidence to begin to feed − and this is not to mention the drop in catch average which will result from the introduction of a load of over-stressed fish.

Many of these dangers can be overcome by the creation of holding and/or rearing facilities at the fishery. Some of the most consistently productive fisheries achieve these results by buying in fish at around 8 or 9 inches and growing on from there, while others simply hold their stock fish for a week or two in ponds created for the purpose so that the fish can acclimatize themselves to the characteristics of the water and can recover from the stress of transportation.

As the price of stock fish rises, more and more fisheries are installing facilities which enable them to rear their own stock. While there is no doubt that this policy can be extremely effective in keeping down costs, it must be remembered that it is not without its drawbacks. For instance, since little poaching occurs these days without the risks being weighed against the potential rewards, it follows that commercial poachers will find a fishery which has densely populated stock ponds much more attractive than one which has not.

Normally, a fishery manager is not much concerned by the risk of disease among the stock since his fish are widely dispersed and therefore any disease which does appear is unlikely to spread. This is not so, however, once rearing facilities are constructed − immediately the fishery manager is faced with all the problems which afflict anyone who rears large numbers of animals in high density. If disease appears, it is difficult to eradicate and if mortality is high enough to force the unfortunate manager back on to the open market looking for fish in mid-season, he is unlikely to find what he needs at short notice.

Speaking of disease, most new fishery managers tend to panic if signs of an outbreak appear among their stock but experience shows that there is little or nothing which can be done to treat disease in the average fishery. It also shows that rarely, if ever, is disease, as opposed to stress or pollution, responsible for high mortality in a fishery. Most experienced fishery managers, when faced with disease among their fish, simply bide their time, remove afflicted fish as quickly as possible and re-stock appropriately when the disease has run its course. While no fish farmer will readily acknowledge that his farm was the source of the disease, straight looks and hard bargaining can often produce some sharing of the burden of cost between the fishery and its supplier.

Before leaving the subject of stocking, we should consider the question of density and here the major factors are rod pressure, surface accessibility (i.e. that proportion of the total surface area which can be covered by fishermen either from the bank or from boats), required bag average and natural food availability. Generalizations are suspect but, on this question, a good rule to adopt is that the clearer the water the lower the density should be. Among the reasons for this are the facts that in more coloured water fish are not easily stalked and that, once hooked, they do not so readily frighten their brethren. Last, but not least, is the simple fact that in clear water large concentrations of fish can easily be spotted by the fishermen, who will often gather there and harass the fish to the detriment of subsequent rods.

For many reasons, the best advice in this respect is to 'suck it and see'. No two fisheries are exactly alike and the best stock density can only be achieved by trial and error. In order to give some guidance, however, it may be helpful to know that most fisheries find that the best fishing is produced by a stock density somewhere between thirty and ninety fish per acre.

One last point worth mentioning while dealing with stock fish is the question of feeding once the fish have been introduced. With certain exceptions, such as the occasional bucket of pellets to over-wintering triploids, the feeding of stocked fish should be abhorred. The object of the exercise is to offer the rods the opportunity to catch fish as close to the wild as is possible in today's conditions. If they are pursuing fish which are regularly fed, then the fishery manager might just as well give them direct access to the rearing ponds and be done with it.

FACILITIES

Few, except the most basic fisheries, can operate satisfactorily without the construction of some additional facilities for the comfort and convenience of the rods. Firstly, and most essentially, adequate, hard, off-road parking must be provided. It is wise to over- rather than under-estimate the average number of rods likely to be using the fishery and to provide car parking facilities accordingly. If this is not done then, inevitably, overspill will occur on a pouring wet day and a number of disgruntled rods will find themselves up to their axles in mud. The construction of a car park need not be a grossly expensive affair and can easily be handled in such a way that the work contributes to the landscaping of the fishery rather than detracting from it. Given the necessary area of reasonably flat ground, it is necessary only to create the access from the road or track which serves the water and then to bulldoze the topsoil evenly around the outside of the site chosen for the car park, using the same machine to landscape the spoil into a surrounding mound which can then be grassed and planted with trees and shrubs to serve as concealment. Assuming that something in the region of 6 inches of topsoil has been removed, this should be replaced with the same depth of some appropriate hardstanding material such as hoggin or roadstone. This can be spread and tracked in by the same machine with the whole job completed over one or at the most two days.

Depending upon the geographical layout of the fishery, it is usually desirable to provide some form of hard path from the car park to the fishing hut, which will normally be a fairly basic building of simple timber construction, large enough to be adequate for use as a shelter by a number of fishermen during heavy rain, sturdy enough to stand for twenty years and, preferably, handsome enough not to be a blot on the landscape.

Commercial fisheries, of course, need more sophisticated buildings, with office facilities, a kitchenette and machinery storage. A decent, easily maintained toilet (usually of the chemical variety) will be needed, no matter how small the fishery. The toilet can be unisex but, in any event, simplicity and cleanliness are essential.

Among its other attributes, the fishing hut should have windows, preferably overlooking the lake so that fishers who are resting or sheltering may indulge in their favourite pastime of looking morosely at the water and commenting on the lack of fly life/lack of rising fish/lack of wind/cloud, etc. The building should also contain facilities for the weighing and recording of the catch but not, repeat not, any piece of equipment into which the rods might be tempted to gut their fish. The practice of gutting fish on the premises should be actively discouraged, even to the point of expulsion from the water or the syndicate if the offence is repeated. Nothing is more offensive than rotting fish entrails for which fishermen, for some unexplained reason, seem to feel no responsibility whatever once the disembowelment has been completed.

The interior of the fishing hut should be made as interesting and as comfortable as is reasonably possible. The chairs should be sound, uniform and practical and the walls should be decorated with photographs, curios, fishery brochures, maps, booklets, posters and pictures. Remember that, on the bad days, the rods will be likely to spend some considerable period of time in the hut and, if the interior is interesting and if there are a few current fishing magazines available to read, this will relieve the boredom and the tendency to criticize the management for their inability to provide ideal fishing weather.

There is one other item which should be made available for rods and guests to read in the fishing hut and that is a copy of the rules. When you draw up your rules be sure that they are simple, unambiguous, brief and few in number. The most important rules are those which concern the number of fish which may be killed and/or returned, the type and size of flies which may be used and the hours between which fishing is permitted. It is also important to insist that all rods enter the details of their catch (including blanks) before they leave the water. Virtually all other rules are determined by the characteristics of the fishery and by the personal preferences of the management but once the rules have been made, take care to see that they are observed. Rule breakers and cheats come from all walks of life, from all age groups and from both sexes. It is common to find that a rod who will break one of the minor rules will display the same disregard for them all.

The subject of bridges, walkways and fishing platforms was covered earlier but among the facilities which a fishery can provide for its rods one, in particular, too often offers scope for criticism or even downright condemnation. This is the boats. Superannuated, clinker built rowing dinghies with ill-matched oars, worn rowlocks and inadequate anchors are an abomination frequently encountered and just as frequently cursed.

Except on the very largest waters, boats are used mainly as stationary fishing platforms and it is therefore wise to acquire well-made boats which are flat-bottomed (and therefore stable), are constructed from a non-degradable material such as aluminium or fibre glass and which are not painted. The boats should be so designed that there are the minimum of projections, both within and without, round which the line may catch when casting or when playing a fish. The thwarts (seats) should be located at gunwale level, thus giving the fishermen the maximum height for casting while remaining seated.

Well maintained, soundly built boats at Blagdon. Those used on smaller lakes should be no less carefully chosen or looked after

A stable, well-made boat is as essential on a small stillwater as on a large one – but should still provide no excuse for standing up, which is both dangerous and counter-productive

Oars and rowlocks should be sound and in good condition. Anchors should be provided fore and aft to allow for anchoring broadside on to the wind. Anchor ropes should be supple, free of knots and of sufficient length comfortably to reach the bottom of the lake in the deepest areas. A yard of chain between the anchor rope and the anchor itself will help to settle the anchor and prevent unwanted drag. Remember to fix anchor ropes to the eyes in the boat so that they are positively irremovable. Unless this is done anchors will inevitably be lost. Remember also that, thanks to the theories developed by the Northampton school of fishermen in the 1970s, every boat angler thinks he knows his boatmanship better than the fishery manager and the anchor ropes should therefore be checked for knots, hitches, warps and bends at regular intervals.

When ordering your boats take care to check the bottom boards. Very few boat designers actually design their boats for stillwater fly fishing and it is therefore common to find that the bottom boards will tip if stepped on at one end and will crash down again, resoundingly, as soon as the weight is removed, causing the bottom of the boat to act as a sounding board and effectively frightening fish for some distance in every direction. Nothing can be done to stop fishermen from hurling anchors noisily into the water instead of lowering them gently but, if the management have done their job properly, it should be possible for the efficient angler to use his boat as stealthily as the old-fashioned gun punts.

POACHING

As soon as a fishery is completed and word of this gets abroad, the fishery manager will face this new problem. It is as well to accept at once that your fishery will be poached. Do not allow yourself to be deluded by the belief that, since it is located at the centre of a large private estate, is surrounded by a well-keepered commercial shoot and is served by a private road, this will be any insurance against poachers. Every rural town and village has its quota of habitual, lifetime game thieves but nowadays the activities of these local intruders are often insignificant in comparison to the predatory raids carried out by well-organized and expensively equipped poaching gangs from the urban areas.

While poaching can never be wholly prevented, by far the best deterrent is the year-round, twenty-four hours a day, on-site presence of the manager, keeper or bailiff. This can only be achieved, of course, if a house goes with the fishery. Where this is not possible, regular night patrols should be organized, bearing in mind that the majority of poaching occurs in the two hours after dusk and in the two hours around dawn.

More often than not, although sophisticated electric and electronic poacher alarms are available, the cost and practicality of installation are questionable. If this can be done, it has undoubted value but where it is not possible some of the old-fashioned remedies merit consideration. Alarm guns, trip wires, signal flares and battery operated security lights are all worthwhile deterrents, but the expense of erection of a security fence is extremely doubtful. The determined poacher will always find a way through barbed wire and over high fences.

However, security fences do come into their own if the location of your fishery permits the installation of a ring fence within which guard dogs may be released. Large, well trained dogs, roaming free at night, are a very effective deterrent indeed. Attractive though this idea may be it does have certain disadvantages. Very costly, high quality fences must be installed together with secure (and therefore usually ugly) gates. Warning notices must be displayed at intervals around the perimeter and adequate steps taken to protect legitimate visitors. All of this paraphernalia generally results in the creation of a fortress-like atmosphere which totally destroys the gentle ambience of a fishery. In most cases, the best idea is to compromise by owning a dog which is large enough to be perceived as a threat by ne'er-do-wells but is disciplined and obedient and therefore does not strike terror into the hearts of your more timid rods.

There is little the police can do either to detect or deter poachers but good relationships with the local police are always desirable and regular visits from the local patrol car — day and night — should be encouraged. In this context, the ready availability of coffee and tea can be a great help. The one area in which the police can be, and usually are, exceptionally helpful is with the prosecution of offenders once they have been apprehended. Remember that, for a prosecution to be successful, poachers must be caught in the act and, if they are to be charged with theft, must be in possession of freshly killed fish which can reasonably be presumed to have come from the water on which they were trespassing.

The apprehension of poachers is a difficult business, fraught with personal danger, and should therefore be undertaken only by those with the stature and self-confidence to be reasonably sure that the incident can be brought to a conclusion without violence on either side. Because of the risks, deterrence is infinitely better than apprehension and it pays to devote the main thrust of the fishery's anti-poaching activities into a deterrent strategy. Much can be achieved in this respect by the judicious dissemination of misinformation through the local pubs and by the development of a reputation for unrelenting prosecution in all cases.

VERMIN

Apart from the activities of the two-legged predators, considerable numbers of fish can be lost to these, their first cousins. While many of the practices advocated by turn-of-the-century game and water keepers are enjoying a remarkable resurgence, it must be acknowledged that the attitude of these gentlemen towards vermin was undeniably murderous. The majority of thinking water keepers and managers now take a fairly tolerant view of most predators and of the other wild life likely to be found around a stillwater trout fishery. As

Cormorant

mentioned earlier, kingfishers, herons and grebes are a joy to the eye, a pleasure to the naturalist and well worth their place in the natural ecology of the lake, regardless of any small damage they may do. As for the other airborne predators, the fish-eating ducks (merganser, goosander, etc.) need watching. The odd one can be a visual attraction but a single pair is enough and, if there are no fish in the water other than trout, even these should be discouraged. Any fishery manager lucky enough to provide a free meal for an osprey should thank his lucky stars for the privilege and make sure that whatever tree the bird may

Mink

choose for feeding or roosting is carefully protected against the woodman's chainsaw. Not so the cormorant or shag. The inclusion of this bird in the list of protected species is roughly equivalent to offering a life peerage to the brown rat. Charmless, ruthless and greedy, the cormorant's only redeeming feature lies in the fact that it can be relatively easily discouraged, by resolute disturbance and harassment, from taking up permanent residence on smallish waters and will normally seek easier pickings, if regularly 'buzzed', even on the larger waters.

Among the predatory animals, only the otter and the mink present any threat to fish stocks and, of these, the former will figure high on almost anyone's list of rare and delightful creatures. Any appearance should be kept secret, encouraged by all possible means and treated as a cause for rejoicing. Unfortunately, it is all too easy for the inexperienced fishery manager to mistake a mink for a young otter but any tolerance displayed towards mink is misplaced. Fearless to the point of foolhardiness, aggressive, persistent and prolific, the mink will resist all attempts to wipe him out and the best strategy that can be adopted is the intensive use of cage and Fenn traps in the early spring to catch the adults before they reproduce and again in the late summer and early autumn when the litters break up and the kits will appear, seeking new territory. Do not be tempted to trap continuously. Mink are among the easiest creatures to catch when traps are first set but any mink not caught after two weeks will never be trapped and can be eliminated only by shooting or by poisoning. Intensive trapping, over short periods, is by far the best method of mink control.

In the lake itself, the only creature likely to be included in the category of vermin is the pike. Most trout fishery managers prefer to have no pike at all in their water and, if you are lucky enough to start from a position in which there is a zero pike population, it is probably best not to play with fire. If, however, pike already exist, there are strong arguments for pursuing a policy under which all small pike (under 10 lb) are removed while larger fish are reduced in numbers, by the selective culling of either males or females, until the water contains no more than one big pike for every 3 or 4 acres of water and all such fish are of the same sex. Remember that large pike are lazy feeders and that, while almost every fish that goes into your lake may be fit, healthy, full-finned and with 20/20 vision, inevitably some will be damaged, diseased, blinded or over-stressed. These fish, if caught by the rods, will be damaging to the reputation of the fishery but they will also be easy prey for your large pike and such natural control of stock quality is well worth the loss of a few healthy fish as well.

COARSE FISH

Discussion of the pros and cons of pike brings us naturally to the consideration of the merits and demerits of coarse fish. Once a stillwater fishery is well established then, by accident or design, some coarse fish species will almost inevitably appear. Here again, most trout fishery managers prefer to be without them and many go to great lengths to keep their water free of any species other than trout, but a balanced ecology can certainly gain great benefits from the existence of other species and it is generally true to say that, unless there is an excessive population of coarse fish, there is little real competition for food.

Working upwards in size through the coarse fish species, minnows and sticklebacks should always be regarded with favour since they offer no competition to the trout but form a valuable item in their diet. Roach, rudd, perch and bream can be a nuisance since they are, for the most part, mid-water feeders and will therefore compete with the trout for some of the same food. They are also fairly readily caught on the fly and this can cause some tooth-sucking among the less tolerant rods. Nevertheless, they are prolific breeders and will provide the trout with much more food than they steal, in the form of their own offspring. Provided their numbers are controlled, none of these species need be viewed with too jaundiced an eye.

The tench is probably the most valuable under-stock it is possible to find in a trout water. Beautiful, entirely inoffensive, unseen, uncompetitive and uncatchable (as far as the fly fisher is concerned) he will reproduce busily, will feed exclusively on the bottom and will provide a valuable and readily saleable cash bonus whenever the lake is drained or netted.

In terms of cash value, of course, nothing equals the carp, but carp are notably more finnicky about their sexual activities, often refusing to spawn for several years in succession. If they are present in the fishery in any numbers they can colour the water and will often adopt a distressingly high profile in times of hot weather. As it is at these times that your trout population will be at its least visible, the surface cruising carp can be the cause of some caustic and wounding comments from the less successful rods. Since these same people will, no matter what you do, find plenty of other opportunities for the exercise of their questionable humour, it is best, on balance, to eliminate carp from the water.

Of the remaining species, orfe, being surface-feeders and highly visible, are not desirable.

Tench

The same applies to chub and dace while the grayling is usually unhappy in stillwater and deserves better than to be subjected to such discomfort. For practical purposes, it is beyond the wit of man either to encourage or to discourage eels. They will inhabit the lake if they wish to do so and if they do not no power on earth will keep them when they wish to leave. If present, however, they fall into the same happy category as tench, representing an excellent cash crop which, if there is an outflow from the lake, can be relatively easily harvested by trapping in the autumn.

Two other waterborne creatures which deserve mention are those efficient scavengers the crayfish and the swan-mussel. In common with the tench and the eel the crayfish can, if the habitat is suitable, form a valuable undercrop, but rainbow trout are very partial to young crayfish, which, like eels, are great escapers when they set their minds to it. In most cases, the attractive idea of an under-stock of crayfish has proved to be nothing more than an expensive way of learning these two simple facts. The swan-mussel, on the other hand, is neither edible nor notably mobile. If introduced to a lake with a mud bottom, they will reproduce rapidly, will render an invaluable cleansing service and, unlike the crayfish, will not walk out on you when you need them most. One word of caution: during the early spring and late autumn when the water is cold and fly fishers are using heavy, sinking lines, the swan-mussel will quite frequently be caught because he will snap shut as the line passes across him. Be prepared for unusual, interesting and often very funny reactions from the rod concerned.

CONCLUSION

The successful fishery manager needs to be patient, tolerant, good-humoured and equipped with a deep understanding of the ways of nature. Every aspect of his life is concerned with unpredictables ranging from the weather through fly hatches to the behaviour of the fish themselves. This means that the most careful planning and the most detailed organization can frequently be brought to nothing by factors completely beyond the control of the management. Such regular frustration brings considerable strain upon the manager and causes him to call upon his greatest reserves of tact when dealing with the rods who, for the most part, know nothing whatever about the problems of fishery management and simply expect to pay their money and find their sport.

The mention of money brings to mind one final comment. No attempt has been made here to deal with the financial elements of running a trout fishery. This is because the private proprietor will not be seeking a financial return, while for a syndicate operator the sums are simple — the total costs are divided equally among the syndicate members and the resultant figure, with a small addition for contingencies, represents the annual subscription. For those contemplating commercial fishery management, however, the sums are much more complex and all such would be well advised to give due weight to the following considerations:

1. Run properly, a stillwater trout fishery demands exactly the same management skills as any other business — planning, organization, accounting, sales promotion, marketing, advertising, media relations and public relations. It also carries great risk and is therefore not a suitable business for those of faint heart or who lack commercial experience.
2. Generally speaking, in terms of comparative business investment, a trout fishery will not provide an adequate bottom-line return and will be lucky to make a true operating profit.
3. The market is already over-subscribed, with very few areas of the country left in which a new fishery will not find itself in competition with many others which are

already well established and from whom it will usually prove to be exceedingly difficult to wrest an adequate share of trade.

Nevertheless, the management of a stillwater trout fishery can be one of the pleasantest and most rewarding tasks it is possible to undertake, having much in common with the old Chinese proverb, 'If you want to be happy for a day — get drunk; if you want to be happy for a year — get married; if you want to be happy for a lifetime — build a garden (fishery).'

Further reading

Rupert Barrington, *Making and Managing a Trout Lake* (Fishing News Books Ltd, 1983).

Alex Behrendt, *The Management of Angling Waters* (Andre Deutsch, 1977).

W. E. Frost and M. E. Brown, *The Trout* (Collins, 1967).

D. Macer Wright, *The Fly-Fisher's Plants* (David & Charles [Holdings] Ltd, 1973)

Robin G. Templeton (ed.), *Freshwater Fisheries Management* (Severn Trent Water Authority).

APPENDIX A
THE FLY FISHER'S KNOTS

The reel knot — for attaching backing to reel

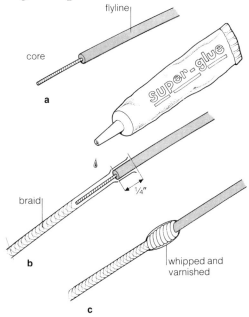

Attaching the fly line backing or nylon mainline to the reel spool

The glued splice

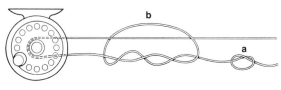

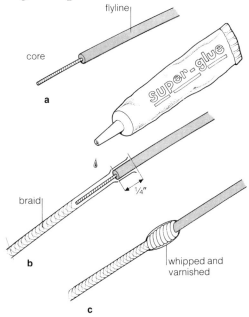

Attaching braided monofilament to the fly line

The double grinner knot

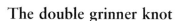

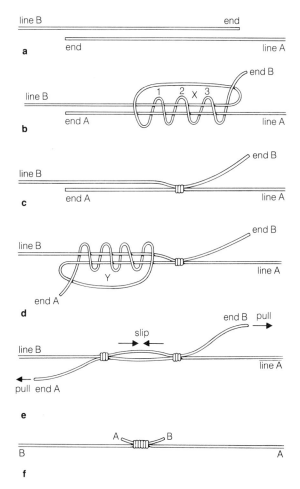

The nail knot

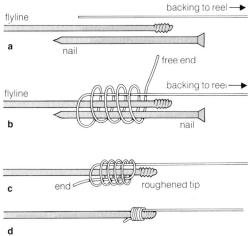

Attaching the backing line to the fly line

The needle knot

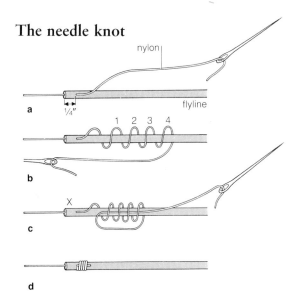

Attaching monofilament to the fly line

The blood knot

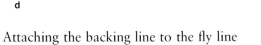

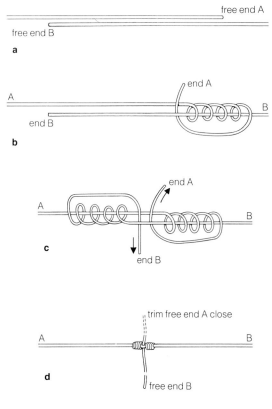

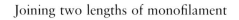

Joining two lengths of monofilament

The turle knot

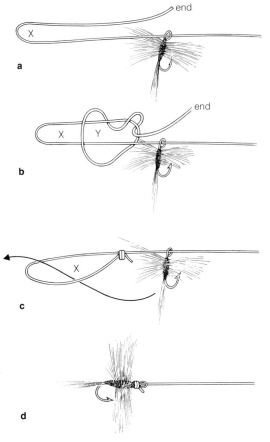

The water (or cove knot)

a

b

c

d

Making droppers in leaders

The grinner knot (or duncan loop knot or uni-knot)

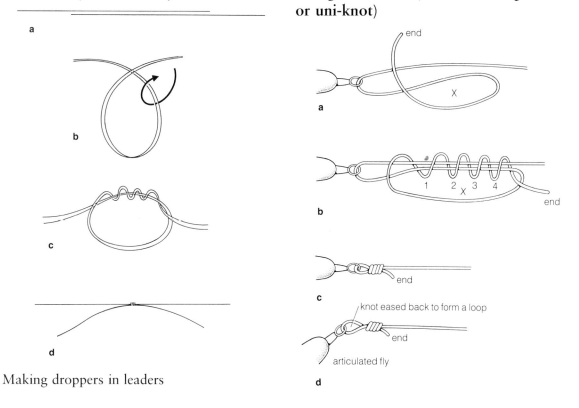

end

a

b

end

c

end

knot eased back to form a loop

end

articulated fly

d

The tucked half-blood knot (or clinch knot)

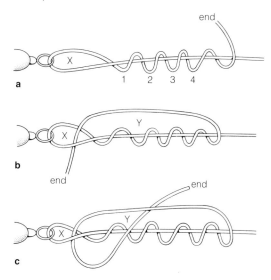

end

a

1 2 3 4

X

b

Y

X

end

c

Y

X

end

Attaching a fly to a header

APPENDIX B
USEFUL ADDRESSES

Sources of tuition

The Association of Professional Game Angling Instructors (Secretary, Donald Downs), The Mead, Hosey, Westerham, Kent, TN16 1TA.

The National Anglers' Council, 11 Cowgate, Peterborough, PE1 1LZ.

Fly dressing materials and tackle

There are, of course, numerous tackle shops and mail order houses selling tackle and fly dressing materials. We have found the following to be consistently helpful and reliable.

D.J. Hackle Farm, Hattons Lodge, Braydon, Swindon, Wilts, SN5 0AB.

Fisherman's Feathers, Hill End Farm, Brandsford, Worcestershire WR6 5JT.

Rare Feathers Ltd, Kaledna, Garras, Morgan-in-Meneage, Helston, Cornwall, TRI2 6LP.

Sportfish Ltd, Lion Street, Hay-on-Wye, Near Hereford HR3 5AD.

Tom C. Saville Ltd, Unit 7, Salisbury Square, Middleton Street, off Ilkeston Road, Radford, Nottingham, NG7 2AB.

Out-of-print fishing books

John and Judith Head, The Barn Book Supply, 88 Crane Street, Salisbury, Wilts.

Associations and societies

Every angler has a duty to join *The Anglers' Co-operative Association*, Midland Bank Chambers, Westgate, Grantham, Lincs, which is wholly dedicated to prosecuting those who pollute our angling waters.

The Grayling Society (Membership Secretary, Mrs M.C. Pickover, 20 Somersall Lane, Chesterfield, S40 3LA) brings together those interested in the grayling and in grayling fishing and promotes appreciation of the grayling as a game fish in its own right.

The Fly Dressers Guild (Hon. Secretary, H.A. Reid, Esq., 18 St Michael's Crescent, Pinner, Middlesex, HA5 5LG) is a friendly association with branches throughout the country for those interested in the craft of fly dressing.

The British Field Sports Society, 59 Kennington Road, London SE1 7PZ, seeks to represent the interests of all field sports men and women in Britain.

The Salmon and Trout Association, Fishmongers' Hall, London EC4R 9EL, seeks to represent game fishing interests throughout the United Kingdom.

INDEX